ASIAN-AMERICAN EDUCATION

Prospects and Challenges

Edited by
Clara C. Park and Marilyn Mei-Ying Chi

BERGIN & GARVEY
Westport, Connecticut • London

Library of Congress Cataloging-in-Publication Data

Asian-American education : prospects and challenges / edited by Clara
  C. Park and Marilyn Mei-Ying Chi.
       p.   cm.
    Includes bibliographical references and index.
    ISBN 0–89789–602–5 (alk. paper).—ISBN 0–89789–603–3 (pbk. :
alk. paper)
       1. Asian Americans—Education.   2. Language arts—United States.
    3. Sociolinguistics—United States.   I. Park, Clara C., 1944– .
    II. Chi, Marilyn Mei-Ying, 1949–
    LC2632.A847   1999
    371.82995′073—dc21   98–55902

British Library Cataloguing in Publication Data is available.

Library of Congress Catalog Card Number: 98–55902
ISBN: 0–89789–602–5
       0–89789–603–3 (pbk.)

First published in 1999

Bergin & Garvey, 88 Post Road West, Westport, CT 06881
An imprint of Greenwood Publishing Group, Inc.
www.greenwood.com

Printed in the United States of America

♾™

The paper used in this book complies with the
Permanent Paper Standard issued by the National
Information Standards Organization (Z39.48–1984).

10 9 8 7 6 5 4 3 2 1

Copyright Acknowledgments

The authors and publisher gratefully acknowledge permission for use of the following material:

Tables 2.1–2.4 and Figure 2.1 from *Mandarin Chinese: A Functional Reference Grammar* by Charles Li
and Sandra Thompson. Berkeley: University of California Press. Copyright © 1981 The Regents of the
University of California.

Contents

Preface

Over the last three decades, the number of Asian immigrants has increased almost six fold, from a mere 0.5% of the U.S. population in 1960 (877,934) to 2.9% (7,237,662) in 1990. At the same time, the ethnic composition has become increasingly diversified from what was once a primarily East Asian population to an extremely diverse group comprised of various Asian groups with diverse linguistic and sociocultural backgrounds.

Today, in 1999, Asian-Americans comprise nearly 4% of the U.S. population. However, there is still a dearth of literature on the education of Asian-American students available for use by educators of all grade levels. It is the intent of this book to provide the much-needed information on Asian-American students and to help shape the educational programs, practices, and policies for Asian-American students.

Asian-American Education: Prospects and Challenges was first conceived at the annual conference of National Association for Asian and Pacific American Education held in San Francisco in the spring of 1996. Subsequently, we invited experts in the field to contribute chapters on the linguistic and sociocultural aspects of Asian-American education. Many of the contributors are immigrants themselves and have lived through many of the experiences discussed in this book. Additionally, each contributor, as a teacher educator or an educational practitioner, is intimately aware of both the prospects and challenges of educating the particular Asian group he or she discusses.

As the first comprehensive survey of major Asian-American groups for educators, this book expounds upon both the linguistic and sociocultural aspects of seven Asian-American groups: Cambodian, Chinese, Filipino, Japanese, Korean, Hmong, and Vietnamese. There are two chapters on each of the seven Asian-American groups, one linguistic and one sociocultural. This book provides a sense of how each group is faring in our public schools and illuminates the unique educational issues, needs, and challenges faced by each group. Furthermore, this book provides practical and insightful suggestions for teachers, administrators, teacher educators, and support service providers in the public schools. Finally, it is important to note that this book is specifically designed to meet the needs of relatively recent Asian immigrant students. Accordingly, throughout the book, we use the term "Asian-American" rather than "Asian American" or "Americans of Asian origins." In addition, in Chapters 11 and 12 we use the terms "Hmong" and "Mong" respectively, to refer generally to all members of the ethnic Hmong-Mong tribes from Laos; and "Mong" to refer to the language used by the Mong Leng (Blue Mong) in Chapter 12. The sizes of the Hmong (White Hmong) and Mong (Blue Mong) groups in the United States are about equal; and their dialects are mutually intelligible; however, there are significant and noticeable differences in pronunciations between the two.

Asian-American Education: Prospects and Challenges is the product of the contributions of many dedicated individuals. The co-editors are deeply grateful to the chapter authors for their unique contributions and multiple revisions. Our thanks also goes to Grace K. Park for providing editing assistance; to Alan K. Chi for formatting and paginating the camera-ready final manuscript; and to Jane Garry, Deborah Whitford, and other editors at Greenwood Publishing Group for their continuous support throughout this project. Finally, we extend our warmest thanks to our families for their extraordinary support and understanding throughout the undertaking and completion of this project. This book would not have been possible without the collective efforts and contributions of these individuals.

CHAPTER 1

Sociocultural Adjustment of Chinese-American Students

Li-Rong Lilly Cheng

This chapter provides a brief overview of Chinese-American immigration, with a focus on the education of recent immigrant families. This chapter also provides an introduction to the Chinese family in transition and discusses religion and values, motivation for immigration, and cultural and historical variables. More specific to the school setting, similarities and differences between American and Chinese schools, differences in expectations of American teachers and Chinese parents, barriers to classroom interactions, and classroom discourse rules are explained. Furthermore, the chapter discusses the sociocultural adjustment process of new immigrants, the identity formation process, maintenance of the home culture, and adaptive strategies used by immigrants. Finally, this chapter concludes with working suggestions to enhance parent participation, student empowerment, and teachers' influence on student motivation.

IMMIGRATION HISTORY OF CHINESE-AMERICANS

The history of Chinese-American immigration cannot be discussed without a brief discussion of Asian-Pacific immigration. Asian-Pacific-Americans originate from Pacific Asia or are descendants of Asian-Pacific Islander immigrants. Numbering 7.2 million in the United States, Asian Pacific-Americans (APA) are the fastest growing segment of the U.S. population, representing 2.9% of the nation and 10% of California (U.S. Bureau of the Census, 1993). APA are fast becoming an influential presence socially, politically, and economically.

According to the U.S. Census 1990 (U.S. Bureau of the Census, 1993), Chinese comprise the largest number of Asian immigrants to the United States. The Chinese first immigrated to the United States two centuries ago, with records documenting the arrival of Chinese in the United States in 1785. Chinese immigrants came in greater numbers beginning in 1848, and many worked as miners, farmers, or as railroad constructors. They eventually settled on the West Coast in San Francisco and Los Angeles, or remained in the mining towns and in the towns along the railroads. Chinese from the coastal provinces of Canton and Fukien, the earliest generation of Chinese who left their hometowns to make a living somewhere else in the world, were the first group to establish a tradition of "overseas Chinese." Many Cantonese voyaged to the United States, while the Fukienese mostly journeyed to Southeast Asia.

Beginning in the late part of the nineteenth century, the U.S. Congress began to enact immigration acts with the purpose of excluding Chinese from immigrating to the United States. Among these were the 1882 Chinese Exclusion Act and the 1924 Oriental Exclusion Act (Yu, 1995). These exclusion acts severely limited the growth of the Chinese population in the United States.

In recent decades, however, the number of Chinese immigrants steadily increased. Since World War II, Chinese, mostly from Taiwan and Hong Kong, have been immigrating to the United States to study, to join their families, or for business ventures. After the Vietnam War, thousands of ethnic Chinese from Southeast Asia (mainly from Vietnam) came to the United States. In the two decades since President Nixon's Ping-Pong Diplomacy, more Chinese from the People's Republic of China have entered the United States. Although the exit policy in China was tightened after the 1989 Tienanmen Square incident, many Chinese immigrants entered the United States under political asylum.

In the 1990s, immigrants from the People's Republic of China have constituted one of the largest groups of immigrants. Most recently, the return of Hong Kong to the Chinese government in 1997, as well as the changes in United States immigration policies regarding the quota system will both undoubtedly impact immigration patterns and change the immigration profiles of Chinese-Americans.

The following are selected statistics concerning the place of residency, age, educational background, and language use of Chinese-Americans (Cheng, 1996b; Yu, 1993):

- The top five states chosen by Chinese immigrants for intended residence were California, New York, New Jersey, Massachusetts, and Illinois (Shinagawa, 1996).
- Among the Chinese immigrant population at large, 48% reside in the Pacific region, and 25% reside in the Mid Atlantic region.
- Fifty-nine percent of Chinese-Americans born in the United States are under 19 years of age, while only 14% of immigrant Chinese-Americans are younger than 19.
- Fifty-one percent of Chinese-Americans born in the United States have a bachelor degree or higher, compared to 39% of the immigrants.
- Forty-eight percent of the U.S. born reported speaking only English, while only 5% of the immigrant population reported speaking only English.
- Thirty-one percent of the immigrant population reported speaking no English or little English.

THE FAMILY IN TRANSITION

As immigrants arrive in their new country, they experience major transitions. It is a time of trial and error, of sadness and joy, of uncertainty and excitement, of expectations and disappointments, of rejection and adjustment. It is a time of imbalance and mental disequilibrium. The following section discusses the Chinese family in transition with attention to religion and values, motivations for immigration, and cultural and historical background.

While this chapter describes general characteristics of Chinese-Americans, it is important to note that there is diversity among Chinese-Americans in each of these areas.

The Family

Chinese culture places a heavy emphasis on respect for elders and the family as a unit. Traditionally, in a Chinese family, each member has a role that is clearly defined by an intricate kinship system. As a rule, the father is responsible for all family members, with the mother having direct responsibility for the children, and the oldest son having responsibility for the care of his younger siblings. In recent decades, the changing role of women and China's zero-population-growth policy have changed the way of life dramatically. Traditionally, women were expected to devote themselves to being mothers. As recently as the 1950s, women who bore many children were honored as "Glory Mothers" (Min, 1994). The onset of the one-child-per-family policy, however, effectively negated the traditional and early Communist respect for woman as childbearer. Today, many women in China join the workforce and have gained a measure of equality. However, the sudden role reversal of women in Chinese society has been a difficult adjustment.

Religion and Values

There are over fifty-five different ethnic groups that reside in China. These groups practice various religions including Buddhism, Taoism, Catholicism and other forms of Christianity, and Islam.

Most Chinese believe in Confucianism, which has a great deal of influence in China as well as in other parts of Asia. The doctrine of *The Analect* provides fundamental principles that guide behavior such as the proper treatment of one's parents, teachers, siblings, spouse, and children. These guidelines, which dictate Chinese-American students' behavior at home, may be in conflict with the new culture dominant in the public schools. The new generation of Chinese, as they face the competition of the global market, may be more competitive and assertive in contrast to the older generation, who seem more passive and "silent" (Cheng, 1995).

Other aspects of Confucianism which are hallmarks of Chinese culture include filial piety and respect for elders, and the pursuit and maintenance of harmony. Filial piety refers to the unquestioned obedience to parents expected of children. This includes being polite and not talking back to or challenging the wishes of one's parents. Respect for elders refers to the general deference on the part of the Chinese to the wishes and needs of anyone older than themselves. The strong emphasis on harmony in Chinese culture can be seen in the high value placed on outward calmness and control of undesirable emotions such as anger, jealousy, hostility, aggression, and self-pity. Open expressions of emotion and confrontation are viewed as being inappropriate and undesirable.

Chinese graduate students from Taiwan during the 19760s and 1970s were highly motivated and academically successful because they had had a competitive education. Many of them completed doctoral studies and subsequently sought a better life in the United States. The children of these Chinese graduate students have been often referred to as "model minority," with media reports and stories of school success which have amplified the impression of Asians being ideal students and citizens. However, such a stereotype may be detrimental for some Chinese-American students, whose needs may be overlooked because they are quiet, resulting in poor school performance or behavioral problems (Chang, Lai, & Shimizu, 1995).

Chinese students who have immigrated recently from Taiwan have had experiences that differ significantly from students who immigrated from the People's Republic of China. In recent decades, however, a large number of "parachute students" from Taiwan have immigrated and live mostly on the West Coast of the United States. Typically, these students are in their early teens and are generally unsupervised, since in many cases, their parents live in Taiwan and come to visit them only occasionally. These unsupervised youth present a unique problem for the schools. First, their parents or legal guardians are often unavailable for consultation as they do not live in the United States on a permanent basis. Furthermore, these unsupervised youth have little guidance in terms of homework and extracurricular activities. As a consequence, they tend to congregate in malls, party all night, and are generally negligent about schoolwork. The number of these children has decreased significantly in the last year or two due to a tightening of immigration regulations.

Cultural and Historical Background

One important factor to consider in the adjustment process is cultural difference. People from various cultural backgrounds differ in their adjustment. All Chinese people have five thousand years of Chinese history in common. However, there are marked cultural differences among Chinese from different regions of China. Immigrants from the People's Republic of China have been exposed to five decades of communism. Immigrants from Hong Kong have been under British rule and have different social, cultural, and linguistic orientations. Immigrants from Taiwan have lived half a century under the ruling party Kuomingtang. Taiwan was ruled by Japan from 1895 to 1945, during which time the official language was Japanese. All these cultural and historical experiences have influenced the profiles of the immigrants coming from these different regions.

The new Chinese-American immigrants vary greatly in age. Of course, the age at the time of entry into the United States is critical to how they fare in United States school. Older students are more likely to have had wider exposure to and broader experiences in their own culture and language. Younger students may adjust more quickly to United States schools, perhaps due to lower degrees of inhibition and the relatively fewer number of experiences in their first culture and language.

Motivation for Immigration

One motivating factor for Chinese immigration is the quality and flexibility of education in the United States. Another key motivating factor is the opportunity for advancement. In Hong Kong and China, where the academic systems are highly selective, large numbers of qualified individuals cannot obtain entry to local institutions. So they choose a different route by going abroad. Despite tightened immigration policies and other restrictions, Chinese immigrants are still coming through sponsorships and business visas. Their children are in our schools and their educational challenges need to be addressed. Their identity as well as adjustment must be understood in the context of their environment. Some of them live in crowded tenements in Chinatowns where living standards are low, though their parents work hard to provide better opportunities for them.

Upon completing their course of study, many Chinese students decide to stay and live in the United States The voluntary nonreturn of students following completion of their study constitutes a brain drain in their home country. The brain drain is no longer a serious threat to Taiwan and Hong Kong, but it is quite likely that it remains a challenging situation for China.

SIMILARITIES AND DIFFERENCES BETWEEN CHINESE AND AMERICAN SCHOOLS

The Confucian tradition places strong emphasis on the importance of education. In China as well as in Taiwan, entrance examinations are required for admission into the universities. Most traditional Chinese families expect their children to do well in school; Chinese parents do not praise their children readily, even when they excel, since excellence is expected (Cheng, 1991). If a child does poorly in school or needs special attention, the parents often feel ashamed, perceiving the difficulties as a sign of their own failure. Broadly speaking, primary schools are generally co-ed, while middle schools are either co-ed or exclusively for boys or girls. Competition is keen for gaining admission into the best universities. (More information about the school systems in China and Taiwan can be found in Lin and Fan [1990], and Chen, Seitz, & Cheng [1987].)

Chinese-Americans work hard to overcome linguistic and cultural challenges in order to obtain a good education. In addition to regular schooling, many Chinese-American parents expect their children to learn the Chinese language and maintain the Chinese culture, and many enroll their children in weekend Chinese community schools. In the greater Los Angeles area alone, there are over eighty Chinese language schools, with a total enrollment of about fifteen thousand students. In the San Jose area, there are over two thousand students in one Chinese language school (C. Y. Su, personal communication, September, 1995).

Table 1.1
American Teachers' and Chinese Parents' Expections

American Teachers' Expectations	Chinese Parents' Expectations
Education is interactive and spontaneous.	Education is formal.
Teachers and students work together in the teaching-learning process	Teachers should tell students what to do.
Students learn through participation and interaction. Homework is only part of the process.	Students learn through doing a lot of homework.
Teaching is an active process; students are not passive learners.	The teacher should teach and students should study.
Factual information is readily available; problem solving, creativity and critical thinking is more important.	Factual information is important, fantasy is not.
Teachers should facilitate and model problem solving; students learn by being actively engaged in the process.	Students should be taught steps to solve problems.
Teachers need to be questioned and challenged.	Teachers should not be challenged.
Reading is a constructive process.	Reading is the decoding of information and facts.

Cultural conventions for classroom participation and interaction, such as respect for the teacher and behaving in a quiet and orderly manner in class, are clearly defined for and obeyed by Chinese school children. New Chinese immigrant students might be confused by the spontaneous and outspoken behavior of their peers in American classrooms. In Chinese classrooms, volunteering information and answers is generally considered to be bold and even daring. Students mostly learn through listening, observing, reading, and imitating. The teachers' questions are generally derived from textbooks and lectures, and examinations generally require the recall of factual information. This is in direct contrast to the heavy emphasis on student-centered instruction and encouragement of responses and questions in American classrooms.

Cheng (1991) has analyzed the incongruencies between American teachers' expectations and Asian parents' expectations (Table 1.1). The following is an expansion of the analysis, comparing the expectations of American teachers and Chinese parents at the level of general observations and tendencies (these should *not* be viewed as invariable).

Cultural Differences and Barriers to Classroom Interactions

New Chinese-American students possess various levels of English language proficiency, due to the variety in pre-immigration backgrounds. Some use English at home as well as at school, while others speak the native language at home, seldom speaking English outside the classroom environment. Those students with limited opportunities to speak English may experience difficulties conducting even basic school discourse due to their lack of English language proficiency, lack of awareness of linguistic and social rules, and insufficient opportunities for practice and support of the English language outside the school setting. School discourse is generally more formal and is guided by a set of rules. Some examples of these rules include raising the hand to be acknowledged; waiting to speak until called on, and then speaking clearly and loudly enough to be heard by the other children; and not engaging in conversation with classmates except during cooperative endeavors. Lack of proficiency and opportunities to engage in a variety of discourse clearly present a strong barrier to school success (Cheng, 1994). Chinese children who live in ethnic enclaves such as Alhambra, Monterey Park, and Little Saigon in southern California, and use English in limited environments, experience tremendous difficulty in gaining both basic interpersonal communicative skills (BICS) and cognitive academic linguistic proficiency (CALP) in English, as described by Jim Cummins (1981).

Frequently, ESL students find classroom discourse and its rules, be they oral, written, or nonverbal messages of interaction, incomprehensible and difficult. These rules exist both inside and outside of the classroom. In *Life In Classrooms*, Jackson (1968) defined the hidden curriculum as "the crowds, the praise, and the power that combine to give a distinctive flavor to classroom life collectively for a hidden curriculum which each student (and teacher) must master if he is to make his way satisfactorily through the school" (pp. 33-34). This description speaks to the particular set of values, beliefs, and attitudes teachers, students, and parents bring to schools, and to the fact that each group views their own values as being central to the education process.

Classroom Discourse Rules

Pang (1988) maintained that some students actively engage in verbal discourse with their teachers while other students are disenfranchised during classroom discussions. Pang further reported that there is a tendency for teachers to differentially engage in verbal interactions with students who are more aggressive. This is but one example of hidden school discourse rules that require deeper understanding of the overall school discourse structure. Chinese students, typically, are less aggressive than their peers. As a result, in addition to learning the English language, Chinese-American immigrant students must face the challenges of learning about the hidden school discourse rules before they can become cross-culturally competent (Cheng, 1990) and succeed in the classroom.

The discourse rules that are in operation in American classrooms differ greatly from those that are practiced in Chinese classrooms. Major differences lie in the way classroom interactions are anticipated and managed. Cheng (1991, 1994) pointed out the incongruencies between the expectations of American teachers and Chinese parents. For example, American teachers usually expect students to be interactive, creative, and participatory. Many Chinese-American children, however, are taught at home to be quiet and obedient, and to not challenge or question teachers. Understandably, many Chinese-American children experience both ambivalence and confusion in the classroom due to such conflicting messages and their lack of knowledge of the hidden curriculum, classroom discourse rules, and United States English. American teachers may interpret this confusion as being deficient, disordered, aberrant, and undesirable. The following is a catalogue of classroom behavior which can easily be misunderstood:

- Delay or hesitation in response
- Frequent topic shifts and poor topic maintenance
- Confused facial expressions, such as a frown signaling concentration rather than displeasure
- Short responses
- Use of a soft voice
- Avoiding risk
- Lack of participation and volunteering of information
- Differences in nonverbal messages, such as avoiding eye contact with adults; differences in body language, such as avoiding being hugged or kissed
- Embarrassment over praise
- Different greeting rituals, which may appear impolite, such as looking down when the teacher approaches
- Use of Chinese-influenced English, such as the deletion of the plural or past tense

These are just a few examples of the observed behaviors which may be misinterpreted by teachers. Chinese-American children may be orally proficient and fluent in English but behave according to the discourse rules from their home culture by speaking softly to persons in authority, looking down or away, or avoiding close physical contact.

Surface-level assessment of linguistic and pragmatic functions is insufficient to determine the communicative competence of children and may mislead teachers in their evaluation, interaction, and decision-making process as related to Chinese-American students. Teachers can better instruct and serve Chinese-American students by exploring the home culture and discourse rules of these students. Teachers need to explicitly explain and repeatedly model school discourse rules before Chinese-American children can fully master the socialization process into American schools (Cheng, 1989, 1996a). For example, a script utilizing school discourse rules may be constructed and used for role play. The following is an example: Teacher: "Good morning, Mei Ling." Mei Ling: "Good morning, Miss Smith." Teacher: "I like your dress, it's very pretty." Mei Ling: "Oh, thank you very much. This is my favorite dress. My grandmother bought it for me."

ADJUSTMENT TO LIFE IN THE UNITED STATES

In the process of becoming Americanized, the Chinese-American child must deal with linguistic, cultural, social, and ethnic identity. There are many generational differences between recent immigrants and those whose families have been in the United States for more than one generation. The newcomers face discrimination and often are not accepted as "Americans." They may be asked "Where are you from?" or "Can you repeat what you just said? I cannot understand you." On the other hand, American-born Chinese children may look Chinese, but they grow up speaking English and have limited information about China or the Chinese culture. They are often asked "Where are you from?" "I mean, where are you really from?" "Where did you learn English?" and "How come you speak English so well?"

In *Strangers from a Different Shore* (1989), Ronald Takaki talked about his personal experiences as a Japanese-American growing up in Hawaii and clearly described the perception of mainstream Americans that people with Japanese names and appearance must know Japanese and may not speak English well, not realizing that many are monolingual English speakers. In *The Woman Warrior* (1977), Maxine Hong Kingston described the difficulties Chinese girls face in American schools. Students of Chinese heritage who grew up in the United States are puzzled by the lack of acceptance and their relegation to second-class status as "hyphenated Americans" (Young, 1997). The process of becoming an American is worthy of discussion. How does one become a member of American society?

For recent immigrants, *The First Suburban Chinatown*, by Timothy Fong (1994), recounts the story of recent Chinese immigrants in Monterey Park, California. This account portrays how many Chinese-Americans feel marginalized, even as other Chinese-Americans have gained political clout or political positions. Lily Chen's election to the seat of mayor of the City of Monterey Park, and her leadership and establishment of policies to meet the needs of the Chinese-American community, chronicles well the journey and transformational process that took place from being an immigrant to an Americanized Chinese-American with bicultural characteristics.

Identity Formation

Scholars from a variety of disciplines including psychology, sociology, linguistics, anthropology, and education have long been interested in the topic of identity formation. The following sections describe three distinct notions of identity formation that are useful for understanding Chinese-American students. They are marginality, bicultural identity, and multiple perspectives.

Marginality. The concept of marginality was introduced by Park (1928), who believed that the process of civilization could best be studied in the mind of the "Marginal Man." Stonequist (1935) defined the Marginal Man in the context of cultural conflict and racial prejudice, recognizing that living in two cultures produces dual identities and dual loyalties. Chinese-American children often struggle to belong to two or more groups at the same time. DeVos and

Romanucci-Ross (1975) noted that a sense of inferiority may also arise when a person wishes to assimilate into the dominant society but is not accepted because of race. For example, Chinese students who speak fluent English are often asked "Where did you learn to speak English so well?"

Bicultural Identity. Du Bois' (1903) writings about the double consciousness of the African American experience is a good example of expositions on the notion of bicultural identity. In his book *The Souls of Black Folk*, he eloquently analyzed the psychology of ethnic identity in the following manner: "The Negro is a sort of seventh son, born with a veil, and gifted with second-sight in this American world—a world which yields him no true self-consciousness, but only lets him see himself through the revelation of the other world. It is a peculiar sensation, this double-consciousness, this sense of always looking at one's self through the eyes of others, of measuring one's soul by the tape of a world that looks on in amused contempt and pity. One ever feels this two-ness—an American, a Negro; two souls, two thoughts, two unreconciled strivings; two warring ideals in one dark body, whose dogged strength alone keeps it from being torn asunder" (p. 3).

Chinese-Americans who were born in the United States may have similar experiences in their identity formation process. They, too, may feel the sense of double consciousness as described by Du Bois (1903) and Delgado (1995). They may feel like their peers in many ways, but nonetheless be made to feel different, viewed as outsiders, or unincluded.

Multiple Perspectives. In *The Rodrigo Chronicle* (1995), Delgado discussed the notion of multiple consciousness. In post-modern theory, binaries and dichotomies are to be avoided in order to prevent stereotyping. In other words, a Chinese-American is not simply the combination of being Chinese and American, but rather the sum of his or her personal experience, parts of which may be neither Chinese nor American in origin. The notion of multiple consciousness might very well work better with individuals who grow up with diverse experiences. An example might be a Chinese-American specializing in African American musicology who is touring Europe with his band making music based on the African theme. This young person's interests are indicative of the unique events experienced in his lifetime. Another example might be a Chinese-American girl who grew up in San Diego and Tijuana speaking fluent Spanish and English, who cannot speak much Chinese, and who is very involved with the activities of the Tijuana Mexican community, the San Diego mainstream community, as well as the San Diego Chinese community. These two vivid examples speak to the fact that it is neither a simple nor easy task to assess the complex and multiple dimensions of identity when striving to meet the needs of a Chinese-American student.

Maintenance of the Home Culture

Although Chinese-American individuals may experience life in multiple perspectives, there is still a tendency for them to be "mainstreamed." This push to be part of American mainstream life may conflict with the pull from their family to retain cultural roots and traditions. Typically, Chinese parents expect their children to follow the rules of filial piety, obedience, and other Confucian values. *The Joy Luck Club* by Amy Tan and *The Woman Warrior* by Maxine Hong Kingston, that describes the struggles faced by American-born Chinese, are two good examples of recent literature. Other works poignantly depict the struggle to become an American, such as Richard Rodriquez's *Hunger of Memory* (1982) and David Mura's *Becoming Japanese* (1991).

ADAPTIVE STRATEGIES

Some newcomers find their new areas of residence comfortable and welcoming, while others encounter very different experiences. Some newcomers find that their new country far exceeds their expectations, while others are disappointed by their new surroundings or even feel a sense of betrayal. They may find that the demands of day-to-day living and acculturation are tremendously taxing and trying.

Research on adjustment problems has recurrently addressed the question of why some refugee and immigrant groups adapt readily to the American way of life, while others do so more slowly (Cheng, 1996c.) In *Myth or Reality: Adaptive Strategies of Asian Newcomers in California*, Trueba, Cheng, and Ima (1993) describe the adaptation process newcomers undergo and explain the cultural conflict immigrants typically experience, utilizing the notion of stages first used by George and Louise Spindler (1971, 1990). The adaptive strategies of different immigrant individuals can be classified into the following types of response to cultural conflict:

1. Reaffirmation: characterized by efforts to revive native cultural traditions, accompanied by rejection of the mainstream culture.
2. Synthesis: a selective combination of various cultural aspects of one group with those of the other in particular domains of life.
3. Withdrawal: a rejection of both cultures in conflict, accompanied by a transitional stage with no commitment to any specific set of cultural values.
4. Biculturalism: full involvement with both cultures, requiring a position of effective code-switching (cultural and linguistic).
5. Constructive marginality: a position of tentative acceptance of two conflicting cultural value systems, in which one keeps a conscious distance from both cultural systems through moderate participation in both cultures.
6. Compensatory adaptation: thorough mainstreaming into the dominant culture and rejection or avoidance of identification with, or display of, their native culture.

In summary, Spindler and Spindler (1971, 1990) have argued that new immigrant groups experience different levels of adaptation as related to their degree of cultural conflict. Some reaffirm their native traditions by attempting to revive and maintain them; for example, they may assist in the building of a temple and attend Sunday services there. Others may subscribe to their native-language newspaper or magazines, listen to native-language radio stations, and rent native-language movies and TV videos while rejecting the mainstream culture. Some may choose to combine selected aspects of one culture with those of the other. Others withdraw and reject both conflicting cultures. Those who desire to embrace both mainstream and home cultures learn cultural and linguistic code-switching abilities in order to function well within the two cultures.

Chinese-Americans are good examples of immigrants who code-switch. They bring to the United States practices in child rearing, kinship support, religion, medicine, and education which are quite different from if not directly in contrast to those of mainstream U.S. society (Cheng, 1991). It is typical for their perceptions of reality, work ethics, and styles of interaction to undergo constant challenge in the face of mainstream culture. Meanwhile, other Chinese-Americans consider themselves to be fully American and feel frustrated when regarded as strangers or outsiders (Mura, 1991; Takaki, 1989). In sum, the Chinese students' school experience and progress with acculturation vary greatly with the students' length of residence in the United States, as well as the unique qualities particular to their areas of residence.

An understanding of Chinese-American student backgrounds and adaptive strategies can lend significant insight to the arena of the classroom and the interactions which take place there. That is, educators can better manage and facilitate the academic and social codes of the classroom, cultural clashes or discourse which may stem from fundamentally different or opposite assumptions students and teachers hold, as well as personal and emotional issues arising out of differing or contradictory academic (American) and home (Chinese) contexts which effect academic behavior. Further, by learning about the backgrounds of Chinese-American students and the adaptive strategies they employ, educators themselves can empower these students by guiding them to discovery of how classroom interactions are greatly influenced by culture and adaptation strategies.

PROVIDING ACCESS FOR CHINESE-AMERICAN PARENTS AND STUDENTS

Schools and families need to establish a partnership in order to ensure success. Although "foreigners" have greater access to becoming bicultural more easily in open societies such as the United States, where cultural rules, mores, and traditions are discussed openly, than in societies such as China, where "foreigners" are not expected to enter society completely and are held at a distance from the culture, foreign-born individuals may still experience difficulty for both cultural and linguistic reasons. Schools need to reach into the community and establish contact with students' families, even as community leaders need to encourage parents to become involved in school activities. Ultimately, all students, parents, and teachers will benefit when, as a result of these multiple interactions, Chinese-American students and parents feel less marginalized and view themselves as constructive members of the school community.

Providing Access for Parents

Understandably, parents who face difficulties of their own in adapting to a new language and culture often feel inadequate and ill equipped to help their children with schoolwork and with social issues. Yet it is critical that students' families be involved in education. Parents can inform teachers about students' use of home and school languages, the literature available at home, and the community resources available to the students. Parents can be a significant resource, as they play a vital role in the students' social, language, and literacy development (Chang, Lai, & Shimizu, 1995).

Parents need to be encouraged to support literacy at home and school; expectations for language use, as well as classroom, social, and academic skills must be explained. The following are some specific suggestions for parental involvement in their children's schools:

- Volunteer for school activities, such as book fairs or multicultural events
- Drive students to field trips
- Help in the office, the library, and the classroom
- Prepare food for bake sales, dances, and clubs
- Be active in the PTA
- Run for Site Council

When Chinese parents gain access to schools and the educational system, their children will benefit both directly and indirectly in academic, social, and emotional aspects.

Providing Access for Students

Students, teachers, specialists, and administrators can work together to contribute to Chinese students' academic success. "They can collaborate across disciplines to provide meaningful learning experiences within comprehensible learning environments" (Cheng & Chang, 1995, p. 19). They can emphasize the attitudes and values of a multicultural society and combat the racism that students encounter in school and outside of school. They can help prepare Chinese students to translate academic success into occupational success after completing their education by providing resources or educating them in nonacademic issues which are important for the students' future, such as accent reduction and professional networking.

Rethinking and changing our patterns of relations and intervention strategies for Chinese-American students can improve communication between Chinese students and teachers, ensure access to the core curriculum, facilitate understanding of school discourse, and ensure that Chinese students become authentic members of the community. The following are some suggestions toward this end:

- Increase vocabulary: use words in children's literature, trade books, and school textbooks.
- Nurture the development of a bicultural identity: stories of famous people both from Asian and other ethnic groups can be shared.
- Practice colloquial and ritualistic patterns of interactions and discourse: for example, with scripted role plays.
- Provide opportunities for exposure to various narrative styles: read letters, stories, and poetry to children; have students act in skits.

- Explain the written and unwritten rules that govern writing styles across different disciplines, genres, and periods: use examples noteworthy in U.S. history to demonstrate good writing, such as the "Gettysburg Address."
- Provide explicit comparisons and contrasts between languages: for example, that Chinese is tonal and non-inflectional, and English is intonational and inflectional.
- Learn to value cultural beliefs, perceptions, and values: multicultural books can be used to foster appreciation of different cultures.
- Join school activities, such as after school clubs and sports, school plays, and bake sales.
- Read a wide variety of literature: fairy tales, newspapers, magazines, biographies, best-sellers, poetry, and so on.

WORKING SUGGESTIONS

Teachers, administrators, counselors, and other service providers need to consider the foregoing suggestions, reexamine their current methods and strategies in servicing the truly diverse student population in our schools today, and recognize the importance of cultural pluralism and move it to the fore. Institutions must redefine and reaffirm their multicultural components and, in keeping with the rich, diverse fabric of the American tapestry, recommit themselves to improving the quality of education for all students, including students of diverse linguistic and cultural backgrounds.

Suggestions for Teachers

The challenge of identifying the sources of students' educational difficulties is compounded by the possible combination of factors linguistic, cultural, social, psychological, emotional, and neurophysiological in nature, which may operate in an individual (Cheng & Chang, 1995). Teachers need support in their attempts to examine the cultural dimensions of interaction between themselves and their students. While trying to comprehend cultural differences, teachers must also guard against stereotyping children by relying on stereotypes of cultural patterns.

The following are some tips and suggestions for creating an optimal, language-learning environment in the classroom and for reducing the level of difficulty both students and teachers may experience in communication (Cheng, 1996c):

- Make no assumptions about what students know or do not know; anticipate their needs and the greatest challenges they may face.
- Expect frustration and possible misunderstandings.
- Encourage students to participate in activities such as student government, social and academic clubs, and other organizations to increase their exposure to different types of discourse. Language is a social tool and students should be provided with a variety of situations in which to use different kinds of language to fulfill a variety of functions.
- Facilitate students' transition into mainstream culture through activities such as role-playing by preparing scripts for common activities or situations such as a birthday party or a Thanksgiving celebration and by using cultural experiences as topics for discussions (Cheng, 1989).

- Nurture the development of a bicultural identity. Introduce multicultural elements not only in phonology, morphology, and syntax, but also in pragmatics, semantics and ritualistic patterns. For example, the child who speaks Chinese at home and practices Buddhism needs to learn something about Christian holidays such as Easter and Christmas. However, the inclusion of Chinese or Buddhist topics in instruction will foster an additive, not subtractive and inclusive, not exclusive, approach to learning.
- Work with individual parents and with the PTA.

Suggestions for Administrators, Counselors, and Other Service Providers

Administrators, counselors, and related service providers need to gain a better understanding of the various communities their students come from. The following suggestions were proposed by Cheng, Chen, Tsubo, Sekandari and Alfafara-Killacky (1997) toward fostering a multicultural or pluralistic perspective in learning:

- Know yourself: Explore your own cultural background first. This will assist in the understanding of your attitudes both toward your own culture and toward other cultures.
- Put the individual first, diversity second: There are ways to incorporate the Chinese student's culture into instruction in an effective manner. First, focus on the individual rather than on a particular group as a key to improving the quality of service provided in school settings.
- Be aware of the wider context(s): Are Chinese students being situated in the proper context for facilitating certain skills development? Are educators aware of all the different contexts that a particular student encounters? Are educators aware of sudden or critical changes in students' contexts and how or why the changes occurred? Are the students and individuals significant to the students aware of these changes?
- Practice honesty: Do not hesitate to say that you don't know something about Chinese students or their culture. Take advantage of an opportunity to learn and invite students to share or ask appropriate questions.
- Show interest: Information about a student's background is key to developing interventions against student alienation or low achievement. Be interested in the unique backgrounds of the Chinese students in your classroom or school.

CONCLUSION

Given the complexity of the Chinese-American student population, it is difficult to acquire in-depth knowledge of every student's linguistics, cultural, and social background. However, general cross-cultural communicative competence, or the ability to communicate effectively across cultures, can be developed and integrated into all facets of educational practice (Cheng, 1989) and widely benefit students, educators, and parents. Towards this end, the notion of cultural therapy, described by Trueba, Cheng, and Ima (1993), requires that one first recognize and understand one's cultural biases, particularly as they influence perceptions of others of different cultures; this essential prerequisite makes possible reflections on issues about cultural interactions and relations.

Powerful things can happen when teachers, students, and parents work together. Immigrants and refugees come to the United States to pursue the

American dream and to share that dream: a dream to be free, to have economic security, to pursue a better life, and to have an equal opportunity to succeed. The adaptive strategies of immigrants are manifested not only in schools but in other social institutions. As an institution with which immigrants have a sustained and ongoing relationship, schools, by learning the backgrounds and adaptive strategies of Chinese-Americans, can model and foster the kind of partnership for other institutions to emulate and help build a stronger community of diverse groups who strive to understand, esteem, and equip each other.

REFERENCES

Chang, J. M., Lai, A., & Shimizu, W. (1995). LEP, LD, poor and missed learning opportunities: A case of inner city Chinese children. In L. Cheng (Ed.), *Integrating language and learning for inclusion* (pp. 265-290). San Diego, CA: Singular Publishing.

Chen, Y. H., Seitz, M., & Cheng, L. (1987). Special education. In D. Smith (Ed.), *Modernization of education in Taiwan.* (pp. 189-213). Taipei, Taiwan: Pacific Cultural Foundation.

Cheng, L. (1989). Service delivery to Asian-Pacific LEP children: A cross-cultural framework. *Topics in Language Disorders* 9(3):1-14.

Cheng, L. (1990). Recognizing diversity: A need for a paradigm shift. *American Behavioral Scientist* 43(2): 263-278.

Cheng, L. (1991). *Assessing Asian language performance: Guidelines for evaluating limited English proficient students.* Oceanside, CA: Academic Communication Associates.

Cheng, L. (1994). Difficult discourse: An untold Asian story. In D. N. Ripich & N. A. Creaghead (Eds.), *School discourse problems*, 2nd ed., (pp. 156-170). San Diego, CA: Singular Publishing.

Cheng, L. (1995). *Integrating language and learning: An Asian Pacific focus.* San Diego, CA: Singular Publishing.

Cheng, L. (1996a). Beyond bilingualism: A quest for communicative competence. *Topics in Language Disorders* 16(4): 9-21.

Cheng, L. (1996b). *Bridging theory and practice: Balancing academic achievement and social growth.* Paper presented at annual convention of Chinese-American Education Research Development Association. San Jose, California.

Cheng, L. (1996c). Enhancing communication: Toward optimal language learning for limited English proficient students. *Language, Speech and Hearing Services in Schools* 28 (2): 347-354.

Cheng, L., & Chang, J. M. (1995). Asian-Pacific Islander students in need of effective services. In L. Cheng (Ed.), *Integrating language and learning for inclusion* (pp. 3-30). San Diego, CA: Singular Publishing.

Cheng, L., Chen, T., Tsubo, T., Sekandari, N., & Alfafara-Killacky, S. (1997). Challenges of diversity: An Asian Pacific perspective. In J. M. Novak & L. G. Denti (Eds.), *Multicultures, 3,* 114-145.

Cummins, J. (1981). The role of primary language development in promoting educational success for language minority students. In California Department of Education (Ed.), *Schooling and language minority students: A theoretical framework* (pp. 3-49). Los Angeles: Evaluation, Dissemination and Assessment Center, California State University, Los Angeles.

Delgado, R. (1995). *The Rodrigo chronicle: Conversations about America and race.* New York: New York University Press.

DeVos, G., & Romanucci-Ross, L. (1975). *Ethnicity*. Palo Alto, CA: Mayfield.

Du Bois, W. E. B. (1903). *The souls of Black folk.* Greenwich, CT: Fawcett.

Fong, T. P. (1994). *The first suburban Chinatown: The remaking of Monterey Park, California*. Philadelphia: Temple University Press.

Jackson, P. (1968). *Life in classrooms*. New York: Holt, Rinehart.

Kingston, M. H. (1977). *The woman warrior: Memoirs of a girlhood among ghosts*. New York: Vintage International.

Lin, B., & Fan, L. (1990). *Education in mainland China: Review and evaluation*. Taipei, Taiwan: National Chengchi University.

Min, A. (1994). *Red azalea: Life and love in China*. New York: Pantheon Books.

Mura, D. (1991). *Becoming Japanese*. New York: Doubleday.

Pang, V. (1988). Ethnic prejudice: Still alive and hurtful. *Harvard Education Review* 58(3)(August): 375-379.

Pang, V. & L. L. Cheng (Eds.), *Cherihed hopes: Educating asian Pacific American students*. New York: SUNY Press.

Park, R. E. (1928). Human migration and the marginal man. *American Journal of Sociology* 33(6): 881-893.

Rodriquez, R. (1982). *Hunger of memory: The education of Richard Rodriguez—an autobiography*. Boston, MA: David R. Godine.

Shinagawa, L. H. (1996). The impact of immigration on the demography of Asian Pacific Americans. In B. O. Hing & R. Lee (Eds), *The state of Asian Pacific America: Reframing the immigration debate* (pp. 59-126). Los Angeles, CA: Leadership Education for Asian Pacifics (LEAP), Inc.

Spindler, G., & Spindler, L. (1971). *Dreamers without power: The Menomini Indians*. New York: Holt, Rinehart and Winston.

Spindler, G., & Spindler, L. (1990). *The American cultural dialogue and its transmission*. London, England: Falmer Press.

Stonequist, E. V. (1935). The problem of the marginal man. *American Journal of Sociology,* 41(1): 1-12.

Takaki, R. (1989). *Strangers from a different shore*. Boston: Little, Brown.

Tan, A. (1989). *The joy luck club*. New York: Putnam.

Trueba, H., Cheng, L., & Ima, K. (1993). *Myth or reality: Adaptive strategies of Asian newcomers in California*. Philadelphia, PA: Falmer Press.

U.S. Bureau of the Census (1993). *1990 Census of populations: Asians and Pacific Islanders in the United States*. Washington, DC: U.S. Government Printing Office.

Young, R. L. (1997). Finding one's roots in uncertain lands: How the Asian Pacific American child copes. In V.O. Pang & L. L. Cheng (Eds.), *Cherished Hopes: Educating Asian Pacific American students*. New York: SUNY Press.

Yu, E. (1993). *Issues in studying Asian-Pacific Islander Americans*. Paper presented at the Biostatistics Conference, December, San Diego State University, California.

Yu, R. (1995). Chinese-American contributions to the educational development of Toisan 1910-1940. In D. T. Nakanishi & T. Y. Nishida (Eds.), *The Asian American educational experience* (pp. 42-57). New York: Routledge.

CHAPTER 2

Linguistic Perspective on the Education of Chinese-American Students

Marilyn Mei-Ying Chi

Asian Americans are the fastest growing ethnic group in the United States (O'Hare & Felt, 1991). Among this group, Chinese-Americans is the largest subgroup. Chinese-Americans are a very diverse group. Like other ethnic groups, the diversity of Chinese-Americans is the result not only of differences in immigration history and experience, but also of differences in their regions of origin, as well as linguistic, educational, religious, and socioeconomic backgrounds. In this chapter, the linguistic considerations on the education of Chinese-American students is presented in four main areas: (1) linguistic backgrounds of Chinese-American students in the United States, (2) differences and similarities between Chinese and English, (3) typical difficulties encountered by Chinese-speaking students learning English, and (4) practical suggestions for educators working with Chinese speakers learning English at the K-12 levels.

LINGUISTIC BACKGROUNDS OF CHINESE-AMERICAN STUDENTS IN THE UNITED STATES

Immigrant and American-Born Chinese-American Students

Chinese people arrived in the United States as early as 1785, and to California in 1815 (Chinn, 1967). Between 1820 and 1965, an estimated 417,000 immigrants came to the United States from China (Sung, 1967). Immigrants during this period were primarily from the southeast coastal province of Guangdong. They spoke Cantonese, one of the seven major dialect groups in China. From 1966 to 1977, an estimated 255,092 immigrants came to the United States from Hong Kong and Taiwan (California State Department of Education, 1989). The majority of immigrants from Hong Kong spoke Cantonese, whereas the immigrants from Taiwan spoke Mandarin (so-called

Putonghua) and the Min dialect (so-called Taiwanese). In the 1980s, a large wave of highly educated professionals and business persons immigrated to the United States from Hong Kong and Taiwan. Many of them were fearful of the People's Republic of China's takeover of Hong Kong in July, 1997. Presently, the majority of this wave reside in California, particularly in Southern California, and in the East Bay areas of San Francisco (e.g., Cupertino, Fremont, San Jose) and Los Angeles (e.g., Alhambra, Cerritos, Monterey Park). In 1979, the United States and the People's Republic of China announced normalized diplomatic relations. Since then, many educated Chinese have come to the United States as exchange scholars or as graduate students. Most of them speak Mandarin, with some variations in tone, pronunciation, and vocabulary.

Chinese Language Variation

China is a great country with five major ethnicities—Han, Manchu, Mongol, Muhammadan, and Tibetan-each having its own language and writing system. Generally, however, when we speak of the Chinese language, we mean the language spoken by the Han people, who constitute approximately 94% of the Chinese population.

The Han language can be subdivided into hundreds of dialects, it is traditional to speak of the varieties of Chinese as dialects, even though they may be "different" from one another to the point of being mutually incomprehensible to other groups. For example, Cantonese and Mandarin differ from each other roughly as do the Romance languages Portuguese and Rumanian (Li & Thompson, 1981). It should be noted that Portuguese and Rumanian are referred to as different "languages" because they are spoken in different countries. On the other hand, because Cantonese and Mandarin are spoken in the same country, they are called different "dialects." Accordingly, in this chapter, the author adheres to this convention and refers to Cantonese and Mandarin as dialects.

The Chinese phonologists have classified the Chinese languages into seven major dialect groups as shown in Table 2.1 and Figure 2.1. The map in Figure 2.1 shows the geographical spread and the locales of the representatives of the different dialect groups, as well as some major cities in China.

The word *Mandarin*, denoting the major dialect of China, is an established linguistic term in the West. It represents the speech of Beijing, which for centuries has been recognized as the official language of China, due to the political and cultural significance of the city. In 1955, the government of the People's Republic of China proclaimed it as the national language. Mandarin comprises the grammar of northern Mandarin, the pronunciation of the Beijing dialect, and the vocabulary of modern vernacular literature. The national language has since been known as *Putonghua*, which means the "common language." In the 1950s, the government of the Republic of China in Taiwan also proclaimed the Beijing dialect as the national language. This dialect is called *Guoyu*, which means the "national language." Thus, the term *Mandarin* refers to both *Putonghua* and *Guoyu*, depending upon who the speaker is (Chao, 1968; Li & Thompson, 1981).

Table 2.1
The Seven Major Dialect Groups in Chinese

DIALECT FAMILIES	GEOGRAPHICAL SPREAD	REPRESENTATIVE LOCALE	TOTAL POPULATION (%)
Mandarin	Northern	Beijing	70
	Northwestern	Taiyuan	
	Southwestern	Chengdu	
	Lower Yangzi	Nanjing	
Wu	I	Suzhou	8.4
	II	Wenzhou	
Xiang	Old	Shuangfeng	5
	New	Changsha	
Kan		Nanchang	2.4
Hakka		Meixian	4
Min	Northern	Fuzhou	1.5
	Southern	Chaozhou	
Yue	Yue-hai	Zhongshan	5
	Qin-lian	Lianzhou	
	Gao-lei	Gaozhou	
	Si-yi	Taishan	
	Guei-nan	Yulin	

Source: Li & Thompson. (1981, p. 3).

In this chapter, the author will mainly discuss Mandarin, including Putonghua and Guoyu. The majority of Chinese who immigrated after 1965, regardless of their place of origin (i.e., China, Hong Kong, Taiwan) and preferred home dialect (e.g., Cantonese, Taiwanese, Wu), speak at least some Mandarin.

While the Chinese language is rich in dialects that are mutually incomprehensible, fortunately, there is only one writing system used by all Chinese speakers. It is not uncommon for Mandarin-speaking Chinese shopping in the Cantonese-populated San Francisco Chinatown to write Chinese characters or to speak English when communicating with the shopkeeper. This writing system has been utilized for more than 3,000 years and is the chief means of communication in Chinese communities throughout the world.

DIFFERENCES AND SIMILARITIES BETWEEN CHINESE AND ENGLISH

The Chinese language is genetically classified as an independent branch of the Sino-Tibetan language family (Anderson & Jones, 1974). All the Chinese dialects, including Mandarin, Cantonese, and Taiwanese, are known as tonal, monosyllabic, and noninflectional languages. For example, in Mandarin, "house" is *wu,* 屋 and "mountain" is *san,* 山. Additionally, in word formation, there is very little morphological complexity in the Chinese language. In English, a large number of words are made up of morphemes such as the root, affix, and/or inflectional endings. For example, in the English word, "books,

Figure 2.1
Chinese Dialect Map

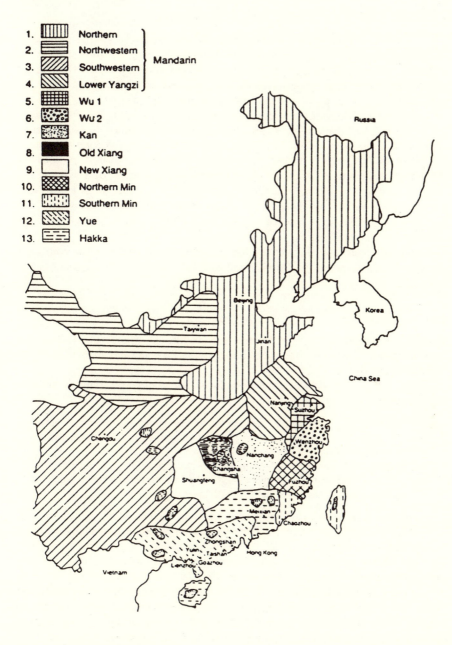

Source: Li & Thompson. (1981, p. 4).

"book" is the root word, and "-s" is an inflectional ending, indicating the plural form; whereas in Chinese, *shu,* 書 can refer to either "book" or "books."

Phonology

In terms of sound structure, Mandarin has a relatively simple consonant system and a rather complicated vowel system as compared with English. In traditional Chinese phonology, a syllable is divided into an initial, a final, and a tone (Chao, 1968; Li & Thompson, 1981). The initial in Mandarin is equivalent to the consonant in English, and the final, equivalent to the vowel.

Consonants. The *initial* represents the consonantal beginning of a syllable. For example, *j* in *ji,* "a last name" and *zh* in *zhan,* "a last name." A small number of syllables such as *an,* "calm," and *yan,* "party," do not begin with a consonant. These are said to begin with the "zero initial." Since Mandarin does not have consonant clusters (e.g., *bl, pl, gr*), the consonantal beginning of a syllable can only be a single consonant. Including the zero initial, Mandarin has twenty-two initials. The initials of Mandarin are provided in Table 2.2 using the International Phonetic Alphabet (IPA) and Pinyin (the national phonetic alphabet adopted in China).

In terms of the key differences between Mandarin and English consonant sounds, listed below are the English consonantal phonemes that do not exist in Mandarin.

Examples:
/th/ (voiceless) as in **thin**   /th/ (voiced) as in **this**

Neither the voiceless nor the voiced /th/ occurs in Mandarin. The closest approximations would probably be the /t/ as in *Taiwan,* and the /d/ as in *du,* "knife," respectively.

Other differences between the sounds of Mandarin and English are less significant, such as the following:

- The Mandarin *l* is pronounced by rapping the tongue against the upper gum ridge and then flat to the front; whereas the English *l* is produced by having the tongue form a hollow from which sides the air flows.
- The Mandarin *r* is produced by curling the tongue upward, almost touching the roof of the mouth, and with the mouth closed; whereas, the English *r* is produced by curling the tongue downward with the mouth open.

As mentioned, Mandarin does not have consonant clusters (also known as consonant blends). The common blends in English combine consonants with *l, r,* and *s,* such as *bl, cl, fl, gl, pl; br, cr, dr, fr, gr;* and *sl, sn, st, scr, spl, spr, sch.* The lack of consonant clusters in Chinese pronunciation generates a very big problem for Chinese speakers learning English.

Vowels. The *final* in Mandarin is the part of the syllable excluding the initial. There are thirty-seven finals that are respectively equivalent to vowels in English. They are listed in Table 2.3. The rules following the correspondences between the IPA vowels and the Pinyin vowels are shown in Table 2.4 (Li & Thompson, 1981).

Table 2.2
Initials (Consonants) in Chinese Mandarin

PLACE OF ARTICULATION \ MANNER OF ARTICULATION	UNASPIRATED STOPS		ASPIRATED STOPS		UNASPIRATED AFFRICATES		ASPIRATED AFFRICATES		NASALS		FRICATIVES		VOICED CONTINUANTS	
	IPA	Pinyin	IPA	Pinyin	IPA	Pinyin	IPA	Pinyin	IPA	Pinyin	IPA	Pinyin	IPA	Pinyin
Bilabials	p	b	p^h	p					m	m				
Labio-dentals											f	f		
Dental-alveolars	t	d	t^h	t	ts	z	ts^h	c	n	n	s	s	l	l
Retroflexes			.		tʂ	zh	$tʂ^h$	ch			ʂ	sh	ɻ	r
Palatals					tɕ	j	$tɕ^h$	q			ɕ	x		
Velars	k	g	k^h	k							x	h		

Source: Li & Thompson, (1981 p.5).

Table 2.3
Finals (Vowels) in Chinese Mandarin

ˉ. ˊ. ˇ	A	ə	o		ai	ei	au	ou	an	ən	aŋ	əŋ	
i	iA			iɛ			iau	iou	iɛn	in	iaŋ	iŋ	
u	uA		uo		uai	uei			uan	uən	uaŋ	uŋ	uəŋ
y				yɛ			.		yɛn	yn			

Source: Li & Thompson. (1981, p. 6).

The velar nasal [ŋ] occurs only as part of a final, never as an initial. In Pinyin, it is represented by *ng*. The finals, as seen in Table 2.4, are composed mainly of vowels. The *only* two consonants that occur in a Mandarin syllable final are the alveolar nasal [n] and the velar nasal [ŋ].

Tones. In contrast to English, a stress language, Mandarin is a tonal language. The musical quality of the spoken Chinese language is due to the fact that almost every syllable must carry one of four basic tones. These tones are indicated by diacritical marks over the vowels. For examples, the syllable *wen*, when spoken in high falling tone, means "to ask" (*wèn*, 問); but it means "to kiss" when spoken in a dipping/falling-rising tone (*wěn*, 吻) or "to smell" when spoken in a high rising tone (*wén*, 聞). Therefore, the sentence, "May I ask you?" can be mispronounced as "May I kiss you?" The Mandarin tonal system is relatively simple in comparison with those of the southern Chinese dialects such as Cantonese and Taiwanese. The four tones are shown in Table 2.5.

The descriptions and graphs in Table 2.5 were devised by Y. R. Chao (1948, 1968) in order to illustrate the time-pitch of the voice. In the example column, the four tones are indicated by diacritical marks over the vowels in Pinyin.

Morphology

When any dialect of the Chinese language, including Mandarin, Cantonese, and Taiwanese, is compared to other languages, one of the most obvious features is the relative simplicity of the word formation; that is, a typical word is not made up of component parts, called "morphemes," but is rather a single morpheme. The lack of inflection and derivation is a critical characteristic of the Chinese language. This is not to say there is none. In fact, there is very little morphological complexity in any of them. Such a language has been referred to as an isolating or analytical language, or a language in which most words consist of just one morpheme and cannot be further analyzed into component parts (Karlgren, 1949).

Number Agreement. In English, it is necessary to make the singular and plural distinction, as in *book/books, box/boxes, child/children*. In Mandarin,

Table 2.4
Correspondences Between IPA and Pinlyn Vowels in Chinese Madarin

IPA VOWEL SYMBOLS	PINYIN SYMBOLS	CONTEXT	EXAMPLES
|A|		all	lā = [lÃ] 'pull'
|a|	a	all	bān = |pān| 'move'
|ɛ|		between {|i| |y|} and |n|	lián = |lién| 'connect' yuǎn = |yěn| 'far'
|o|		all	mó = |mó| 'grind'
|u|	o	before |ŋ| or after |a|	lóng = |lúŋ| 'dragon' láo = |láu| 'toil'
|y|		all	lè = |lý| 'happy'
|e|		before |i|	léi = |léi| 'thunder'
|ɛ|	e	after |i| or |y|	liè = |liè| 'arrange in order' lüè = |lyé| 'vile'
|ə|		before |h| or |ŋ|	gēn = |kᴣn| 'root' gēng = |kᴣŋ| 'till'
|ᴣ|	er	all	ér = |ᴣ| 'son'
|e|	φ	after |Cu|	duì = |tuèi| 'correct'
|ə|	φ	after |Cu|	dūn = |tuān| 'squat'
|i|		with any initial except zero	li = |li| 'depart'
|ʅ|	i	after |tʂ|. |tʂʰ|. |ʂ|. |ɻ|	shī = |ʂʅ̄| 'poetry'
|ɿ|		after |ts|. |tsʰ|. |s|	sī = |sɿ̄| 'think' |cī| = |tsʰɿ̄| 'female'
|u|		with any initial except zero	lú = |lú| 'stove'
|y|	u	after |tɕ|. |tɕʰ|. |ɕ|	xū = |ɕȳ| 'false' qù = |tɕʰȳ| 'go'
|y|	ü	after |n| and |l|	lǘ = |lý| 'donkey' nǚ = |nỹ| 'daughter'
|y|	yu	after zero initial	yú = |ǘ| 'fish' yuán = |yén| 'garden'
|i|	y	after zero initial but not in isolation	yào = |iàu| 'want'
|i|	yi	in isolation	yī = |ī| 'one'
|u|	w	after zero initial but not in isolation	wén = |uᴣn| 'smell'
|u|	wu	in isolation	wǔ = |ǔ| 'five'

Source: Li & Thompson. (1981, p. 7).

Table 2.5
Tones in Chinese Mandarin

Tone	Description	Graph	Example		
1	high level	⌐	*wen*	溫	"warm"
2	high rising	⌐	*wén*	聞	"smell"
3	dipping/falling-rising	⋁	*wěn*	吻	"kiss"
4	high falling	⌐	*wèn*	問	"ask"

"book/books" are the same form as *shu*. The lack of plural inflectional endings does not mean that there is no such concept and function of plurality in Mandarin. In Mandarin, plurality is typically expressed by a separate word such as *yixie,* "some," or *xuduo,* "many," and involves no morphological change within a word. In Mandarin, plurality is only marked on pronouns and human nouns. With pronouns, the suffix *-men* serves this function.

Examples:

Singular		Plural	
ta	"s/he"	*ta-men*	"they"
ni	"you"	*ni-men*	"you"
wo	"I"	*wo-men*	"we"

With human nouns, the suffix *-men* also serves the same function.

Examples:

xiongdi-men	"brothers"
jiemei-men	"sisters"
pengyou-men	"friends"

Subject-Verb Agreement. In English, it is also necessary to have subject-verb agreements, for example, in the third person singular present tense. In contrast, the subject-verb agreement inflectional ending (i.e., *-s* and *-es*) does not exist in Mandarin.

Examples:

wo	*du*	*shu*	(first person)
I	read	book	

I read a book.

ta	*du*	*shu*	(third person)
he/she	read	book	

S/he reads a book.

Tense and Aspect Marker. In English, there are inflectional endings (i.e., *-ed* and *-ing*) to signal the time of a stated event relative to the time of speaking (i.e., tense) or the duration or completion of a stated event relative to other events (i.e., aspect).

Example:
a. I *walked.*
b. I *am walking.*

and Filipino students, who had minor preferences for it, as observed in a separate study (Park, 1997c).

Korean-American students' placement in English as a second language (ESL) classes or their length of residence in the United States did not appear to be related to their preference for visual learning (Park, 1997c); that is, Korean-American students' preference for visual learning was comparable, whether they were enrolled in regular English or in an ESL class, and whether they had been in the United States for a few years or for more than ten years. Park's findings mean that teachers who incorporate more visual materials (charts, graphs, semantic maps, graphic organizers, and character webs, etc.) in instructional activities most likely enhance learning by Korean-American students (Park, 1997b; 1997c).

Korean-American students also indicated a major preference for kinesthetic learning (Park, 1997b, 1997c); therefore, teachers should try to provide experiential and interactive learning activities that require total physical involvement for Korean-American students. Research findings suggest that Korean-American students' preference for kinesthetic learning increases with their length of residence in the United States and their acculturation to American classrooms (Park, 1997c).

Korean-American boys and girls were also found to have a minor preference for tactile learning regardless of their length of residence in the United States and whether they were enrolled in regular English or in ESL classes (Park, 1997b, 1997c). Thus teachers should provide Korean-American students with many opportunities for hands-on learning activities. Building models, doing laboratory experiments, or using manipulatives are some suggestions. Using geoboards, electroboards, content-related computer games, and algebra or integer tiles in math would also be beneficial.

Finally, Korean-American students showed a negative preference for group learning (Park, 1997b). This may be a reflection of Korean students' sense of individualism or competitive spirit, or it may be due to the lack of exposure to small group activities in Korean classrooms prior to their immigration to this country. It could also be a reflection of the relatively limited exposure to such instructional activities since their immigration (Park, 1997c). This finding suggests that teachers should try to minimize the use of small group activities for Korean-American students, especially during their initial adjustment period to American classrooms.

SIMILARITIES AND DIFFERENCES BETWEEN KOREAN AND AMERICAN SCHOOLS

Observations and experience in Korean and American educational settings have revealed significant differences as well as some similarities between the two. This section briefly compares the two systems and describse the nature of pre-immigration schooling experiences of Korean students. Tables 3.1-3.4 provide comparisons of the school systems, curricula, school organization, and instruction and evaluation, respectively.

Table 3.1
School Systems

Korean Schools

Free, universal, and compulsory education is provided for grades one through six and for a limited number of students in grades 7- 9 in rural areas or on remote islands. Kindergarten is optional, and offered only in private schools. Assignment to tuition-supported middle schools (7 - 9th grade), whether public and private, is lottery-based.

Students buy their own text books.

Girls and boys go to separate all-girls or all-boys middle schools, with the exception of a handful of middle schools affiliated with teachers' colleges.

Admission to high school is determined by a citywide or regional entrance examination. Once students pass the exam, they are assigned to a high school in their residential district by lottery.

High school education depends completely upon the financial resources available to parents Students must pay for the entrance fee, tuition, and all books.

There are three different types (streams) of high schools: academic high schools with a college preparatory curriculum and some components of general education; vocational high schools (commercial, technical, fishery and marine, and agricultural); and special high schools (fine arts, science, sports, foreign language, etc.). This system resembles the German model in that each stream has a different curricular emphasis.

Admission to a university is based primarily on student performance on a national examination. Since 1996, students' high school grade point average and character development are also taken into account. College admission policies are determined by the Ministry of Education and apply to both public and private institutions.

Tuition and costs at private and public four-year colleges are similar. Scholarships and other forms of financial aid are very limited.

American Schools

Free, universal, & compulsory education is provided for children from ages six to sixteen. Education from kindergarten to grade twelve is tuition free.

Students do not buy their own textbooks.

Girls and boys go to a coed middle school in their neighborhood.

Admission to high school is open to all students who successfully complete middle school. Assignment to a specific school is based on one's place of residence.

American students do not pay an entrance fee or tuition. They do not have to buy textbooks.

Comprehensive high schools offer academic, general, and vocational courses from which students can choose as they please. Students can change their career goals and choose to take courses that suit them even after they have begun high school. Unlike students in Korea who are almost precluded from transferring to a different track after beginning high school, students in the United States have more flexibility and a wider range of elective courses to choose from.

Admission to a university is determined by the university's admission policies. Among the generally considered criteria are the high school grade point average, performance on the Scholastic Aptitude Test (SAT), as well as participation in extracurricular activities.

Tuition at public four-year colleges is minimal, while tuition at private institutions is high. Scholarships and other forms of financial aid are available based on students' academic merit and need.

Table 3.2
Curricula

Korean Schools	American Schools
Almost uniform curriculum is provided for everyone with a few electives available. Variation in the program depends on the type of school a student attends; that is, academic (general), special, or vocational. Students take up to fourteen courses per semester.	All high school students select six or seven courses per semester from a wide variety of available courses with the assistance of a counselor.
Curriculum content is established by the Ministry of Education for all public and private schools.	Curriculum content is established by each school district from the recommendations contained in the Model Curriculum Standards and the curriculum frameworks adopted by the State Board of Education.
Moral education, improving students' ability to make sound judgments about the nation and society, is a required subject at each grade level in elementary, middle, and high schools.	Understanding the democratic process and civic values are supplemental concepts that are integrated with the teaching of history-social science at the elementary and secondary levels.
English as a foreign language is required each year for all students in grades seven through twelve. Students in grades ten through twelve also choose an additional foreign language such as French, German, or Japanese. An English conversation class is offered two hours per week in grades three and above in elementary schools.	One year of foreign language or one year of visual and performing arts is required for high school graduation.
In middle schools (grades seven through nine), concepts from biology, physics, and chemistry are combined in one science course; in mathematics courses, concepts from algebra, geometry, and trigonometry are integrated. In high school, all subjects are separated.	In middle and high schools, subject areas are usually separated and taken at different grade levels.

Table 3.3
School Organization

Korean Schools

The homeroom is a key element in Korean schools and serves as a forum for developing class identity and personal relationships, dealing with disciplinary problems, and motivating students to excel. The homeroom teacher acts as the students' academic and social counselor.

Students have a staggered schedule everyday. They have some subjects only on some days, not everyday; they may have seven classes on some days and six classes on other days, and so on.

The Korean academic year begins on March 1 and ends on February 28 of the following year. Summer vacation is 35 days long and stretches from the third week of July until the fourth week of August. Winter vacation is 45 days long and is from the third week of December to the first week of February the following year. Korean students attend school 222-225 days during each academic year which includes four hours on Saturdays.

Students in middle and high schools (7-12th) remain in their homeroom for most subjects for the entire academic year, with teachers rotating among classrooms.

Elementary school classrooms are self-contained.

American Schools

The homeroom is decreasing in significance and even completely disappearing in some schools. Where it exists, the homeroom period is short and a forum for mostly administrative details and announcements.

Students have the same number of classes and a uniform schedule everyday.

The American academic year begins roughly in mid-September and ends in mid-June with three months of summer vacation and two weeks of winter vacation. Students go to school 180 days during each academic year; they do not attend school on Saturdays.

Students in middle school and high school change classrooms for most subjects.

Elementary school classrooms are self-contained, although students may rotate for certain subjects such as Language Arts.

Table 3.4
Instruction and Evaluation

Korean Schools	American Schools
Students learn by rote memorization and mental discipline. Few opportunities are provided to develop analytical and higher level thinking skills.	Students learn by problem-solving methods. Many opportunities are provided to develop analytical and higher level thinking skills.
Few individual discussions and questions are allowed. The teacher addresses the entire class during most of the instructional time.	Students are encouraged to hold animated and spontaneous discussions about lessons. Students may ask questions freely anytime.
The teacher instructs the whole class most of the time. Ability grouping and group activities are rarely utilized.	The teacher is a facilitator of learning. The teacher frequently instructs or helps individual students. Independent learning is encouraged. Mixed or homogeneous ability grouping and other forms of group activities are common.
The classroom is structured for didactic teaching. The classroom arrangement rarely changes.	The classroom is less structured. The classroom arrangement is changed according to needs.
Interaction with the teacher is formal. Students are always obedient.	Interaction with the teacher is informal. Students generally maintain a friendly relationship with the teacher.
There are few disciplinary problems. The family usually takes care of disciplinary problems in order to save face.	There are many disciplinary problems with which the teacher and school have to cope, with or without parental cooperation.
Little positive reinforcement is provided as is typical of Korean families.	Sufficient positive reinforcement is provided as is the case in most American families.
Korean students' motivation to learn comes from the home, which strongly emphasizes learning and academic achievement.	The teacher is primarily responsible for motivating the students to learn.
For evaluation, students in middle and high schools are ranked individually against peers in their homeroom class and in their entire grade level according to their average performance in all subjects. They also receive number and letter grades for individual subjects.	For evaluation, students are not ranked individually against their peers. They receive number and letter grades in individual subjects. Overall performance is recorded as a student's grade point average.

The Korean education system is modeled after the American education system. Like the American system, the Korean system consists of a six-year primary school; a three-year middle school; and a three-year high school. After secondary school, students may opt to attend a two-year junior or vocational college, or they may choose a four-year college or university and go on to graduate school to earn a master's or doctoral degree. The Korean education system is much more centralized than its American counterpart in almost all respects: financing, governance, curriculum decisions, textbook adoptions, and teacher certification procedures.

In Korea, children first attend school at age seven. Free, universal, and compulsory education is provided for all children between the ages of seven and twelve years. Kindergarten is not part of the public school system. One notable difference between U.S. and Korean schools is that, in Korea, all middle school and high school students pay tuition and buy their own textbooks. The average class size in Korea is fifty students at all grade levels (Ministry of Education, 1995). Many Korean immigrant students end up skipping one grade upon arriving in the United States, because American educators place them in a particular grade level according to their age, without realizing that Korean students began attending school at age seven, not six.

HELPFUL STRATEGIES IN WORKING WITH KOREAN-AMERICAN STUDENTS

If at all possible, teachers, counselors, and administrators may provide a school orientation to Korean students who are new to this country and their parents with a Korean interpreter. The organization of instructional activities in American schools is quite different from that of Korean schools, especially in secondary schools. It may be very confusing to Korean students to have to change classrooms each period because they do not have to change classrooms after each period in Korea. School personnel should also explain the locations and functions of the attendance office, counselors' office, principal's and main office, library, cafeteria, health office, and so on.

Teachers, counselors, and administrators should strive to develop cross-cultural competence. First, they should learn to explicitly articulate the characteristics of American culture. Second, they need to examine the cultural biases they may have. This would entail first attempting to understand their own culture, since they are products of their own culture. Furthermore, they should try to learn about Korean culture and the social and educational backgrounds of Korean students in their schools as much as possible.

Teachers, counselors, administrators, and other educators should try to incorporate their knowledge about Korean culture and the social and educational issues relevant to Korean students into instruction and other educational services. While holding an international fashion show or food festival which displays traditional Korean costumes or cuisine is certainly one way of celebrating cultural differences, such events create a postcard effect at best because these extracurricular activities treat Korean culture as an addendum to the core curriculum. Incorporating Korean and Korean-American history into the social studies curriculum and teaching Korean and Korean-American literature during language arts or in English class can significantly promote the self-concept of Korean students and expand the instructional repertoire of teachers. Teachers could read *Halmoni and the Picnic* (Choi, 1993) to children in primary grades and *Finding My Voice* (Lee, 1992), *If It Hadn't Been for Yoon Jun* (Lee, 1993), or *Saying Goodbye* (Lee, 1994) to students in middle or high schools. They could assign students to read and report on *The Three Day Promise: A Korean Soldier's Memoir*, an autobiography by Donald Chung for a deeper understanding of the Korean War (1989) in a world history class, *Quiet Odyssey,* by Mary Paik Lee (1990), or *The Dreams of Two Yi-min*, by Margaret Pai (1989). Autobiographies of Korean-American women are also great for use in U.S. history or California history classes for learning about Korean-American experiences, perhaps for extra credit.

Teachers, counselors, administrators, and other service providers should wait before passing judgment on Korean students' behavior. Instead, they should try to understand Korean students' behavior in terms of Korean culture, not their own. They may try to learn about the Korean culture and the sociocultural and educational backgrounds from Korean students. At the same time, they can take time to explain American culture and how it is different or similar to Korean culture to Korean students. In other words, they should prepare to act as cultural brokers when necessary.

Teachers, counselors, administrators, and other service providers should try to display some Korean cultural posters or objects in their classrooms, hallways, or offices, so that Korean students would feel that their culture is adequately recognized and that they are not inferior to other ethnic groups. Furthermore, learning a few Korean greetings and using them when interacting with Korean students or parents can be very helpful and effective icebreakers.

Teachers, counselors, administrators, and other service providers should encourage Korean students to participate in extracurricular activities sponsored by school and in other activities such as community sports. This will help develop and expand their English skills and social competence, since different types of activities require the use of different types of discourse. Furthermore, Korean students can gain a wide range of experiences which they cannot acquire in the classrooms. Besides, participating in a wide variety of extracurricular activities both inside and outside of schools enhances their application to prestigious universities. These prestigious universities usually consider such participation to be important. The majority of Korean-American parents are new immigrants, have a very limited exposure to information concerning such opportunities and believe in cognitive development, but not social development. In fact, to most of Korean-American parents, studying is equated with becoming a bookworm. Therefore, educators should encourage and guide Korean students to participate in such activities to gain experience from sources other than books alone.

Teachers, counselors, administrators, and other service providers may act as community liaisons and provide orientations about the community to Korean students, such as encouraging them to take advantage of various community and library services. Being new to this country, Korean-Americans may not be aware of many services available to them or know how to utilize them.

PARENT ATTITUDES TOWARD SCHOOL

Schools and teachers can consider the Korean community as a new partner in the education of Korean-American students. Various approaches are necessary to encourage Korean parents to get involved in school affairs.

Korean parents have a deep respect for school administrators and teachers. They believe in assisting the school by deferring to the authority of teachers and administrators. They depend upon teachers for their wisdom and expertise. Parents believe that their role is to listen, respect, and follow the professional judgment of teachers and administrators. Thus while Korean parents generally keep track of their children's schoolwork and actively monitor their children's homework, they may be rather reluctant to participate in school functions and confer with teachers. Other reasons for Korean parents' minimal involvement in schools is their lack of confidence in their ability to speak English and their long work hours. Unfortunately, such attitudes may be misunderstood as a lack of interest and responsibility in school affairs.

Korean parents are willing to sacrifice almost anything for their children's education and to tolerate adverse conditions, as is evidenced in many parents' underemployment, extended work hours, and social isolation in the United States. Korean parents do not mind hardship, as long as their children can receive a good education and grow in a positive school environment.

EFFECTIVE STRATEGIES IN WORKING WITH KOREAN PARENTS

Korean parents believe that teachers will successfully manage their children's education toward academic success. To win the cooperation of Korean parents, teachers must utilize effective channels of communication that involve more than fliers and letters. Teachers who take a more personal approach and demonstrate a knowledge of Korean culture will be most successful in maintaining a good line of communication with Korean parents. The following suggestions will help teachers, counselors, administrators, and other service providers to work more effectively with Korean-American parents.

Korean-American parents are eager to learn about the American education system and college admission policies. As a matter of fact, many of them are not aware that American secondary schools have ability tracking. Many of them believe that, just like in Korea, a uniform curriculum is offered to every student in a given secondary school. Therefore, teachers, counselors, administrators, and other service providers need to provide parent education workshops to inform them of the American education system and strategies to help their children at home and prepare them for college. Since the majority of Korean-American parents' primary concern is their children's school achievement, schools should often plan such parent education workshops and help them become true and informed partners in their children's education. Some recommended topics for parent education workshops are effective parenting skills, which can help develop democratic yet authoritative parenting skills, since many of them tend to be authoritarian; effective communication skills, to develop active listening skills and the ability to have open and frank communication with their children; American holidays and American customs; and orientation to local schools and the neighborhood community. As new immigrants to this country, Korean parents need to learn about the various community services and functions, such as libraries, recreational centers, historical sites, and organized sports activities. Where possible, schools can provide Korean interpreters for such workshops and send letters in Korean home so that parents are not shut out by the language barrier. Additionally, school personnel should be aware that, although many Korean parents may not speak English fluently, many can read English, since most of them have had English instruction in Korea. Therefore, when Korean parents have a comprehension problem during a conversation in English, teachers can write down some of the troublesome words and communicate that way.

Schools may also occasionally set up meetings for only Korean parents, in order to spare them from the embarrassment that often results from meetings with culturally mixed groups. Meetings for Korean parents may elicit the involvement of those who are typically reluctant to come to meetings because they do not speak English and are not yet familiar with American customs. Schools may schedule meetings around business hours, since many Koreans manage their businesses over extended hours. Koreans generally do not mind weekend activities that relate to school or education.

Schools will most likely get a good response by using Korean community agencies and news media to announce school and community activities in Korean. Newspapers such as the Korea Times and the Joongang Daily News in Los Angeles, San Francisco, Chicago, and New York; and Radio Korea and Korean Television Enterprises in Los Angeles and San Francisco are some examples of news media that can be contacted. Schools may also try to contact Korean community agencies, Korean language schools, or churches to locate interpreters for school meetings or translation jobs, or to advertise positions for a classroom instructional assistant or a qualified teacher.

Schools can also establish a hot line at the school with prerecorded information in Korean to announce current events of interest to parents. It may also be possible to get a Korean parent to coordinate a telephone tree by grade level, so that Korean parents can network with one another about school and community events.

Schools may arrange social and cultural events to ensure that Korean parents have a role in school affairs. Some examples might include an international fashion show, food festival, or games. This helps overcome the alienation they often feel due to their lack of facility in English.

CONCLUSION

Korean-American students are an emerging ethnic group in U.S. public schools. Most of them have arrived in this country over the last two and a half decades. Only a small percentage of them have been raised in this country from birth.

Korean-American students come from diverse sociocultural and educational backgrounds. They come with cultural advantages that put a strong emphasis on learning. Typically, they receive strong parental support for their academic achievement. However, their learning styles and classroom interaction patterns are significantly different from those of their American counterparts, due to their distinct cultural background.

When East meets West, it is almost inevitable that culture clashes occur. This chapter has tried to assist the transition of Korean students into U.S. schools by shedding some light on the sociocultural and educational characteristics of Korean-American students. Teachers and other educators would do well to consider these factors when planning educational activities for Korean-American students and ensuring their adjustment to American public schools.

REFERENCES

Bonaciche, E. (1987). Making it in America: A social evaluation of the ethics of immigrant entrepreneurships. *Sociological Perspectives* 30 (October): 446-466.

California Department of Education. (1983). *A Handbook for Teaching Korean Speaking Students*. Sacramento, CA: California Department of Education.

Choi, S. N. (1993). *Halmoni (grandmother) and the picnic*. Boston: Houghton Mifflin.

Choy, B. Y. (1979). *Koreans in America*. Chicago, Il.: Nelson-Hall.

Chung, D. K. (1989). *The three day promise: A Korean soldier's memoir*. Tallahassee, FL: Father & Son Publishing.

Crane, P. S. (1967). *Korean Patterns*. Seoul, Korea: Hollym.

Daniels, R. & Kitano, H. H. L. (1970). *American racism: Exploitation and the nature of prejudice*. Englewood Cliffs, NJ: Prentice-Hall.

Education Week. (1997). 4th graders do well in math, science study. June 18, pp. 1-5.

Hurh, W. M. (1989). Employment of Korean immigrant wives: The burden of double roles. *Korean and Korean-American Studies Bulletin* 6 (spring/summer): 17-19.

Hurh, W. M., & Kim, K. C. (1979). *Korean immigrants in America: A structural analysis of ethnic confinement and adhesive adaptation*. A final report submitted to National Institute of Mental Health, U.S. Department of Health and Human Services, Grant No. 5R01 MH 30475-02.

Institute for International Education. (1988). *Open doors: Report on international education exchange*. New York: Institute for International Education.

Kim, B. L. (1978). *The Asian-Americans: Changing patterns, changing needs*. Montclaire, NJ: Association of Korean Christian Scholars in North America.

Kim, B. L. (1980). *The Korean-American child at school and at home: An analysis of interaction and intervention through groups*. Project Report submitted to Administration for Children, Youth, and Families, U.S. Department of Health, Education, and Welfare, Grant No. 90-c-1335 (01).

Kim, I. H., & Jung, S. M. (1974). *Korean culture and education* (in Korean). Seoul, Korea: Ewha Woman's University Press.

Kim, R. (1989). *Clay Walls*. Sag Harbor, NY: Permanent Press.

Kim, O. K. (Ed.). (1972). *History of Korean women*. Vols. I and II. Seoul, Korea: Ewha Woman's University Press.

Kim, S. J. (1995). *The effect of parenting styles, cultural conflict, and peer relations on academic achievement and psychosocial adjustment among Korean immmigrant adolescents*. Paper presented at the California Association for Asian and Pacific American Education Conference. March, Los Angeles, CA.

Lee, C. (1975). The United States immigration policy and the settlement of Koreans in America. *Korean Observer* 6 (2): 412-451.

Lee, M. G. (1992). *Finding my voice*. Boston, MA: Houghton Mifflin.

Lee, M. G. (1993). *If it hadn't been for Yoon Jun*. Boston, MA: Houghton Mifflin.

Lee, M. G. (1994). *Saying goodbye*. Boston, MA: Houghton Mifflin.

Lee, M. K. (1969). Rural people and their modernization, In C. I. E. Kim (Ed.), *Aspects of social change in Korea* (pp.70-92). Detroit, MI: Research and Publication.

Lee, M. P. (1990). *Quiet odyssey*. Seattle, WA: University of Washington Press.

Lyu, I. Y. (1977). Korean nationalist activities in Hawaii and the continental U.S., 1900-1975: Part I: 1900-1919, *Amerasia Journal* 4 (1).

McCune, S. (1956). *Korea's heritage*. Tokyo, Japan: Charles E. Tuttle.

Min, B. Y. (1985). *One hundred years of Korean immigration: Early immigrants* (in Korean). Los Angeles, California: *Korea Times* Publication Bureau.

Min, P. G. (1989). The social costs of immigrant entrepreneurship: A response to Edna Bonaciche, *Amerasia Journal* 15 (2): 187-194.

Ministry of Education. (1995). *Education in Korea*. Seoul, Korea: Ministry of Education.

Ministry of Education. (1996). *North America Educational Directors' Conference Materials*. Seoul, Korea: Ministry of Education.

Pai, M. K. (1989). *The dreams of two yi-min*. Honolulu: University of Hawaii Press.

Paik, H. K. (1969). The Korean social structure and its implications for education, In C. I. E. Kim (Ed.), *Aspects of social changes in Korea* (pp. 32-43). Ann Arbor, MI: Korean Research and Publication.

Park, A. K. (1980). *An analysis of names*. Seoul, Korea: Sung Kyoon Kwan University Journal.

Park, C. C. (1981). *Ethnic identification, sociocultural adjustment and school achievement of Korean-American youth in Los Angeles*. Unpublished doctoral dissertation, University of Southern California, Los Angeles.

Park, C. C. (1997a). *A comparative study of educational and occupational aspirations between Asian-American and Anglo students in secondary schools*. Paper presented at the 1997 American Educational Research Association Annual Meeting. March, Chicago, Illinois.

Park, C. C. (1997b). Learning style preferences of Korean, Mexican, Armenian-American and Anglo students in secondary schools. *National Association for Secondary School Principals* 81(January): 103-111.

Park, C. C. (1997c). Learning style preferences of Asian American (Chinese, Filipino, Korean, and Vietnamese) students in secondary schools. *Equity and Excellence in Education* 30 (September): 68-77.

Park, C. C. (1998). Educational and occupational aspirations of Korean youth in Los Angeles. In R. Endo, C. Park, & N. Tsuchida (Eds.), *Current issues in Asian and Pacific American education*. West Covina, CA: Pacific Asia Press.

Passin, H. (1964). Society and education in Japan. In G. Z. F. Bereday (Ed.), *Comparative Education Studies*. New York: Columbia University Press.

Patterson, W., & Kim, H. C. (1992). *Koreans in America*. Minneapolis, MN: Lerner Publications.

Sohn, I. S. (1978). *The values of Koreans: A new discovery of educational values* (in Korean). Seoul, Korea: Mun Eum Sa.

Takaki, R. (1989). *Strangers from a different shore: A history of Asian Americans*. New York: Penguin.

Underwood, H. G. (1977). *The Korean way*. Seoul, Korea: Christian Literature Society of Korea.

U.S. Bureau of the Census. (1993a). *1990 Census of population*. Washington, DC: Government Printing Office.

U.S. Bureau of the Census. (1993b). *1990 Census of population: Asians and Pacific Islanders*. Washington, DC: Government Printing Office.

Yu, E. Y. (1988). The Korean-American communities and their institutions: An overview. *Korean Culture* 9: 33-45.

Yu, E. Y. (1979). The Korean-American family. *The Hankook Ilbo* (March): 21-22.

Yun, T. R. (1978). *The Koreans: Their consciousness structure* (in Korean). Seoul, Korea: Hyun Am Sa.

Linguistic Perspective on the Education of Korean-American Students

Harold Chu

LINGUISTIC BACKGROUNDS OF KOREAN STUDENTS

Although recent immigration has greatly increased the diversity of the U.S. population, native-born Americans constitute half of the people in the United States, age 5 and older, who speak languages other than English in their homes. In 1990, the number of Koreans living in the United States was 797,304, an increase of 125.3 % over the 1980 figure (U.S. Bureau of the Census, 1993). The age distribution of Koreans who speak Korean at home was as follows: 116,000 ages 5-17; 478,000 ages 18-64; and 32,000 ages 65 and older. These figures represent a dramatic increase in the number of Koreans who speak Korean at home, which grew by 135% between 1980 and 1990 (Waggoner, 1993). According to Lapham (1990), the estimated number and percentage of the Korean-born population aged 5 years and older who speak Korean at home was 520,000 (92.5%), with 348,000 (67%) of Koreans who indicated experiencing difficulty in speaking English.

The above data suggest that almost every Korean-American family speaks Korean at home. Korean children born in the United States are brought up under the influence of Korean language and culture at home. The enculturation process of these children in their first language and culture is certainly different from their experiences at school. Many students experience varying degrees of culture shock, adjustment stress, and sociocultural disruption, caused largely by their distinctive culture and language, limited English proficiency, and unique physical characteristics. Indeed, these problems have been most severe for members of the younger generation, or individuals caught in the middle of transition as they exist between the rather different worlds of school and home.

The Korean language shares its genetic origin with the family of Altaic languages, including Manchu, Mongolian, Turkish, and Japanese (Lee, 1967; Poppe, 1965; Ramstedt, 1949). A number of features common among the Altaic languages are present in Korean: words are built by agglutinating affixes; the vowels within a word follow certain rules of harmony; and articles, relative pronouns, conjunctive words, explicit gender markers, and auxiliary words are absent. Until the alphabetic script (Hangul) for writing Korean was invented by King Sejong in the fifteenth century, only Chinese characters were used for writing. Because of the continuous use of the Chinese characters, and the consequent massive influx of Chinese loan words, more than half of the Korean vocabulary consists of such loans (Kim, 1992).

The Japanese language may be considered a distant relative. Some basic words for body parts, clothing, and agriculture are shared by both languages, suggesting some degree of linguistic-family relationships. Many other similarities between the two languages exists; that is, both have the common features of the Altaic family, and the grammatical structures of both languages are so close that word-for-word translation of Korean into Japanese and vice versa is easily done (California Department of Education, 1994).

The ten basic vowels and fourteen simple consonants in Hangul expand to twenty-one vowels and nineteen consonants for a total of forty symbols in combination. The smallest unit of pronunciation is a syllable that contains at least one vowel. There are six types of syllables:

1. Vowel
2. Consonant + vowel
3. Consoant + vowel + consonant
4. Consonant + vowel + consonant + consonant
5. Vowel + consonant
6. Vowel + consonant + consonant

COMPARATIVE ANALYSIS OF KOREAN AND ENGLISH FOR ENGLISH LEARNERS

This section presents a comparative description of Korean and English in terms of selective and pragmatic comparison in the acquisition of English as a second language (ESL) for Korean students with limited English proficiency.The comparison is conducted at four levels of linguistics: phonology, lexicon, syntax, and sociolinguistic aspects. In an attempt to clarify the differences between the two languages and to alleviate the possible problems that Korean students encounter in learning English, the analysis is selective; that is, only certain major differences between the two languages are arbitrarily chosen for discussion. The selection was pragmatically made in the sense that the analysis was designed to provide practical assistance to the classroom teacher. Thus, this section is not as concerned with the theoretical niceties of contrastive analysis as it is with the practical application of the analysis to actual or potential learning or teaching problems which may arise from the linguistic interferences (Chu, 1978, 1983).

This analysis is ESL specific in the sense that it focuses on differences that may pose problems for Korean students learning English as a second language. Hence, this analysis is unidirectional. Children tend to transpose many language rules and concepts of their first language onto their learning in English. If ESL or bilingual teachers become more aware of the degree to which structural differences between Korean and English interfere with a smooth transition, they can properly plan to meet the instructional needs of Korean students rather than allowing the differences to hamper learning in English.Teachers can more fully understand the reasons for errors in oral English and confusions in English silent reading. They can formulate hierarchies with which to clarify the language differences and be better equipped with techniques for facilitating a smoother and more accurate transition into speaking English.

Phonological Comparison

In this section, phonological interferences between the two languages are discussed, especially as they relate to (1) individual sounds (or phonemes), (2) sounds (or phonemes) in sequence, and (3) stress and intonation.

Individual Sounds. /p/ vs. /f/: English has the p/f distinction while Korean does not. Consequently, Koreans often have difficulty in distinguishing between these two English sounds. Thus, they often find it hard to discriminate between *pine* and *fine, pile* and *file,* or *leap* and leaf. Since Korean does not have /f/ and since /pʰ/ happens to be the closest thing that Korean has to the English /f/, Korean students often use the Korean /pʰ/ for the English /f/. Thus, they often say *pound* for *found, pour* for *four,* or *pin* for *fin.* Since they also often transfer /pʰ/ for the English /p/, the /p/f/ contrast is often lost entirely in their English.

/b/ vs ./v/: English has the b/v distinction, but Korean does not. As a result, Korean students often experience difficulty in differentiating between these two English sounds. They often find it hard to discriminate between *ban* and *van, bow* and *vow, bat* and *vat,* and so on. Since Korean students often use Korean /b/ for the /v/ in English, the b/v 3contrast is often lost in their English.

/s/ vs. /z/: English has the s/z distinction while Korean does not. However, Korean students do not seem to have difficulty hearing the difference between the two sounds, probably because one is distinctly voiced while the other is distinctly voiceless.

Korean does not have the /z/ sound. Since the Korean /s/ is preempted for the English /s/, and further since /ch/ is the closest thing left to /z/, Korean students often transfer the Korean /ch/ to the English /z/. As a result, they often say *chipper* for *zipper,* **chest** for *zest,* **chow** for *zoo,* and so on. It is notable here that the Korean /ch/ is often transferred for the English /j/ as well. The result is that Korean students often make no distinction between /z/ and /j/ in English.

/l/ vs. /r/: English has the l/r contrast while Korean does not. Consequently, Korean students often have difficulty in hearing the differences between these two English sounds. Thus, they often cannot discriminate *light* from *right, load* from *road,* and *lead* from *read.* Furthermore, since Korean has one sound that is at the same time similar to the English /l/ and /r/, Korean students often transfer this in-between sound to both /l/ and /r/ in English. The result is that the l/r distinction is often lost or mixed up in their English.

/th/: The English /th/, either voiced or voiceless, is nonexistent in Korean. As such, it is often difficult for Korean students to distinguish /s/ from the voiceless /th/ in English and to properly pronounce the voiceless /th/ sound. Since /s/ is the closest sound Korean has to the English voiceless /th/, Korean students often use the Korean /s/ for the voiceless English /th/. Thus they often say *sin* for *thin, sing* for *thing, sree* for three, and often find it hard to tell *sick* from *thick, sigh* from *thigh,* and so on.

Since /d/ is the closest consonant Korean has to the voiced English /th/, Korean students often use /d/ for the voiced English /th/. They will say *dis* for *this, dem* for *them,* and *dat* for *that.* Korean students also often find it hard to discriminate between the voiced /th/ and /d/, which they often identify with the Korean /d/. Thus, they often have difficulty in discriminating between *den* and *then, does* and *thus,* and so on.

Short vs. long /i/: The contrast between the short and long /i/ is lost in some dialects of Korean and is fast disappearing in most dialects of Korean. On the other hand, the contrast between the long and short /i/ is fairly productive in English, as is attested by word pairs such as *beat/bit, heat/hit,* and *seat/sit.*

Korean students who speak Korean dialects wherein the contrast between the long and short /i/ is already lost find it difficult to hear the difference between the two varieties of /i/ in English. They also find it hard to produce the two varieties of /i/ in English correctly.

Short vs. long /u/: Like the distinction between the long and short /i/, the distinction between the long and short /u/ is difficult for Korean students. As a result, Korean students often have difficulty in discriminating the long and short /u/ in English as in *pool* and *pull, fool* and *full,* and *food* and *foot.* Also, they often fail to pronounce the short /u/ as in *pull, full, foot,* and so on.

/e/ vs. /ae/: The contrast between /e/ as in *met* and /ae/ as in *mat* is lost in many of the dialects spoken in South Korea today. Thus, Korean students often find it difficult to differentiate between these two sounds in English in both listening and speech production. For example, it is often difficult for them to distinguish *bed* from *bad, set* from *sat,* and *peck* from *pack.*

Open and closed /o/: English makes the distinction between the open and closed /o/ as in *brought* and boat and *caught* and *coat.* No comparable distinction exists in Korean. Thus Korean students often find it hard to hear the difference between the two vowels and fail to pronounce them correctly.

Sound in Sequence

Consonant Clusters. English abounds in consonant clusters. On the other hand, Korean allows only a few consonant clusters, with no word-initial consonant clusters and a limited number of clusters in the middle and at the end of words. Of the allowed clusters, those that occur at the end of words appear to be disappearing.

Thus Korean students often have difficulty with English consonant clusters, especially when they occur at the beginning or at the end of words. When they produce a consonant cluster, they often insert a barred /ɨ/ (or i) between the consonants in the cluster. In other words, they tend to use the barred /ɨ/ to decluster the cluster. Thus, they often say *s ɨ tay* for *stay, s ɨ t ɨ rike* for *strike, mis ɨ t* for *mist,* and so on.

Note that this insertion of /i/ is only natural, because the standard canonical syllable in Korean takes the form of consonant (C) + vowel (V) + consonant (C) and because the least salient vowel in Korean is /i/. Note that here CVC means that a standard Korean syllable consists of an optional initial consonant, an obligatory vowel, and an optional final consonant. Thus, we may say that Korean students often restructure the English consonant clusters in such a way as to make them conform to the standard Korean syllable structure by using the least salient Korean vowel.

/n/ & /l/ sequence: In Korean, /n/ becomes /l/ when it is followed immediately by an /l/. Korean students often transfer this to English. Thus they often mispronounce *only* as *olly, manly* as *mally,* or *keenly* as *keelly.* Recall that the Korean /l/ is similar to both /l/ and /r/ in English. This may explain why Korean students often mispronounce the English /n/ + /r/ sequence as something like /l/ + /l/, that is, they often mispronounce *Henry* as *Helly, weaponry* as *weapolly, green robe* as *greel lobe*, and so on.

/p/t/k/ + /m/n/ sequence: In Korean, p/pʰ/pp, t/tʰ/tt, and k/kʰ/kk become /m/ and /n/, respectively, when they are followed immediately by the /m/ or /n/ sound.   Korean students often transfer this nasalization rule to English.   Thus they often mispronounce *Take me with you* as *Taying me with you, Hug me* as *Hung me, He hit me* as *He hin me, He bade me go* as *He bane me go, Keep me company* as *Keen me company, Deep mines* as *Deem mines*, or *Dont rub my hair* as *Dont rum my hair*.

m/ ŋ   + /l/ sequence: In Korean, /l/ becomes /n/ when it immediately follows either the /m/ or / ŋ   / sound.   Korean students often apply this nasalization rule when they speak English.   Thus they often mispronounce *Hamlet* as *Hamnet, kingly* as *kingny, home run* as *home nun*, or *long run* as *long nun*.

/n/ insertion: In Korean, /n/ is often inserted between two words if the first word ends in p/pʰ/pp, t/tʰ/tt, k/kʰ/kk, /m/, /n/, or / ŋ   / and if the second word begins with the /i/ or /y/ sound.   Korean students often transfer this rule on /n/ insertion when they speak English.   Thus they often mispronounce *Keep your fingers crossed* as *Keem nyour fingers crossed, Kick your ball* as *King your ball, Sing your song* as *Sing nyour song*, and so on.

/n//s/ + /i/ sequence: In Korean, /n/ and /s/ become palatalized when they are followed immediately by /i/.   In other words, when followed by /i/, /s/ becomes /sh/ as in *shy* while /n/ becomes the kind that we have in the second syllable of such English words as *onion, canyon*, and *Bunyan*.

Korean students often transfer this rule of palatalization when they speak English.   Thus they often pronounce *sin* as *shin*, *sit* as *shit*, *sick* as *shick*, and so on.   The symbol **n** designates the palatalized /n/ such as that found in the second syllable of *onion*.

/w/ + /u/ sequence: The English sequence /wu/ as in *woman* or *would* does not exist in Korean.   The simple /u/ without the preceding /w/ is the closest thing Korean has to the English sequence in question.   Thus Korean students often transfer this simple /u/ for the English /wu/.   As a result, they often mispronounce *woman* as *uman*, or *ooman*, or *would* as *ud* or *ood*.

Since Korean does not have the wu/u distinction as does English, Korean students often find it difficult to discriminate between /wu/ and /u /in English as in *woos* and *ooze*, *swoon* and *soon*, and so on.

/y/ + /i/ sequence: The English sequence /yi/ as in *yeast* does not exist in Korean. The simple /i/without the poreceding /y/ is the closest thing Korean has to the English /yi/.   Thus, Korean students often transfer this simple /i/ for the English /yi/ and have trouble telling /yi/ from /i/. As a result they often pronounce *ye*ast as *e*ast, *yield*, as *eeld, ye* as *ee*, and so on.

Stress and Intonation

Stress. English is a stress-timed language in the sense that the time it takes to make an utterance in English depends upon the number of stressed syllables in the utterance in question. The following expressions, despite differences in length, take about the same amount of time to utter:

a.   *It's Bob.*
b.   *It's Elizabeth.*
c.   *It's Pennsylvania.*

d. *It's North Carolina.*

On the other hand, Korean is syllable-timed language in the sense that the time that it takes to make a Korean utterance is determined by the number of syllables in the utterance in question. In this respect, Korean is very much like Japanese, Spanish, or Portuguese. For example, the following Korean utterances take different amounts of time to utter because they each contain a different number of syllables:

e. 가자   kaja *Let's go.*
f. 빨리가자   ppalli kaja *Let's go home quickly.*
g. 빨리 집으로 가자   ppalli chibrokaja *Let's go home quickly.*
h. 빨리 보스톤으로 가자   ppalli pos toniro kaja *Let's go to Boston quickly.*

Note that every syllable in a syllable-times language is more or less evenly stressed while only certain syllables are stressed in a stress-times language. Thus certain syllables in a stress-times language are unstresseed or very weakly stressed. The result is that Korean students often transfer their syllable-timing habit to English. They often assign an even level of stress to every syllable in an English utterance.

Stress vs. Unstressed Vowels in English. In English, stressed vowels are quite clearly and prominently enunciated while unstressed vowels are blurred or very faintly pronounced. Unstressed vowels in English are typically reduced to the barred i($/i/,/e/,/+/$) or schwa $/ \partial /$.

In contrast, there is no distinction in Korean between stressed and unstressed vowels because every vowel receives about the same amount of stress. As a consequence, every vowel in a Korean utterance is uttered rather cleary and prominently. Consequently, Korean students often fail to blur (or reduce to the barred /i/ or schwa) an unstressed vowel when they speak English.

Intonation. Korean intonation may sound monotonous to native English speakers, due to the fact that every syllable is evenly stressed. In normal Korean speech, there is little or no noteworthy rise and fall in pitch in the middle of a Korean utterance; the only significant rise and fall in pitch comes at the very end. The general rule is that the voice rises at the end of a yes-no question, while it falls at the end of other types of sentences. Korean students often use a similar intonation when they speak English, which may sound odd to native speakers of English.

Lexical Comparison

The lexicon is the most idiosyncratic part of any language. It is also the bulkiest of all linguistic levels. Thus, there are typically more contrasts between languages on the lexical level than on any other level. In fact, there are so many lexical contrasts between any two languages that it is extremely difficult or next to impossible to exhaustively study the differences. Hence the list of lexical contrasts that follows is highly fragmentary.

Korean Words with More than One English Equivalent. 먹다 /m ∂ kta/ vs. eat, drink, and smoke: The Korean verb/ m ∂ kta/ is ordinarily used in the sense of *eat.* However, many Koreans use this verb in the sense of *drink* or even in the sense of *smoke.* For these Koreans, it is perfectly natural to say such things as /kop^{h}il+1 + m ∂ kta/ *to eat coffee* or /tampel+1 + m ∂ kta/ *to eat a cigarette.* This may help explain why many Koreans produce verb phrases such as *eat water, eat a cigarette*, and so on.

호박 /hopak/ vs. pumpkin, squash, and zucchini: The Korean noun /hopak/ has three English equivalents, as shown. It may not be so surprising, then, that Korean students often find it hard to distinguish among the three English equivalents. Most Korean students learn the word *pumpkin* before they do the other two and associate it with the Korean /hopak/. Before and unless they learn the other two words, they are bound to use *pumpkin* to refer to a squash or a zucchini. This should help explain why many Korean students refer to a squash or a zucchini as a pumpkin.

차/chha/ vs. car, station wagon, sedan, pick up, van and truck: The Korean noun /ch^{h}a/ has many English equivalents. *Car* is the most common, and Korean students tend to learn this equivalent before they do the rest. The result is that, until and unless they learn to use the other equivalents here, they are likely to use *car* to refer to all of the many equivalents of /ch^{h}a/. This should explain why Koreans often refer to all sorts of vehicles as simply car.

듣다/t+tta/ vs. hear, and listen: Korean students often have difficulty in discrimination between the two English equivalents of /t+tta/. *Hear* is more common than *listen*, and Koreans tend to learn it before they do the other word and associate it with the Korean /t+tta/. Thus until and unless they learn the other word, they are likely to use *hear* for *hear* as well as for *listen*. For example, Korean students tend to say *heard the recorded message* and *I listended to the recorded message* interchangeably.

보다/pota/ vs. see and look: See is the more common of the two equivalents of /pota/, and it is likely that Korean students learn it before they learn *look*. Until and unless they learn to use *look* as well, they are likely to use *see* for both *see* and *look*. This should explain why Korean students sometimes say, for example, *you saw her* when they really want to say, *you looked at her.*

찾다/chhachta/ vs. find and look for: *Find* is more common than *look for*, and Korean students tend to associate it first with the Korean /ch^{h}achta/. Until and unless they learn to use *look for* as well, they are likely to use *find* for both *find* and *look for*. For example, Korean students say *They found John* when they really mean to say *They looked for John.*

빨리/ppalli/ vs. early and quickly: The Korean adverb /ppalli/ has English equivalents, *early* and *quickly*. Thus Korean students often find it hard to discriminate between the two English equivalents, and often use *early* for *quickly and fast* and vice versa.

뛰다/ttuita/ vs. jump, run, skip, hop, and leap: Since *jump* is the more common of the various English equivalents, Koran students are likely to learn it before they do the other equivalents and associate it with the Korean /ttuita/. Thus until and unless they learn the other equivalents, they are likely to use *jump* for the other equivalents as well. This should help explain the tendency among Korean students to use *jump* for all the English equivalents of /ttuita/.

English Words with More than One Korean Equivalent. Put on vs. 입다/ipta/, 신다/sinta/, 끼다/kkita/, 쓰다/ss+ta/, 차다/chhata/. The English verb *put on* or *wear*, as in *put on your coat* or *wear your shoes,* has five Korean equibalents. In Korean, the choice among the five verbs depends on the referent of the object noun that follows the verb. Korean students must get used to the fact that, regardless of the reference of the object noun that follows the verb in question, English uses only the verbs *put on* or *wear.*

Wash vs. 빨다/ppalta/, 씻다/ssissta/, and 닦다/takkkta/: Which of the three available Korean equivalents is used depends on the referent of the object noun that follows the verb. Korean students must get accustomed to the fact that English uses only one verb regardless of the referent of the object noun in question.

Wall vs. 담/tam/ and 벽/pi∂k/: The English noun *wall* has two Korean equivalents. /pi∂k/ refers to the wall of a room or a hall, while /tam/ refers to a wall surrounding a house or a building. Korean students must get used to the fact that this distinction between different types of walls is not made in English.

Brother vs 동생/toŋ saeŋ/ and 형/hi∂ŋ/: The English word *brother* has two Korean equivalents: /toŋ saeŋ/ is used to refer to the younger brother, while /hi∂ŋ/ is used to refer to an older brother. Korean students must get used to the fact that English does not make this distinction lexically, although it does make the distinction phrasally, that is, *younger brother* and *elder brother.*

Brother-in-law vs. 처남/chh+nam/, 동서/toŋs∂/, 매형/ maehi∂ŋ/, 매제 /maeche/, and 형부/hi∂ŋpu/: The English word *brother-in-law* has many Korean equivalents as shown here. (처남/ch^h∂nam/) refers to the brother of one's wife: (동서/toŋs∂/) refers to the husband of a sister of one's wife: (매형 /maehi∂ŋ/) refers to the husband of one's older sister, as spoken by a male: (매제/maeche/) refers to the husband of one's younger sister, as spoken by a male:(형부/hi∂ŋpu/) refers to the husband of one's elder sister, as spoken by a female. Korean students must grow accustomed to the fact that English does not make this kind of distinction at all, at least lexically. Every other *in-law* word in English has more than one equivalent in Korean. In this sense, every other *in-law* may pose a confusion for Korean students during the initial stage of English development. However, eventually Korean students will find it much simpler than its Korean counterparts.

Korean Words with Polysemic English Equivalents. This section addresses instances where one Korean word has an English equivalent with more than one meaning, only one of which is the same as the meaning of the Korean word in question.

상자/saŋcha/ v. box: The Korean word /saŋcha/ has the meaning of a box as a container. On the other hand, the English word *box* may mean not only a container but also a seating area in a theater or an embarrassing or perplexing situation, among others. Korean students tend to find it easiest to learn to use the English word *box* in its sense as a container, perhaps because *box* as a container is closest to the meaning of the Korean/saŋcha/, and it is the most commonly used.

방/paŋ/ v. room: The Korean word /paŋ/ has the meaning of a room as in *This is my bedroom.* On the other hand, the English word *room* means not only a room as part of a house but also room in scope or space as in *There is room for improvement.* Consequently, Korean students find it easiest to use *room* in its sense as a part of a house both because room is closest in meaning to the Korean /paŋ/, and because it is the most common use of the word *room.*

손/son/v. hand: The Korean word /son/ has the meaning of a hand as an extension of the human arm beyond the wrist. On the other hand, the English word *hand* means not just the part of the human arm beyond the wrist but also a pointer on the dial of a watch, or a person who assists with a particular task. Korean students tend to find it easier to use *hand* int the first sense. The reason may be that this definition is closest in meanig to the Korean word /son/, and it is also the most commonly used definition of the word *hand.*

학교/hakkio/v. school: The Korean word /hakkio/ has the meaning of a school as a place of learning. On ther other hand, the English word *school* refers to not just a place of learning but also to a group of fish, a group of artists who follow a certain style or the like. Korean students tend to find it easier to use *school* in their sense of a place of learning than in its other senses, perhaps because this sense is closest to the meaning of the Korean word /hakkio/, and it is the most commonly used of the many defintions of *school.*

Syntactic Comparison

Word Order Difference Between English and Korean. English is an SVO (subject-verb-object) language and Korean is an SOV (subject-object-verb) language. This inversion pattern often confuses Korean students learning English.   For example, for the English sentence *I went to New York by car yesterday,* Korean students might say the following sentences:

a. *I to New York by car yesterday went.*
b. *To New York by car yesterday I went.*
c. *By car yesterday to New York I went.*
d. *Yesterday to New York by car I went.*

The four word components, *I, to New York, by car,* and *yesterday,* are interchangeable in Korean and thus it is possible to make many more sentences.   The English prepositions *to* and *by* are also inversed in Korean. Thus, *New York to car by yesterday I went.*

Expletive It and There. The so-called expletives *it* and *there* are frequently used in English while they are often omitted in Korean.   Thus Korean students find it rather difficult to learn to use expressions that contain one of these expletives, such as the following and other similar expressions:

a. *I like it here.*
b. *It was cold last winter.*
c. *It is important that I pass this test.*
d. *It is kind of you to come.*
e. *He made it clear that he would come.*
f. *Its cold enough for there to be ice on the window.*
g. *There was not a single book in his room.*

Yes/No to Negative Questions.   In response to negative questions such as *Aren't you hungry?* in English one would say *no* when he wants to answer in the negative while one would say *yes* when he wants to answer in the affirmative.   On the other hand, in response to a negative question in Korean one would say *yes* when he wants to answer in the negative while one would say *no* when he wants to answer in the affirmative. That is, in Korean, a *yes* response would   mean, *No, I am not hungry,* and a *no* response would mean, *Yes, I am hungry.*   *Yes* and *no* indicate *what you've said is correct* and *what you've said is incorrect.*   Thus if you state a question in the negative, the Korean response would be the opposite of the English response.

Let us take the Korean question /ankaass pnikka/ *Did you not go?* as an example.   Korean will say /ye ankass pnita/ *Yes, I did not go* if they want to answer the question in the   negative; they will say /anio kass pnita/ *No, I went* if they want to answer the same question in the affirmative.

Korean students often transfer this Korean habit of responding to negative questions when they speak English.   Thus they often use *yes* and *no* in the wrong way when they answer negative questions in English. For example, the negative question *Didn't you do it?* is likely to elicit either, *Yes, I didn't do it,* or *No, I did it.*

Verb + Adjectival Complement or Verb + Object + Adjectival Complement.   Many English verbs take adjectival complements.   Among such verbs are *feel,* as in *I feel happy; appear,* as in *She appears to be happy; seem,* as in *She seems to be happy, look,* as in *She looks happy; smell,* as in *It smells good; sound,* as in *It sounds good;* and *taste,* as in *It tastes good.*   Many English verbs take an object followed by an adjectival complement.   Among such verbs are *consider,* as in *I consider him to be great; think,* as in *I think him to be good;* and *regard,* as in *I regard him as good; make*, as in *I made them bigger; render*, as in *This will render him powerless.*

Korean also uses complements with such verbs. However, Korean uses adverbial complements rather than adjectival complements. Thus *I feel happy* would be translated into Korean as *I feel happily.* This may explain why Korean students often use adverbial, instead of adjectival complements for such English verbs. Consider the following sample sentences:

Sentences	Possible Sentences Rendered by Korean Students
a. It tastes *nice.*	a. It tastes *nicely.*
b. It smells *nice.*	b. It smells *nicely.*
c. It looks *nice.*	c. It looks *nicely.*
d. It sounds *nice.*	d. It sounds *nicely.*
e. It appears *to be nice.*	e. It appears *nicely.*
f. It seems *to be nice.*	f. It seems *nicely.*
g. Make him *happy.*	g. Make him *happily.*
h. Render him *powerless.*	h. Render him *powerlessly.*

Countable v. Uncountable Nouns. English makes the distinction between countable and uncountable nouns. In English, many nouns can take both countable and uncountable forms. For example, *pine* is countable when it refers to a tree or trees, while it is uncountable when it refers to the wood obtained from the pine tree. On the other hand, Korean does not make a similar distinction. Grammatically, every Korean noun may be used as a countable noun. This may explain why Korean students often have trouble using uncountable nouns or make the required distinction between countable nouns and uncountable nouns in English. This may also help explain why Korean students often distort uncountable English nouns such as *news, information, evidence, testimony,* and *intelligence,* and say such things as *many news, one evidence, a few testimony, several informations, an information,* or *intelligences,* or *I had a lamb for dinner* instead of *I had lamb for dinner.*

Thus, Korean students quite frequently fail to distinguish between the countable and uncountable uses of the same noun in English. They may fail to see the difference between the two uses of nouns such as the following:

Noun	Countable Use	Uncountable Use
cow	*an animal*	meat from the animal
chicken	*a fowl*	meat from the fowl
oak	*a tree*	wood from the tree
pine	*a tree*	wood from the tree

Predicative v. Attributive Adjectives. According to its position, an adjective may be predicative, attributive, or both. If an adjective may occur only as verbal complement, it is predicative. If an adjective may occur as a prenominal modifier only, it is attributive. If an adjective may occur in either position, it is both predicative and attributive. All Korean adjectives may be used either attributively or predicatively. On the other hand, we may think of English adjectives as belonging to one of the following three types. First, some English adjectives are used only predicatively. We may say *I saw a boy who was afraid,* but we may not say *I saw an afraid boy.* Second, some English adjectives may be used only predicatively. We may say *This is the main reason,* but not *This is the reason that is main.* Finally, most English adjectives may be used either attributively or predicatively. We may say either *I know a man who is sick* or *I know a sick man.*

The first two types of English adjectives do not have their counterpart in Korean while the third type does. The first two types pose potential learning problems for Korean students. Korean students may use predicative-only English adjectives attributively; that is, they produce such phrases as *aflame house, ablaze mountains, adrift boats,* or the like. Korean students may use attributive-only English adjectives predicatively. That is, they may say *This reason is main, The problem is major, The president is former, The administration is previous.*

Definite and Indefinite Articles. In most of their uses, the English articles *the, a,* and *an* do not have counterparts in Korean. Korean students often find it extremely difficult to learn to use the English articles correctly. They often either mix up one article with another or leave out an article where they should use one, as in the following cases.

The in a set name: When a set consists of more than one member such as that a member may be called X, the set is often referred to in English as *the Xs.* Some examples are *the Rocky Mountains, the Philippine Islands, the three Rs, the Carolinas, the Americas,* and so on. Korean students often drop *the* in such set names, often along with the plural-marking *s.*

Korean v. the Korean language: Often in English, a proper noun may be rewritten as the + proper adjective + common noun. Thus *Korean, Christianity,* and *Rome* may be rewritten as *the Korean language, the Christian faith,* and *the Roman Empire.* Korean students often leave out *the* in the construction.

Ten dollars v. an even ten dollars: When an English noun phrase takes the form of adjective + plural numeral + plural noun, it is preceded by an article, either definite or indefinite. Some examples are noun phrases such as *an even ten dollars, the usual 100 percent, the customary two dollars,* and so on. Korean students often omit the article from noun phrases of this sort.

The in proper names: Certain proper names such as names of rivers or hotels are frequently preceded by the definite article (*the*) in English. Some examples are proper names such as *the Potomac, the Potomac River, the Nile, the Nile River,* and so on. Korean students often omit the definite article from the type of proper name.

The + adjective: In English *the* + adjective is frequently used as a noun phrase that refers to either a set or group of certain things or a certain quality. *The beautiful* may be used as a noun phrase which, depending on the context, refers to either a set of beautiful persons or the quality of being beautiful, that is, beauty. Korean students often find it difficult to learn to use this type of noun-phrase construction in English; they also find it difficult to assign correct meaning to such a construction.

Relative Pronouns. Relative pronouns and relative clauses of English do not have their equivalents in Korean. Korean lacks relative pronouns. Relative clauses precede their head nouns directly, without being preceded or followed by relative pronouns or conjunction. For example, /melika   ss   n ph   ncin   n cemiitta/ is rendered *Mary writes letters interesting is* in Korean for *The letters that Mary writes are interesting* in English. As a consequence, Korean learners often experience difficulty in learning to use relative pronouns and relative clauses in English.

Gender. English makes the distinction between masculine, feminine, and neuter gender in its third-person singular pronouns. *She, her,* and *hers* are feminine; *it* and *its* are neuter; and *he, him,* and *his* are masculine.

Korean does not make a similar distinction. The gender distinction in the third-person singular pronouns of English often poses a problem for Korean students. In many instances, they mix up the masculine pronoun with the feminine pronoun. This can perhaps be attributed to the fact that masculine pronouns are more commonly used or more dominant than their feminine counterparts.

Number Agreement between Subject and Verb. In English, the subject of a sentence must agree in number with the main verb of the sentence. In Korean, a similar agreement does not seem to be operative, although the subject of a sentence has to agree in number with the subjective complement if the subjective complement is a noun.

Pre-modification v. Post-modification. The modifier of a noun in English may either precede or follow the noun that it modifies. Thus we may have either *a valuable book* or *a book of value.* In Korean, a noun modifier must precede the noun that it modifies. Thus *a valuable book* has its equivalent in Korean while *a book of value* does not. This suggests that Korean students may find modifications following a word in English to be problematic. Phrases such as *a book of value* or *a book which is valuable* may be rather difficult for Korean students, whereas *a valuable book* would not be as difficult for them. It is notable that particular English phrases require postword modifications and do not allow preword modifications, for example, an adjective phrase modifies such *indefinite* pronouns as *something, somebody, someone, nothing, nobody, no one, anything, anybody, anyone, everything, everybody, everyone,* and so on. Understandably, Korean students often use preword modifications, in cases where only postword modifications are allowed, producing ungrammatical English strings such as *good something* instead of *something important.*

Subject-Verb Inversion. This often occurs in English when a statement is turned into a question. For example, subject and verb change places when we transform *Professor Jones will teach somebody.* into either *Whom will Professor Jones teach?* or *Will Professor Jones teach somebody?* This phenomenon of subject-verb inversion is not found in Korean. This may help explain why Korean students often produce sentences such as *Whom Professor Jones will teach?* instead of the grammatically correct *Whom will Professor Jones teach?*

Irregular Verbs, Nouns, Adjectives, and Adverbs. Many English verbs form their past tense/past participle forms irregularly; many English nouns form their plural forms irregularly, and many adjectives and adverbs form their comparative and superlative forms irregularly. Korean verbs, nouns, adjectives, and adverbs are by and large regular. Thus the English irregular verbs, nouns, adjectives, and adverbs do not have counterparts in Korean. This, coupled with the general tendency to make regular what is irregular, may explain why Korean students often produce such forms as *goed* instead of *went* or *gone; gooses* instead of *geese; gooder* or *more good* instead of *better;* and *iller* instead of *worse.*

Sociolinguistic Aspects

Sociolinguistic competence might include knowledge of sociocultural rules or appropriateness of use of language varieties, domains, repertories, skills, roles, statuses, attitudes, settings, topics, channels, registers, styles, and so on (Briere, 1979; Troike, 1982).

In any language, there are linguistic and nonlinguistic devices that express the speakers attitude toward the person spoken about or to whom the speech is addressed.   Therefore, when Korean-speaking students are placed in an English-speaking environment, a variety of sociolinguistic blunders are expected. Understanding the root causes of these blunders will help teachers and other service providers develop strategies to effectively interact with and teach Korean students proper skills.

Korean has four different levels of speech   (higher honorific, simple honorific, simple familiar, and lower familiar) to show respect or intimacy among speech partners, relative to the degree of social and age superiority. For example, to address teacher, parent, or an elderly person (a social superior), a special honorific particle may be attached to an honorable subject; and an honorific infix is inserted in the verb of the honorable subject. Use of an inappropriate sociolinguistic level of speech is socially unacceptable and normally interpreted as having a special message, such as intended formality (e.g., use of the honorific level when the familiar is acceptable) or disrespect or contempt to a social superior (e.g., use of the familiar level when the honorific is appropriate).   One sometimes may have to evaluate the degree of intimacy with the speech partner before choosing the appropriate level of speech. This speech level system is an important linguistic feature characterizing interpersonal relationships in the Korean culture. Korean children acquire the basic rules of honorifics by the time they enter elementary school.

Compared to the rigid forms of Korean honorifics, English does not appear to have linguistic devices to show politeness. As a result, new immigrant Korean students may wonder how they can dare to use the same *you* to address their teachers as well as their classmates. In fact, English has other linguistic devices to show respect and to be polite to a speech partner; and it takes time to master these skills.   Korean students may not realize that there are other ways to express politeness to social superiors, e.g., the use of   *would* and *could* instead of *will* or *can*, and so on.   For example, a request may begin with *May I ask you to . . .* to be polite or formal to the speech partner; one would say *pass away* instead of *die* to express respect for the person who died.

Teachers should be aware that native Korean speakers expressions for offers or requests could sound too direct in most situations and even rude and demanding to non-Korean speakers. And this could result from a literal translation of Korean request such as *kajo wayo* (Bring it)   instead of saying *Would you please bring it?*   Also, Korean students are not familiar with the use of questions by American teachers which are actually indirect commands, because they are used to direct commands of Korean teachers and parents, who may sound drill sergeants to native speakers' ears.

English pragmatics is another area of difficulty for Korean students   to overcome. Korean students may not realize that one can interrupt a conversation by saying *Excuse me* instead of waiting until it is over. Or, they may interrupt others conversation without even saying *Excuse me.* For greetings, Koreans tend to use *Have you eaten yet?* or *Where are you going?* when native speakers would simply say *How are you doing?* or *How is it going?* or simply *Hi!* This is not because they are prying into others privacy, but due to their age-old habit of Korean greetings. Therefore, Korean students need to understand why those types of greetings are inappropriate and to practice proper forms.

Korean students are not accustomed to light compliments such as *That jacket looks great on you*, or *You have done a good job*. They would not know how to respond to these comments and would most likely simply smile a little to recognize these compliments. It is because Koreans do not tend to say *Thank you* as often as Americans do, unless the degree of thankfulness is really high and deserves a verbal acknowledgment. Therefore, it would be a good idea to provide a role play and help Korean students practice saying *Thank you* in these situations. In addition, Korean students need to be taught that *No, thank you* is used in a quite different situation.

PRACTICAL SUGGESTIONS FOR ESL AND OTHER EDUCATORS

Understanding the processes involved in acquiring a second language is as essential to effective teaching as anything else that teachers may study. Familiarity with the basics of second language acquisition theory and research can help teachers to better understand the strength, abilities, and needs of language minority students. Cummins (1989, 1994) draws on psychoeducational research as well as second language acquisition theory and research to develop a set of principles that teachers can use to guide program development. The first principle, conversational-academic language proficiency, draws attention to the significant distinctions between social and academic language skills.The second principle, linguistic interdependence examines the relationship between the first and second language. The third, the additive bilingualism enrichment, focuses on the importance of the primary language in developing second language proficiency.

Language proficiency encompasses linguistic and communicative competence. To be proficient in a second language, learners must internalize the underlying structures of the new language, adjust their language to make it appropriate socially and culturally in different situations, and master the dynamics of interaction. They must also develop strategic competence by learning to use verbal and nonverbal techniques to compensate for limitations in proficiency.

Ovando and Collier (1998) define teaching by means of the active, inquiry-based, interdisciplinary teaching style. Students actively engaged in solving a problem discovering new ways of perceiving their world, intensely applying learning strategies to the next task, developing family-like community among classmates, sharing the excitement of a special discovey—these glimpses of invigorating, deep learning occurs naturally in a classroom that promotes active learning.

Cooperative learning is one element in an active learning classroom that is crucial to management of an interactive class. However, according to Park (1997), Korean students in secondary school do not prefer group learning. Cooperative learning is recommended after they are well acculturated. The cognitive academic language learning approach (CALLA) trains teachers how to focus on students explicit acquisition of learning strategies, at the same time that language is being taught through content (Chamot & OMalley, 1994). CALLA is designed to meet the academic needs of limited-English-proficient students. Whole language approaches focus on use of authentic language that is meaningful to students, proceeding from whole to part, integrating development of multiple language modes (listening, speaking, reading, writing). Whole language focuses on using language, focusing on meaning first, getting students to write early and often, accepting invented spelling for beginners but expecting conventional spelling as students advance in the writing process, exposing students to high-quality literature and authentic texts from diverse writing genres, allowing students to make choices in reading, and encouraging all to be various readers (Willis, 1995).

CONCLUSION

To be effective, instruction must meet the academic, linguistic, intellectual, social, and individual needs of all students in culturally and linguistically diverse classrooms. Instruction must enable students to experience education in the fullest sense of the term, to be enriched through the formation of habits of judgment and the development of character, the elevation of standards, the facilitation of understanding, the development of taste and discrimination, the stimulation of curiosity and wondering, the fostering of style and a sense of beauty, the growth of a thirst for new ideas and visions of the yet known (Bracey, 1993).

The acculturation of Korean parents and their children are determined by an interaction of forces, some of which are rooted in Korea and others that are newly encountered in the United States. Among these forces are three key relationships that influence the educational process: the parent-child relationship, the educator-student relationship, and the parent-educator relationship. By understanding and improving these relationships, each stakeholder can enhance the educational experiences and adjustment of Korean-American children (California Department of Education, 1994; Chu, 1995).

REFERENCES

Bracey, G. W. (1993). The third Bracey report on the condition of public education. *Phi Delta Kappan* 75 (2): 104-117.

Briere, E. J. (1979). *Language development in bilingual settings.* Los Angeles: National Evaluation, Dissemination, and Assessment Center, California State University.

California Department of Education. (1994). *Handbook for teaching Korean-American students.* Sacramento, CA: California Department of Education.

Chamot, A. V., & O'Malley, J. M. (1994). *The CALLA handbook: Implementing the cognitive academic language learning approach.* Reading, MA: Addison-Wesley.

Chu, H. (1978). *A contrastive analysis between Korean and English for ESL teachers.* Arlington, VA: Arlington Public Schools.

Chu, H. (1983). Linguistic interferences in acquisition of English as a second language for Korean limited English proficient students. In R. V. Padilla (Ed.), *Theory, technology and public policy on bilingual education,* 15 (pp. 231-252). Rosslyn, VA: National Association for Bilingual Education.

Chu, H. (1995). The Korean Americans. In C. A. Grant (Ed.), *Educating for diversity: An anthology of multicultural voices,* (pp. 139-157). Boston: Allyn and Bacon.

Cummins, J. (1989). *Empowering minority students.* Sacramento, CA: California Association for Bilingual Education.

Cummins, J. (1994). Primary language instruction and the education of language minority students. In California Department of Education (Ed.), *Schooling and language minority students: A theoretical framework.* 2nd ed. (pp. 3-46). Los Angeles: Evaluation, Dissemination and Assessment Center, School of Education, California State University.

Kim, N. K. (1992). Korean. In W. Bright (Ed.), *International Encyclopedia of Linguistics,* (pp. 282-285) Vol. 2.

Lapham, S. (1990). *1990 profiles of foreign-born population, selected characteristics by place of birth.* Washington, DC: U.S. Bureau of the Census.

Lee, K. M. (1967). Foundations of the Korean language. *History of Korean Culture* 5: 9-112.

Ovando C. J. & Collier, V. P. (1998). *Bilingual and ESL classrooms: Teaching in multicultural contexts.* New York: McGraw-Hill.

Park, C. (1997). Learning style preferences of Asian American (Chinese, Filipino, Korean, and Vietnamese) students in secondary schools. *Equity & Excellence in Education* 30 (2): 68-77.

Poppe, N. (1965). *Introduction to Altaic linguistics.* Wiesbaden: Otto Harrassowitz.

Ramsteadt, G. J. (1949). *Studies in Korean etymology.* Helsinki: Suomalais-Ugrilainen Seura.

Troike, R. D. (1982). Zenos paradox and language assessment. In S. Seidner (Ed.), *Issues of language assessment: Foundations and research,* (pp. 3-5). Evanston, IL: Illinois State Board of Education.

U.S. Bureau of the Census (1993). *1990 Census of population.: Asians and Pacific Islanders in the United States.* Washington, DC: Government Printing Office.

Waggoner, D. (1993). Numbers of speakers of Asian languages lead in increase of multiculturalism. In D. Waggoner (Ed.), *Numbers and Needs.* Vol. 3, 5-6, (pp. 1-21). Washington, DC: U.S. Bureau of the Census.

Willis, S. (1995). Whole language: Finding the surest way to literacy. *Association for Supervision and Curriculum Development Update,* 1-8.

Meeting the Educational and Sociocultural Needs of Japanese Students in American Schools

Tina Yamano Nishida

As the Asian-Pacific-American population continues to grow, it is becoming increasingly diverse. The broad term "Asian-American" can be misleading because it suggests that the backgrounds, experiences, and needs of the twenty ethnic groups it represents are homogenous (Ono, 1995). In order to best meet the diverse educational needs of the various Asian-American groups, we must become acquainted with and acknowledge the similarities and differences between these groups.

While Japanese-Americans share similarities with other Asian-American groups, the group is truly unique in its history and characteristics. Japanese-Americans have endured a history of discrimination, segregation, and exclusion (Daniels, et al., 1991; Kitano, 1976; Nakanishi, 1988). Siu (1996) reports that, while most Asian-Americans are currently foreign-born, the Japanese-Americans are the only group with a larger United States-born than immigrant population. They have succeeded in many avenues, educational and otherwise, and their success has been often generalized to other ethnic minorities.

The experiences of individuals and subgroups within the Japanese-American population are wide and varied as well. There are generational differences with regard to assimilation, acculturation, language ability, and ethnic identity (Miyoshi, 1994; Nagata, 1993; Yamano, 1991) among Japanese immigrants, American-born Issei, Nisei, Sansei, and Yonsei (first-, second-, third- and fourth-generation, respectively). Japanese visiting scholars, Japanese-born women who have outmarried and are living permanently in the United States, and young children who have parents of two different backgrounds (California Department of Education, 1987) are still other groups with unique characteristics and needs. Thus it is most important to consider the tremendous diversity among Japanese-Americans.

The model minority myth has portrayed Asian-Americans as being academically, economically, and socially superior to other ethnic groups. Burstein and Hawkins (1992) concur that virtually every article written about the achievements of Japanese students highlights their exceptional performance, especially in science and mathematics. Newsworthy success stories containing convincing data, as well as the belief held by some Asian-Americans themselves that they are indeed successful, make the model minority myth difficult to discredit.

However, this can mask the various social and psychological needs and problems among those Asian-American students who are not performing well (Chun, 1995; Crystal, 1989; Divorky, 1988; Hsia, 1988; Nakanishi, 1995; Leadership Education for Asian Pacifics, 1995; Pang, 1990; Siu, 1996). For example, while Asian-Americans have been able to move up steadily in the hierarchy of occupations (Hsia, 1988), stereotypes that characterize them as quiet and nonassertive have led to persistent underrepresentation of Asian-Americans in leadership positions. Further, the misleading myth has created differential treatment by quota systems at universities across the country or render the numerous Asian-Americans who are "at risk," including some Japanese-Americans and recent Japanese immigrants, invisible.

By broadly highlighting the educational issues, needs, and concerns of recent Japanese immigrants,[1] this chapter provides a window to understanding the difficulties Japanese immigrant students face when matriculating in the U.S. educational system. More specifically, this chapter provides important information on background and cultural traits that affect the interaction between home and school for Japanese immigrants. In addition to assisting educators and support service providers to develop greater awareness, the author's main goal is to improve Japanese students' sociocultural adjustment to schools.

The chapter is divided into the following sections: a brief historical overview of Japanese immigration including the establishment of the Japanese-American family in transition; similarities and differences between Japanese and American schools, including cultural differences in classroom interaction; and lastly, parental attitudes toward school and school participation, with suggestions for greater parental involvement.

A HISTORICAL OVERVIEW OF JAPANESE IMMIGRATION TO THE UNITED STATES

Issei: The First Generation

Japanese immigrants first came to America in the 1880s. Ichioka (1988) divides the history of Japanese immigration into two broad periods: 1885 through 1907, and 1908 through 1924. The first period was characterized by Japanese laborers who left their native homeland with intentions of staying only long enough to earn money and return home.

"The land of the promise" was in the minds of many young Japanese who came to America to fulfill their dreams at the beginning of the twentieth century, according to Akemi Kikumura in *Through Harsh Winters* (1981). Beginning in

1908, Japanese immigrants began to settle on agricultural land, making the transition from laborers to farmers. Many of these young Japanese men settled along the Pacific Coast and found employment in the areas of domestic service and farm labor.

Although the early Japanese-Americans made great efforts to orient themselves to the new environment, they were hindered by their inability to speak English. Their dreams were quickly shattered by the harsh realities of racism, segregation, and discrimination. Yuji Ichioka's *The Issei: The World of the First Generation Japanese Immigrants, 1885-1924* (1988) documents the struggles of Japanese immigrants in their attempts to survive in a hostile land where Asians were viewed as being racially inferior and undesirable.

According to Hirabayashi (1991), "racism was a fact of life for Japanese-Americans" (p. 47). Japanese immigrants suffered from the anti-Japanese exclusion movement. They were the excluded aliens, ineligible for citizenship from 1885 to 1924. Denied naturalization rights, these Japanese immigrants never won the power to defend themselves in the political arena. Their plight was compounded by laws that prohibited aliens from purchasing or leasing land. Ichioka (1988) observes that "this state of powerlessness is a central theme in Japanese immigrant history" (p. 2).

Among the many other problems prompted by racial discrimination was that of marriage. Japanese government regulations did not allow laborers to summon wives from Japan, but they did allow farmers and businessmen to do so. Since the majority of the young men who immigrated wanted to marry and start families, they made arrangements to send for "picture brides" from Japan. Thus, the immigrant family unit emerged as the key foundation underlying permanent settlement; the birth of children gave new meaning to their American residency (Ichioka, 1988).

In 1907, the U.S. government responded to the increased threats of violence towards the Japanese who resided in California by passing the Gentlemen's Agreement of 1907. Under this law, Japan promised to limit the number of unskilled laborers entering the United States from Japan in exchange for respectful treatment of Japanese citizens already in the United States. In addition to being denied admittance to the United States, the Issei were prohibited from owning or leasing land by racial obstacles such as the California Alien Land Laws of 1913 and 1920. This was just one method used to drive the Japanese out of agriculture; without citizenship, one could not become a tenant farmer. Anti-Oriental sentiment continued to escalate, resulting in the passage of the Exclusion Act of 1924, which barred Asian immigration to the United States entirely (Ichihashi, 1969).

During the exclusion movement, in spite of widespread racism and discrimination, Japanese immigrants worked hard to adapt to American society: they accepted the primacy of an American public school education for their children, and assigned a secondary educational role to the private Japanese-language schools which they had established (Ichioka, 1988). Moreover, in the belief that anti-Japanese sentiments were rooted in ignorance, they attempted to educate the American public about Japanese immigrants. Although the 1924

Exclusion Act symbolized total rejection of all Asian groups including the Japanese by the United States, they still hoped for a better future for their American-born children (Ichioka, 1988).

Nisei: The Second Generation

With the onset of World War II and the Japanese attack on Pearl Harbor, Nisei children soon faced new anti-Japanese sentiment and mounting racial tension. "All the racial fears, antagonism, and distrust culminated in an order[2] from the President of the United States [Franklin D. Roosevelt], which was stamped with legal approval by the United States Supreme Court and supported by public sentiment, to evacuate more than 110,000 Japanese, aliens and citizens alike, from the West Coast internment and to concentrate them into camps located in the interior on desolate government land" (Kikumura, 1981, p. 120; see also Daniels, et al., 1991).

Not only did the internment strip Japanese-Americans of virtually all of their land and possessions, it also destroyed the system of community networks, business establishments and churches, and brought the Japanese society to a sudden halt. Issei leaders were arrested, and all Japanese assets, including bank accounts, were frozen, adding to the wartime atmosphere of insecurity (Kimura, 1988). All Japanese language schools were closed (Hawkins, 1978) for the duration of World War II and never regained their popularity. As a result, the Japanese language was no longer spoken in the home, and many Japanese-Americans grew up unable to speak Japanese.

Some Japanese-Americans went out of their way to prove their loyalty to the United States by volunteering to join the 442nd Regimental Combat Team. In addition, Kimura (1988) states that, in their effort to eliminate anything that would identify them with the enemy, they felt compelled to destroy cultural artifacts such as brocaded *obi* (kimono sashes), letters, personal photographs of their relatives, their books, as well as the Japanese flag and portraits of the Emperor and Empress of Japan. Many were ashamed to say they were Japanese and, in their desperate efforts to be identified as Americans, placed portraits of George Washington, Abraham Lincoln, and President Roosevelt, as well as American flags in their homes, restaurants, barbershops, and other business establishments. They tried to prove that any suspicion of national disloyalty was groundless (Ueda, 1974).

World War II brought great changes among Japanese-American families (Kimura, 1988). For example, the Issei (first generation) became enemy aliens, although their Hawaiian-born children were U.S. citizens; this often meant changed parent-child roles and the loss of parental authority over children. Ironically, since public use of the Japanese language was prohibited, the Issei had to depend on their children's interpretations of the regulations concerning enemy aliens. As a result, the Issei, who spoke only their native tongue, kept silent, even at home.

Despite all the hardship and discrimination the Issei endured, they accepted the fact that their children were American citizens and expected a better future for them. This sentiment was strongly expressed in the letters of the internees,

instructing their wives to conduct themselves solely as the mothers of American citizens or instructing their sons to conduct themselves as loyal Americans and not to let their fathers' internment interfere with their duty to their native land (Kimura, 1988). Nevertheless, many were concerned about how internment affected their children. They did not want them to feel humiliated by the internment, nor did they want them to think that their internment was because of any subversive activities on their part, but rather that it was "due to the war." They wanted them to think and behave as proud U.S. citizens despite the fact that it was the U.S. government that was committing the misdeed (Kimura, 1988).

The Effects of World War II on Subsequent Generations

Many Japanese-Americans fought hard to gain reparations and apology for the wrongdoings of the U.S. government in World War II (Commission on Wartime Relocation and Internment of Citizens, 1982; Daniels, et al., 1991; Naito & Scott, 1990; Weglyn, 1976). Finally, in 1980, the Commission on Wartime Relocation and Internment of Civilians was established to review the facts and assess the circumstances of Executive Order (E.O.) 9066. In 1982, the commission concluded that E.O. 9066 was not justified by military necessity and resulted in part from racism and ignorance at all levels of government; hence it was a personal injustice to loyal citizens (Kitano, 1991). Ultimately, the long fight for redress brought due compensation of $20,000 to each survivor and a formal apology signed by President George Bush, which acknowledged that money and words cannot restore lost years or erase painful memories (Daniels, 1991).

Despite the reparations and a formal apology from the United States government forty years after the closing of the camps, Japanese-Americans' lives were forever altered psychologically, culturally, and linguistically (Mass, 1991; Yamano, 1994). Although more than 80,120 redress payments have been made, thousands of evacuees and internees have yet to receive compensation (Ochi, 1997). Most importantly, this significant event in Japanese-American history substantially affected the ethnic identity of subsequent generations. For many Japanese-Americans, the internment experience triggered a reevaluation of their ethnic identity. Many decided to abandon their ethnic heritage and become completely Americanized. Some even refused to eat Japanese food, to prove to others that they could be trusted as loyal Americans. In order to prove their loyalty, many spoke only English and did not participate in Japanese cultural events. The Nisei (second generation), who suffered greatly from discrimination, wanted their children to be accepted by other Americans, so they hastened the process of acculturation and assimilation by cutting ties to Japan, familial traditions, and so on. As a result, many unique qualities of the Japanese were quickly diluted or abandoned.

Kitano (1991) asserts that one of the most visible cultural changes among Japanese-Americans is the increasing rates of outmarriages.[3] Interestingly enough, the younger generations of Sansei and Yonsei are trying to revive their cultural heritage by taking multicultural courses or by getting involved with various Buddhist churches, the Japanese American National Museum, and other Japanese associations (Miyoshi, 1994; Nagata, 1993; Yamano, 1991). Unfortunately, increases in the number of "Japan bashing" incidents in recent years have caused some Japanese-Americans to fear that another era of intense racial discrimination may flare up, despite their American identity.

The difficulty of the Japanese-American experience has often been trivialized or ignored outright. Some of the most harsh experiences have been glossed over and instead used to validate justice and equality in American society (i.e., despite all obstacles, they have become successful [Fujita, 1987]). Further, the primarily Eurocentric curriculum that dominates the United States' public schools often excludes the contributions made by Japanese-Americans and other Asian-Americans (i.e., textbooks in U.S. history do not reflect the diversity of its people). This inaccurate portrayal and instruction about the Japanese-American experience and history is made more problematic by the lack of Asian American faculty. Thus many Americans believe that Asian-Americans (and all other ethnic minorities) are marginal or insignificant, and many Asian-Americans are robbed of ethnic pride and cultural and historical identity.

Our educational system plays a critical role in making future generations aware of significant events that have occurred in the Japanese-American and collective Asian-American histories. We need to create school curricula that reflect the diverse experiences and histories of Asian-Americans and other minority students, so that the detrimental and irreversible consequences of racism will not repeatedly affect future generations.

Recent Trends in Japanese Immigration

Japanese immigrants continue to comprise a significant portion of the population in both California and the United States. According to the Japanese Consulate of Los Angeles, as of October, 1996, there were 264,000 Japanese nationals (including green card and visa holders) in the United States. In California, there are approximately 68,500 Japanese nationals, with roughly 37,500 in Los Angeles County (R. Yanagi, personal communication, February 7, 1997). In 1996, there were 5,042 students of Japanese ancestry in California public schools who were classified as having limited English proficiency (California Department of Education, 1997b).

These figures may seem high, but the number of Japanese nationals immigrating to the United States is in fact decreasing for various reasons. One reason is that the average Japanese national has more job security in Japan than in the United States. Historically, corporate Japan has provided lifetime employment for its workers; although this practice has begun to change. Another reason is that many married men with families prefer to stay in Japan if they have a good job there. Further, Japanese companies are becoming increasingly reluctant to send personnel to the United States, since many of these companies have not seen a significant number of returnees. The Japanese economy is a contributing factor as well. In the late 1980s, when the Japanese economy was very strong (the "bubble period"), Japanese companies were more than willing to send Japanese personnel and capital to the United States. Recently, however, the prolonged economic recession in Japan has reversed this trend.

Recent Japanese immigrants include ambitious single men who are looking for work, and women who desire a different lifestyle from that available in the male-dominated society of Japan. Currently, most Japanese businessmen who are sent by their companies to stay in the United States for three to four years send their children to U.S. public schools during the week and to Japanese language schools (or "Saturday schools") on the weekends. Many of the Saturday schools are sponsored by the Japanese government and offer the Japanese curriculum. According to Nezu (1986), a Japanese Ministry of Education (*Monbusho*) study that documented the level of parental anxiety related to their children's potential academic problems as returnees, 75% of the parents had sent their children to both local public schools and supplementary Japanese schools during their residency in the United States.

Recently immigrating Japanese nationals, often living in America for business purposes, hope that when they return to Japan, their children will matriculate into (or, in certain cases, re-enter) the Japanese school system. Thus, Japanese children need to prepare themselves for two separate and equally demanding curricula: (1) they need to adapt to American schools, and (2) they must prepare themselves to return to Japan. Previously, students who were educated in the United States suffered from "returnee syndrome"; they were regarded as different, and therefore had difficulties with administrators and classmates upon their return to Japan. Fortunately, in recent years the Japanese educational system has become more accepting of, and lenient toward, returnees. A special entrance exam has been devised for those who have studied abroad (T. Hashimoto, personal communication, February 7, 1997). According to the *Handbook for Teaching Japanese-Speaking Students* (California Department of Education, 1987), the ministry operates special assistance programs in designated schools throughout Japan in order to help returnees readjust to the Japanese curriculum.

SIMILARITIES AND DIFFERENCES BETWEEN JAPANESE AND AMERICAN SCHOOLS

Confronting the Stereotypes

Could it be true that all Japanese schools conform to the stereotyped image of intense, high-pressure education in which children learn by rote memorization from a demanding teacher? As a result of these teaching methods, are all children robot-like and lacking the creativity and problem-solving skills of their American counterparts? A comparison study of Japanese and American elementary schools found no support for these stereotypes of Japanese schools. In fact, the researchers found that Japanese educators considered these stereotypes to be very outdated (Lee, Graham, & Stevenson, 1996)[4] and that far from emphasizing rote memorization, choral, response and drill learning, the lessons in Japanese elementary schools encourage conceptual problem-solving approaches to learning. In actuality, the preferred method of teaching in Japan involves frequent dialogue and interaction between and among students and teachers (Stevenson, 1991).

According to Lewis (1995), "Both Japanese and Americans have expressed concern about whether 'creativity' is fostered by Japanese education, but careful studies are lacking. Originality is associated with academic achievement in the United States, whereas persistence predicts academic achievement in Japan" (p. 12). Stevenson (1991) found that many Japanese parents were critical of and dissatisfied with their children's education in Japan, citing the inadequate attention paid to individual children, especially in large classes where it was difficult for teachers to spend class time attending to individual needs. Also, Japanese schools fail to provide supplementary materials for children with special needs. The absence of special education in much of the literature on Japanese education reflects the relatively low attention paid to these students.

Articles in both the Japanese and the American popular press suggest that Japanese preschool children go through "examination hell" as early as age two in order to gain admission to prestigious kindergartens that will subsequently lead them to prestigious elementary schools, middle schools, high schools, and universities. These publications claim that the examination system is souring the entire educational system. Although the focus is directed toward high school students, its effects overflow into the elementary school system (Stevenson, 1991). A recent article published in *The Los Angeles Times*, entitled "In Japan, Even Tots Must Make the Grade" (Efron, 1997), characterized all Japanese kindergartners and their mothers[5] as obsessively examination-oriented and highly competitive. Lois Peak (1991), in her book *Learning to Go to School in Japan*, contends that this is another myth about Japan that has entered contemporary American folklore, which has persisted to obscure American perceptions of Japanese preschools. She claims that very few Japanese children experience entrance examinations before they enter high school at the age of fifteen.

Another myth involves the use of Spartan discipline practices in Japanese schools. Peak attests that news reporters tend to see Japanese preschools at their most formal, but that what they see are actually carefully planned exhibitions of classroom activities. She adds that, although Japanese preschools foster and value such formal behavior, they also encourage lively and even boisterous child-initiated play. A related common misconception is that Japanese children are "naturally" tractable and easier to discipline because their mothers require them to exhibit cooperative and polite behavior at home. In reality, children are encouraged to freely demonstrate their feeling of *amae,* the desire to be indulged, in the privacy of their homes because in other settings it would be labeled as evidence of selfishness, regressive dependence, and irritability (Doi, 1962; Peak, 1991).

Contrary to the common belief that Japanese high school students spend more hours in *class,* in actuality they simply spend more hours in *school* (participating in various extracurricular activities and school festivals) than their U.S. counterparts (Irish, 1994). Irish concluded that, unlike high schools in the United States, the Japanese high school is like a second home, playing a greater role in students' lives not only as an educational institution but also as an instrument of socialization. Although the Japanese educational system has come under attack for requiring students to spend time cleaning classrooms, these cleaning chores are seen as activities central to teaching the responsibility and social cohesion necessary for basic character development (Quinn, 1995). Japanese educators seek to develop well-rounded, whole individuals by emphasizing qualities such as perseverance, kind-heartedness, healthiness, and diligence (Cummings, 1980; Stevenson, 1991).

After World War II, the Japanese imported many ideas from the United States, with the result that Japanese and United States school curricula are more similar than they are different. However, because their teaching methods are very different, it may be advantageous for Japanese and American teachers to learn about each other's ways to provide help to the children, who are caught in the middle (T. Hashimoto, personal communication, February 7, 1997). When we compare our educational system with that of Japan, the Japanese educational landscape contains many familiar features, for example, a lengthy period of compulsory education, a high rate of high school attendance, and diverse preschool options. However, the many features that differ sharply from the U.S. educational system include "the Ministry of Education's control over textbooks and instructional hours, the avoidance of ability grouping and tracking during the compulsory education years, and the downward pressure of college entrance examinations on elementary and even pre-elementary education" (Lewis, 1995, p. 17).

The Structure of the School System

The structure of the Japanese school system shares numerous similarities with the American system. In fact, the present Japanese school system uses the United States' system as its model: nine years of compulsory education, with six years of elementary school followed by three years of lower secondary school education (junior high school) and three years of upper secondary school (senior high school) (Ishizaka, 1990). Unlike the U.S. school year, the Japanese school year begins on April 1 and ends in March of the following year. Japanese children must be six years of age before they enter first grade on April 1. Interestingly, unlike elementary and high school, kindergarten is not compulsory for children ages three to five. The elementary and junior high schools have three terms (April to July, August to December, and January to March). High schools are either on a three-term schedule or follow the two-term schedule used by the Japanese universities (California Department of Education, 1987). Vacations are scheduled in summer, winter, and at the end of the school year. Further, as in the United States, school attendance and textbooks are free to all public school students in grades one through nine in Japan.

In Japan all children are automatically passed on to the next grade level in elementary schools, whereas in the U.S. student retention is an option (Stevenson, 1991). Therefore, regardless of their academic performance, students in Japan remain with their classmates throughout elementary school. Each teacher and his or her students are considered a unit that stays together for most or all subjects in the school day, including music, science, physical education, and lunch, in order to develop a sense of community (Lewis, 1995). The elementary and junior high students stay together for all subjects, while high school students are together for most subjects (California Department of Education, 1987).

Japanese and American schools differ substantially with respect to their treatment of gender. In Japan, prior to World War II, schools did not integrate the sexes. Despite the 1947 Fundamental Law of Education and other postwar educational reforms that called for the adoption of coeducation at all levels, many students still attend single-sex schools. The majority of urban public schools are coeducational, but suburban schools in northern Kanto and Tohoku regions are still significantly single-sex institutions. According to Fujimura-Fanselow and Imamura (1991), over 60% of the private high schools in Japan are still single-sex schools. As mandated by federal law, most public schools in the United States are coeducational.

Although women's access to education has improved considerably in Japan, gender differentiation in educational participation and level of attainment has persisted. Gender differences are more obvious at the secondary level than at the compulsory elementary and lower secondary school levels. There has been a significant increase in the number of women entering four-year universities over the years, but a substantial number still chooses to enroll in women's junior colleges by attending affiliated high schools, where they are not required to undergo rigorous entrance examinations (Rohlen, 1983). Conversely, males are found almost exclusively in four-year universities. According to Fujimura-Fanselow and Imamura (1991), parents perpetuate gender inequalities because they feel that the rigorous competition and preparation costs for examinations are imperative for their sons but unnecessary for their daughters. As a result, women often forgo the competitive preparations for university admission, lower their ambitions, and decide to attend two-year junior colleges. Investigative studies have also revealed that many public high schools practice discriminatory admission regulations that require higher examination scores for women or maintain quotas for admitting Japanese women (Fujimura-Fanselow & Imamura, 1991).

Generally speaking, schools in Japan require student conformity and have stricter rules regarding appearance than the public schools in the United States. Japanese students often wear some form of school identification. For example, kindergartners may wear matching hats or smocks, while elementary school children wear identification badges. Elementary school students are not required to wear uniforms; junior and senior high school students do wear them, and they must follow a code of behavior while in their school uniforms as they commute to and from school (California Department of Education, 1987). In addition, school rules apply to personal appearance: girls are not allowed to wear makeup or nail polish and may not have chemically treated hair (colored or permed), and long hair on boys is unacceptable. Differences are not welcome because they do not enhance group-minded behavior.

The Teaching Profession

Teaching holds a respected position in Japanese society and is a profession that is attractive to both men and women. Perhaps this societal attitude is reflected in individual attitudes. Lee, Graham and Stevenson (1996) found that Japanese teachers spent more time at school than their American counterparts (approximately three additional hours per day).

One way that Japanese teachers spend the additional hours is in learning and receiving help from fellow teachers. Japanese teachers confer with each other on all aspects of teaching including preparing lessons, working with individual students, and correcting student work. Even the placement of teachers' desks facilitates group orientation. A typical staff room might have two rows of desks pushed together with the sides touching. This "island" in the middle of the room optimizes the teachers' ability to gather, prepare materials, hold meetings, and socialize with one another (Peak, 1991; Stevenson, 1992). Quinn (1995) noted that while inservice professional development activities are common practices in both the United States and Japan, teachers in Japan create study groups to research their own areas of interest and review the practices and ideas of their colleagues. In contrast, American teachers often work alone in their classrooms during the entire time they are at school; sharing their research ideas is neither a common practice nor an expectation of American teachers.

In Japan, large class sizes of roughly forty students are the norm, and Japanese teachers are expected to handle classes independently; parents are never called upon to help in class (Lee, et al., 1996). In contrast, American elementary schools have corresponding class sizes of twenty-eight students, and teachers often have assistance from parents or aides. Lewis (1995) found that while Japanese elementary classes are large by U.S. standards, they are steadily being reduced.

Curriculum and Instruction

In contrast to the United States, curriculum and instruction in Japanese schools are highly centralized. The Japanese Ministry of Education (Monbusho) defines the curriculum whereby all Japanese schools interpret a set of guidelines to fit their own needs. According to Lewis (1995), Monbusho prescribes national instructional goals and hours, approves textbooks, and strongly shapes many other aspects of educational policy. Therefore, every Japanese public school student studies the same subjects using similar or identical textbooks for approximately the same number of hours per year. In addition to the nine basic subjects (Japanese, math, social studies, science, English, music, health, physical education, home economics) taught per week in Japanese middle schools (twenty-sevem hours of instruction), five additional hours per week are allocated to health and moral and occupational guidance (Fukuzawa, 1996). English is a compulsory subject for almost all first-year junior high school students until they finish high school (California Department of Education, 1987). Unlike the schools in the United States, Japanese schools provide moral education until the ninth grade and art, music, and English as part of every student's course of study until the twelfth grade (Burstein & Hawkins, 1992).

Japanese schools lack the high degree of local autonomy that U.S. schools enjoy. Teachers in the United States may tailor their curriculum to make it more relevant to their students. While Japanese teachers develop their own approaches to teaching the content of the text required by the local educational authorities (Lee, Graham & Stevenson, 1996), they must adhere strictly to the national curriculum, which is the basis of the high school entrance examination. Any deviation from the ministry-approved guidelines and textbooks would handicap their students in their competition for high school placement (Fukuzawa, 1996). Many middle school classrooms, therefore, are fact based, routinized, teacher centered, and textbook oriented. Students are not encouraged to express opinions or to discuss the readings and their relevance to contemporary issues, and individual interests or abilities may often be overlooked (Fukuzawa, 1996).

Since the contemporary Japanese philosophy of education is egalitarian in nature, usage of whole-class instruction helps teachers handle large numbers of students within the limited quarters of Japanese classrooms (Lee, et al., 1996). It is believed that the whole-class method allows all children to receive the same type and amount of instruction from the teacher. Teachers assume that all children can master their coursework as long as topics are presented slowly and thoroughly. Tracking and ability grouping are foreign ideas in a Japanese classroom. Gifted students or students with special needs must attend private tutorial schools commonly known as *juku*[6] or have their needs met through after-school clubs. The *juku* often compensates for the public school system's lack of individualized instruction, and some public school teachers feel that juku undermines their authority, since they are bound to follow the curriculum and not express the extent of their knowledge (Fukuzawa, 1996). Moreover, the concepts of reading disabled, learning disabled, and emotionally impaired have only recently been open to discussion (Stevenson, 1991). In contrast, students in United States schools are often grouped according to ability level and may be required to repeat a grade.

The Role of Testing and Standards

Japanese high schools are ranked on the basis of their success rate in preparing students for admission to the most prestigious universities (Fujimura-Fanselow & Imamura, 1991). Due to the extreme pressure placed on children from age three to age nineteen, the entrance examinations that numerous elementary, junior, and senior high school students experience require them to go beyond what their school curriculum provides. Often, students enroll in the *yobiko,* commercially operated profit-making preparatory schools, and the juku, local private classes, to improve their chances of passing the entrance examinations (Duke, 1986). This form of admission is different from the U.S. admission policy, which is typically based on a combination of grade point average and standardized test scores. The competitive entrance examinations leading to hierarchically ranked high schools and universities define Japanese students' school life, since much of their time is academically oriented (Irish, 1994).

In stark contrast to institutional entry measures in Japan, most high schools in the United States do not require entrance examinations (Ellington, 1992). While American secondary and higher educational institutions have examinations for entry, many universities in the United States require scores on standardized exams such as the Scholastic Aptitude Test and the Graduate Record Examination, which measure aptitude rather than content mastery (Ellington, 1992). Moreover, public schools in the United States are typically ranked not according to college placement rates but according to student achievement on norm-referenced tests. School rankings on these tests are often published in local newspapers.

The Role of Cultural Differences in Classroom Interaction

It may be both undesirable and futile to hope that Americans become more like the Japanese (or vice versa), yet there is much that we can learn from each other. At the very least, understanding another culture can encourage us to reexamine our own cultural approaches and assumptions (Peak, 1991, p. 191).

Although we run the risk of stereotyping when we attempt to distinguish between Japanese and American educational systems, students, and teachers, the following explanation of characteristics may provide a context for determining the best ways to meet the needs of Japanese-American youth. As noted above and in the *Handbook for Teaching Japanese-Speaking Students* (California Department of Education, 1987), Japanese youth may resort to cultural behaviors when interacting with teachers in United States schools.

Cultural differences between Japanese and Americans define classroom interaction in dinstinct ways. For example, group behavior and cooperation, important cultural concepts in Japanese society, are taught and learned in preschool. Peak (1991) professes that learning to go to school in Japan is primarily defined as training in group life or *shudan seikatsu*. These cultural traits help Japanese children to understand what it means to be a member of Japanese society (Quinn, 1995; Peak, 1991). Lewis (1995) asserts that "students didn't just work *in* groups, they worked *as* groups" (p. 81). Teachers create groups and group activities in ways that help children enhance one another's strengths and overcome one another's weaknesses. They combine ability levels and mix outgoing children with more introverted children. Putting together children who can learn from one another academically and socially is often the central principle that Japanese teachers use to organize groups. According to Lewis's observation of group activities in various elementary school classrooms, children ate, played and worked in these small, fixed, family-like groups several times a day for weeks, months, or even years. These groups were fundamental in helping children develop socially, emotionally, and intellectually and in helping them to build a sense of belonging and to recognize one another's positive qualities, as well as providing opportunities to receive feedback from their peers (Lewis, 1995).

In Japanese classrooms, leadership is not a privilege afforded to the well-behaved few; it is a regular responsibility of all children who are members of the group. This leadership system (known as *toban)* seems to capitalize on children's natural need for attention, prestige, and a chance to lead others, as well as giving them a sense of responsibility. For example, the designated *toban* may lead meetings, evaluate other students' behavior, lead the class in performing tasks or solving disputes, and manage other mechanics of classroom activities (Lewis, 1995).

Cultural traits and values regarding respect and deference to authority instilled in a child at an early age govern that child's actions in school and as a member of the greater community. For example, *enryo,* or respectful hesitation, governs a child's behavior when in the presence of his or her superiors. Japanese educators' tendency to emphasize socialization of appropriate emotions conflicts with American educators' emphasis on self-expression (Lewis, 1995). Whereas American teachers often expect their children to vocalize their needs and request assistance, Japanese children have a tendency to hesitate because they believe that they would be bothering their teacher. This behavior (and other behavior traits) reflects their cultural upbringing. Therefore, many Japanese children appear to be unassertive and reluctant to express their needs, when they are actually displaying respect. Japanese children have been taught to respect their teachers, and part of that respect is not to bother their teachers. In addition, Japanese children are often taught to show respect for their elders by choosing a particular vocabulary of polite address to a "superior" (this includes adults and teachers), as well as not to initiate conversation with an elder. They are taught to address instructors as *sensei* (teacher) rather than by their surnames. American students do not use particular word choices to demonstrate respect and are encouraged to address their teachers as Mrs. Jones or Mr. Smith (California Department of Education, 1987). Further, U.S. students do not necessarily view adults as superior, and are encouraged to interact with their elders. Another expression of respect for Japanese students is avoiding eye contact with one's superiors. Unfortunately, cultural signals are not always clear; for instance, when Japanese students hesitate to make eye contact with their American teachers out of respect, such behavior is often interpreted as being deceitful, aversive, or insecure.

These cultural differences regarding what constitutes respect have important implications for the classroom. For example, Japanese youth will uphold the "silence is golden" rule, especially when their comments might expose the imperfect teaching skills of their teachers. Fearing to appear to criticize a teacher's efforts by saying, I don't understand, students will instead nod politely and attribute their lack of comprehension to their own lack of diligence. Their hesitation to express opinions is deeply rooted in the notion that their thoughts might sound presumptuous or be contradictory to the feelings or thoughts of the teacher. They must never openly disagree with anyone and should defer to the judgment of their superiors (California Department of Education, 1987). On the contrary, their American counterparts are encouraged to speak up whenever they do not understand, and they are praised for trying their best rather than for always being correct. American youth do not have to be well-versed in the subject matter in order to state their opinions. Overall, they are encouraged to develop an independent viewpoint and to defend their statements to their teachers or fellow students (California Department of Education, 1987). The U.S. culture encourages assertiveness, independence, and leadership, but for the Japanese student who may be trying to acculturate, ingrained cultural traits make behavioral changes difficult. Hence, when a Japanese immigrant child is quiet during a lesson, this does not necessarily mean that he is not disengaged or uninterested.

Another cultural difference is the nature of communication. Japanese students, especially those who have immigrated more recently, are often unaccustomed to having teachers come close to them. Japanese students may consider loud, excited, classroom dialogue improper or even boisterous. These students may appear intimidated or shy, but it is quite possible that these children are experiencing culture shock. Educators can help by asking students about their needs and eliciting unspoken student perceptions.

Concluding Remarks about the Differences between Japanese and American Schools

What these differences between Japanese and American schools suggest is that for Japanese immigrants to make a successful transition to U.S. schools, a reciprocal relationship must be fostered. American educators would benefit from being educated about the cultural and social differences of the Japanese. Ideally, teachers can function as cultural translators, who can interpret and attribute specific behavior to their individual cultural foundations and use it to address the individual needs of their diverse student body. At the same time, Japanese parents and children must become more aware of U.S. culture and expectations regarding classroom behavior.

Parental Attitudes toward School and School Participation

Although every parent hopes his or her child will do well in school, such sentiment is even stronger among the Japanese, because in the Japanese culture, the success or failure of young children reflects upon the family as a whole. While Japanese who have lived in the United States for many years or decades have a good understanding of the public school system, immigrant Japanese parents may not be clear on the roles of parents in education in the United States. Many of these recently arrived immigrants are here on temporary business assignments and are living in the United States for an undetermined period of time. They may enroll their Japanese immigrant children in American public schools with the hope that their children will become bilingual and bicultural. However, these immigrant students often experience difficulties in the classroom while they are acquiring English language skills. Hashimoto, principal of Sigma school (T. Hashimoto, personal communication, February 7, 1997), observed that "these children may be very intelligent and have good learning habits; however, since they do not know any English, they feel incompetent. Inevitably, it changes the child's attitude and self-confidence." He suggests that, in order to equip these immigrant children, educators may offer intensive ESL classes at Japanese language schools where bilingual Japanese teachers can explain difficult English terminology in Japanese.[7] Programs such as Sigma admit newly arrived students and teach them English for four months, equipping them for transition to American public schools. This helps to ensure that they will "swim" rather than "sink."

In addition to dropping their children into U.S. schools without a basic grasp of the English language, many Japanese parents are not familiar with the American education system. They may compare the unknown to what they know—that is, the way they were educated in Japan. Japanese parents need to learn how the U.S. educational system works and become informed about significant differences between the two systems. For example, some parents ask the principal how to read an American report card. In sum, parents who move to a foreign country need to have a cross-cultural understanding of education, because the educational system has an effect on their children.

Suggestions for Parental Involvement

Before making suggestions for greater involvement by Japanese immigrant parents in their children's K-12 education, the perspective of Japanese educators and their expectations of parents in Japan must be understood. Many Japanese educators exclude parents from their elementary school classrooms for what they see as justifiable reasons. They believe children need to establish independence from the close, indulgent, parent-child relationship. They also feel that inequities develop among children when some (but not all) parents volunteer in the classroom. In addition, due to the diverse ways in which parents relate to children, parents may be regarded as a threat to the classroom culture created by the teachers (Lewis, 1995). This model of the parent-school relationship is very different from the U.S. model, where parent participation in the classroom is often strongly encouraged.

In general, although parents' concerns and ideas are welcomed by teachers in Japan, Japanese parents are reluctant to offer their ideas to school administrators and teachers because they regard them as professionals who know how to educate children. Parents also believe that teachers are the authorities on what children need and that teachers' concerns should set the agenda for parent-teacher conversation.

Japanese parents do not have informal opportunities for parents to volunteer at school as tutors, classroom helpers, library aides, or other roles familiar to American parents (Lewis, 1995). Peak (1991) asserts that mothers avoid entering the classroom while class is in session, except on carefully planned observation days for parents. Japanese teachers believe that the presence of mothers in their classroom inhibits the development of children's independence, friendships, and peer interaction. Hence, the behavior appropriate to mother-child interaction is not appropriate to group life in the classroom.

On the other hand, while not participating in the classroom, parents (i.e., mothers) are expected to be active in school-related activities such as monthly parent-teacher association (PTA) meetings and PTA-sponsored mothers' clubs (Duke, 1986; Peak, 1991). This is feasible because the percentage of working mothers in Japan is much lower than that in the United States. Further, Japanese mothers may hold office (approximately one out of every five mothers has held an administrative position within the PTA) or attend meetings held during school hours for group activities such as needlecraft and hiking. Parents may also participate in parent-teacher interviews, which are conducted in children's homes, enabling teachers to gain a better understanding of students' personalities and behavioral patterns within their home settings. This reinforces the intricately woven triangular relationship between the teacher, parent, and student in Japan (Duke, 1986; Peak, 1991).

Although Japanese mothers and teachers desire close and open communication, they rarely discuss children's adjustment problems (Peak, 1991). Peak believes that frank mother-teacher communication about a child's problems is relatively rare because most mothers and teachers have a general expectation that problems will arise and eventually will be solved. She adds that the main reason for this lack of communication probably involves Japanese cultural norms of interpersonal communication, which strive to maintain a positive and harmonious relationship at all costs. According to Peak (1991), a child's adjustment to school can be attributed to many other aspects of Japanese culture and society, such as Japanese family life, childrearing techniques, the establishment of the individual's psychological relationship to the group, the exercise of authority and conflict management.

For students who have transferred from a Japanese to an American school, oftentimes conflict and tension develop due to the inconsistencies of behavior among their parents, American school teachers and Japanese school teachers. For example, parents expect their children to be studious and well-disciplined; Japanese school teachers expect group-oriented and cooperative behavior; and American school teachers expect them to demonstrate more assertiveness and independence. The following recommendations for educators, service providers and school administrators will assist the Japanese immigrant students in adapting to the U.S. school system (and to gain more parental participation): (1) offer an orientation in Japanese about school procedures and expectations for students and parents, (2) translate all school correspondence that relates to the welfare of the students into the parents' native language, (3) staff English as a Second Language classrooms with culturally sensitive teachers, (4) make teaching strategies highly interactive and visual, whenever possible, (5) since learning a new language is a lengthy process, encourage teachers to be patient and give students plenty of time to acquire English skills, (6) encourage teachers to incorporate literature that accurately depicts the diverse experiences of Asian-Americans and integrate multicultural aspects into their curricula (Cowart & Cowart, 1994). Since basic literacy in English is a prerequisite for adequate parental involvement in children's schooling, expansion of adult education programs is also crucial (Tran, 1995).

Clearly there is a need for additional research on Asian-American parental involvement in their children's education, but the existing data suggest that

Asian-American parental involvement is very different from that of other cultural groups (Siu, 1996). Siu reveals that Asian-American families enhance their children's school performance by asking children about school, providing financial support, reducing household chores, assisting children with homework, as well as creating homework when none has been assigned. Despite this type of academic support, most of Asian-American immigrant parents do not fit the school's definition of active parents (Siu, 1996). Some roadblocks to Japanese parent involvement in U.S. schools may include unfamiliarity with the educational system, inflexible work schedules, language barriers, and different perspective of their role as parents compared to the role of teachers. In addition, school personnel may inadvertently create barriers by not providing translation or interpretation through parent groups, welcome signs, or outreach and follow-up programs. Unfortunately, because many Asian parents believe it is more important to show their concern by providing a nurturing home environment rather than appearing frequently at school, they miss important information, and their lack of participation often is misinterpreted as uncaring or "not advocating for their children's needs." This, according to Siu (1996), is not beneficial for the students.

CONCLUSION

In-depth qualitative studies such as case studies and structured interviews of Japanese students, parents, and educators would provide further insight to this issue. By comparing and contrasting the educational systems of both the United States and Japan, we better equip ourselves to help sustain and stimulate Japanese immigrant children in our school system. In an era of continuing immigration by Asian-Pacific-American students, educators, and service providers can benefit and facilitate these students' transition into American classrooms by recognizing the tremendous diversity of this group.

In our rapidly changing communities, educators and service providers have a great responsibility to address the needs of various foreign students. Schools that offer bilingual education often overload bilingual teachers, who may speak English and one other language, with *all* foreign-speaking children. Ideally, a bilingual teacher for every ethnic group would help children make the transition from their home countries to the United States; however, it is an impossible request to make of our American school system because of the increasing diversification of our student bodies. Therefore, we recommend that teachers focus on each child as an individual and try to be aware of his or her unique differences. A good teacher learns to communicate intuitively with the child's inner self, as well as to guide the expression of the child's feelings into an appropriate form (Peak, 1991). Although our schools claim to accept diversity, we lack a concrete approach to understanding our children's differences. Tran (1995) concurs that, despite the current fashion of multiculturalism and the appreciation of racial and cultural diversity in schools, conformist assumptions persist. Hence, immigrants are expected to shed their cultural uniqueness and acquire American values as preconditions to their acceptance and success.

Perhaps it is because of these assumptions that we must embark on discovering alternative ways to ease immigrant adaptation.

Since their early immigration in the 1890s, the Japanese have persevered, despite extreme forms of racism, to become one of the most assimilated and acculturated ethnic groups in the United States. Although many have succeeded despite racial discrimination, their current mythic reputation as the model minority has caused some resentment in other minority groups, which has escalated racial tensions. To create and maintain an informed and vigilant public, the Civil Liberties Public Education Fund, with board members appointed by President William Clinton, has accepted more than 200 grant applications for public educational activities about the Japanese-American internment (Yen, 1997).

The model minority myth and other stereotypes, such as that of the Japanese being nonassertive and group oriented, can mask various problems children face in schools and hinder Japanese-Americans from assuming leadership roles. Teachers often use them as role models, thinking they have no problems. Many assume they are whiz kids in every subject (especially mathematics), and the students do not get the help or counseling they need.

Japanese immigrant children are often caught between cultures. Their homeland schools, where group activities were stressed, differ from their new American classrooms where teachers often expect them to be well-disciplined, assertive, and independent. Like other new immigrants to this country, they should be given our time, patience, counseling/support, and native-language materials because acquiring a new language and adapting to a new environment are challenging tasks.

To teach these children more effectively, we should stay abreast of current issues they face as a minority group and continue to educate ourselves about the diverse community in which we live. Preservice and inservice educators can add new dimensions to their profession by increasing their awareness of educational practices outside their own countries. By becoming more knowledgeable, they may recognize similarities within their own practices. Educators are encouraged to seek opportunities for international experiences, to learn the ways of others, and to look for similarities between their own educational efforts and the efforts of international partners (Quinn, 1995).

As a final point, the inadequate representation of Asian-Pacific-Americans in textbooks needs to be remedied by educators who are aware of the diversity of the student body. Incorporating the histories of Asian-Americans into the curricula will help make other people aware of their differences and will promote tolerance of diversity. President Clinton's keynote address at the University of California commencement ceremonies in San Diego (1997, June 14) is noteworthy: he addressed the necessity of reconciling antagonisms between races and uniting people together in *one* America and advocated *using our diversity* to make progress as one people in the twenty-first century (University of California, San Diego Commencement Homepage, 1997).

In teaching values to students, teachers influence the way young people respond to established patterns of behavior (Cummings, 1980). Here is a window of opportunity to dismantle racial prejudice and raise awareness concerning diversity. As educators, we need to share with each other invaluable lessons on appreciating individual differences, collective histories, and multicultural backgrounds, enriching not only the students' but our own minds and lives. We need to equip our students with indispensible skills for building a better world.

NOTES

1. Due to the limited nature of this chapter, the general term "Japanese immigrants" includes short- and long-staying Japanese nationals (*chusaiin* are Japanese nationals who stay an average of three years and have business visas or green cards; *eijyusha* are those who stay longer than ten years and have obtained permanent residency). While some immigrants become U.S. citizens, many choose to keep their alien status.
2. Executive Order 9066 authorized the secretary of war to exclude civilians from designated areas in order to secure them against espionage or sabotage by enemy sympathizers. While protection of Japanese-Americans from angry mobs whose call for their removal took on ugly racial overtones, the chief rationale was for "national security" (Naito, 1990). Although controversy remains about its wartime necessity (see Commission on Wartime Relocation and Internment of Citizens, 1982; Irons, 198;, Weglyn, 1976; Daniels et al., 1991), there are few who would dispute that racism was at least one of its major underlying motives (Nakanishi, 1988).
3. Outmarriage, as defined by Kitano (1991), refers to a Japanese individual who chooses a non-Japanese mate. The proportion of outmarriages among Japanese-Americans is well over 60%.
4. Lee, et al.'s (1996) conclusions were based on their observation of ten elementary schools in Sendai, Japan and twenty elementary schools in the Chicago metropolitan area.
5. According to Stevenson (1991), mothers are more strongly involved than fathers primarily because the fathers are drawn away from the home due to business. The Japanese "educational mother" or *kyoiku mama* is strictly dedicated to her child's education (p. 116).
6. *Juku*, private institutions that offer after-school classes in various subjects such as mathematics, science, calligraphy, and music, have gained popularity during the past two decades. The major function of juku is to enrich the child's learning experiences (Stevenson, 1991).
7. According to Hashimoto (1997), the Palos Verdes and Torrance Unified School Districts have translated their school handbooks into Japanese and have made them available to interested parents. In addition, twenty-one course guides have been prepared in English-Japanese (bilingual format) and are available from the Torrance Unified School District (Park, 1987-89).

REFERENCES

Burstein, L., & Hawkins, J. (1992). An analysis of cognitive, noncognitive, and behavioral characteristics of students in Japan. In R. Leestma & H. J. Walberg (Eds.), *Japanese educational productivity*. Ann Arbor: Center for Japanese Studies, University of Michigan.

California Department of Education. (1987). *Handbook for teaching Japanese-speaking students*. Sacramento, CA: California Department of Education.

California Department of Education. (1997a). *Fact Book 1996-97: Handbook of education information.* Sacramento, CA: California Department of Education.

California Department of Education. (1997b). *Language census 1996.* Sacramento, CA: California Department of Education.

Chun, K. (1995). The myth of Asian American success and its educational ramifications. In D. T. Nakanishi & T. Y. Nishida (Eds.), *The Asian American educational experience: A Source book for teachers and students.* New York: Routledge.

Clinton, W. J. (1997). Commencement speech. University of California, San Diego, Commencement Homepage.

Commission on Wartime Relocation and Internment of Citizens. (1982). *Personal justice denied.* Washington, DC: Commission on Wartime Relocation and Internment of Citizens.

Cornelius, W. (1995). Educating California's immigrant children. In R. Rumbaut & W. Cornelius (Eds.), *California's immigrant children: Theory, research, and implications for educational policy.* San Diego: Center for United States Mexican Studies.

Cowart, M., & Cowart, R. (1994). Breaking the cycle of violence. *The Education Digest* 59, no. 7 (March): 34-37.

Crystal, D. (1989). Asian Americans and the myth of the model minority. *Social Casework* 70, no. 7 (September): 405-413.

Cummings, W. K. (1980). *Education and equality in Japan.* Princeton, NJ: Princeton University Press.

Daniels, R. (1991). Redress achieved, 1983-1990. In R. Daniels, S., Taylor, & H. Kitano (Eds.) *Japanese-Americans: From relocation to redress.* London: University of Washington Press.

Daniels, R., Taylor, S., & Kitano, H. (Eds.). (1991). *Japanese-Americans: From relocation to redress.* London: University of Washington Press.

Divorky, D. (1988). The model minority goes to school. *Phi Delta Kappan* 70 (3): 219-222.

Doi, T. L. (1962). Amae: A key concept for understanding Japanese Personality Structure. In R. J. Smith & R. K. Beardsley (Eds.), *Japanese culture: Its development and characteristics.* Chicago: Aldine Publishing.

Duke, B. (1986). *The Japanese school: Lessons for industrial America.* New York: Praeger.

Efron, S. (1997). In Japan, even tots must make the grade: Japanese students learn to cram early. *The Los Angeles Times,* February 16, pp. A1, A16.

Ellington, L. (1992). *Education in the Japanese life-cycle.* New York: Edwin Mellen Press.

Fukuzawa, R. E. (1996). The path to adulthood according to Japanese middle schools. In T. Rohlen, G. K. Le Tendre (Eds.), *Teaching and learning in Japan.* Cambridge: Cambridge University Press.

Fujimura-Fanselow, K., & Imamura, A. E. (1991). The education of women in Japan. In E. R. Beauchamp (Ed.), *Windows on Japanese education.* New York: Greenwood Press.

Fujita, T. Y. (1987). Better Americans in a greater America? Japanese American education, occupation, and income, 1940-1960. Ph.D. dissertation, University of California, Los Angeles.

Hawkins, J. N. (1978). Politics, education, and language policy: The case of Japanese language schools in Hawaii. *Amerasia Journal* 5 (1): 39-56. Reprinted in D. T. Nakanishi, & T. Y. Nishida (Eds.). (1995). *The Asian American educational experience: A source book for teachers and students.* New York: Routledge.

Hirabayashi, L. R. (1991). The Impact of incarceration on the education of Nisei school children. In R. Daniels, S. Taylor, & H. Kitano (Eds.), *Japanese-Americans: From relocation to redress*. London: University of Washington Press.

Hsia, J. (1988). *Asian Americans in higher education and at work*. New Jersey: Lawrence Erlbaum Associates.

Ichihashi, Y. (1969). *Japanese in the United States*. New York: Arno Press.

Ichioka, Y. (1988). *The Issei: The world of the first generation Japanese immigrants, 1885-1924*. New York: Free Press.

Irish, A. B. (1994). Why does Japanese high school education work? *NASSP Bulletin* (May): 31-35.

Irons, P. (1983). *Justice at war.* New York: Oxford University Press.

Ishizaka, K. (1990). *School education in Japan*. Tokyo: International Society for Educational Information.

Kikumura, A. (1981). *Through harsh winters: The life of a Japanese immigrant woman*. Los Angeles, CA: Chandler and Sharp.

Kimura, Y. (1988). *Issei: The Japanese immigrants in Hawaii*. Honolulu: University of Hawaii Press.

Kitano, H. L. (1976). *Japanese-Americans: The evolution of a subculture*, 2nd ed. Englewood Cliffs, NJ: Prentice-Hall.

Kitano, H. L. (1991). *Race relations*, 4th ed. Englewood Cliffs, NJ: Prentice-Hall.

Leadership Education for Asian Pacifics (LEAP) Asian Pacific American Public Policy Institute. (1995). *Common ground: Perspectives on affirmative action and its impact on Asian Pacific Americans*. Los Angeles, CA: Leadership Education for Asian Pacifics.

Lee, S., Graham, T., & Stevenson, H. (1996). Teachers and teaching: Elementary schools in Japan and the United States. In T. P. Rohlen & G. K. LeTendre (Eds.), *Teaching and learning in Japan*. New York: Cambridge University Press.

Lewis, C. C. (1995). *Education hearts and minds: Reflections on Japanese preschool and elementary education*. New York: Cambridge University Press.

Mass, A. I. (1991). Psychological effects of the internment experience. In R. Daniels, S. Taylor, & H. Kitano (Eds.), *Japanese Americans: From relocation to redress*. London: University of Washington Press.

Miyoshi, N. (1994). Identity crisis of the Sansei and the concentration camp. Special report. Alameda, CA: Sansei Legacy Project.

Nagata, D. K. (1993). *Legacy of injustice: Exploring the cross-generational impact of the Japanese-American internment*. New York: Plenum Press.

Naito, C., & Scott, E. (1990). Against all odds: The Japanese Americans' campaign for redress. Case program. John F. Kennedy School of Government, Harvard University.

Nakanishi, D. T. (1988). Seeking convergence in race relations research: Japanese-Americans and the resurrection of the internment. In P. A. Katz & D. A. Taylor. (Eds.), *Eliminating racism*. New York: Plenum.

Nakanishi, D. T. (1995). Growth and diversity: The education of Asian/Pacific Americans. In D. T. Nakanishi & T.Y. Nishida (Eds.), *The Asian American educational experience: A source book for teachers and students*. New York: Routledge.

Nezu, T. (1986). Japanese parents' perceptions of educational objectives and ideal solutions for their children in the United States. Ph.D. Dissertation, University of California, Los Angeles.

Ochi, K. A. (1997). Redress update: Only 18 months left for the final big push! *Banner NCRR* (winter): 1.

Ono, K. A. (1995). Re/signing "Asian American": Rhetorical problematics of nation. *Amerasia Journal* 21 (1, 2): 67-78.

Pang, V. O. (1990). Asian American children: A diverse population. *The Educational Forum* 55: 49-65.

Park, C. C. (Ed.). (1987-89). Torrance Unified School District: 21 Bilingual Course Guidebooks. Torrance, California.

Peak, L. (1991). *Learning to go to school in Japan: The transition from home to preschool life*. Berkeley, CA: University of California Press.

Quinn, L. F. (1995). Having new eyes: The international experience. *Journal of Teacher Education* 46, no. 1 (January/February): 29-34.

Rohlen, T. (1983). *Japan's high schools*. Berkeley: University of California Press.

Siu, S. (1996). *Asian American students at risk: A literature review*. Report No. 8. Baltimore, MD: Johns Hopkins University, Center for Research on the Education of Students Placed at Risk.

Stevenson, H. W. (1991). Japanese elementary school education. *The Elementary School Journal* 92, no. 1: 109-120.

Stevenson, H. W. (1992). Learning from Asian schools. *Scientific American* 267, no. 6 (December): 70-76.

Tran, M. (1995). Korean and Russian students in a Los Angeles high school: Exploring the alternative strategies of two high-achieving groups. In R. G. Rumbaut & W. A. Cornelius (Eds.), *California's immigrant children: Theory, research, and implications for educational policy*. San Diego, CA: Center for United States Mexican Studies.

Ueda, R. (1974). The Americanization and education of Japanese-Americans: A psychodramatic and dramaturgical perspective. In E. G. Epps (Ed.), *Cultural pluralism*. Berkeley: McCutchan.

Weglyn, M. (1976). *Years of infamy*. New York: William Morrow.

Yamano, T. K. (1991). UCLA Japanese students: Ethnic identity and language revitalization. Master's thesis, University of California, Los Angeles.

Yamano, T. K. (1994). Brooding silence: A cross-generational study of informal learning, socialization and child rearing practices in a Japanese American family. Ph.D. dissertation, University of California, Los Angeles.

Yen, Janice. (1997). Civil liberties public education fund board to disburse funds. *Banner NCRR* (winter): 3.

CHAPTER 6

Teaching English to Native Japanese Students: From Linguistics to Pedagogy

David Whitenack and Kunie Kikunaga

This chapter considers key linguistic aspects of Japanese for K–12 educators of native Japanese speakers in the United States. It briefly explains the Japanese language and contrasts some of its key features with those of English, considers some difficulties that native Japanese speakers typically encounter when learning English, and offers some practical suggestions for educators of native Japanese speakers learning English in the K-12 U.S. system. While Japanese is rich in dialectical variation, this chapter considers only standard Japanese, in which all Japanese students are educated.

JAPANESE LANGUAGE STRUCTURE AND USE

This section first considers the origins of Japanese. Next, we examine the phonology, or sound system, of Japanese.[1] A discussion of Japanese morphology, or word formation, follows. Later, we explore Japanese syntax, the way that words are combined to form sentences. Finally, we consider the pragmatics of Japanese; that is, how it is used in social contexts.

Origins of Japanese

Japanese is the only major world language of which scholars have yet to trace the genealogy conclusively. Many scholars believe that Japanese and Korean are related and that both are related to the Altaic languages (e.g., Turkish, Mongol, Manchu). Scholars of Japanese trace the origins of Modern Japanese, or 現代日本 *Gendai Nihongo*, to the year 1868, the beginning of the Meiji Era (Miller, 1967).

Phonology

The Japanese sound system includes vowels, consonants, mora (a unit of duration), and pitch.

Vowels. Standard Japanese (similar to Tokyo dialect) contains five vowel sounds: /a/, /i/, /u/, /e/, and /o/.[2] The Japanese /a/ sounds like the English vowel sound /o/ in the word *cot*.[3] The Japanese /i/ sounds like the English /ee/ in *keep*. The Japanese /u/ resembles the /oo/ in *boot*. The /e/ in *bet* approximates the Japanese /e/, and the Japanese /o/ sounds like the /oa/ in *boat*. Japanese vowels essentially make the same sound in all cases.

Consonants. The English consonantal phonemes (and example words) that do not exist in Japanese are listed below.

(1) a. /f/ as in **f**ood
    b. /l/ as in **l**ip
    c. /r/ as in **r**ed
    d. /th/ as in **th**atched (voiceless "th")
    e. /th/ as in **th**e (voiced "th")
    f. /v/ as in **v**ent
    g. /z/ as in a**z**ure (as opposed to /z/ as in **z**ap)

The closest Japanese approximation to the English /f/ is /h/ as in 富士山 *Hujisan* (Mt. Fuji).[4] This /h/ is made by holding the lips together loosely and blowing air through them. As for the English /l/ and /r/, the Japanese /r/ sound lies somewhere in between these two English sounds. The Japanese /r/, as in *romaji* (the characters of the Roman alphabet used to write Japanese), is made by quickly flapping the front of the tongue against the hard pallet of the roof of the mouth. The closest approximation to the voiceless "th" would probably be the /t/, as in 東京 *Tookyoo* (Tokyo).[5] The /d/, as in ドア *doa* (door), comes closest to the voiced "th." The Japanese /b/, as in ビル *biru* (building), comes closest to the English /v/, and perhaps the Japanese /j/, as in 柔道 *judo*, most nearly approximates the English /z/ in azure.

Table 6.1 lists single vowels (e.g., *a, i,* etc.), consonant-plus-vowel clusters (e.g., *ka, gi,* etc.), consonant-plus-semivowel [y]-plus-vowel clusters (e.g., *kya,* etc.), and single consonants. The *n* appears only at the end of words, and it is the only one of the five consonants listed that can appear by itself. The phonemes /k/, /s/, /t/, and /p/ only appear directly before the respective consonant-plus-vowel clusters with which they can pair to form double consonants (e.g., はっきり *hakkiri* [clearly]).

Table 6.1
The Sounds of Japanese

a	ka	ga	sa	za	ta	da	na	ha	ba	pa	ma	ya	ra	wa	
a	*ka*	*ga*	*sa*	*za*	*ta*	*da*	*na*	*ha*	*ba*	*pa*	*ma*	*ya*	*ra*	*wa*	
i	*ki*	*gi*	*shi*	*ji*	*chi*	–	*ni*	*hi*	*bi*	*pi*	*mi*	–	*ri*	–	
u	*ku*	*gu*	*su*	*zu*	*tsu*	–	*nu*	*hu*	*bu*	*pu*	*mu*	*yu*	*ru*	–	
e	*ke*	*ge*	*se*	*ze*	*te*	*de*	*ne*	*he*	*be*	*pe*	*me*	–	*re*	–	
o	*ko*	*go*	*so*	*zo*	*to*	*do*	*no*	*ho*	*bo*	*po*	*mo*	*yo*	*ro*	*wo*	*n*
	kya	*gya*	*sha*	*ja*	*cha*	–	*nya*	*hya*	*bya*	*pya*	*mya*	–	*rya*	–	
	kyu	*gyu*	*shu*	*ju*	*chu*	–	*nyu*	*hyu*	*byu*	*pyu*	*myu*	–	*ryu*	–	
	kyo	*gyo*	*sho*	*jo*	*cho*	–	*nyo*	*hyo*	*byo*	*pyo*	*myo*	–	*ryo*	–	
	k		*s*		*t*					*p*					

Source: Table adapted from Maynard (1990, p. 4).

The Mora. Japanese features a unit known as the mora, which is one beat of duration and differs from the more familiar (to English speakers) syllable (Maynard, 1990). Each sound in Table 6.1 receives one beat (mora) when pronounced in Japanese. Thus, /a/ and /byu/ are uttered for equivalent lengths of time. The Japanese word for book~ 本 *hon* contains two morae: ほ *ho* and ん *n.*

Perhaps the importance of the mora can be appreciated best by looking at a pair of words with divergent meanings that differ by only a single mora.

(2) 伯母[6]   お祖母さん
     おばさん   おばあさん
     obasan   *obaasan*
     aunt   *grandmother*[7]

The Japanese words for aunt and grandmother above differ by the mora /a/.

Pitch. Rather than stress, pitch accent marks Japanese words (California Department of Education, 1987). For example, あめ *ame* can mean either 雨 rain or 飴 candy depending on pitch accent. This difference in pitch accent, however, is not a matter of saying, *A*me or a*ME,* which would be typically the two different ways to stress a two-syllable English word. The stress on both morae is the same; it is a question of saying them with different pitch depending on the meaning of the word. For あめ *ame,* meaning 雨 rain, the pitch of the two syllabes is the same. For あめ *ame,* meaning 飴 candy, however, the pitch rises in the second syllable.

Morphology

Here we consider Japanese lexical categories, or types of words; affixation, or the adding of prefixes, suffixes, and other affixes to words; and two types of words, verbs and adjectives.

Lexical Categories. Japanese includes nouns, verbs, adjectives, demonstratives, conjunctions, and two categories of words that do not occur in English and other European languages: adjectival nouns and verbal nouns (Shibatani, 1990). The latter two categories merit mention because loan words typically belong to them. Foreign adjectives usually become Japanese adjectival nouns, such as タフだ *tahu da* (tough). Foreign verbs usually become Japanese verbal nouns, such as ゼロックスする *zerokkusu-suru* (to xerox) (Shibatani, 1990).

Affixation. Japanese words incorporate prefixes, suffixes, and other affixes. Some affixes are case specific; that is, they do not function with all words in a given class of words. Other affixes can be more universally applied. For example, nouns are made into honorific nouns by adding the prefix お *o-,* as shown below.

(3) 箸   お箸
     hashi   *ohashi*
     chopsticks   *chopsticks (polite speech)*

There are many other more specialized cases of Japanese affixation that exceed the scope of this chapter.

Verbs. Table 6.2 is not exhaustive; it lists direct verb forms without considering the corresponding humble and honorific forms that exist for certain inflectional categories. One can see that Japanese expresses certain ideas through verb inflection that English expresses using combinations of verbs. The negative form listed, 書かない *kakanai* (to not write), can be inflected further as discussed in the following adjective section.

Adjectives. Japanese adjectives inflect by changing the い *-i* (no translation) ending of the imperfective form to the various other endings shown in bold in Table 6.3. Since the negative form in Table 6.3, おもしろくない *omoshirokunai* (is not interesting), derives from the imperfective, おもしろい *omoshiroi* (is interesting), it is the negative imperfective form. There are also negative forms of the gerund, perfective, conditional, representative, and provisional inflectional categories of Japanese adjectives. These are derived from

Table 6.2
Inflectional Categories of Japanese Verbs and Their English Translations

Inflectional Category	*Japanese*	*English*
Imperfective	書く kaku	to write
Gerund	書いて kaite	(varies with context)
Perfective	書いた kaita	wrote, did write
Conditional	書いたら kaitara	if (one) writes
Representative (alternative)	書いたり kaitari	(varies with context)
Provisional	書けば kakeba	provided that (one) writes
Consultative	書こう kakoo	let's write
Imperative	書け kake	write (command)
Negative imperfective	書かない kakanai	to not write
Potential imperfective	書ける kakeru	to be able to write
Desiderative	書きたい kakitai	to want to write
Causative imperfective	書かさせる kakasaseru	to cause to write
Passive imperfective	書かれる kakareru	to be written
Passive causative imperfective	書かさせられる kakasaserareru	to be made to write

Note: The endings of the Japanese verb forms are written in bold text for emphasis only.

the negative imperfective form by changing the い *-i* ending and adding the same ending listed for each of the inflectional categories in Table 6.3. For example, the negative perfective is:

(4) おもしろくなかった
     omoshiroku nakatta
     was not interesting

As seen in Table 6.3, various forms of Japanese adjectives express the same ideas that English represents with adjectives plus verbs, and sometimes other words, too.

Syntax

Key considerations in Japanese sentence formation include word order; postpositional particles, or words that mark the function of the words that precede them in a sentence; number (singular and plural); counters (noun countability); articles and pronouns; unstated subjects; and verb tenses.

Word Order. Japanese has the basic word order of subject-object-verb (SOV). This pattern is actually quite flexible. Example 5b expresses the same meaning as 5a even though it uses an object-subject-verb pattern.

(5) a. 学生は本を読んだ。
         Gakusei wa hon o yonda.
         <u>student (subject case marker) book (object case marker) read</u>
         The student read the book.

     b. 本を学生は読んだ。
         Hon o gakusei wa yonda.

Table 6.3
Inflectional Categories of Japanese Adjectives and Their English Translations

Inflectional Category	*Japanese*	*English*
Imperfective	おもしろい omoshiro**i**	is interesting
Stem	おもしろく omoshiro**ku**	interesting
Gerund	おもしろくて omoshiro**kute**	(varies with context)
Perfective	おもしろかった omoshiro**katta**	was interesting
Conditional	おもしろかったら omoshiro**kattara**	if (it) is interesting
Representative	おもしろかったり omoshiro**kattari**	(varies with context)
Provisional	おもしろければ omoshiro**kereba**	provided that (it) is interesting
Negative	おもしろくない <u>omoshiro**ku nai**</u>	<u>is not interesting</u>

Note: The endings of the adjectival forms are written in bold for emphasis only.

book (object case marker) student (subject case marker) read
The student read the book.

It makes no difference in this case which comes first, the subject 学生 *gakusei* (student) or the object 本 *hon* (book). The sentence still carries the same meaning. In contrast, if we were to switch the subject and object of the English sentence, we would have the nonsensical The book read the student.

In Japanese, relative clauses do not exist, and all other modifiers precede the modified word. Thus, the Japanese adjective-noun pattern follows the same order as that of English, as shown in the following example.

(6)　　黄色い鉛筆
　　　kiiroi enpitsu
　　　yellow pencil

Particles. The particles used in the Japanese language allow for the word-order flexibility described above. Particles indicate the functions of various words in sentences. They follow the words with which they correspond. Subjects are marked by the particles が *ga* and は *wa*.[8] The particle を *o* marks direct objects; で *de* indicates where an action takes place; に *ni* denotes location or destination (both in the geographic sense and in terms of intended recipient); か *ka* is used at the end of interrogatives; and よ *yo* comes at the end of exclamations. The use of these particles can be seen in the following examples. Regardless of whether a Japanese sentence is a statement, a question, or an exclamation, the final punctuation mark is the small-circle period (。).

(7)　a.　クラスでだれが本を読んだか。
　　　　Kurasu de dare ga hon o yonda ka.
　　　　classroom (locative case marker) who (subject case marker) book (object
　　　　　　case marker) read (question indicating particle)
　　　　Who read the book in class?

　　b.　学生は手紙を書いて先生に出したよ。
　　　　Gakusei wa tegami o kaite sensei ni dashita yo.
　　　　student (subject case marker) letter (object case marker) wrote teacher
　　　　　　(object case marker [to]) turned in (particle)
　　　　The student wrote a letter and turned it in to the teacher!

Singular and Plural. Japanese nouns typically use the same form for both the singular and the plural, as illustrated in the sentence below. Note that the noun 鉛筆 *enpitsu* (pencil) does not change in the Japanese sentence regardless of whether it refers to one object or five. While the plural does exist in Japanese, the way it is marked—in the minority of instances when it actually is marked—varies from case to case.[9]

8)　　学生は鉛筆を一つ持っているが、
　　　先生は鉛筆を五つ持っている。
　　　Gakusei wa enpitsu o hitotsu motteiru ga, sensei wa enpitsu o itsutsu motteiru.
　　　student (subject case marker) pencil (object case marker) one has but teacher
　　　　(subject case marker) pencil (object case marker) five has
　　　The student has one pencil, but the teacher has five pencils.

The use of one noun form to represent both singular and plural in Japanese has other consequences. While we distinguish in English between <u>this</u> and <u>these</u>, these two ideas are typically expressed the same in Japanese.

Countability. Japanese makes no distinction between count and noncount nouns, and the Japanese translation for both <u>much</u> and <u>many</u> is たくさん *takusan.*

Articles and Pronouns. Japanese employs neither definite nor indefinite articles as seen in example 9.

(9)   本がテーブルにある。
         Hon ga teeburu ni aru.
         <u>Book (subject case marker) table (location case marker) there is</u>
         There is a book on the table.

Neither 本 *hon* (<u>book</u>) nor テーブル *teeburu* (<u>table</u>) is accompanied by any word akin to the English definite or indefinite article.

While the pronouns I, me, mine, my, you, he, and so on exist in Japanese, they are rarely used in polite communication, and they tend to be avoided in writing. Instead, particular noun and verb forms often serve the same function that a pronoun would in English. The two different representations of <u>mother</u> shown below illustrate this phenomenon.

(10)   母   お母さん
          haha   *okaasan*
          <u>mother</u>   <u>(honorable) mother</u>
          my mother   *your mother*

In practice 母 *haha* (<u>mother</u>) is only used when speaking to someone else about one's mother. One would not properly address one's mother using this form, but instead would use お母さん *okaasan* (<u>honorable mother</u>).

Unstated Subjects. Japanese sentences often do not include an explicit subject. In polite speech, certain verb forms indicate whether or not the speaker is talking about herself or about her conversation partner. In other cases, context usually obviates the subject of an utterance. Maynard (1990) calls this avoidance of stated subjects a non-agent orientation and connects it to the Japanese worldview, which attributes most events to natural forces rather than specific agents or subjects.

Verb Tenses. Japanese divides time between past and nonpast. Context determines distinctions between the present and the future in Japanese. There are, of course, more than two verb tenses in Japanese, as shown in Table 6.2.

Pragmatics

Key cultural factors influence the way that the Japanese use language. First, there is the Confucian tradition emphasizing deeds over words. Persuasion of others through language tends to be discouraged, and direct confrontation is generally avoided (Shibatani, 1990). Japanese communication patterns reveal a preference for conveying intended meaning indirectly. The listener is expected to draw the appropriate conclusion based upon what the speaker says (Shibatani, 1990).

In practice, these cultural elements influence language use in that Japanese tend to avoid straightforward responses. One example of this tendency is the Japanese expression (shown in example 11) that has become famous in international business circles.

(11)   考えておきます。
          Kangaete okimasu
          <u>*think in advance*</u>
          I'll think it over.

If a Japanese businessman closes a meeting with this phrase, he actually means <u>No</u>!

Written Systems of Japanese

The Japanese developed the written form of their oral language by adopting many Chinese characters to represent Japanese words.

Components of Written Japanese. Written Japanese consists of four components: *hiragana, katakana, kanji,* and *romaji.* ひらがな *Hiragana* and カタカナ *katakana* are both syllabaries, or systems in which a written figure represents a syllable as opposed to a single sound. 漢字 *Kanji* (literally "Chinese letters") are logographs, or characters that represent words, derived from Chinese characters. Written Japanese can also be represented using ローマ字 *romaji,* which is a romanize alphabet.[10] The figures of Aみ らがな *hiragana* and カタカナ *katakana* generically are called 仮名 *kana.*

Table 6.4 contains the figures from the ひらがな *hiragana* and カタカナ *katakana* syllabaries, some sample logographs, and the corresponding ローマ字 *romaji,* which were also presented in Table 6.1. As partially shown in Table 6.4, each Japanese sound listed in Table 6.1 can be represented by a figure of ひらがな *hiragana* and the corresponding figure of カタカナ *katakana.*

Functions of the Four Components. In contemporary writing, 漢字 *kanji* typically are used for content words, and ひらがな *hiragana* tend to serve grammatical functions. An example of these respective uses can be seen in the sentence below.

(12)   本を読んだ。
          Hon o yonda.
          <u>*book (object case marker) read (past tense)*</u>
          (Unstated subject) read (past tense) a/the book.

Note that 本 *hon* (<u>book</u>) is written using 漢字 *kanji,* as is the stem 読 *yo-* of the verb 読んだ *yonda* (<u>did read</u>). The particle を yo and the verb ending -んだ, both of which serve grammatical functions, are written using ひらがな *hiragana.* Words of Japanese origin normally written in 漢字 *kanji* can also be written using ひらがな *hiragana.* For example, the Japanese word 水 *mizu*

Table 6.4
Hiragana and Katakana Syllabaries, Corresponding Romaji, and Sample Kanji

Key:	R = ローマ字 *romaji*	漢字 = *kanji*
	H = ひらがな *hiragana*	E = English
	K = カタカナ *katakana*	

R	a	ka	ga	sa	za	ta	da	na	ha	ba	pa	ma	ya	ra	wa
H	あ	か	が	さ	ざ	た	だ	な	は	ば	ぱ	ま	や	ら	わ
K	ア	カ	ガ	サ	ザ	タ	ダ	ナ	ハ	バ	パ	マ	ヤ	ラ	ワ

R	i	ki	gi	shi	ji	chi	di	ni	hi	bi	pi	mi		ri	
H	い	き	ぎ	し	じ	ち	ぢ	に	ひ	び	ぴ	み		り	
K	イ	キ	ギ	シ	ジ	チ	ヂ	ニ	ヒ	ビ	ピ	ミ		リ	

R	u	ku	gu	su	zu	tsu	du	ru	fu	bu	pu	mu	yu	ru	
H	う	く	ぐ	す	ず	つ	づ	ぬ	ふ	ぶ	ぷ	む	ゆ	る	
K	ウ	ク	グ	ス	ズ	ツ	ヅ	ヌ	フ	ブ	プ	ム	ユ	ル	

R	e	ke	ge	se	ze	te	de	ne	he	be	pe	me		re	
H	え	け	げ	せ	ぜ	て	で	ね	へ	べ	ぺ	め		れ	
K	エ	ケ	ゲ	セ	ゼ	テ	デ	ネ	ヘ	ベ	ペ	メ		レ	

R	o	ko	go	so	zo	to	do	no	ho	bo	po	mo	yo	ro	wo
H	お	こ	ご	そ	ぞ	と	ど	の	ほ	ぼ	ぽ	も	よ	ろ	を
K	オ	コ	ゴ	ソ	ゾ	ト	ド	ノ	ホ	ボ	ポ	モ	ヨ	ロ	ヲ

R														n
H														ん
K														ン

R	kya	gya	sha	ja	cha	dya	nya	hya	bya	pya	mya	rya
H	きゃ	ぎゃ	しゃ	じゃ	ちゃ	ぢゃ	にゃ	ひゃ	びゃ	ぴゃ	みゃ	りゃ
K	キャ	ギャ	シャ	ジャ	チャ	ヂャ	ニャ	ヒャ	ビャ	ピャ	ミャ	リャ

R	kyu	gyu	shu	ju	chu	dyu	nyu	hyu	byu	pyu	myu	ryu
H	きゅ	ぎゅ	しゅ	じゅ	ちゅ	ぢゅ	にゅ	ひゅ	びゅ	ぴゅ	みゅ	りゅ
K	キュ	ギュ	シュ	ジュ	チュ	ヂュ	ニュ	ヒュ	ビュ	ピュ	ミュ	リュ

R	kyo	gyo	sho	jo	cho	dyo	myo	hyo	byo	pyo	myo	ryo
H	きょ	ぎょ	しょ	じょ	ちょ	ぢょ	にょ	ひょ	びょ	ぴょ	みょ	りょ
K	キョ	ギョ	ショ	ジョ	チョ	ヂョ	ニョ	ヒョ	ビョ	ピョ	ミョ	リョ

漢字	一	二	日本	手紙	学生
H	いち	に	にほん	てがみ	がくせい
R	*ichi*	*ni*	*nihon*	*tegami*	*gakusei*
E	*one*	*two*	*Japan*	*letter*	*student*

(water) can also be written as みず using the ひらがな *hiragana* for み *mi* and ず *zu*.

The カタカナ *katakana* syllabary is used primarily to form words borrowed from other languages. For example, in Japan it is possible to eat at マクドナルド *Makudonarudo* (McDonald's), which is made up of the マ *ma* + ク *ku* + ド *do* + ナ *na* + ル *ru* + ド *do* of the カタカナ *katakana* syllabary. カタカナ *Katakana* can also be used for artistic effect. ローマ字 *Romaji* can be used for addressing letters, and they are used on road signs.

Traditional Japanese writing is done vertically from top to bottom, and the lines are written from right to left. Today, writers of Japanese use both this traditional way of writing and the left-to-right, horizontal style of English and many other Western languages.

Reading Japanese

It is worth noting that reading Japanese is quite complicated from the perspective of a native English speaker owing to the fact that there are two or more ways to read most 漢字 *kanji*. No systematic way exists to determine the readings for the various 漢字 *kanji*. The readings must be memorized. Typically, Japanese nationals who have completed high school are expected to be able to write about 1,700 漢字 *kanji*, having gradually learned them in grade-level sets. In order to read a Japanese newspaper, one requires a working knowledge of over 3,000 漢字 *kanji*.

NATIVE JAPANESE SPEAKERS LEARNING ENGLISH: TYPICAL DIFFICULTIES

Japanese students tend to have trouble with certain aspects of English, particularly pronunciation, word recognition and spelling, grammar, meaning, and communicative competence in oral and written discourse.

Pronunciation

Japanese does not have the long (e.g., kite) and short (e.g., kit) vowels and other variations in vowel pronunciation that exist in English. Thus, native Japanese speakers tend to confuse ship and sheep; pool and pull; and cat, cot, and cut (Ervin-Tripp, 1973). Native Japanese speakers tend to pronounce the different words in these word groups as if they were the same word, because they use the Japanese vowel sound that most closely approximates the English vowel sounds.

Other pronunciation difficulties occur with the aforementioned English consonant sounds that do not exist in Japanese. Japanese learners of English have trouble distinguishing /l/ and /r/ in English. For Japanese speakers, mastering the English /r/ is more laborious than the /l/ (Cochrane, 1980). Mastering the voiceless /th/, as in **th**umb, and the voiced /th/, as in **the**se, is also difficult for Japanese speakers.

Consonant clusters, two or more consonants in succession within a word (e.g., pencil), do not exist in Japanese. Japanese speakers of English tend to insert a vowel sound between the consonants to avoid the clustering (Thompson, 1987). Hence, English words containing consonant clusters, such as <u>trouble</u>, become トラブル *toraburu* (toe-rah-boo-roo).

Word Recognition and Spelling

Fourth graders in Japan are formally introduced to the English alphabet for the purposes of writing their own names as well as those of certain places (Tokyo, Kyoto, etc.). English as a subject is officially introduced in the seventh grade. Japanese children are also exposed to English words widely used in advertisements. They typically have little difficulty recognizing printed English words and spelling them.

Understanding spoken English, on the other hand, can be difficult for native speakers of Japanese. For example, <u>rap</u> and <u>lap</u> are likely to sound the same to a Japanese ear. Shimamune and Smith (1995) found that it was easier for Japanese speakers to pronounce words correctly than it was for them to distinguish correctly between words that they heard.

Grammar

Japanese speakers seem to have particular trouble with the following grammatical features in English: definite and indefinite articles (<u>a/an</u> and <u>the</u>), plurals, mass and countable nouns, number agreement, subject-verb agreement, and certain verb tenses. These difficulties and others can be seen in Figure 6.1, which presents two samples of written text.

The first sample text is by a student who had been living in the United States for one and a half years at the time she wrote it during the summer before she entered the tenth grade. She completed the eighth grade in Japan. A Japanese boy who had been living in the United States for two years produced the second text during the summer before he entered the tenth grade. This sample also includes editing by the student's teacher. Readers will note in both samples that certain passages that are not coded for grammatical difficulty might nevertheless sound awkward to a native speaker of English.

The two sample texts in Figure 6.1 provide a context for the grammatical features of English that tend to be most difficult for native Japanese speakers. Regarding articles, Kubota (1994) found that Japanese speakers of English acquire and are able to use definite articles more accurately than indefinite articles. Even Japanese natives who have been speaking English for many years may continue to have trouble using articles properly in spoken and written discourse. Perhaps because Japanese does not have articles, Japanese natives acquire English articles more slowly than do native speakers of languages such as French and German, which have article systems (Park, 1996). In Yoon's (1995) research, when Japanese speakers thought that an English noun was countable, they used the indefinite article in context. Conversely, they did not use any articles with nouns that they judged as uncountable.

In the realm of verbs, Japanese has no aspects such as the present perfect (e.g., **I have seen** her before.), past perfect (e.g., <u>My parents **had traveled** to New Orleans before I was born</u>.), or future perfect (e.g., <u>You **will have heard**</u>

Figure 6.1
Two Samples of Native Japanese-Speaking Students' Writing Coded by Typical Features of Grammatical Difficulty

Key:	A = articles	C = noun countability	N = number agreement	P = plurals
	S = subject-verb agreement		V = verb tense	X = other

Codes   *Writing Samples*

A — When I see the person who is always mad, I will guess
she is nasty. If the person was always smiling,

V,X — I think she is very kind and nice.   The person

A — had white skin before the vacation but after vacation if

V — she was red or brown, I think she went to a pool or

A,V — sea. If she was sleeping during the class, I think

X — she was studying hard last night or just playing
a game or something. Girls who always wear boyish

C,A — stuff might play sports very well. The person who is

A — always reading books might want to be novelist.

X,A — When I see people in rug, I will think they

V — are very dirty and poor. But if they always wore

X — big-name brand goods, I will change my mind and
will think they are very rich. Sometimes, there are

X — people who are always wearing hats. They might don't have
hair or they might worry about their bad hair style.

N — I think we can make many assumption about
the people.

"You must know everything" can be bothersome

N,V — to children of my ages. We, teenagers are already

V — suited ourselves to a life of TV, a comfortable
home, and nutritious meals like they naturally

V — happen from the beginning of time. Therefore,
the story makes teenage readers notice the big

X — differences of young and old generations. I don't
like to say what the grandmother told the child

X — was wrong, but there is a complete opposite

S — ways of living between us and them.
When I recall my grandmothers, who overcame
a hard, cruel, and intense period of time, I
seen very strong strictness in them. They used
to tell me that they were forced to work in
a factory, manufacturing guns, airplanes, and
other horrible weapons all day long. But now
my generation doesn't encounter those kinds of

X — experiences, rather lives in a far more comfortable

A — life than theirs. We don't strongly feel importance
of education like they do, and that is all because

X,A — of how our lives are on daily basis.

N — We might find every incident in a different order
of importance from theirs. Most important, everybody's

N — single lives are greatly involved in changes, I feel
that adapting to each change that is being
made in lives should be the best way to spend
one generation in a period of time.

of it by next week.). Consequently, Japanese speakers have more trouble acquiring these forms than they do other English verb tenses. In addition, the transfer from Japanese to English of the different forms and functions of passives often leads native Japanese speakers to produce awkward and incorrect English sentences (Watabe, 1991).

Meaning

There are a substantial number of loan words in Japanese that have an English origin. These are not likely to be comprehensible to English speakers, however, because they are transformed in such a way that native speakers of English often cannot identify the original English word, especially in writing. English words are typically transformed by using one or a combination of the tactics shown in example 13.

(13)   a.   Pronunciation modification.
              コンピューター *konpyuutaa* (computer).
        b.   Abbreviation.
              マスコミ *masukomi* (mass communication = mass media).
        c.   Modification of original meaning.
              コンセント *konsento* (consent = electric socket).
        d.   "Japanglish" (Japanese-made English-like words)
              スキンシップ *sukinshippu* (skin ship = physical attachment.)

In addition, a number of loan words originate from other European languages.

Communicative Competence in Oral and Written Discourse

Kaplan (1966) attempted to describe patterns of thought of several different languages. For example, Kaplan characterized the English pattern of thought as a straight line from the original topic to the conclusion and the patterns of Asian languages as a spiral. Kaplan explained that the Asian pattern is "marked by 'indirection,' employing 'a variety of tangential views' that may be said to be 'turning and turning in a widening gyre'" (in Bialystok and Hakuta, 1994, p. 176). Thus, Japanese speakers may have trouble expressing themselves in the linear fashion typical of English discourse. On the other hand, Shishin (1985) reports that neither English nor Japanese writers are limited to one rhetorical pattern, and that both linear and nonlinear rhetorics are universal.

Another potentially troublesome point is that the sequencing of information in Japanese discourse tends to differ from the typical sequence in English (Nishiyama, 1995). Odlin (1989) describes a Japanese written form called 起承転結 *ki-shoo-ten-ketsu.* The first two parts (起 *ki* and 承 *sho*) have patterns of development similar to English, but the third part (転 *ten*) suddenly shifts away from the original topic "to introduce a subtopic that is only indirectly related to the first two parts" (p. 63). The fourth part is the 結 *ketsu,* or conclusion, and it serves the same function as its English counterpart. Unaware of these differences, Japanese students may attempt to transfer the *ki-shoo-ten-ketsu* pattern of thought into English when writing.

English relative clauses (e.g., The girl **who came** was Yoko.) also can create problems for Japanese students when they write in English; thus, they attempt to avoid using relative clauses (Yao, 1985). Japanese students tend to use simple sentence structures leading to choppiness in English (Odlin, 1989).

In oral discourse, Japanese speakers sometimes apply their norm in speaking English. It is documented that they inappropriately overuse excuse me and I'm sorry because "expressions of gratitude are often formulated with terms that in other languages only express apologies" (Odlin, 1989, p. 54). Fukushima (1990) found that native Japanese speakers' expressions for offers and requests tend to be too direct in most situations and sound rude to non-Japanese speakers even when they are intended to be polite. This could result from a literal translation of a Japanese request, such as 食べて下さい *Tabete kudasai* (Please eat this), which is stated as a command from the perspective of a native English speaker.

Even Japanese speakers at an advanced level of English competence may have trouble with pragmatics. Overall, speakers with a greater verbal ability in Japanese tend to succeed in learning English more rapidly (Harada, 1996).

NATIVE JAPANESE SPEAKERS LEARNING ENGLISH: PRACTICAL SUGGESTIONS

For Japanese students to benefit most from their experience in American schools, it is crucial for educators to ask parents how long the students will stay in the United States and how much English they expect to acquire during their sojourn. Some parents may actually choose to focus on maintaining Japanese and may be content with their children's minimal survival skills in English, given a short sojourn. Other parents may expect their children to attain the level of English proficiency equivalent to that required by prestigious universities.

Japanese children typically arrive in April, the beginning of an academic year in Japan, and they usually receive a substantial amount of ESL instruction until the summer. What becomes problematic for these students is that they are often retained at the same level of ESL during the subsequent academic year.

One possible solution is to advise Japanese families to seek help outside of school. Counselors and teachers may suggest private tutors or intensive ESL courses at private institutions to accelerate students' English acquisition. Summer schooling is an excellent option for developing English proficiency intensively. In addition, educators should be aware that on weekends, many Japanese students attend some form of Japanese school where they study Japanese language and participate in other cultural, academic, and social activities.

Classroom Teachers

Age of arrival and length of residency in the United States are crucial factors in teaching Japanese students English. Schooling experience in Japan and Japanese literacy levels are also important factors that teachers should keep in mind. In their studies investigating Japanese students' (grades 2–8) proficiency in both English and Japanese in Canada, Cummins, Harley, Swain, and Allen (1990) found that (1) when controlled for the effect of sojourn length, the older students showed stronger reading skills in English and (2) the length of their sojourn correlated with vocabulary knowledge as well as academic skills in English.

Age of arrival also affects the acquisition of English phonology. Linguists agree that a critical period around puberty may exist in regard to phonology (Bialystok and Hakuta, 1994). Thus, adult learners of second languages rarely attain native-like proficiency in terms of accent.

To help overcome the pronunciation difficulties, teachers might try some of the following strategies. One technique for practicing the /r/ is raising the tongue until its sides touch the tooth ridge toward the back of the mouth. Kinetic exercises to make Japanese speakers use the whole mouth may be effective as a preparation for teaching them English phonetics (L. Yoshida, personal communication, January 16, 1997). For example, students may be asked to speak out the vowel sounds by exaggeration, to yawn, or to mime biting and chewing an apple as warm-up exercises prior to practicing oral drills suggested in textbooks. In addition, Yao (1985) suggests minimal-pairs drills to highlight the difference between similar words, such as lead and read.

To learn the voiced and voiceless /th/, traditional textbooks on pronunciation often suggest sticking the tongue out slightly, which is not always an easy task for the Japanese for technical and psychological reasons. Others (Avery and Ehrlich, 1992; Stevick, 1989) suggest that stressing the necessary contact between the tongue and the teeth may appeal to Japanese.

Avery and Ehrlich (1992) propose techniques to facilitate the pronunciation of consonant clusters. By saying an English word more and more quickly, a Japanese speaker will lose the inserted vowel as the speed increases. Another helpful technique is to give Japanese students a work sheet with several sentences in English. Then have them cross out the final consonants with a pen. Finally, have them read those sentences aloud. For example, taking Read throughout the book, students would cross out d, t, and k as follows: Read throughout the book. When they read aloud, students will say, ree-sue-roo-a-oo-za-boo. This method should be used only to encourage students to omit the addition of vowel sounds and should be limited to the initial stage so that students do not systematically omit every final consonant when reading English. In preparation for a reading exercise, teachers could hand out a work sheet with several sentences to Japanese students and ask them to draw arcs that connect a word's final consonant with the first letter of the next word beginning with a vowel sound. For the sentence Put it on the table, students connect t in put to i in it, and t in it to o in on (draw arcs between t and i, and t and o), and then say, pu-ti-ton-za-teh-boo-roo, which more closely approximates the intended Put it on the table.

It is worth mentioning that Madden (1983) found no significant effects resulting from pronunciation instruction. Students' pronunciation improved over time, but the improvement could not be attributed to pronunciation. In addition, while Underbakke (1993) reported that listening practice improved the pronunciation of /r/ and /l/ among native Japanese speakers, Takagi and Mann (1995) found that even extended exposure to authentic spoken English did not ensure native Japanese speakers' perceptual mastery of the /r/ and /l/ sounds. With these findings in mind, it might be advisable for teachers to focus on pronunciation only when it inhibits the communication of the speaker's intended message.

Kubota (1994) suggests that teachers need to keep in mind that indefinite articles are difficult for Japanese speakers of English to acquire. Teachers need to encourage Japanese students to make a conscious and constant effort to check their use of articles, particularly in their writing. The same holds true for verb tenses and usage patterns. Teachers can use peer editing groups to address many of these writing issues, and pair Japanese students with native English speakers.

Teachers need to remind Japanese students of the differences between English and Japanese. For example, students may have to refer to a dictionary of loan words in Japanese. Some students tend to assume that all loan words come from English, and this can lead them to use "English" words that do not actually exist. Teachers also need to introduce an English written discourse pattern to students and to show them how it differs from what they are accustomed to using. To help Japanese students understand and use English discourse patterns, teachers can have students first read examples of a given genre and then write something in the same genre.

Teachers can use role-playing to teach students usage patterns, such as appropriate expressions for gratitude and requests. These can take the form of mini-dialogues on very basic exchanges, such as using the words please and thank you and asking someone for information. The teacher can provide a brief dialogue model for the students to practice. Students can then develop their own skits to expand the ideas being covered and to link them to their own experiences.

In the classroom, teachers should understand that the passive behavior of Japanese students reflects Japanese school culture. In Japan, students are expected to be quiet and attentive to and respectful of their teachers. American teachers should gradually encourage these students to speak in class by providing them with a nonthreatening environment. Suggestions for encouraging more speaking include role-playing and other activities that require speaking, explicit teacher requests for students to speak, and additional reading skills development (Dwyer & Heller-Murphy, 1996). It is important that some of these speaking opportunities be more informal, less structured, peer-play-type situations (Rescorla & Okuda, 1987; Ross & Berwick, 1988). It may also be necessary for teachers to adjust their expectations somewhat and allow more silence during the Japanese students' period of adjustment.

These various activities designed to elicit student speech should be accompanied by explicit metalinguistic information (Kubota, 1996), or teachers' comments that help students to think about what they are saying. Such comments might include grammar explanations by the teacher when appropriate (Kubota, 1995). Japanese students have also been found to benefit from peer tutoring with native English-speaking classmates (Ward, 1995).

Japanese newcomers are sensitive to their teachers' attitudes and care, which influence their motivation. A potentially important contributor to teachers' attitudes about native Japanese speakers is their sensitivity to the underlying reasons for these students' errors in English (Yao & Hwang, 1987). Teachers need to understand that errors usually result from factors related to linguistic differences between English and Japanese, not from some inherent student deficiency.

Regarding literacy, Carson (1990) found that reading and writing skills transferred from Japanese to English with the transference of reading skills occurring more easily. During reading instruction, teachers should provide background information, give students a purpose for each reading task, encourage faster reading, teach about English discourse organization, have students practice basic reading skills, use activities based on real experiences, provide multiple opportunities for discussion, encourage further cultural or topical study, and avoid exercises requiring that students replace Japanese words with English words (Kitao & Kitao, 1986). Readings should be well organized, with concrete information chosen to suit content-area goals. Certain passages may require exercises to improve reading comprehension and spoken English. Difficult vocabulary should be accompanied by explanations in easy English. Activities for motivating students include allowing students to select their own reading materials, providing computer-assisted instruction, and using newspapers for extensive reading (Kitao, 1994).

Day (1991) found that Japanese students of English could learn vocabulary incidentally while reading silently for entertainment in the classroom. In addition, Ross, Shortreed, and Robb (1988) found that journal writing helped native Japanese speakers improve their English skills.

Finally, teachers need to keep in mind that Japanese speakers are more likely to be able to distinguish between similar sounding spoken words (e.g., rake and lake) when visual representations, such as pictures or objects, accompany written texts. For this reason, teachers should provide as many visual cues and sound-print connections as possible in their instruction.

Counselors

School counselors are important because they often build bridges between Japanese students and classroom teachers when trouble is encountered. Hence, counselors need to provide students with a place where they feel free to drop in and express their concerns. Coker (1988) suggests directive rather than group counseling for Japanese and other Asian students, which reflects sensitivity to their cultural differences.

In developing an academic schedule, counselors should consult with students and their parents to understand each student's needs and objectives. To grasp what the students have learned in Japan, counselors should review the students' core Japanese textbooks in subjects such as mathematics, science, and English. Generally, Japanese students who have completed grade 9 in Japan have covered all aspects of English grammar.

Counselors should also encourage participation in nonacademic activities such as art, music, and sports. These activities can provide wonderful opportunities for Japanese students to socialize with some of their English-speaking peers and to learn colloquial English.

Administrators

Typically, Japanese students have been served by ESL programs or have been mainstreamed (Yao, 1985). Multilevel instruction using different methods and materials within the same ESL classroom is an alternative that allows teachers to accommodate students with various objectives and from diverse backgrounds. Additionally, Yao (1988) recommends education for Asian parents, more reliable research on Asian students of limited English proficiency, and proper representation of Asian staff and personnel.

It might be useful for some administrators to know that only a small proportion of the native Japanese adults coming to the United States are experienced teachers. Those who are teachers usually seek employment in higher education (California Department of Education, 1987).

Other Service Providers

Japanese parents need to be informed that their active involvement is highly expected in American schools. American parents or neighbors are a useful resource for Japanese families seeking to obtain the necessary information about typical parental involvement at the school in their community, including volunteer activities.

There are likely to be other education-related services available to Japanese students and their parents in most major urban areas in the United States where there are significant Japanese populations. Information about these services and others may be available from companies hosting Japanese employees in the United States.

CLOSING REMARKS

As Lee (1988) notes, Asian-Americans often defy stereotypes. The same can be said for native Japanese students. Educational service providers need to consider each student individually. As a first step toward working with a Japanese population, it is recommended that educators examine their personal feelings, prejudices, and expectations concerning native Japanese students and their parents. Then counselors and teachers need to consult with individual students and their parents to find out about each student's educational background, goals, and needs. Educational personnel, students, and parents can then collaboratively plan a course of study and other activities that will provide an enriching learning experience for these students.

Finally, to truly meet the needs of native Japanese, other Asians, Asian-Americans, and, indeed, all students, the government must alter the direction of bilingual education so that students are not inappropriately mainstreamed or served with English-only programs (Yao, 1988). With the increasing importance of Asian markets in the global economy, it seems sensible to offer two-way bilingual programs in Japanese and other Asian languages wherever possible.

ACKNOWLEDGMENTS

The authors thank Kenji Hakuta, Mary McDevitt, and Ryoko Winter for their assistance in bringing this projectto fruition. We are especially grateful to Phyllis Ogata for her thoughtful comments on drafts of this work and her technical assistance with the manuscript. Finally, we are deeply indebted to Linda Yoshida and her students for sharing their time, work, and ideas with us.

NOTES

1. The authors have tried to accompany linguistic terms with laypersons' terms throughout.
2. All letters within slashes represent the sound made by a given letter or letters in a given example.
3. We distinguish between Japanese phonemes, e.g., /a/, and English phonemes, e.g., /a/. All Japanese is written in italics.
4. Examples of Japanese words in the main text follow this format: (1) written Japanese, (2) romanized Japanese in *italics*, (3) English translation <u>underlined</u> (in parentheses).
5. The romanization *Tookyoo* uses double vowels to represent long vowels. This style of *romaji* is more typically used by linguists.
6. This *kanji* representation of <u>aunt</u> refers to an elder sister of either parent. Other *kanji* can be used to represent other <u>aunts</u>, such as a parent's younger sister.
7. For indented examples of Japanese writing, this format is used: (1) Japanese writing (including *kanji*, if any), (2) Japanese *kana* (when necessary in certain examples), (3) romanized Japanese in *italics*, (4) <u>underlined</u>, *italicized* literal English translation (when different from vernacular), (5) English vernacular translation in *italics*.
8. These are not necessarily used interchangeably. The specifics of when each is used exceeds the scope of our discussion.
9. Although unrelated to the singular-plural issue, one can also note in example 8 that commas in written Japanese slant down from left to right (、) and follow the conjunction.
10. The system of *romaji* that is widely used in Japan is called the Hepburn system (or *Hebon-shiki* in Japan). It is based on the system used by James Curtis Hepburn in the third edition of his Japanese-English Glossary (*Wa-ei gorin shuusei*), published in 1886 (Shibatani, 1990).

REFERENCES

Avery, P., & Ehrlich, S. (1992). *Teaching American English pronunciation*. Oxford: Oxford University Press.

Bialystok, E., & Hakuta, K. (1994). *In other words: The science and psychology of second–language acquisition*. New York: Basic Books.

California Department of Education. (1987). *Handbook for teaching Japanese–speaking students*. Sacramento, CA: California Department of Education.

Carson, J. E. (1990). Reading–writing relationships in first and second language. *TESOL Quarterly* 24(2): 245–266.

Cochrane, R. M. (1980). The acquisition of /r/ and /l/ by Japanese children and adults learning English as a second language. *Journal of Multilingual and Multicultural Development* 1(4): 331–360.

Coker, D. M. (1988). The Asian student in the classroom. *Education and Society* 1(3): 19–20.

Cummins, J., Harley, B., Swain, M., & Allen, P. (1990). Social and individual factors in the development of bilingual proficiency. In Harley, B., Allen, P., Cummins, J., & Swain, M. (Eds.), *The development of second language proficiency*. New York: Cambridge University Press.

Day, R. R. (1991). Incidental EFL vocabulary learning and reading. *Reading in a Foreign Language* 7(2): 541–551.

Dwyer, E., & Heller–Murpy, A. (1996). Japanese learners in speaking classes. *Edinburgh Working Papers in Applied Linguistics* 7: 46–55.

Ervin–Tripp, S. (1973). *Language acquisition and communicative choice*. Stanford, CA: Stanford University Press.

Fukushima, S. (1990). Offers and requests: Performance by Japanese learners of English. *World Englishes* 9(3): 317–325.

Harada, Y. (1996). Judgments of politeness in L2 acquisition. *Kansas Working Papers in Linguistics* 21: 39–56.

Kaplan, R. B. (1966). Cultural thought patterns in inter–cultural education. *Language Learning* 16: 1–20.

Kitao, K. (1994). Getting students to read actively. *Doshisha Studies in English* 63: 49–78.

Kitao, K., & Kitao, S. K. (1986). *Difficulties Japanese have in reading English*. (ERIC Document Reproduction Service No. ED 278 214).

Kubota, M. (1996). The effects of instruction plus feedback on Japanese university students of EFL: A pilot study. *Bulletin of Chofu Gakuen Women's Junior College* 18: 59–95.

Kubota, M. (1995). Teachability of conversational implicature to Japanese EFL learners. *IRLT (Institute for Research in Language Teaching) Bulletin* 9: 35–67.

Kubota, M. (1994). *Acquisition of English articles by Japanese EFL learners*. (ERIC Document Reproduction Service No. ED 397 642)

Lee, E. Y. (1988). Working effectively with Asian immigrant parents. *Phi Delta–Kappan* 70(3): 223–225.

Madden, E. H. (1983). The effect of training on pronunciation. *ORTESOL Journal* 4: 69–80.

Maynard, S. K. (1990). *An introduction to Japanese grammar and communication strategies*. Tokyo: The Japan Times.

Miller, R. A. (1967). *The Japanese language*. Chicago: University of Chicago Press.

Nishiyama, S. (1995). Speaking English with a Japanese Mind. *World Englishes* 14(1): 27–36.

Odlin, T. (1989). *Language transfer*. Cambridge: Cambridge University Press.

Park, K. (1996). *The article acquisition in English as a foreign language*. (ERIC Document Reproduction Service No. ED 397 647)

Rescorla, L., & Okuda, S. (1987). Modular patterns in second language acquisition. *Applied Psycholinguistics* 8(3): 281–308.

Ross, S., & Berwick, R. (1988). Scripted and unscripted information exchange tasks: Two approaches to learner negotiation in the foreign language classroom. *PASAA* 18(1): 21–31.

Ross, S., Shortreed, I. M., & Robb, T. N. (1988). First language composition pedagogy in the second language classroom: A reassessment. *RELC Journal* 19(1): 29–48.

Shibatani, M. (1990). *The languages of Japan*. Cambridge: Cambridge University Press.

Shimamune, S., & Smith, S. L. (1995). The relationship between pronunciation and listening discrimination when Japanese natives are learning English. *Journal of Applied Behavior Analysis* 28(4): 577–578.

Shishin, A. (1985). Rhetorical patterns in letters to the editor. *Journal of the Aichi Institute of Technology* (20): 17–28.

Stevick, E. W. (1989). *Teaching and learning languages*. Cambridge: Cambridge University Press.

Takagi, N., & Mann, V. A. (1995). The limits of extended naturalistic exposure on the perceptual mastery of English /r/ and /l/ by adult Japanese learners of English. *Applied Psycholinguistics* 16(4): 379–405.

Thompson, I. (1987). Japanese speakers. In Swan, M., & Smith, B. (Eds.). *Learner English* (pp. 212–223). Cambridge: Cambridge University Press.

Underbakke, M. E. (1993). Hearing the difference: Improving Japanese students' pronunciation of a second language through listening. *Language Quarterly* 31(1–2): 67–89.

Ward, A. M. (1995). An examination of Salem–Teikyo University's Conversational Tutoring Program: Perceptions of a cross–lingual tutoring program. Paper presented at the 29th Annual Meeting of the Teachers of English to Speakers of Other Languages, March 26–April 1, 1995, Long Beach, CA.

Watabe, M. (1991). Transfer of discourse function: Passives in the writing of ESL and JSL learners. *IRAL* 29(2): 115–134.

Yao, E. L. (1988). Roles of federal government for Asian LEP students. *Contemporary Education* 59: 169–172.

Yao, E. L. (1985). Adjustment needs of Asian immigrant children. *Elementary School Guidance and Counseling* 19(3): 222–227.

Yao, E. L., & Hwang, C. C. (1987). Teaching English to Asian immigrant children. *Educational Horizons* 66: 43–45.

Yoon, K. K. (1995). Challenging prototype descriptions: Perception of noun countability and indefinite versus zero article use. *IRAL* 31(4): 269–289.

CHAPTER 7

Learning in America: The Filipino-American Sociocultural Perspective

Edmundo F. Litton

Filipino-Americans are unique among immigrant groups in the United States. They are one of the least understood and most often forgotten group of Asian immigrants (Heras & Revilla, 1994). While the Philippines is in South East Asia, Filipinos do not fit the "oriental" profile generally attributed to the Chinese or Japanese (Cordova, 1973; Wagner, 1973). This is partly due to the fact that the Philippines was a colony of the United States for the first half of the twentieth century. After the Philippines gained independence in 1946, American influences continued to affect life in the Philippines (Karnow, 1989).

The past colonial relationship between the United States and the Philippines is one of the primary reasons Filipinos have assimilated relatively easily into American society (Galang, 1988). Yet Filipino-Americans face unique problems and concerns in their adjustment to American society and the American school system. Although most Filipinos come to the United States with some proficiency in English (Galang, 1988), they must still negotiate various sociocultural difficulties and stress factors associated with moving to another country. This chapter addresses some of these sociocultural issues related to immigrant life among Filipino-Americans in the United States and discusses some concrete steps educators can take in working with Filipino-American students and their families.

Filipinos comprise one of the largest and fastest growing immigrant groups in the United States (Strobel, 1996; Fermin, 1991), second only to that of Mexican immigrants. According to the 1990 U.S. census, the San Francisco Bay area has the largest Filipino population outside of the Philippines (McLeod, 1993). The United States Immigration and Naturalization Service estimates that about 168,000 Filipino immigrants were legally admitted to the United States between 1993 and 1995. Barringer, Gardner, and Levin (1993) project that by the year 2000 there will be about two million Filipinos in the United States, comprising approximately 21% of the Asian-American population. Filipino immigration can be classified into different *waves,* with each wave having its own set of economic, political, and social reasons for coming to the United States.

PRE-1900: EARLY PRESENCE

Filipinos resided in the United States long before the United States became a nation. As early as 1565, Filipinos were recruited as crewmen in the Spanish galleons that plied the trade route from Manila to Acapulco, Mexico, during the Spanish occupation of the Philippines. Many of these crewmen were badly treated and jumped ship when they arrived in Mexico. Eventually, many of these Filipinos made their way to Louisiana (Macaranas, 1983; Mayberry, 1990; Stern, 1989). These "Manilamen" made their living by fishing in the bayous of Louisiana. In 1870, the first documented Filipino organization, the *Socidedad de Beneficia de los Dispano Filipinos de Nuevo Orleans*, was formed in Louisiana. By the end of the nineteenth century, there were about 2,000 Filipinos in the New Orleans area (Macaranas, 1983).

The *Pensionados* of the First Wave

Massive Filipino immigration to the United States started during the American occupation of the Philippines from 1898-1946. In the early 1900s, Governor-General William Howard Taft developed an educational program for the Philippines, which provided Filipino students with pensions for higher education in the United States. These students became known as the *pensionados*. Macaranas (1983) classifies these Filipinos as "potential immigrants." Many of the pensionados who had been either invited or coaxed to study in the United States (Stern, 1989) did not want to remain in the United States after completing their education. Many returned to the Philippines and assumed leadership roles. By 1910, most pensionados had returned home.

The pensionados inspired other Filipinos to come to the United States and enroll in American universities. These new students, however, did not receive government aid. Many of these Filipinos contended with discrimination and experienced difficulty in their academic pursuits due to the language barrier or poor academic preparation (Galang, 1988). Instead of returning to the Philippines and facing being branded as failures, many of these Filipinos chose to the stay in the United States and work as unskilled laborers (Strobel, 1996).

THE LABORERS OF THE SECOND WAVE

The Filipino immigrants of the second wave were predominantly male laborers hoping to earn money in the United States and return to the Philippines. Many of them settled in Hawaii, Alaska, and on the West Coast. Prior to this influx, inexpensive labor was provided by the Chinese and the Japanese. The Chinese Exclusionary Act of 1882 and the Gentlemen's Agreement with Japan (1907-1908) restricted Chinese and Japanese immigration, and the Filipinos filled the need for inexpensive labor (Agbayani-Siewert & Revilla, 1995).

Filipino immigrants to the United States during the colonial period were classified as American nationals (Takaki, 1989). This classification allowed Filipinos to enter the United States but did not allow them to become naturalized American citizens (Mayberry, 1990). Because they were American nationals, Filipinos were automatically excluded from restrictive immigration acts like those above.

Filipino immigrants worked in various occupations. Those in Hawaii worked on sugar plantations, while those who settled in Alaska worked in salmon canneries. The work was often difficult and backbreaking. Most who settled in California and Washington were employed in the service industry as busboys, bellboys, or in domestic service as chamber boys, valets, and so on.

The experiences of Filipinos in these various sectors differed from one another. On the West Coast, Filipino immigrants often competed with European-Americans for the same jobs. This situation fostered resentment and racism among European-Americans, who believed that Filipinos posed an economic threat to the dominant European-American group. Filipinos suffered greatly from the tremendous amount of anti-Filipino sentiment on the West Coast. (Matsouka & Ryujin, 1991). Filipinos in Hawaii did not face the same kind of racial discrimination; however, Filipinos in Hawaii were often pitted against Japanese laborers. During this time, there was much labor unrest, because of extremely harsh working conditions (Takaki, 1989).

Filipino immigration to the United States slowed in 1934 when the U.S. government passed the Tydings McDuffie Act. This law changed the status of Filipinos from nationals to aliens. The immigration quota for Filipinos was limited to fifty per year. There was a strong repatriation movement against Filipinos, and they were offered free passage to hasten their return to the Philippines. Only 2,000 of the 45,000 eligible Filipinos accepted the offer (Strobel, 1996). Despite the presence of strong anti-Filipino sentiment in the United States, most Filipinos did not want to return to the Philippines without money in their pockets, since there were no jobs waiting for them in the Philippines (Takaki, 1989). It is noteworthy that, despite the racism Filipinos endured, some of the Filipinos who remained joined the armed forces and fought for the United States during World War II.

THE PROFESSIONALS OF THE THIRD WAVE

With the passage of the Immigration Reform Act of 1965, the immigration quota for Asians was increased to 20,000 per annum. The Filipino population in the United States more than tripled as a result during the post-1965 third wave of immigration. The new immigration law included an occupation-based preference. The 1965 law also had a provision for family reunification. Family members of Filipinos who had come during the second wave were now allowed to immigrate to the United States. Strobel (1996) notes that this immigration was a result of a commonly held, if exaggerated concept of economic opportunities in the United States. This notion was a product of the dominance of American popular culture in the Philippines, through which many Filipinos were led to believe that America was the land of milk and honey.

The Filipino immigrants of the third wave were highly educated professionals. Most were doctors, nurses, teachers, and engineers. Furthermore, instead of single men (as in the second wave), the Filipino immigrants were made up of family units. There were also political exiles in the third wave, many of whom moved to the United States because of their opposition to the government of Ferdinand Marcos (Mayberry, 1990).

THE FILIPINO-AMERICAN COMMUNITY OF THE 1990s

Filipinos are still coming to the United States in great numbers. Most Filipino immigrants come to the United States under occupation-based immigration or family reunification quotas.

In line with the multicultural movement in the United States, there is a growing sense of Filipino identity among Filipino immigrants. There are Filipino organizations all over the United States, most of which are in California. Colleges and universities are seeing a growth of Filipino student organizations. Classes in Filipino (Tagalog) are now being offered in the University of California, Berkeley, the City College of San Francisco, San Francisco State University and Loyola Marymount University.

The growing number of Filipinos born in the United States also contributes to this search for identity. Currently, the Filipino-American community is undergoing a process of decolonization (Strobel, 1996), in which it examines and acknowledges the past and considers how the colonization period has affected who they are today. Decolonization manifests itself in various ways, such as greater involvement in community and political activities, appreciation of Filipino-American heritage, and assumption of leadership positions.

Filipino-Americans have made notable progress in the political arena in the United States, which has given them greater visibility and empowerment through representation. Filipino-Americans have served the U.S. government as governors, mayors, senators, and congressmen. Hawaii Governor Ben Cayetano is one example. In 1995, Michael Guingona became the first Filipino mayor of Daly City (a city in Northern California with a large Filipino population). In 1999, Pete Fajardo won re-election as the mayor of the City of Carson in Southern California. Lorelie Olaes served as a councilwoman in the City of Carson for six years. Filipino-Americans have also held advisory positions in the White House under President William J. Clinton. Some of these notable Filipino Americans are Maria Haley (Member, Board of Directors of the Export-Import Bank of the U.S.), Paula Bagasao (Senior Policy Advisor to the Administrator, U.S. AID), Irene Natividad (Chair, National Commission on Working Women), and Josie Natori (Commissioner of White House Conference on Small Businesses).

A significant factor that may change the immigration patterns of Filipinos in the United States is the political-economic situation in the Philippines (Stern, 1989). Since the early periods of immigration, Filipinos have immigrated to the United States to escape economic and political hardship. In 1992, democracy was restored in the Philippines through a peaceful transition of political power, and most Filipinos have enjoyed the healthy economic growth which has followed (Elliott, 1996; Koretz, 1996). Such conditions could prompt many Filipino immigrants to return home. Currently, increasing numbers of Filipinos are choosing to work in areas closer to the Philippines, such as the Middle East and Hong Kong. These factors may change the pattern of Filipino immigration to the United States.

THE FILIPINO-AMERICAN FAMILY IN TRANSITION

The Filipino-American immigrant family is often composed of immigrant parents with children who were either born in the United States or immigrated to the United States at a young age. The resulting differences in the acculturation process among the older and younger generations often lead to individual and family distress (Heras & Revilla, 1994).

Filipino families not only experience disharmony from the generation gap, but from the cultural gap between Filipino and American cultures (Agbayani-Siewert, 1994). Filipino values that may be a part of the lives of Filipino parents are often alien to Filipino children, who readily learn the ways of mainstream American culture.

Foreign Influence on Filipino Society and Culture

Ponce (1980) notes that there are three major factors that have influenced Philippine society and culture. The Malay influence is seen in the Filipino's beliefs in magic, animism, fatalism, clannism, and group affinity (the extended family). The Spanish influence can be discerned in the Filipino's major religion (Catholicism), language, consciousness of class rankings, and profound respect for and obedience to authority figures. The American influence is noticed in the Filipino's desire for democratic ideals, the use of English as a major language, and the adoption of American styles of dress, music, and art. These multiple influences make the Filipinos difficult to understand at first glance. Many of the values embedded in these influences are often contradictory. On the surface, the American influence is seen in the way Filipinos dress and in their conversation. The Spanish component is most evident in the form of religious practices and attitudes, acceptance of class differences, and a belief in the superiority of anything foreign. When the Malay influence dominates, Filipinos may be superstitious, animistic, and fatalistic. As a result of these conflicting influences, which often operate simultaneously, "the Filipino can be seen—even by other Filipinos—as inconsistent and contradictory" (Ponce, 1980, p. 160).

The Filipino Family

A major factor that shapes Filipino values is the family. Guthrie and Jacobs (1967) explain that an understanding of the Filipino family system is important to comprehending Philippine society. The key component in the Filipino family is kinship (Jocano, 1972). Kinship groups are formed "through blood, or consanguineal relationships; through affinity, or marriage relations; and through fictional or fictive processes, such as adoption and religious rituals, as in the cases of baptism and confirmation" (Mendez & Jocano, 1974, p. 56). The extended family is a result of the *compadre* system. Other people, who may not be blood relatives, are incorporated into the family through religious ceremonies such as baptisms or weddings. The Filipino kinship system can be described as bilateral (Jocano, 1972; Guthrie & Jacobs, 1967). In a bilateral kinship system, the child equally recognizes kinship relationships on both the mother's and father's sides (Jocano, 1972). Thus, the child has an extended network of relatives that influences how he or she is raised. Such an extended family offers protection and the members of the family can rely on one another, but it may also hinder the Filipino child's development of independence and self-reliance (McLeod, 1975). Thus, a Filipino child can best be understood in the context of this matrix of relationships in which most decisions are made. Each child is taught from early on to be sensitive to the needs of others and to make an effort to minimize conflict (Guthrie & Jacobs, 1967).

The Filipino family plays a primary role in the development of the child. In Philippine society, children are considered to be a gift from God (Guthrie & Jacobs, 1967; Sevilla, 1982). Filipino parents see their role of raising their children as part of a divine calling. De la Torre (1992) notes that a newborn immediately becomes the center of the household because the Philippines is a child-centered society. Panopio, Cordero, and Raymundo (1978) enumerate the different functions of the family in the shaping of the Filipino child. The family plays an important biological function by being the unit for reproduction and regulator of sexual behavior. The family also performs the function of biological maintenance, where the parents are responsible not only for the physical well-being of the child, but also for any extended family members who may be aged, unemployed, or widowed.

The family provides an identity for its members; it gives a child a name and a lineage (Panopio, et al., 1978). To maintain its good status, the family exerts pressure on its members to conform to what is considered acceptable behavior. The family exerts its control over the members' relationships with other people, morals, etiquette, and religious and political functions. Obedience to authority is a lesson that is taught early in life to the Filipino child.

The family is the primary socializing agent of the child (De la Torre, 1992; Mendez, et al., 1984; Panopio, et al., 1978; Jocano, 1972). The family transmits the culture and values of the community through example and indoctrination, and prepares the child for its future role in society.

Age is a significant factor in the hierarchy of the Filipino family. Age may not necessarily translate to authority (Agbayani-Siewert, 1994), but older members of the family are respected by the younger members. Older members of the family are often consulted on important issues and may help support the family economically. The most evident sign of respect for elders is in the language used to address older members of the family. An older sibling is often addressed as *ate* (older sister), or *kuya* (older brother). Grandparents are called *lolo* (male) or *lola* (female). Aunts and uncles are referred to as *tito* (male) or *tita* (female). Because of this respect for elders and the extended family network, even older family friends are addressed as *tito* or *tita*. When addressing older members of the family, the younger members may also use the respect markers *po* or *ho*.

Filipino Values

Among the values Filipino families teach their children are *amor propio* (self-esteem), *hiya* (shame or embarrassment), *utang na loob* (debt of gratitude), *pakikisama* (getting along harmoniously), and *bahala na* (what will be, will be). Ponce (1980) observes that *amor propio* often "exhibits itself as an exaggerated sense of personal worth which, underneath, the individual secretly recognizes to be overdrawn" (p. 161). Ponce further notes that this fragile sense of self-worth makes the Filipino sensitive to negative remarks from others and dependent on signs that indicate his or her status in the group. *Amor ropio* makes it difficult for Filipinos to accept compliments. When receiving a compliment, a Filipino may respond that the action was a duty or that it may have not have entailed any difficulty and, thus, the good deed should be overlooked.

Hiya (shame and embarrassment) is related to *amor propio*. Andres (1989) defines *hiya* as "a Filipino trait with emphasis on fear of losing face" (p. 137). The concept of *hiya* is exhibited in several Tagalog sayings such as *Di baling saktan mo ako, huwag mo lang akong hiyain* (I would not mind if you hurt me physically, just don't shame me) or *Ang sugat ng itak ay mas mahinay kaysa sugat ng masamang pangungusap* (The wound from a knife is more bearable than the wound from an offensive word). Indeed, an offensive comment may well trigger a negative reaction from a Filipino.

Jocano (1972) observes that *hiya* is evident in the way Filipinos prefer to approach sensitive situations in an indirect manner. Verbal clashes are often avoided because Filipinos regard confrontations to be rude behavior (Agbayani-Siewert, 1994). Andres (1989) also notes that *hiya* often leads to monetary debt because many Filipinos borrow money to impress their friends with lavish clothing or parties. It is considered an embarrassment, or *hiya*, if a gift or gathering is simple. Andres (1989) further states, however, that *hiya* also dictates payment of debt. A person risks being shamed if the individual is capable of settling the debt, yet fails to do so.

Utang na loob, or debt of gratitude or reciprocal obligation, refers to a favor which must be returned (Ponce, 1980; Agbayani-Siewert, 1994). *Utang na loob* is incurred when an individual voluntarily helps another, without being asked (Jocano, 1972). The person who received the favor is expected to reciprocate at a later time. If the favor is not repaid when help is needed, the person who incurred the favor is said to be *walang hiya* (no shame). However, it is difficult to know if a debt has been adequately repaid since *utang na loob* is often based on services rather than goods. In the family, children are expected to have eternal *utang na loob* to their parents for giving them life (Agbayani-Siewert, 1994).

Pakikisama is a very important underlying current in any Filipino relationship. Lynch (in Andres, 1989) defines *pakikisama* as "the ability to get along with others in such a way as to avoid signs of conflict" (p. 150). It is important to maintain smooth interpersonal relationships among Filipinos. Thus, every effort is made to avoid direct confrontation, disagreement, and criticism (Ponce, 1980). An integral part of *pakikisama* is *pakiramdam* or the ability to sense other people's feelings and needs by understanding indirect cues such as body language and tone of voice (Agbayani-Siewert, 1994).

Filipino-Americans are a religious people. Most Filipinos are Christians, the majority being Catholics. Consequently, there may be among Filipinos a strong sense of fatalism, or a belief that life is predestined (Yalung, 1992). This belief is reflected in the attitude of *bahala na* (what will be, will be). This value can be manifested in various ways. A strong belief in *bahala na* can lead one to become lazy, irresponsible, or have a lack of initiative. If everything is predetermined, then there is no point to try to shape one's destiny. In a more positive light, *bahala na* allows a Filipino to accept past misfortunes. This allows the Filipinos to face further challenges without dwelling on the past (Church, 1986). *Bahala na* also promotes a high tolerance to ambiguity which allows Filipinos to respond calmly to uncertainty (Chan, 1992).

Sociocultural Adjustment of Filipino-American Families

As with most immigrant groups, Filipino immigrant children tend to adapt to American culture more quickly than the Filipino immigrant parents (Agbayani-Siewert & Revilla, 1995). Conflicts arise when Filipino parents impose their traditional values on their children who have embraced American values. This tension may have dire consequences. A 1993 survey conducted by the San Diego Unified School District revealed that, Filipino-American female students have the highest rate (45.6%) of suicidal tendencies in the county (Marquez, 1995). The same survey found that Filipino-American male students deal with the pressures of living in two worlds by joining gangs (Lau, 1995).

The acculturation process also changes the behavior expectations of Filipino families. In Philippine society, dependence on the family is encouraged. Heras and Revilla (1994) point out that Filipino mothers encourage their children to be dependent on them and resent it when their children show signs of independence. Being dependent is equated with being obedient. The children are expected to conform to this dependent orientation at home, but outside the home, they are confronted with values that preach the very opposite. Naturally, this leads to conflict among Filipino immigrant parents and their children. Filipino children who have acculturated to American society often challenge the authority of their parents (Agbayani-Siewert & Revilla, 1995). When the parents are challenged, they respond by reasserting their power, based on the traditional hierarchy of Filipino families, and accuse their children of being ungrateful. The children react by rebelling even more. It is interesting to note here that Heras and Revilla (1994) also found that Filipino mothers whose children had more traditional Filipino value orientations expressed a greater level of family satisfaction than mothers whose children were more acculturated and had adopted more American values.

Immigration and acculturation also lead to stress in the marital relationship (Agbayani-Siewert & Revilla, 1994). Economic needs often forces Filipino women to work outside of the home, altering the role of the traditional Filipino housewife (who is expected to stay at home). There is also a change in communication patterns between husband and wife. Card (1978) notes that the nature of verbal communication between Filipino immigrant couples changes when they move to the United States. In the Philippines, they discuss personal problems with each other more readily. Filipino couples are not likely to seek advice on their marital problems (Agbayani-Siewert, 1994), because in the Filipino culture, it is thought that family problems should never leave the home. Discussing family problems with others may lead to *hiya*. In the United States, because of the demands of the new life, immigrant Filipino couples often hesitate to discuss their individual problems, many of which are related to acculturation and adaptation to new American values. However, immigrant Filipino couples do discuss problems concerning their children.

Filipino families are also confronted with the economic realities of living in the United States. Like most immigrant groups, both Filipino parents often work outside of the home; thus they are unable to raise their children in the traditional Filipino way. When Filipino parents clash with their Americanized children, they often are heard saying *Palibhasa, laki na sa Amerika kasi* (It is because he/she was raised in America). When these children become problematic, Filipino parents threaten to send their children back to the Philippines where they will be disciplined according to Filipino tradition, which stresses respect for elders and family interdependence (Agbayani-Siewert & Revilla, 1995).

Loss of status is another factor that leads to social stress among Filipino immigrants in the United States (Chan, 1992). Filipino immigrants who enjoyed high status and respect in Philippine society often lose this privilege in the United States. Family names which may have commanded respect and status in the homeland mean little or nothing in the United States. Many Filipino immigrants lose status in their own eyes when they are forced to take jobs for which they are overqualified. Training and credentials received in the Philippines are usually not recognized in the United States. This compounds the level of stress felt by the immigrant family.

Filipino immigrants in the United States have created many support groups within their communities to help deal with stress factors related to acculturation (Matsouka & Ryujin, 1991). These community groups, based on similarities in language, region of origin, or religion, also provide a forum in which Filipinos can share their cultural heritage through celebrations, music, and the arts. Cordova (1983) notes that Filipinos are noted for being "fun people." Social gatherings are a prominent part of Filipino life and provide a way of dealing with the stress and adjustment related to immigration. The community organizations are also a good source of news from the Philippines, provide advice on immigration and social services, and serve as a means for making or renewing social connections with other Filipinos.

FILIPINO STUDENTS IN THE UNITED STATES

To address the needs of Filipino students in the United States, it is important to distinguish between Filipino students born in the Philippines and those born in the United States. In a study by Strobel (1996), a Filipino participant makes a distinction between these two groups:

My idea, at the time, of Filipino culture and identity was split into two distinct groups. The FOB and the Filipino-American. The FOB (fresh off the boat) was someone to be despised, laughed at. I didn't associate with FOBs. They were backwards, had accents, and just acted weird. . . . Then, of course, there was me, the "non-FOB," spoke perfect English, was born and raised here, had only white friends, did the same kind of things they did, wasn't at all close to my relatives because I distanced myself from them. . . . I was "white" in every way except for the color of my skin, my nose, and my eyes. But hey, that can be overlooked if you dress cool and don't have an accent. (p. 94)

Each of these two groups of Filipinos may have different cultural beliefs, different concepts of Filipino identity, and different levels of English-language proficiency (Macarnas, 1983). This section focuses on the needs of Philippine-born immigrants, although some of these issues also apply to Filipinos born in the United States.

Educational Background and Experience in the Philippines

The educational institutions in the Philippines are the most visible reminders of the colonial era. The Spaniards passed decrees that mandated the creation of public schools operated by the Spanish friars (Cortes, 1980; Carson, 1978). The curricula in these early schools were influenced by Catholic doctrine and consisted mainly of prayers and religious songs. The present public school system in the Philippines is based on the American model. This system was established during the American occupation of the Philippines with the arrival of the first American teachers in 1901. During the early part of the twentieth century, most of the teachers in the Philippines were Americans. The educational setting was a vehicle for the dissemination of American values (Strobel, 1996). American textbooks were used and English became the language of instruction.

Although elementary education is compulsory in the Philippines, this policy is often unenforced (Trueba, et al., 1993). Many young Filipino children must help their parents earn a living. Furthermore, there are more students than there is classroom space. Thus, class size in the Philippine tends to be large. Expenditure on education by the national government is also not commensurate with the demands of education (Ronquillo, Peralta, Ramos, et al., 1989) Filipino children spend about ten years in school: six years in the elementary grades, and four in secondary school. The American middle school does not exist in the Philippines except in schools that cater primarily to the children of foreign nationals. Examples of such schools are the International School in Metro Manila and Brent School in Baguio City. Students who attend pre-school and private schools may have a longer period of education. Students in the Philippines study more subjects than students enrolled in American schools (California Department of Education, 1986). However, the bulk of instruction time is spent on language instruction, which may include Filipino, English, or another foreign language such as Spanish. Education in the Philippines is conducted both in English and Filipino. English is used in subjects such as science and math and Filipino is used to teach social studies (Gonzalez & Sibayan, 1988). In areas outside of Metro Manila, the local language may be used to elaborate classroom directions and provide more explanation. This language situation is more complicated when the language spoken at home is not English. Thus, in addition to trying to understand concepts, the students may need to learn English as well. When students are being educated in an unfamiliar language, creativity may be stifled especially in the early school years because they are unable to express themselves. Early on, students are taught self-restraint. Despite the problems associated with being taught in English, a majority of Filipinos still prefer that instruction be conducted in both English and Filipino (Sibayan, et al., 1988). Learning English is seen as an asset because it allows those who want to work abroad to communicate easily with foreigners (Sevilla, 1988). In the United States, the Filipino-American community uses English in formal situations and for status differentiation (Dar, 1983). Proficiency in English is associated with higher social status.

Students in schools in the Philippines are usually taught using the lecture method (California Department of Education, 1986; Carson, 1978). Techniques that teachers use in the classroom may be limited due to lack of educational materials or insufficient classroom space. There is a big focus on retention of facts, and, thus, students are expected to memorize the information for later assessment. In many Philippine schools, teachers are the sole providers of information. Students from the Philippines are not used to working in cooperative groups. The amount and quality of interaction between students and teachers or among students depends on the teacher's initiative. Most progressive teachers encourage student participation and involvement (J. Palma, personal communication, June 18, 1997).

Philippine classrooms are characterized by a high degree of regimentation (California Department of Education, 1986). Classrooms are highly structured. Students are taught to be polite and are encouraged to remain quiet. Thus, many Filipino students are reluctant to speak in class. If one speaks, comments need to be carefully thought out and the students need to be sure of their answers. As teachers are the main focus of control in the classroom, most Filipino students do not perform tasks unless they receive explicit instructions from the teacher.

Filipino schools are generally departmentalized at all levels. Exceptions exist in the early levels of schooling (up to second grade). Although elementary school teachers in the Philippines are expected to be able to teach all subjects, there is a trend towards specialization in a single subject area (J. Palma, personal communication, June 18, 1997). High school teachers are expected to teach only in their areas of specialization. In schools that are departmentalized, the teachers move from one classroom to another to teach their respective subjects except in classes that require specialized learning and teaching tools (such as band instruments for music) [N. Salazar, personal communication, June 27, 1997]. In addition to teaching their classes, a teacher may also be assigned a homeroom class. The homeroom teacher provides information regarding school policy or acts as an advisor when a student is experiencing academic and personal difficulties (J. Palma, personal communication, June 18, 1997). A teacher's desk may be located in this homeroom classroom. A school may also designate a special work area for teachers of the same grade level or teachers of the same subjects, which facilitates socialization and meetings.

When looking at the educational experience of Filipinos in the Philippines, it is important to note the differences between private and public schools. Most private schools in the Philippines are operated by Catholic religious orders and tend to be more rigorous in their demands for academic achievement. Some of these private schools are operated by the Brothers of the Christian Schools (La Salle Green Hills and La Salle Alabang in the Metro Manila area), the Society of Jesus (Ateneo de Manila), the Religious of the Assumption (Assumption College), or the Sisters of St. Paul (St. Paul's College). Private schools typically stress English instruction. Entrance into these schools is highly competitive. To enter these schools, students often must take a standardized test (mostly U.S.-developed tests such as the California Achievement Test). Thus, Filipino students who come from private schools in the Philippines are often better prepared to deal with the academic expectations of the American classroom.

Most elementary schools and high schools are coeducational. Only a few, private, Catholic schools maintain single-gender classes. Single-gender colleges and universities are rare. In coeducational institutions, students may be separated when they take classes in physical education and vocational skills (e.g., automobile maintenance, sewing, cooking). The entire curriculum in elementary schools and high schools is mandated by the Department of Education, Culture, and Sports (J. Palma, personal communication, June 18, 1997).

There are a number of institutions of higher education in the Philippines. Most of these are privately owned. Acceptance into prestigious private universities such as De La Salle University, Ateneo de Manila University and the government-run University of the Philippines is extremely competitive. In addition to having the applicants take the government-administered National Secondary Achievement Test (NSAT), these colleges administer their own entrance examinations. Applicants to institutions of higher education must pass the NSAT before they can be considered for enrollment in any college or university in the Philippines. Students who are not accepted into a prestigious university often enter colleges with lower academic standards. These colleges accept candidates on the basis of the individual's ability to pay tuition rather than potential scholastic achievement (J. Palma, personal communication, June 18, 1997). Most college students rely on family support to pay for these educational expenses (Sanyan, et al., 1981).

A few schools cater to special needs children in the Philippines. There are schools for children with visual and hearing impairments, such as the School for the Deaf and Blind in Metro Manila. There are also schools providing programs for the academically gifted, such as the Philippine Science High School and the Philippine School for the Arts. Parents and teachers provide assistance to students who experience academic difficulty. Those students who cannot meet the demands of academic classes, pursue their education in vocational or technical schools (J. Palma, personal communication, June 18, 1997). Special education classes, however, are increasing since the University of the

Philippines introduced a teacher preparation program in special education (N. Salazar, personal communication, June 24, 1997).

Schools in the Philippines are large. Some private institutions (such as the Ateneo de Manila), have an elementary school, high school, and a university on a multi-acre campus. It is possible for a Filipino student to spend an entire educational career on the same campus. Most public schools have separate campuses for elementary school and high school.

The Filipino Educational Experience in the United States

Despite the differences in the educational experience of Filipino immigrants, the Filipino community of the 1990s is one of the most highly educated immigrant groups in the United States (Barringer, et al., 1995; Chan, 1992; Stern; 1989). This is primarily due to the fact that most Filipino immigrants have a professional background. High educational attainment, however, does not necessarily lead to a high-paying job in the work force. Most Filipino immigrants are employed in clerical and service jobs despite their high educational attainment and proficiency in English (Strobel, 1996). Even with their positive attitudes towards education, many second-generation Filipino-Americans do not feel that their education will lead to the economic upward mobility they desire (Agbayani-Siewert & Revilla, 1995). As a results, many Filipino-Americans drop out of high school and college (Azores, 1987).

Filipino immigrant students may also have different economic backgrounds. Many Filipinos in the Philippines, 80% in 1985, live below the poverty line (Ronquillo, et al., 1989). Students who live in poverty may be malnourished and may be helping their parents earn a living; academic development is not a priority when children are struggling to survive. Poverty prevents schools and parents from purchasing educational materials. Filipino immigrant children who come from the lower socioeconomic classes in the Philippines may have received only minimal academic preparation prior to immigrating to the United States and may be ill equipped to meet the academic demands of American schools.

Culture plays an important role in the educational experience of Filipinos in the United States. In recent years, many researchers have begun looking at the effect of culture on cognitive development and cognitive style. Hansen (1979) defined cognitive style as "an individual's characteristic pattern or strategy for acquiring and processing information" (p. 17). Other researchers such as Lancy (1983), Cole and Means (1981), Halverson (1979), Ginsburg (1978), Baecher (1976), Ramirez and Castaneda (1974), and Chiu (1972) found that, while not having examined Filipino children in particular, people of different cultures clearly have different thought patterns.

There are few studies that describe how Filipino children learn. Fermin (1991) and Litton (1994) conducted studies that attempted to illustrate the learning styles and strategies of Filipino students in the elementary school. Park (1997) and Ingham and Price (1993) explored the learning styles of Filipino students in secondary school. These studies revealed some of the different dimensions of learning in Filipino-American students, and further showed that a linear, westernized approach may not be an effective way to describe how Filipino-American children learn.

Fermin (1991) studied the cognitive styles of field dependence and field independence of Filipino children using the same conceptual framework in the research of Ramirez and Castaneda (1974). Fermin wanted to find out if the students' cultural background affects their disposition towards being field dependent or field independent. Fermin observed and interviewed ten Filipino children enrolled at the Filipino Education Center in San Francisco, California. In addition to interviews and observations, Fermin administered the Children's Embedded Figure Test (CEFT) developed by Karp and Konstadt in 1963.

Fermin (1991) concluded that it is not meaningful to describe the selected Filipino immigrant children in terms of a characteristic cognitive style. She draws this conclusion from the data that showed that Filipino-American children tend to be field independent and data derived from the interview that showed that these same children were leaning towards a field dependent orientation. Fermin stated that the findings "can only be suggestive and tentative because the sample was small and the measures used were different...the instruments were not correlated to each other" (p. 104). However, Fermin did find that most Filipino children "arrive in American classrooms with backgrounds that nurture a field dependent orientation, or at least a field sensitive orientation" (p. 122). The study indicates the real need for American educators to understand that Filipino children "do not manifest the cultural behaviors that are overtly and covertly expressed by the majority of their classmates" (p. 134).

Park (1997) studied the learning style preferences of Filipino-American students and three other Asian-American groups enrolled in high schools in the United States. Park compared the reported learning styles of Asian-American students with European-American students with similar academic achievement and gender. One of the hypotheses being tested in the study is, "the learning style preference of Asian-American students would be significantly different from those of Anglo students because of their Asian cultural background" (Park, 1997, p. 71). A survey was administered to the participants of the study. The instrument measured the students' learning style preferences for visual, auditory, kinesthetic, tactile, group learning, and individual learning.

Park found that Filipino-Americans have learning style preferences that may be different from other Asian-American students and European-American students. In the area of auditory learning, Filipino-Americans showed a minor preference for auditory learning. This finding is similar to the Korean-Americans and the European-Americans. Filipino-Americans exhibited a greater preference for visual learning when compared to their European-American counterparts. For kinesthetic learning, there were no statistically significant differences between preferences of the Asian-American students and the European-American students. However, Asian students who have been in the United States for a longer period of time showed a major preference for kinesthetic learning in comparison to Asian students who have resided in the United States for a brief period of time. Thus, Asian students who have acculturated to the American classroom have a higher preference for kinesthetic learning. No statistically significant differences were found for tactile learning. Filipino-Americans, however, showed a minor preference for group learning. Thus, cooperative learning activities may match the learning style preference of Filipino-Americans. There is a high preference for individual learning by native-born Filipinos and other Asian-American students.

Ingham and Price (1993) studied the learning style preference of Filipino high school students in the Philippines and compared the results with European-American students enrolled in high schools in the United States. Ingham and Price noticed significant differences between the learning style preferences of Filipinos and the European-American students. The study shows that Filipino students have a preference for learning through their visual and kinesthetic senses, are more teacher motivated, and prefer to learn in a variety of ways. The Filipino students in the study were also more persistent than their European-American counterparts.

Litton (1994) compared the learning strategies that were perceived to be effective by Filipino-American and European-American children enrolled in private elementary schools in the San Francisco-Bay area. One of the purposes of the study was to determine if students from these two cultural backgrounds have different perceptions on the effectiveness of specific learning strategies in completing routine school tasks such as reading from a social studies textbook, working in groups, or working on a mathematics assignment. The Learning Strategies Questionnaire (Nolen, et al., 1986) was administered to 152 children enrolled in the fourth, fifth, and sixth grades. In addition, randomly selected students were interviewed.

Litton (1994) found consistent differences in student perception of the effectiveness of various learning strategies between Filipino-American students and European-American students. The most notable difference was found in selective attention. The mean for the activity of reading from a science or social studies textbook was significantly higher for Filipino-American students than European-American students, indicating that Filipino-Americans find it more effective to utilize the selective attention strategies of reading slowly and carefully, looking up unknown words, and memorizing the important parts of what is being read.

Differences were also found between the two groups for the ineffective strategy of plunging in. While neither group viewed the strategy as being effective, this study found higher mean scores for this strategy among Filipino-American students. This result can be explained by the observation that Filipino-American students tend to rate the strategies, effective or not, higher than European-American students. The strategy of plunging in may also be related to Filipino-American students' belief in *bahala na* (what will be, will be). This, however, does not mean that Filipino-Americans have a preference for starting school work without doing any kind of planning.

Another hypothesis in this study was that there would be differences in learning strategies used for working in small groups, with lower mean scores among Filipino-American students. The findings from this study did not lend support to McLeod's (1975) earlier observations that suggested that most

Filipino children are shy and docile in the classroom. Many of the Filipino-American students who were interviewed showed a high preference for working with their friends. This ability to work with others is a manifestation of the Filipino value of *pakikisama* (getting along harmoniously). Further research is needed to show to what extent this Filipino value influences the way Filipino-American children work with their peers.

Chattergy (1992) notes that numerous teachers in the United States have expressed a common observation that Filipino students are not assertive in the classroom. Teachers may associate passivity with a lack of academic ability (Macaranas, 1983), but this may be a result of educational factors in the Philippines described earlier in this chapter. Chattergy also points out that many Filipino children have not had experience in presenting themselves in a public forum such as the classroom. The students' limited English-speaking ability may also cause the students to be self-conscious and quiet.

WORKING WITH FILIPINO-AMERICAN STUDENTS AND PARENTS

An awareness of the cultural values Filipino students and parents bring to the educational setting can equip and empower school personnel who work with Filipino-Americans to provide better services. A person looks at the world through the schema constructed by his cultural background. School personnel can help Filipino-Americans view their rich cultural heritage as an asset to their future.

Strategies for Helping Filipino-American Students Succeed in School

One of the most important steps school administrators and teachers can take to help Filipino-American students succeed in school is to provide role models for Filipino-American students (Manuel, 1989). Despite the rapid rise in the number of Filipino-American students in California, Filipino teachers comprise only about 1% of public school teachers (Cordova, et al., 1997). The participants in a study by Strobel (1996) noted that the mere presence of a Filipino teacher can be empowering for Filipino students. Often, a Filipino-American teacher is able to share knowledge that can only be gained by experience. A Filipino-American teacher can also help Filipino students deal with confusion over their ethnic identity and may inspire and guide other Filipinos to become teachers. Unfortunately, due in part to both the inadequate salary and low prestige associated with the teaching profession in the United States, few Filipino-Americans enter the teaching profession. In a private interview, the principal of a Catholic elementary school with a large Filipino-American population stated that she has tried to recruit Filipino teachers over the last five years but has been unable to find any candidates. In another private interview, a Filipino-American student enrolled in a teacher preparation program at a major California university stated that she had never had a Filipino teacher prior to entering the teacher education program. A participant in the Strobel study also noted that there was only one Filipino teacher in a California school district with a large Filipino-American population. Filipino-Americans need greater professional representation in the educational system in the United States for the curriculum to be balanced with the Filipino perspective.

There are Filipino teachers who have immigrated to the United States. Should these teachers decide to teach in America, they must become familiar with the educational structure and practices of the United States. Filipino teachers need to learn about different pedagogy, as well as legal issues in American schools. An orientation to teaching in the United States is necessary for Filipino teachers to succeed.

The development of bilingual education programs in Filipino is another strategy that can help Filipino students succeed in school. Researchers have shown the social, academic, and psychological value and advantages of learning a second language. An additive approach to language instruction can help Filipino-Americans communicate more effectively in their families. Bilingual programs in Filipino and English can ensure access to academic content, as Filipino-American students acquire English.

There are a number of factors, however, that make the implementation of bilingual education programs in Filipino difficult. First, there are few materials available in Filipino. Another major hindrance to the successful implementation of Filipino bilingual programs is the attitude among some Filipino-American parents towards the maintenance of Filipino. A Filipino parent who participated in a study by Juarez (1997) stated that educating Filipino children in two languages is important but opposed the use of Filipino in bilingual programs. This participant preferred Spanish-English bilingual programs and associated these two languages with greater prestige. Some Filipino-American parents also fear that their children will become functional illiterates if they do not learn English (Asimov, 1996). In order to ensure the success of Filipino bilingual programs, Filipino parents need to believe that it is possible for immigrant students to become fully competent bilinguals (Aivazian, 1991), given that such success is highly dependent on parental support. Further, school administrators and teachers need to actively involve Filipino-American parents in all aspects of the program.

In the classroom, teachers can help Filipino-American students by making explicit the rules of the classroom. Chattergy (1992) has pointed out that teachers should not assume that basic classroom rules are automatically known or understood by all students, since classroom rules are not the same for all cultures. For example, cultural values such as respect for the teacher as an authority figure may prevent Filipino-American students from asking the teacher to clarify procedures or instructions. Teachers should thoroughly discuss all classroom procedures with Filipino-American students to ensure access to academic content.

Teachers can help Filipino-American students by allowing them to demonstrate their understanding of subject matter through nonverbal means. Silence should not be equated with indifference or the inability to think (Chattergy, 1992). Filipino students may be hesitant to respond out of fear that their answers may be incorrect and out of the need to avoid *hiya*. An incorrect answer may displease the teacher, who is an authority figure.

Teachers can encourage and elicit student response by learning to engage Filipino-American students rather than talk down to them (Strobel, 1996). Teachers can go beyond cultural sensitivity by, for example, becoming active participants in the Filipino community. Finally, teachers can provide a forum in which students can share their cultural knowledge in the classroom.

Parental Attitudes Towards School

Generally speaking, Filipino parents have a favorable attitude towards school. Filipino parents are highly supportive of their children's education for various reasons. Education is seen as a vehicle for economic advancement, and high status is attached to college education (Galang, 1988). Filipinos also view a solid education as a source of pride and honor for the family (Yalung, 1992).

Filipino parents expect their children to do well in school. Parents help their children succeed in school and are willing to sacrifice their financial resources to ensure that their children are highly educated. A child's failure in school is a source of *hiya*. Filipino parents feel that their children's success or shortcomings in school reflect back on them (California Department of Education, 1986).

This reverence for education is shown in the respect Filipino parents show for teachers. However, cultural elements definitely influence the way Filipino parents act when they associate with school personnel. Filipino parents believe that, when it comes to matters concerning their children's education, the teacher knows best. Thus, many Filipino parents may not question what their children's teachers are doing. The school personnel may view the Filipino parents' deference to teachers and noninvolvement in school as a sign that these Filipino parents do not care about their children's education. School personnel find when they ask, however, that Filipino parents are quite willing to participate in various programs and activities.

Filipino-American parents may have two different views concerning their children's learning disabilities, physical disabilities, and counseling for their children. These attitudes are influenced by cultural factors. There are almost no special education classes in the Philippines, mainly due to financial considerations. Some Filipino-American families consider a disability as a gift from God and, therefore, view it as a sign of good luck (Yalung, 1992). Thus, many Filipino parents are hesitant to attempt to change or to take care of this disability. This view is related to the cultural value of *bahala na*.

On the other hand, a disability may be seen as a source of *hiya*. There is usually a stigma attached to any form of disability. Chan (1992) and Church (1986) explain that a disability may be associated with the supernatural. In some instances, children with disabilities are considered to be possessed by evil spirits.

The values of *bahala na* and *hiya* also influence the way parents view counseling or any form of intervention by anyone who is not a family member. Parents may hesitate to change the status quo and prefer to keep family problems within the family.

Strategies for Encouraging Parent Participation in School

Filipino parents need to be empowered to participate in the education of their children. A principal who works with Filipino-American parents stated that most of the Filipino-American parents in her school do not like to participate in school because they do not feel that they can help. Thus, educators need to encourage parent participation by helping parents believe and understand that their participation is essential.

A personal invitation is necessary to encourage Filipino-American parents to participate in schools. School administrators can expect more parent participation if personal invitations are extended to each parent and if tasks are made specific. Many Filipino-American parents are unfamiliar with what is expected in school. Thus, administrators and teachers need to take the time to educate parents on the kind of role they need to play to enhance their children's education.

In some instances, counseling or some other form of intervention may be necessary. As stated earlier, a disability or counseling may have negative connotations. Thus, interventionists also need to be sensitive to the cultural values that influence how Filipinos see counseling. Interventionists or teachers need to consider the existence of the extended family in Filipino culture (Agbayani-Siewert, 1994). Interventionists may receive initial contact from members of the extended family (Chan, 1992).

Teachers and other interventionists should avoid direct confrontations with Filipino parents. The values of *hiya* and *amor propio* may make it difficult for Filipino parents to accept direct questions or criticism (Agbayani-Siewert, 1994). Filipino parents may respond indirectly through nonverbal means (Chan, 1992). This response may be frustrating to someone who is used to western directness when dealing with problematic situations. However, teachers and other interventionists who are aware of the cultural aspects underlying this behavior may better tolerate this indirect way of dealing with problems. Teachers and other interventionists would benefit by learning about the Filipino value of *pakiramdam* and by learning to "listen" to what their Filipino-American clients are not saying.

To involve Filipino parents in their children's education, teachers and administrators need to invite them to become part of the educational process. Teachers and administrators need to make Filipino parents aware that their contributions can and do make a difference.

CONCLUSION

Filipino-Americans have been part of life in the United States for many years. If educators expect Filipino-Americans students and parents to participate more in the educational process, they need to first consider the rich history and major cultural aspects of Filipino-Americans. It is important to remember that Filipino-Americans come to the United States with different cultural perspectives and languages. Members of the American community need to better understand the internal diversity within the Filipino-American community. Further, it is equally important for Filipino-Americans to understand and appreciate their own history properly. By exploring their past, Filipino-Americans will discover cultural pride, realize greater achievement in school, and build a better future.

REFERENCES

Aivazian, C. R. (1991). *A participatory study of the reflections and attitudes of Filipino high school additive and subtractive bilingual students toward the maintenance of Filipino*. Doctoral dissertation, University of San Francisco.

Agbayani-Siewert, P. (1994). Filipino American culture and family: Guidelines for practitioners. *Families in Society: The Journal of Contemporary Human Services* 75 (7): 429-438.

Agbayani-Siewert, P., & Revilla, L. (1995). Filipino Americans. In P. G. Min (Ed.), *Asian Americans: Contemporary trends and issues* (pp. 134-168). Thousand Oaks, CA: Sage.

Andres, T. (1989). *Positive Filipino values*. Quezon City, Philippines: New Day.

Asimov, N. (1996). Rojas meets with Filipino group—reporters ousted. Controversy over bilingual education. *San Francisco Chronicle*, September 13, p. A17.

Azores, T. (1987). Educational attainment and upward mobility: Prospects for Filipino Americans. *Amerasia Journal* 13 (1): 39-52.

Baecher, R. E. (1976). Bilingual children and educational cognitive analysis. In A. Simoes, Jr. (Ed.), *The bilingual child* (pp. 41-61). New York: Academic Press.

Barringer, H. R., Gardner, R. W., & Levin, M. J. (1993). *Asian and Pacific Islanders in the United States*. New York: Russell Sage Foundation.

Barringer, H. R., Takeuchi, D. T., & Xenos, P. (1995). Education, occupational prestige, and income of Asian Americans. In D. T. Nakanishi & T. Y. Nishida (Eds.), *The Asian American educational experience* (pp. 146-164). New York: Routledge.

California Department of Education (1986). *Handbook for teaching Pilipino-speaking students*. Sacramento, CA: California Department of Education.

Card, J. (1978). Correspondence of data gathered from husband and wife: Implications for family planning studies. *Social Biology* 25 (3): 196-204.

Carson, A. L. (1978). *The story of Philippine education*. Quezon City, Philippines: New Day.

Chan, S. (1992). Families with Pilipino roots. In E. W. Lynch & M. J. Hanson (Eds.), *Developing cross-cultural competence* (pp. 259-300). Baltimore: Paul H. Brookes.

Chattergy, V. (1992). Bridging two worlds: The teacher and the immigrant Filipino student. *The Kamehameha Journal of Education* 3 (2): 23-28.

Chiu, L. H. (1972). A crosscultural comparison of cognitive styles of Chinese and American children. *International Journal of Psychology* 7 (4): 235-242.

Church, A. T. (1986). *Filipino personality: A review of research and writings*. Manila, Philippines: De La Salle University Press.

Cole, M., & Means, B. (1981). *Comparative study of how people think: An introduction*. Cambridge, MA: Harvard University Press.

Cordova, F. (1983). The Filipino American: There's always an identity crisis. In S. Sue & N. N. Wagner (Eds.), *Asian-Americans: Psychological perspectives* (pp. 136-139). Palo Alto, CA: Science and Behavior Books.

Cordova, J. M. T., Cordova, F., & Cordova, D. L. (1997)). Filipino American experiences. In *Unfamiliar partners: Asian parents and U.S. public schools*. National Coalition of Advocates for Students report. Boston: National Coalition of Advocates for Students.

Cortes, J. R. (1980). The Philippines. In T. N. Postlewaite & R. M. Thomas (Eds.), *Schooling in the ASEAN region: Indonesia, Malaysia, the Philippines, Singapore, Thailand*. New York: Pergamon Press.

Dar, R. (1983). *Language usage among multilingual Filipino high school students*. Doctoral dissertation, University of San Francisco.

De La Torre, V. (1992). *The Filipino child: Images and insights*. Makati, Philippines: Tower Book House.

Elliott, D. (1996). The newest Asian tiger: The Philippines is learning, at last, how to prosper without depending on the United States. *Newsweek*, December 2, p. 45.

Fermin, P. (1991). *A descriptive analysis of the cognitive style(s) of selected Filipino immigrant children at the Filipino Education Center*. Doctoral dissertation, University of San Francisco.

Galang, R. (1988). The language situation of Filipino-Americans. In S. L. McKay & S. C. Wong (Eds.), *Language diversity, problem or resource* (pp. 229-251). San Francisco: Newbury House.

Ginsburg, H. (1978). Poor children, African mathematics, and the problem of schooling. *Educational Research Quarterly* 2 (4): 26-44.

Gonzalez, A., & Sibayan, B. (1988). *Evaluating bilingual education in the Philippines*. Manila, Philippines: Linguistic Society of the Philippines.

Guthrie, G. M., & Jacobs, P. J. (1967). *Child rearing and personality development in the Philippines*. Manila, Philippines: Bookmark.

Halverson, C. (1979). Individual and cultural determinants of self-directed learning ability: Straddling an instructional dilemma. In D. Delia-Dora & L. Blanchard (Eds.), *Moving towards self-directed learning* (pp. 53-65). Alexandria, VA: Association for Supervision and Curriculum Development.

Hansen, J. (1979). *Sociocultural perspectives on human learning*. Prospect Heights, IL: Waveland Press.

Heras, P., & Revilla, L. A. (1994). Acculturation, generational status, and family environment of Pilipino Americans: A study of cultural adaptation. *Family Therapy* 21 (2): 129-138.

Ingham, J. & Price G. E. (1993). The learning styles of gifted adolescents in the Philippines. In R. M. Milgram, R. Dunn, & G. E. Price (Eds.), *Teaching and counseling gifted and talented adolescents: An international learning style perspective*. Westport, CT: Praeger.

Jocano, F. L. (1972). Filipino social structure and value system. *Silliman Journal* 19 (1): 59-77.

Juarez, L. (1997). *Attitudes of Filipino parents in the United States towards bilingual education*. Doctoral dissertation, University of San Francisco.

Karnow, S. (1989). *In our image: America's empire in the Philippines*. New York: Random House.

Koretz, G. (1996). Asia's 'sick man' is thriving. *Business Week*, September 30, p. 200.

Lau, A. (1995). For Filipino girls who have considered suicide. *Filipinas* 4 (September): 39-40.

Lancy, D. F. (1983). *Cross cultural studies in cognition and mathematics*. New York: Academic Press.

Litton, E. F. (1994). *Effective learning strategies for private elementary school Filipino American and European American children: Personal perspectives*. Doctoral dissertation, University of San Francisco.

Macaranas, F. M. (1983). Socioeconomic issues affecting the education of minority groups: The case of Filipino Americans. In D. T. Nakanishi & M. Hirano-Nakanishi

(Eds.), *The education of Asian and Pacific Americans: Historical perspectives and prescriptions for the future* (pp. 65-102). Phoenix, AZ: Oryx Press.

Manuel, M. C. Z. (1989). *A participatory study of the attitudes of Filipino parents and their children toward the use of Filipino in school and at home*. Doctoral dissertation, University of San Francisco.

Matsouka, J. K., & Ryujin, D. H. (1991). Asian American immigrants: A comparison of the Chinese, Japanese and Filipinos. *Journal of Sociology and Social Welfare* 18, (3): 123-133.

Marquez, C. C. (1995). A call to action. *Filipinas* 4 (September): 41.

Mayberry, J. (1990). *Filipinos*. New York: Franklin Watts.

McLeod, J. (1975). *The Filipino family*. Paper presented at the Philippine cultural workshop sponsored by the Girl Scouts of America in San Francisco, California.

McLeod, R. G. (1993). High population of Filipinos in the Bay Area. *San Francisco Chronicle,* February 10, p. A18.

Mendez, P. P., & Jocano, F. L. (1974). *The Filipino family in its rural and urban orientation: Two case studies*. Manila, Philippines: Centro Escolar University Research and Development Center.

Mendez, P. P., Jocano, F. L., Rolda, R.S., & Matela, S. B. (1984). *The Filipino family in transition*. Manila, Philippines: Centro Escolar University Research and Development Center.

Nolen, S. B., Meece, J., & Blumenfeld, P. (1986, April). *Development of a scale to assess students' knowledge of the utility of learning strategies*. Paper presented at the annual meeting of the American Educational Research Association, San Francisco.

Palma, J, (1997). Personal communication with the author, dated June 18.

Panopio, I. S., Cordero, F. V., & Raymundo, A. A. (1978). *General sociology: Focus on the Philippines*. Quezon City, Philippines: Ken Incorporated.

Park, C. C. (1997). Learning style preferences of Asian American (Chinese, Filipino, Korean and Vietnamese) students in secondary schools. *Equity and Exellence in Education* 30 (2): 68-77.

Ponce, D. E. (1980). Introduction: The Philippine background. In J. F. McDermott, Jr., W. Tseng, & T. W. Maretzki (Eds.), *People and cultures of Hawaii: A psycho-cultural profile* Honolulu: John A. Burns School of Medicine and the University Press of Hawaii.

Ramirez III, M., & Castaneda, A. (1974). *Cultural democracy, bicognitive development, and education*. New York: Academic Press.

Ronquillo, A. A., Peralta, A. M .R., Ramos, M . M., Salcedo, L. L., Zaide, Jr., C. A., & Espiritu, S. C. (1989). *Social issues and problems: The implications to Philippine national development*. Quezon City, Philippines: Katha.

Salazar, N. (1997). Personal correspondence with the author, dated June 24.

Sanyan, B. C., Perfecto, W. S., & Arcelo, A. A. (1981). *Higher education and the labor market in the Philippines*. New Delhi, India: Wiley Eastern.

Sibayan, B. P., Gonzalez, A., Arong, J., Otanes, F. T., & Moortgat, L. (1988) Measuring achievement and its factors after eleven years of bilingual schooling (1974-1985). In B. P. Sibayan & A. Gonzalez (Eds.), *Evaluating bilingual education in the Philippines (1974-1985)* (pp. 5-61). Manila, Philippines: Linguistic Society of the Philippines.

Sevilla, J. C. (1982). *Research on the Filipino family: Review and prospects*. Manila, Philippines: Development Academy of the Philippines.

Sevilla, J. C. (1988). Level of awareness of the bilingual education policy among parents and among government and non-government organizations. In B. P. Sibayan & A.

Gonzalez (Eds.), *Evaluating bilingual education in the Philippines (1974-1985)* (pp. 99-130). Manila, Philippines: Linguistic Society of the Philippines.

Stern, J. (1989). *The Filipino Americans*. New York: Chelsea House.

Strobel, E. F. M. (1996). *Coming full circle: The process of decolonization among post-1965 Filipino Americans*. Doctoral dissertation, University of San Francisco.

Takaki, R. (1989). *Strangers from a different shore: A history of Asian Americans*. New York: Penguin.

Trueba, H. T., Cheng, L., & Ima, K. (1993). *Myth or reality: Adaptive strategies of Asian Americans in California*. Washington, DC: Falmer Press.

Wagner, N. N. (1973). Filipinos: A minority within a minority. In S. Sue & N. N. Wagner (Eds.), *Asian Americans, Psychological perspectives* (pp. 295-298). Palo Alto, CA: Science and Behavior Books.

Yalung, F. N. (1992). *A cross-cultural counseling framework for Asian parents of children with special needs based on the dynamics of the Filipino family*. Master's thesis, San Jose State University.

CHAPTER 8

Promoting Educational Success for Filipino-American Students: A Linguistic Perspective

Rosita G. Galang

INTRODUCTION

Filipino-Americans, the second largest subgroup of the fastest growing Asian-American group (O'Hare & Felt, 1991), are a diverse population. This subgroup includes immigrants from the Philippines and American-born or naturalized American citizens who are of Filipino ancestry or mixed parentage such as the American Indian Filipinos, Mexican Filipino-Americans, and Chinese Filipino-Americans. It is therefore a myth that Filipino-Americans are only those who were born in the Philippines and came here as immigrants, sojourners, exiles, or expatriates. Like other Asian-Americans, their diversity is a result of differences not only in their immigration history and experience, but also in their regions of origin as well as linguistic, educational, religious, and socioeconomic backgrounds.

The majority of Filipino immigrants grew up in the Philippine society with values different from those held by U.S. society. Many born in the United States grow up in a cohesive Filipino-American community which has a strong sense of belonging to a unique group sharing a certain set of values similar to those held by immigrants. Thus, there are Philippine-born and American-born Filipino-Americans who may be in search of Filipino or American identity and oftentimes are torn between two legacies, the Filipino and the American history, language, and culture. These two groups should be considered when discussing the education of Filipino-Americans.

In this chapter, the linguistic perspective on the education of Filipino-American students is presented in five main areas: (1) linguistic backgrounds of Filipino-American students, (2) their implications for instruction in English, (3) contrastive description of Filipino and English, (4) possible difficulties of Filipino-American learners of English, and (5) strategies and suggestions for English language development.

LINGUISTIC BACKGROUNDS OF FILIPINO-AMERICAN STUDENTS

Diversity of Language Backgrounds

An understanding of the complex language situation in the Philippines is a prerequisite to understanding the linguistic backgrounds of Filipino-American students. There are about 100-150 Austronesian or Malayo-Polynesian languages spoken in the Philippines which consists of approximately 7, 200 islands and islets off the southeast coast of mainland China. Rugged mountain ranges and an array of rivers on the larger islands tend to isolate the population, resulting in linguistic diversity (Llamzon, 1978).

Although there is no agreement among authorities regarding the exact number of Austronesian languages spoken in the Philippines, there is consensus on the eight indigenous languages designated as major languages because they are spoken natively by the eight largest ethnic groups in the country. According to the 1970 census of the Philippines, more than 90% of the population were speakers of these major languages, which can be further broken down into several dialects (Llamzon, 1978). There are also substantial numbers of speakers of Chinese and Arabic (Kaplan, 1982). Table 8.1 shows the number of speakers of the eight major languages (National Statistics Office, 1990).

Five of the major languages (Tagalog, Ilocano, Bicol, Pampango, Pangasinan) are spoken mainly in Luzon, the northern island; the remaining three are spoken in the Visayas, the central islands; and on the northern part of Mindanao, the southern island of the Philippines.

The language history of the Philippines is marked by changing language policies. Although the Spanish colonizers (1565-1898) encouraged the Filipinos to adopt Christianity and give up their religion, they allowed them to retain their languages and encouraged but did not compel them to learn Spanish. After 1688, the policy of encouragement changed to that of obligation, but the policy met with obstacles and was not successfully implemented (Phelan, in Llamzon, 1978). The Spanish missionaries used the mother tongues of the Filipino population for evangelistic purposes. Access to Spanish was limited to native elites, so that in the 1870 census only 2.4 % of the 4.7 million Filipinos spoke Spanish. However, Spanish remained an official language even through the American period, up to 1935 (Gonzalez, 1980).

Table 8.1
Native Speakers of the Eight Major Languages of the Philippines

Language	No. of Speakers	Population (%)
Tagalog	16,910,458	27.9
Cebuano	14,709,844	24.3
Ilocano	5,923,514	9.8
Hiligaynon	5,647,067	9.3
Bicol	3,518,161	5.8
Waray	2,433,180	4.0
Pampango	1,897,319	3.1
Pangasinan	1,164,267	1.9

When the United States took over the Philippines from Spain (1898-1946), English became the common means of communication and was added to Spanish as an official language (Beebe & Beebe, 1981; Sibayan & Gonzalez, 1990). On September 1, 1898, English was introduced as the language of instruction in the Philippines by American soldiers in seven elementary schools in Manila. In 1901 the Americans officially established the public school system, and in 1902 the first boatload of school teachers called the "Thomasites" arrived and started mass education in English (Llamzon, 1978; Sibayan & Gonzalez, 1990). While the 1935 Constitution of the Philippines provided that the law-making body of the country should take steps toward the development of a common national language based on one of the Philippine languages, the Tydings McDuffy Act provided that during the Commonwealth period (1935-1945) an adequate system of public schools be established, maintained, and conducted primarily in English (Sibayan & Gonzalez, 1990). English gradually replaced Spanish in influence so that according to the 1939 Census, more than 26.6 % of the 16 million Filipinos spoke English (Gonzalez, 1980).

On December 5, 1939, Secretary of Public Instruction Jorge Bocobo ordered that the native languages which were barred from the schools would be used as auxiliary media of instruction in grades one and two when the child could not understand what was being taught in English. From 1940, the national language based on Tagalog was taught in the schools (Sibayan & Gonzalez, 1990).

The Japanese forces of occupation (1941-1945) realized the importance of language in the fight against the United States. They took steps to downgrade the teaching of English and encouraged the use of Tagalog in schools and in government. To further replace English, classes in Nippongo were organized for government officials (Sibayan & Gonzalez, 1990).

The tension of competing languages gave rise to various social conflicts, as exemplified in historical controversies over the national language question. The search for a national identity that arose during the Spanish rule in the nineteenth century and continued during the American regime in the twentieth century is closely tied to the need for an indigenous national language.

The name of the national language has evolved from Tagalog or Tagalog-based to Pilipino to Filipino. *Tagalog* was proclaimed as the basis of the national language by President Manuel Quezon in 1939. In 1940 it was declared by the Commonwealth Act to be one of the official languages from July 4, 1946. Tagalog, although only second to Cebuano in the number of speakers, was spoken in the Greater Manila area and was considered by many to be the most studied and highly developed indigenous language. The regional connotations of the term Tagalog and the purist tendencies of the propagators of the national language most likely delayed its acceptance.

The Tagalog-based national language was renamed Pilipino by Secretary of Education Jose Romero in 1959 (Bautista, 1996), in order to free the national language of its ties with a particular ethnic group and to provide the language with the properties of a national symbol. The continuing opposition to Pilipino was evidenced in the constitution in 1973, which provided that "the National Assembly shall take steps toward the development and formal adoption of a common national language to be known as Filipino. Until otherwise provided by law, English and Pilipino shall be the official languages" (Juco, 1977, p. 10). The Philippine Constitution of 1987 declared Filipino the national language and stated that "as it evolves, it shall be further developed and enriched on the basis of existing Philippine and other languages" (Nolledo, 1992, p. 53).

From 1901 to 1956, English was used as the sole medium of instruction in all schools. From 1957 to 1974, the Board of National Education mandated the use of the vernacular[1] as the medium of instruction, the introduction of English and Pilipino as subjects in grades one and two, and the use of English as the language of instruction and Pilipino as an auxiliary medium from the third grade up to high school. This vernacular policy, however, was rigidly implemented only in public schools. Many elite private schools continued using English as the teaching medium from the first grade (Otanes, 1974).

In 1974, the Department of Education and Culture promulgated guidelines for the implementation of the bilingual education policy with the purpose of developing a bilingual nation competent in Pilipino and English. Bilingual education was defined as "the separate use of Pilipino and English as media of instruction in definite subject areas, provided that additionally Arabic shall be used where it is necessary." According to this policy, Pilipino was to be used as the medium of instruction in social studies or social science, character education, work education, health education, and physical education. English was to be used to teach science, math, and English communication arts.

The Bilingual Education Policy enacted by the Department of Education, Culture, and Sports (1987) essentially had the same provisions as the earlier policy enacted by the Department of Education and Culture (1974) except for the following: use of the regional languages (referring to the eight major vernaculars) as auxiliary media of instruction and as initial languages for literacy where needed; task of tertiary level institutions to lead in the continuing intellectualization of Filipino; funds for policy implementation; and a more flexible timeline.

The present language situation in the Philippines presents a dilemma for Filipinos. On the one hand, the imperatives of nationalism demand that Filipino, the national language, be developed not only as a national lingua franca[2] but also as the language of education and scholarly discourse. The trend of its dissemination indicates quite clearly its rapid expansion as the national lingua franca across the archipelago and its expanding use in the domains of Philippine life (Gonzalez, 1988).

However, other considerations dictate the desirability of maintaining English at least for a smaller, but perhaps significant portion of the population. With nearly two million Filipinos abroad and with the Philippine Overseas Employment Administration sending more workers annually because of population growth and unemployment or underemployment in the country, Filipinos need competence in English for employability. Skills in the English language are needed in order to maintain business and international relations, attract local investments, and encourage the transfer of regional offices in other Southeast Asian countries to Manila rather than Hong Kong or Singapore. At present, access to science and technology for Filipinos is possible only through English, which makes knowledge from the West available in the language at an advanced level (Gonzalez, 1988).

Surveys have indicated that among Filipino parents, teachers, government and nongovernment workers, and school administrators, the language of schooling is not equated with nationalism. An instructional scheme which uses both English and Filipino continues to be the majority choice and the choice of the Tagalog-based Pilipino/Filipino is no longer a divisive issue. However, there is now a generation of Filipinos conversant in Filipino, but unable to communicate in English, even after six years of English, math, and science instruction (Gonzalez, 1988).

The National Language: Tagalog, Pilipino, Filipino

The terms *Tagalog*, *Pilipino*, and *Filipino*, which refer to the national language of the Philippines and are often used loosely in the United States, sometimes create confusion among those unfamiliar with the history of the Filipino language (Galang, 1988). Tagalog is the indigenous Austronesian language on which the national language is based. The Tagalog-based national language was officially termed Pilipino in 1959. Pilipino is basically Tagalog enriched with officially recognized words borrowed primarily from English, Spanish, and Chinese; coinages; and revived words which have had differential success in popular usage. Many Filipinos did not perceive differences between Tagalog and Pilipino (Sibayan, 1975), but in fact language planners have exerted conscious efforts to modify the regional language (e.g., by borrowing) to fulfill all the functions of a modern, national language, such as the transfer of scientific and technological information (Beebe & Beebe, 1981; Gonzalez, 1980; Laygo, 1977). Increased use of Pilipino in the schools and mass media has led to the development of regional varieties of the national language which can no longer be identified as the language spoken in the Greater Manila area.

Filipino, the approved national language of the Philippines since the ratification of the 1987 Constitution (Gonzalez, 1996; Nolledo, 1992), is Tagalog-based Pilipino enriched with lexical items from the indigenous and other languages spoken in the Philippines (Gonzalez, 1988). Filipino was predicted to be spoken as a first or second language by at least 82 % of the population by the year 2000 because of its increasing use by the mass media (Gonzalez, 1974). In the remainder of this chapter, Filipino is used to refer to the primary language of many Filipino-American students (whether it is Tagalog, Pilipino, or Filipino). In the absence of an official or published Filipino grammar book (Cruz, 1990), Tagalog and Pilipino grammar books are used as references for the description of Filipino.

Proficiency in the Vernacular, Filipino, and English

Filipino immigrant students have different language backgrounds and different degrees of exposure to the vernacular, Filipino, and English and therefore demonstrate different levels of proficiency in these languages.

Depending on their region of origin in the Philippines, immigrant Filipinos speak natively at least one of the several mutually unintelligible indigenous languages. Students' exposure to Filipino and English may differ depending on their region of origin, socioeconomic status, and educational experience. Typically, students from a high socioeconomic stratum or with private school experience have had greater exposure to English, while those students from a lower socioeconomic stratum or with public school experience are likely to have had greater exposure to Filipino. Furthermore, students from the Greater Manila area most likely have received more exposure to both Filipino and English, since in that area there is greater access to newspapers, radio and television programs, and movies in the two languages.

Similarly, American-born Filipinos may differ in their degrees of exposure to and levels of proficiency in the vernacular, Filipino, and English. Although they may grow up in an English-speaking society, their exposure to the vernacular, Filipino, and English differs according to the linguistic, educational, and socioeconomic backgrounds of their families and friends.

IMPLICATIONS FOR INSTRUCTION IN ENGLISH

Considering the diversity of the linguistic backgrounds of Filipino-American students, assessment of their proficiency in the vernacular, Filipino, and English is necessary in order to identify their linguistic and other educational needs. Although Filipino immigrant children may have been exposed to Filipino at all levels of education, like English it remains a second language to those who come from non-Filipino-speaking regions. Therefore, the focus of instruction in Filipino and English, at least initially, should be on basic interpersonal communication skills (BICS).

Filipino-American students need to be exposed to English in language-rich environments at home, in school, and in the community so that they may attain English fluency. Parents and teachers need to provide students with adequate exposure to English and monitor their progress. In this way, many students can receive enough comprehensible English input necessary for the acquisition of basic interpersonal communication skills. Generally, regardless of the school program, language minority students in the United States acquire basic interpersonal communication skills in English in two or three years (Cummins, 1994; Legarreta-Mercaida, 1981). It is common for Filipino children to speak English with some relatives, especially siblings, at home. Many youngsters often watch children's television programs such as *Sesame Street, Barney*, and cartoons, which are sources of comprehensible second-language input. If one parent has native-like proficiency in English, he or she may serve as an English-speaking model. It is probably wise for family members to maintain consistency as language models and avoid switching or mixing languages to promote optimal development in Filipino and English. If both parents speak Filipino, and proficient bilingualism is desired, they should consider speaking Filipino in the home because exposure to English is adequately available in school and other domains (Cummins, 1994).

Table 8.2
The Sounds of Filipino

Consonant Sounds					
	Labial	Dental	Palatal	Velar	Glottal
Stops, voiceless	p	t		k	
Stops, voiced	b	d		g	
Fricatives, voiceless			s		h
Nasals, voiced	m	n		ng	
Laterals, voiced		l			
Flap, voiced		r			
Semivowels, voiced	w		y		

Vowel Sounds and Diphthongs					
Front		Central		Back	
Vowels	Diphthongs	Vowels	Diphthongs	Vowels	Diphthon
High	I	iw			u	gs
Mid	e	ey			o	uy
Low			A	ay, aw		oy

Filipino students can be assisted in the acquisition of native-like communication skills in English through the following: (1) ESL classes which are communicative-based (Terrell, 1981), (2) specially designed academic instruction delivered in English (SDAIE) classes (formerly known as subject matter classes delivered under special sheltered English conditions), and (3) interaction with peers who are native speakers of English on the playground, in the halls, during assemblies, on field trips, and in regular classes (California Department of Education, 1986).

CONTRASTIVE DESCRIPTION OF FILIPINO AND ENGLISH

Phonology

Table 8.2 presents an inventory of the sounds of Filipino: sixteen consonants, five vowels, and six diphthongs (Ramos & Ceña, 1990).

The differences between the vowel sounds of Filipino and English are nmore complex than the differences between their consonant sounds. Comparing the sounds of the two languages, Hemphill (1962) cites the following:

1. There are sounds in English which are absent in Filipino.

Examples: /f/, /v/, /z/, /sh/, /zh/, /th/, /dh/, /æ/, /ch/, /j/

2. There are sounds in Filipino which are comparable to but different from certain sounds in English, so that there is some difficulty recognizing such sounds.

Examples: /l/, /r/, /t/, /d/, /n/, /s/

Ramos (1971) cites other differences in the sounds of Filipino and English:

1. The sounds /p/, /t/, and /k/ are never aspirated or produced with a puff of air in Filipino but are aspirated in initial positions in stressed syllables in English.

Examples:

Filipino		English
puri	'praise'	pencil
matalas	'sharp'	baton
keso	'cheese'	castle

2. The velar nasal /ng/, though present in both systems, occurs in all positions in Filipino: initial, medial, and final; but occurs only in medial and final positions in English.

Examples:

Position	Filipino		English
Initial	*ngipin*	'tooth/teeth'	___
Medial	*panga*	'jaw'	*singer*
Final	*gulong*	'wheel'	*ceiling*

3. The glottal stop, represented in this chapter by the symbol ('), is produced when the glottis is closed, thus stopping the passage of air from the lungs. Although this sound is present in both languages, it is distinctive only in Filipino, and not in English. The glottal stop, though not represented in writing, distinguishes minimal pairs in Filipino.

Examples:

basa	/basa'/	'wet'
basa	/basa/	'read'
baga	/baga'/	'lung'
baga	/baga/	'live coal'

Other differences between the sounds of Filipino and English are less significant.

1. The Filipino /r/ is produced by rapping the tongue against the upper gum ridge, but the English /r/ is produced by curling up the tongue so that it does not touch the roof of the mouth.
2. The Filipino /l/ is pronounced with the tongue relatively straight and flat from the tip to the back, but the English /l/ is produced by having the tongue form a hollow from which sides the air flows.
3. In Filipino, /t/, /d/, /n/, and /s/ are produced with the tongue tip at the back of the upper teeth but in English they are produced with the tongue behind the upper gum ridge.

Morphology

According to Ramos and de Guzman (1971), these morphological features of Filipino are not present in English:

1. Filipino has a complex system of affixation. Most words consist of roots and affixes which determine their meaning. The roots are substantive, verbal, and adjectival in meaning, and the affixes show aspect, focus, and mode. For example, the root *aral* 'study' denotes different meanings, depending on the affix added.

mag-*aral*	(v.)	'to study'
mangaral	(v.)	'to preach'
makaaral(v.)	'to be able to study'	
makiaral (v.)	'to join in studying'	
palaaral	(adj.)	'fond of studying'

| *aralan* | (n.) | 'place for studying' |
| *aralin* | (n.) | 'lesson' |

2. Almost any root in Filipino may be transformed into a verb by affixation.

Examples:

malinaw	(adj.)	'clear'
linawin	(v.)	'to clarify'
walis	(n.)	'broom'
magwalis	(v.)	'to sweep (the floor)'
tapat	(adj.)	'faithful/sincere'
magtapat	(v.)	'to confess'

3. Reduplication is used extensively in Filipino to show plurality, intensity, and uncompleted action and so on. Note how words or parts of words are repeated to signal different meanings in Filipino.

apat	'four'
apat apat	'by fours'
aapat	'only four'
aapat apat	'the only four' (intensified)

| *makulay* | 'colorful' |
| *maku**kula**y* | 'colorful' (plural) |

sayaw	'dance'
sasayaw	'will dance' (uncompleted action)
sumasayaw	'dancing' (uncompleted action)

Syntax

Below are key syntactic differences between Filipino and English (Ramos & de Guzman, 1971; Schachter & Otanes, 1972):

1. The normal word order of basic sentences in Filipino (i.e., predicate/comment followed by subject/topic) is the reverse of the normal word order in English (i.e., subject followed by predicate).

Examples:
Basic Filipino Sentences

Predicate	Subject
Masarap	*ang pagkain.*
delicious	the food

'The food is delicious.'

| *Nagalit* | *ang nanay* | *sa bata.* |
| got mad | the mother | at child |

'The mother got mad at the child.'

| *Manghuhula* | *ang babae.* |
| fortune teller | the woman |

'The woman is a fortune teller.'

Basic English Sentences

Subject	Predicate
The knife	is sharp.
The students	are taking the test.

There is of course an alternate word order in Filipino similar to the normal word order in English, but it is somewhat formal, less common, and is used to emphasize the first element of the construction. The inversion marker *ay* is also used in sentences in the reverse order. Note how the simple sentences in the normal order above are converted to the reverse word order.

Ang pagkain	*ay*	*masarap.*	
the food	inversion marker	delicious	
'The food is delicious.'			

Ang nanay	*ay*	*nagalit*	*sa bata.*
the mother	inversion marker	got mad	at child
'The mother got mad at the child.'			

Ang babae	*ay*	*manghuhula.*	
the woman	inversion marker	fortune teller	
'The woman is a fortune teller.'			

2. English predicates always include a verb, while Filipino predicates need not.

Examples:

	Predicate/Comment without a Verb	Subject/Topic
Nominal	*Inhinyero*	*siya.*
	Engineer	he/she
	'He/She is an engineer.'	
Prepositional	*Sa New York*	*ang palabas.*
	In New York	the show
	'The show will be in New York.'	
Adverbial	*Bukas*	*ang eleksiyon.*
	Tomorrow	the election
	'The election will be held tomorrow.'	

3. As the above sentences show, there is no equivalent of the linking verb *be* in Filipino. The particle *ay,* which appears to be equivalent to is/are in the English translation of the Filipino sentences, is really a marker for their reverse order.

4. *Focus,* a distinctive feature of Filipino, is a feature of a verbal predicate that indicates on the surface the semantic relationship between a predicate verb and its topic. This feature of verbal predicates is associated with the verbal affix. For example, certain affixes form verbs that occur with topics that express the performer/actor (actor focus) or object (object focus) of the action. Focus is similar to, but not exactly the same, as the active-passive distinction in English. In English, the verb form changes to indicate active or passive voice. In Filipino, the verb form changes to indicate the different focuses, which are all translated as passive voice in English. The verbal affixes in the sentences below indicate, on the surface, different semantic relationships between the predicate verb and its subject/topic:

Relationship	Predicate Verb		Subject/Topic
Actor	*Bumili*	*ng laruan*	*ang Nanay.*

	bought toy	the mother
		(agent or actor)
	'The mother bought a toy.'	
Object	*Hiniwa ng kusinera*	*ang kamatis.*
	sliced the cook	the tomato
		(object)
	'The cook sliced the tomato.'	
Location	*Pinaglabahan ng ale*	*ang planggana.*
	washed in the woman	the basin
		(location)
	'The woman washed (clothes) in the basin.'	
Beneficiary	*Ipinagluto* niya	ang pasyente.
	cooked for he/she	the patient
		(beneficiary)
	'He/She cooked for the patient.'	
Instrument	*Ipinangsulat* ng bata	ang lapis.
	wrote with the child	the pencil
		(instrument)
	'The child wrote with the pencil.'	

Clearly, the topic in Filipino is not limited to the actor or object of the action, but may also apply to the location (locative focus), beneficiary (benefactive focus), or instrument (instrumental focus) of the action.

5. The Filipino verb system does not make true tense distinction like the English distinction between past and nonpast; but it does make aspect distinction like the English distinction between events viewed as completed or not completed, and if not completed, as begun or not begun. All Filipino verbs are inflectable for three aspects: perfective (begun and completed), imperfective (begun, but not completed), and contemplated (not begun, therefore not completed). Some verbs also occur as recent perfective (recently completed). In Filipino, the verb forms that mark these three aspects differ according to the affix of the basic form of the verb. However, certain features are quite consistently present. For example, (1) the sign of incompleteness (which characterizes both imperfective and contemplated aspects) is duplication: usually, the first consonant and first vowel of the verb base, and (2) the sign of events as having been begun (i.e., imperfective and perfective) is an affix that includes the phoneme /n/ (Schachter & Otanes, 1972).

Examples:

nagsulat	'wrote (letter, etc.)'	(begun as signaled by an affix with the phoneme /n/, and completed)
nagsusulat	'writing'	(begun as signaled by an affix with the phoneme /n/, but not completed as signaled by
		duplication of first consonant and first vowel of verb base)
magsusulat	'will write'	(not begun, therefore not completed as signaled
		by duplication of first consonant and first vowel
		of verb base)

6. Linkers or ligatures are used extensively in Filipino, but not in English, to connect

words, phrases, and sentences that are related to each other as modifier and modified. The forms of the major linker are *na* and *-ng*. *Na*, which occurs between the modifier and the modified or vice-versa, is used after consonants. *Ng* is attached to the first member of the construction when it ends in a vowel or *n*. When attached to a word ending in *n*, the *n* of *ng* is dropped.

Examples:

puting   *(puti+ng)*   *papel*
            white+linker   paper
'white paper'

siyam   **na**   *aklat*
nine   linker   book
'nine books'

mahabang   *(mahaba+ng)*   *tula*
             long +linker   poem
'long poem'

madilim **na**   *kuwarto*
dark   inker   room
'dark room'

7. Unlike English, Filipino does not indicate gender in its third person, singular pronouns. There is only one form of the personal pronoun for the third person singular.

Examples:

siya   'he/she'
niya   'him/her'
kaniya   'his/hers'

8. Personal pronouns in Filipino have different forms depending on the markers for the noun phrases they replace. For the sake of simplicity, only the *ang*-pronouns are discussed here. The *ang*-pronouns, which occur as predicates or topics of sentences in Filipino, are listed below.

	Nonplural Forms		Plural Forms	
First person	ako	'I'	kami	'we' (I and others)
Dual	kata	'we' (you and I)	tayo	'we' (you and I and others)
Second person	ikaw	'you'	kayo	'you' (you and others)
	ka	'you'		
Third person	siya	'he/she'	sila	'they' (he, she, and others)

The first person plural pronoun (used when the listener is excluded) and the dual person plural pronoun (used when the listener is included) illustrate the distinction between exclusive and inclusive pronouns, which is not marked in English.

9. Personal pronouns have nonplural and plural forms. The first group of pronouns is called nonplural rather than singular because it includes the dual, meaning literally 'you (singular) and I.' The plural pronouns have, as a group, the meanings of the corresponding nonplural pronouns with the additional meaning 'and others' (or 'and another'). Thus, the first person plural is literally 'I and others,' the dual plural 'you and I and others,' and so forth.

10. While in English the verb is always inflected for number, in Filipino, it is not. The same verb form may occur with both singular and plural nouns/pronouns.

Examples:

English Verb Forms	Filipino Verb Forms	
He/She **is** studying.	***Nag-aaral***	*siya*.
	studying	he/she
	'He/She is studying.'	
They **are** studying.	***Nag-aaral***	*sila*.
	studying	they
	'They are studying.'	

Semantics and Lexicon

The lexicon of Filipino, which consists of polysyllabic words made up of roots and affixes, has been enriched by extensive borrowing from foreign languages (especially Chinese, Spanish, and English) and other indigenous languages in the Philippines. Borrowed words are oftentimes pronounced to conform to the sound system of Filipino.

Examples:

Borrowed Words	Filipino Pronunciation
bag	/bag/
sandwich	/sandwits/
blackboard	/blakbord/
auditorium	/awditoryum/
bungalow	/bunggalo/
cebollas 'onion' (Spanish)	/sibuyas/
ventana 'window' (Spanish)	*/bintana'/*

Writing

Filipino is highly phonetic, having an almost one-to-one correspondence between letter and sound. Except for the glottal stop, every consonant and vowel sound is represented by one letter in the alphabet. The original twenty-letter Roman alphabet and the rules of orthography in Filipino, which were introduced by the Spaniards, were modified by the Institute of National Language (Department of Education and Culture, 1976; Komisyon sa Wikang Filipino, 1995) to respond to the need for modernization and to keep pace with the rapid developments and changes in the Filipino language brought on by the influx of linguistic elements from the different influencing languages, native as well as foreign. The alphabet and rules in orthography of Filipino were again revised (Kagawaran ng Edukasyon, Kultura, at Isports, 1987; Komisyon sa Wikang Filipino, 1995) (Table 8.3) in response to the (1) mandate of the 1987 Constitution regarding the further development and enrichment of Filipino as a national language; (2) guidelines of the 1987 Bilingual Education Policy; and (3) rapid changes, development, and propagation of the national language (Komisyon sa Wikang Filipino, 1995).

While the original twenty-letter Roman alphabet continues to be used with the Filipino words, the additional letters C, F, J, Ñ, Q, V, X, and Z are used in the following:

1. Proper nouns

Examples:
Exequiel (person)
Nueva Vizcaya (place)
Filipinas Hotel (building)
Japan Air Lines (transportation)

2. Technical words that may not be readily assimilated into Filipino because the pronunciation does not closely correspond to the spelling.

Examples:
chemistry
circuit
physics
quartz

Table 8.3
The 1987 Filipino Alphabet

Letters		Letter Names	Filipino Sounds
Capital	Small		
A	a	/ey/	/a/
B	b	/bi/	/b/
C*	c*	/si/	—
D	d	/di/	/d/
E	e	/i/	/e/
F*	f*	/ef/	—
G	g	/dzi/	/g/
H	h	/eyst/	/h/
I	i	/ay/	/i/
J*	j*	/dzey/	
K	k	/key/	/k/
L	l	/el/	/l/
M	m	/em/	/m/
N	n	/en/	/n/
Ñ*	ñ*	/enye/	—
NG	ng	/endzi/	/ng/
O	o	/o/	/o/
P	p	/pi/	/p/
Q*	q*	/kyu/	—
R	r	/ar/	/r/
S	s	/es/	/s/
T	t	/ti/	/t/
U	u	/yu/	/u/
V*	v*	/vi/	—
W	w	/dobolyu/	/w/
X*	x*	/eks/	—
Y	y	/way/	/y/
Z*	z*	/zi/	—

* Does not represent a Filipino sound and was not in the original twenty-letter Roman Filipino alphabet.

3. Words closely associated to the culture of the source language

Examples:
canao (ceremonial dance of the Igorot)
bon voyage
pizza
xylophone

Sociolinguistic Aspects

Language and culture are closely interrelated. Ways in which certain aspects of the Filipino culture are reflected in the Filipino language are discussed below.Courtesy or respect is highly valued by Filipinos. Linguistically, this is manifested in several ways including the following (Ramos, 1978):

1. The respect particle **po'** (or the less formal variant **ho'**) which is roughly equivalent to 'sir' or 'madame' is used for older people, one's superiors, or strangers.

Examples:
Magandang	*(maganda+ng)*	*umaga*	***po'.***
	beautiful+linker	morning	respect particle

'Good morning.sir/madame.'

Ano	***ho'***	*ang*	*kailanganniyo?*
what	respect particle	subject marker	need	you

'What do you need, sir/madame?'

2. The second and third person plural pronouns *kayo* 'you' plural and *sila* 'they' are used in place of the singular form.

Example:
Instead of the second person singular
Kumain	***ka***	*na*	*ba?*
have eaten	you	already	question marker

'Have you eaten yet?'
One of these two forms is used:

Second person plural
Kumainna	*na*	*po*	*ba*	***kayo?***
have eaten	already	respect particle	question marker	you
(plural)				

'Have you eaten yet?'

Third person plural
Kumain	*na*	*po*	*ba*	***sila?***
have eaten	already	respect particle	question marker	they

'Have you eaten yet?'

3. Kinship terms such as *kuya* and *ate* are used to refer to an older brother and sister.

Examples:
Sumali	*sa paligsahan*	*ang*	***ate***	*ko.*
joined	the contest	subject marker	older sister	my

'My older sister joined the contest.'

Kuya,	*umuwi*	*na*	*tayo.*
older brother	go home	already	we

'Let's go home.'

4. Titles such as *Mang, Aling, Doktor, Gobernador,* and so on are used to address an older man, an older woman, a doctor, and a governor, respectively.

Examples:

Aling	*Lorna*
title for an older woman	Lorna

'Lorna'

Mang	*Nestor*
title for an older man	Nestor

'Nestor'

POSSIBLE DIFFICULTIES OF FILIPINO-AMERICAN LEARNERS OF ENGLISH

Filipino-Americans, particularly the immigrants, may speak English with a Cebuano, Ilocano, Filipino, or Pangasinan accent, depending on what part of the Philippines they came from. The phonological, morphological, lexical, and syntactic differences between the structures of Filipino and English may partly explain some of the difficulties or problems Filipino-speaking students may have in learning or speaking English as a second language.

Pronunciation

1. Filipino-American students might have difficulties distinguishing or producing sounds in English which do not exist in Filipino, such as /ae/, /f/, /v/, /z/, and /th/. Thus, they tend to substitute the Filipino sounds /a/, /p/, /b/, /s/, and /t/ for the English sounds since they are the most similar Filipino counterpart sounds. For example, they might pronounce *hat, fail, vie, buzz,* and *thank* as *hot* /hat/, *pail* /peyl/, *buy* /bay/, *bus* /bas/, and *tank* /tank/.
2. Certain consonant clusters in English such as *sk, st,* and *sp* do not occur in Filipino without a vowel preceding it. A Filipino speaker might pronounce *school, stop,* and *spill* as /iskul/, /istap/, and /ispil/ instead of /skul/, /stap/, and /spl/.
3. There are sounds in both languages that are roughly similar but different in some relatively minor way such as in the point or manner of articulation. For example, the English /p/ is aspirated when it occurs as the initial sound of a stressed syllable, but the Filipino /p/ is never aspirated. Use of the unaspirated /p/ not only causes speech to be perceived as having an 'accent,' but might also cause confusion because phonemic boundaries are obscured. An unaspirated /p/ where one expects aspiration may sound more like a /b/ to an English speaker who may hear *pill* as *bill.*
4. Distinctive sounds in English may be nondistinctive variations of a single sound in the Filipino language.

For example, /U/ and /u/ are distinctive in English but not in Filipino. Consequently, Filipino speakers may not only find it difficult to distinguish the two sounds, but may use the sounds inappropriately.

Examples:

English Pronunciation	Filipino Student's Possible Pronunciation
full /ful/	/pUl/ or /pul/
stewed /stud/	/istud/ or /istUd/

5. Similarly, distinctive sounds such as /i/ and /e/ which are never interchangeable in English may be interchangeable in the final position in Filipino. For example, *babae* 'woman' may be pronounced as /*babae*/ or /*babai*/ without changing the meaning in Filipino. A Filipino speaker who is used to ignoring the differences between these two sounds may not easily recognize the difference between the vowel sounds in *bid* and *bed*.
6. In Filipino, length prominence is a primary indicator of stress. A Filipino-American student might use length, instead of pitch and volume, to indicate stress on the stressed syllables of English words.

Grammar

1. Plurality is signaled in English by the morpheme 's' or its variants, as in *plates*, *clothes*, and *children*. In Filipino this is indicated by the word ***mga*** placed before the word to be pluralized or by another word carrying the idea of plural.

Examples:

mga   *lapis*
plural marker   pencil
'pencils'

dalawang   *(dalawa+ng)*   *lapis*
               two+linker   pencil
'two pencils'

maraming   *(marami+ng)*   *lapis*
               many+linker   pencil
'many pencils'

Thus, if the Filipino speaker thinks of English in terms of a Filipino sentence like

Kami	*ay*	*mga*	*dayuhan.*
We	inversion marker	plural marker	foreigner

'We are foreigners.'

he may say

We are **foreigner**.

following the Filipino pattern where plurality is indicated only by the word ***mga*** with the noun not changing in form.

Similarly he might say

You have few **enemy**.

if he thinks in terms of the Filipino sentence

Ikaw	*ay*	*may*	*konting*	*kaaway.*
you	inversion marker	have	few	enemy

'You have few enemies.'

where plurality is indicated only by the word *konting* 'few.'

2. Filipino has only aspect while English has both aspect and tense. Consequently, a Filipino speaker may have difficulty producing the correct verb forms to describe

actions that take place at several times.

She might say

Mother is cooking everyday.

Mother is cooking when I got home.

instead of

Mother cooks everyday.

Mother was cooking when I got home.

since in Filipino there is only one form (imperfective) for both the general present and the present progressive.

Examples:

Nagluluto	*ang*	*Nanay*	*araw-araw.* (imperfective)
cooking	subject marker	mother	everyday

'Mother cooks every day.'

Nagluluto	*ang*	*Nanay*	*ngayon.* (imperfective)
cooking	subject marker	mother	now

'Mother is cooking now.'

Nagluluto	*ang*	*Nanay*	*nang dumating*	*ako*	*sa bahay.* (imperfective)
cooking	subject marker	mother	when arrived	I	at home.

'Mother was cooking when I got home.'

3. The Filipino pronoun *siya,* which refers to the person being spoken about, is equivalent to the two English forms *he* and *she.* The Filipino speaker learning English may mix *he* and *she* and fail to use the appropriate form because in Filipino the same form is used for both.
4. The misuse of *is* and *was* by a Filipino speaker might be attributed to the absence of tense and the linking verb *be* in the native language.
5. In Filipino, there are two alternate forms of the tag question: *hindi ba 'isn't it?'* (reduced to *di ba* in rapid speech) or *ano* 'what/huh.' Consequently, Filipino speakers tend to use *isn't it or huh* in English tag questions regardless of the form of the verb.

Examples:

You play the piano, isn't it?

They are naturalized citizens, isn't it?

You dance the tango, huh?

They're graceful dancers, huh?

Vocabulary

The large-scale borrowing from Spanish and English into Filipino has resulted in lexical interference of various kinds (Goulet, 1971), such as the use of false cognates. Though some cognates have the same range of meaning and can fit into similar frames, their patterns of distribution often are not exactly alike. An incomplete knowledge of the range of meanings and patterns of distribution of cognates often leads the Filipino speaker to construct sentences that are either amusing or incomprehensible to native speakers of English and Spanish. An example is the Spanish *molestar* meaning *'to* worry, vex, disturb, annoy, tease' interpreted in English as *molest 'to* interfere' so as 'to injure, disturb.' Thus, the sentence *Lagi akong minumulestiya ng mga estudyante ko kahi't marami akong trabaho* is often translated as 'My students often molest me even when I'm busy,' instead of 'My students often disturb me even when I'm busy.'

Other examples of Filipino English may be explained by the inappropriate use of certain English words. For instance, *dumaan,* 'to pass,' has different meanings in Filipino: 'to go by, pass by, pick up, stop for, go.' Thus, a Filipino-American may use 'pass' in situations where a native speaker of English will not.

Examples:

Filipino English	American English
1. I'll pass for you at seven.	I'll pick you up at seven.
2. I'll pass Tokyo.	I'll go via Tokyo.
3. I'll pass by the library and borrow a book.	I'll stop by the library and borrow a book.

Another word that is used inappropriately in various situations is *bumaba,* 'to go down,' which may mean 'get out of' or 'get off' in Filipino.

Examples:

Filipino English	American English
1. He got down the cab in a hurry.	He got out of the cab in a hurry.
2. How can we go down the bus?	How can we get off the bus?

Other awkward Filipino English utterances may result from the use of a word for word translation of a Filipino idiom in English such as:

1. 'oiled him/her' which is a translation of
   linangisan   *siya*
   oiled   him/her
   'buttered him/her up'
2. 'His watch is dead' which is a translation of
   Patay   *ang*   *kaniyang relo.*
   dead   subject marker   his/her   watch
   'His watch stopped.'
3. 'Kill the light' which is a translation of
   Patayin   mo   ang   ilaw.
   Kill   you   the   light
   '(You) Turn off the light.'

Spelling and Writing

Filipino has many words borrowed from English. These words may have retained their spelling or may have been respelled to conform to the Filipino alphabet. This may present difficulties to Filipino speakers learning to write in English.

Used to a highly phonetic language like Filipino, Filipino students may spell English words observing an almost one-to-one correspondence between letter and sound. This is even a bigger problem when the English word contains sounds not present in Filipino which may lead the Filipino speaker to substitute the most similar sounds in Filipino.

Examples:
Filipino Student's Possible Spelling
football	*putbol*
vague	*beyg*
school	*iskul*
volume	*bolyum*

Sociolinguistic Aspects

The importance of respect in the Filipino culture might lead Filipino learners of English to punctuate sentences with 'sir' or 'madame' which are the equivalent of the respect particle in Filipino. An overabundance of the translations of this respect particle, which often characterizes a Filipino-American's English speech, gives the impression of extreme humility and, in the American context, may be considered superfluous.

Social conventions in Filipino, when taken literally in English, may lead to misunderstandings. For example, a Filipino speaker might ask 'nosy' questions such as, 'Where are you going?' and 'Did you go to school/work?' which are simply translations of greetings in Filipino and are equivalent to the English 'Hi!' or 'Hello!'

Goulet (1971) cites certain Filipino ways which are tied up with Filipino speech and which when misunderstood might be annoying to native speakers of English.

Examples:
When the Filipino says 'I'll try to come,' it usually means one of three things:
1. I can't come, but I don't want to hurt your feeling by saying 'No.'
2. I'd like to but I'm not sure you really want me to come.
3. I'll probably meet you but I won't say 'Yes.' Something might prevent me from coming.

Instead of responding 'I'll see you at seven' or 'I can't make it tonight' to the invitation 'How about having dinner with me tonight?' the Filipino might just say 'I'll try to come.' The Filipino who feels uncomfortable about accepting what appears to be a casual invitation, unless it is repeated, tends to give the impression that he is not interested.

STRATEGIES AND SUGGESTIONS FOR ENGLISH-LANGUAGE DEVELOPMENT

Strategies

Most Filipino-American students benefit from oral English instruction as soon as they enter school. Students whose primary language is Filipino should be ready to develop their basic interpersonal communication skills (BICS) in English. They should be provided with adequate exposure to English needed for successful acquisition of basic communicative competence in this language without interfering with subject matter instruction and cognitive development.

Filipino-American students can be exposed to English in communicative-based ESL and specially designed academic instruction in English (SDAIE) classes. In communicative-based ESL classes, the focus is on basic communicative competence, not on learning grammar rules. In SDAIE classes, subject matter instruction is delivered in the second language (English), second-language acquirers are grouped together, special materials are provided, and students are allowed to speak in their primary language. However, the teacher always models native speaker or near-native-speaker speech in the second language and uses when appropriate a native speaker-to-nonnative speaker register (known as 'motherese' or 'foreigner talk'). Research suggests that communicative-based ESL instruction and SDAIE promote the acquisition of basic interpersonal communication skills in English (Krashen, 1994; Terrell, 1981). They are effective in promoting the development of BICS in English for students at any age and at any development or academic level except for those who have been diagnosed to have physical challenges or to be suffering from some form of psychological trauma (California Department of Education, 1986).

Grammar-based ESL and submersion classes have been found to be less effective in promoting basic interpersonal communication skills (Krashen, 1994; Terrell, 1981). In grammar-based ESL classes teachers focus on phonology and grammar and emphasize learning the rules of the language through grammar-translation, audio-lingual, or cognitive code methods. In submersion classes, also known as sink-or-swim models, teachers instruct students as if they were all native speakers of English. No special activities are provided to meet the needs of language minority students.

Filipino-American students whose primary language is English should be ready for the development of their cognitive academic language proficiency in this language. Communicative-based ESL, SDAIE, and other natural-language acquisition environments are generally inadequate to promote all of the English-language skills needed by language minority students for academic success. Once students have developed basic interpersonal communication skills and appropriate level of cognitive academic-language proficiency in English (skills learned in primary language, communicative-based ESL, and SDAIE classes), they are ready to benefit from grammar-based ESL and formal reading instruction in English that focuses on those cognitive academic skills specific to English that they have not yet learned (e.g., language that is not part of the common underlying proficiency) (Cummins, 1994). Examples of such skills are some decoding, grammar, and spelling skills. Development of cognitive academic language proficiency in English is more efficient when school personnel build on already acquired cognitive academic-language skills in Filipino.

Alternative Models and Strategies

Filipino-American students are oftentimes exposed to English in grammar-based ESL and submersion classes. At best, grammar-based ESL instruction leads to the development of the language monitor, which assists second language learners in the production of grammatically correct utterances (Krashen, 1994). Submersion classes are even less effective than grammar-based ESL classes because language minority students do not comprehend much of what is said and therefore do not develop their skills in English (Cummins, 1994; Krashen, 1994).

In 1948, an educational experiment was conducted using the vernacular (Hiligaynon) as the language of instruction in the first two grades of the elementary school in Iloilo, Philippines. The test results of the control and experimental groups revealed that the vernacular was more effective than English in teaching reading, arithmetic, and social studies in the first grade. The study concluded that it is best to teach initially in the language of the home for optimum results, even in the teaching of a second language (Davis, 1967; Prator, 1950). When the bilingual education policy was promulgated in 1974, Galang (1977) proposed the use of the vernacular as a primary medium of instruction in the first two grades in the Philippines.

The development of basic interpersonal communication skills in a second language depends largely on the amount of comprehensible second-language input that a student receives under favorable conditions (Krashen, 1994; Terrell, 1981). While communication-based ESL and SDAIE situations provide students with large amounts of comprehensible input under optimal conditions, submersion and grammar-based ESL classes provide students with only very limited amounts of such input (especially in the initial stages) under conditions considerably less favorable for second language acquisition.

Grammar-based ESL and submersion environments often work against English acquisition. Children who have not experienced normal cognitive or academic development do not acquire the cognitive skills needed for learning decontextualized language that characterizes grammar-based ESL and submersion classes. Overemphasis on grammatically correct speech often inhibits second language acquisition. Therefore, submersion environments and grammar-based ESL instruction (audio-lingual, cognitive code, and grammar translation) are not recommended for Filipino-American students before they attain sufficient levels of basic interpersonal communication skills and cognitive academic language proficiency to benefit from such instructional contexts.

Suggestions for Classroom Teachers

The superior results gained from beginning literacy training in the primary language are well documented (California Department of Education, 1981; Leyba, 1994). Therefore, language minority students should begin reading with their primary language-the language through which they have accumulated learning and experience which allows them to take a direct route to understanding meaning.

In a three-year study conducted at the Philippine Normal College Laboratory School (Masangkay et al., 1977), three groups of children who were taught in three different instructional schemes (all English, all Pilipino, and bilingual English-Pilipino) did not differ significantly in performance at the end of the third year in all subject areas, including Pilipino and English language arts. Findings of a six-year study in the Philippines seemingly conflict with the widely held view that beginning reading in a second language is academically disadvantageous (Davis, 1967). Like the immersion studies in Canada (Lambert

& Tucker, 1972) and California (Cohen, 1973), the Rizal study indicates that immediate immersion into the second language, English, promotes simultaneous academic achievement and proficiency in that language. The English immersion group performed better in English proficiency and in content areas than any of the groups instructed in Pilipino. Moreover, the immersion group did as well as the others in Pilipino proficiency (Davis, 1967).

Tucker (1977) and Skutnabb-Kangas (1979) speculate that the academic success of students in such programs could be attributed to certain common features: (1) the students' primary language was also the majority language; (2) the children benefited from a language arts program in their primary language; (3) the teachers held extremely positive expectations of the students; (4) the students did not have negative feelings about their language; and (5) the students experienced an additive form of bilingualism; and (6) these conditions do not usually exist in the United States. Exposure to Filipino, a minority language, is drastically reduced and its speakers have ambivalent feelings towards it. In the absence of supportive influences, literacy training in Filipino is recommended in order to minimize chances of primary language deterioration, poor second language acquisition, and unsatisfactory academic achievement.

Cummins (1994) and Thonis (1994) provide helpful clues regarding the critical levels of oral English proficiency and literacy in the primary language needed before literacy in the second language is introduced. Thonis speaks of the universal aspects of literacy acquisition. There might be a common underlying proficiency (CUP) which Cummins regards as part of cognitive academic language proficiency (CALP). Cummins (1994) speculates that CALP is more critical than BICS in literacy acquisition. He states that for language minority students, the first language reading level is a very stable predictor of eventual attainment in second language reading. Thus, it is recommended that basic interpersonal communication skills in English and cognitive academic language proficiency in Filipino be used as criteria for beginning literacy instruction in English (California Department of Education, 1986).

The Linguistic Society of the Philippines conducted a nationwide evaluation of bilingual education after eleven years of implementation (1974-1985) by testing a national sample of elementary school fourth and sixth graders and fourth year high school students in Pilipino and English as language subjects and in math, science, and social studies as content subjects. The evaluation team discovered a cross-sectional 'deterioration' in achievement of pupils across the country. Further examination of the data showed that this dramatic deterioration in achievement was not so much the effect of bilingual schooling as of factors such as lack of teacher competence, type of community, socioeconomic status, and institutional factors. The findings indicate a systemic problem bigger than just time allocation for language and content subjects in the two languages (Gonzalez & Sibayan, 1988; Sibayan & Gonzalez, 1990).

One of the challenges in the education of Filipino-American students is the assessment of BICS and CALP. Valid and reliable tests in Filipino are few, if not non-existent. Cloze tests, reading tests, and other academic measures can be used to assess CALP skills. Language arts and reading skills continua can be used as indicators of CALP levels. After selecting assessment instruments, achievement level criteria must be set. Oral English language skills form the basis for some aspects of English language reading. A student who scores in the fluent-English-speaking range on BICS measures will probably have most of the prerequisite basic interpersonal communication skills, which, when combined with cognitive academic language proficiency skills, will facilitate progress in English reading.

If the literacy program is properly managed, reading instruction in the first language will support further reading instruction in the second language (Cummins, 1994; Thonis, 1994). Most of the skills in these areas form part of the common underlying proficiency (CUP) (Cummins, 1994). Consequently, most CALP skills developed in Filipino will promote CALP skills in English. Although both Filipino and English use the Roman alphabet, there are some skills which are unique to each language. Therefore, some of the decoding and spelling skills, as well as some mechanical skills, need to be learned separately in each language. However, these important language-specific skills actually represent only a small part of what is considered reading or literacy development.

Cognitive academic language proficiency skills developed in Filipino are most efficiently brought to bear on the task of English reading when individual students have learned, practiced, and mastered a substantial number of skills that form part of the common underlying proficiency. Literal and inferential comprehension appear to be especially critical areas since the learning and practice of such skills lead students to a more complete understanding of the reading process. Usually by the end of the third grade, most students have been exposed to and have learned many of the CALP skills. After adequate practice, full mastery generally occurs during the third grade or later.

Introduction of formal reading instruction in English depends largely on the goal. Where the goal is biliteracy, reading instruction in Filipino usually begins in kindergarten and continues through at least the sixth grade. Since Filipino has one of the most consistent spelling systems in the world, initial reading process in this language is relatively easy and can probably be done in six months or less (Gonzalez, 1971). Formal English reading could be introduced in the second or third grade without causing any cognitive confusion among students, because previously learned CALP skills are reinforced in Filipino in grades three through six until full mastery is achieved. English reading should be introduced when reading skills in Filipino are mastered well enough to transfer to or be applicable to similar reading tasks in English. Such mastery is usually attained at about the fourth grade. At this stage of reading in Filipino, most readiness, comprehension, literacy, and study skills will be applicable to English. In English-only programs, development of CALP takes place exclusively in English. It is unfortunate that many educators do not consider CALP developed in or through Filipino, the primary language, as crucial in literacy acquisition. In the English-only approach, language minority students are introduced to formal English reading instruction once individual students have mastered the prerequisite readiness skills in English. Operationally, this would mean that language minority students must attain levels of BICS and CALP skills in English similar to those attained by native speakers of English when the latter are introduced to formal reading instruction (California Department of Education, 1986).

The instructional approaches described earlier are not equally effective in promoting high levels of achievement in English reading among language minority students. A variety of student, teacher, school, home, and community factors affect the implementation and outcome of instructional activities. Approaches that promote high levels of biliteracy are likely to have positive outcomes. When appropriately implemented, they allow language minority students to experience the benefits of proficient bilingualism and avoid the negative consequences of subtractive or limited bilingualism.

Therefore, effective reading programs in bilingual contexts require that school personnel implement instructional programs that are responsive to student needs and community desires. Regardless of the approach selected, the quality of implementation is an important determinant of outcome. Literacy programs should be evaluated on their effectiveness in producing independent readers at the sixth grade level or higher. Unfortunately, some instructional treatments are discontinued when students perform well in reading in kindergarten through grade three. Recent studies indicate, however, that the effects of special instruction for language minority students are cumulative and that the most positive outcomes appear after five or six years of instruction (Cummins, 1994).

CONCLUSION

Almost all Filipino immigrant students in the United States speak natively one of the indigenous Austronesian languages in the Philippines. Students' proficiency in Filipino and English varies depending on their exposure to these two languages which, in turn, depends on where they come from, their socioeconomic status, and the schools they attended. While the primary language of American-born Filipino students is likely to be English, their exposure to the vernacular, Filipino, and English differs according to the linguistic, educational, and socioeconomic backgrounds of the other members of the family. For both groups of Filipino-Americans, assessment of their proficiency in both Filipino and English (ideally, also in the vernacular when appropriate) is critical in determining their linguistic and other educational needs. Also, instruction in Filipino is recommended for all Filipino-American students for many different reasons. Those whose primary language is Filipino need instruction in this language (1) to gain access to the core curriculum, that is, to learn math, science, and social studies; (2) to acquire English more effectively and speedily; (3) to be able to adjust to the new academic and social environment; and (4) to nurture high self-esteem and pride in their language and culture. Those whose primary language is English also need instruction in Filipino (1) to develop pride in their linguistic and cultural heritage; (2) to enrich their linguistic and cultural experiences; and (3) to communicate with family members and relatives who are more proficient in this language than in English.

Filipino exhibits many phonological, morphological, syntactic, and other differences from English. Knowledge of these differences may help teachers understand not only the students' variety of English but also their possible difficulties in learning this language.

It is unfortunate that many parents and educators have considered the acquisition of basic interpersonal communication skills in English as the only critical need of language minority students. While these skills are very important, the development of cognitive academic language proficiency seems to be even more critical to school success. For Filipino-American students, cognitive academic language proficiency in English can be developed through instruction in Filipino. Unfortunately, opportunities to develop cognitive academic language skills in Filipino are not available to students in most communities in the United States. Therefore, parents and educators must work together to design and implement opportunities in the home, school, and community. On the other hand, opportunities to develop basic interpersonal communication skills in English are naturally present in many language minority homes, most communities, and most schools. However, cognitive academic language skills not learned in Filipino need to be learned in appropriate programs such as communicative-based ESL and SDAIE classes.

Thus, if Filipino-American students are to benefit from their bilingualism, attention to Filipino language development and English language acquisition is necessary. Otherwise, the majority of Filipino-speaking children will continue to have serious language, academic, and cultural problems in school. The task of educating language minority students is not without challenge. Nevertheless, creative and committed educators in partnership with concerned parents can design and implement educational programs for language minority students that will result in (1) high levels of English language proficiency, (2) normal cognitive academic development, (3) positive adjustment to both minority and majority cultures, and (4) high levels of Filipino language development.

NOTES

1. *Vernacular* is the term used to refer to a language or language variety that is spoken by some or most of the population in bilingual and multilingual countries but is not the official or national language of the country. In the Philippines, this term refers to the indigenous languages spoken in the different regions of the country.
2. *Lingua franca* refers to the language that is used for communication between and among different groups of people, each speaking a different language.

REFERENCES

Bautista, M. L. S. (1996). An outline: The national language and the language of instruction. In M. L. S. Bautista (Ed.), *Readings in Philippine sociolinguistics* (pp. 223-227). Manila, Philippines: De La Salle University Press.

Beebe, J., & Beebe, M. (1981). The Filipinos: A special case. In C. A. Ferguson & S. B. Heath (Eds.), *Language in the U.S.* (pp. 322-338). Cambridge, MA: Cambridge University Press.

California Department of Education, Office of Bilingual Bicultural Education. (1981). *Schooling and language minority students: A theoretical framework.* Los Angeles:

Evaluation, Dissemination and Assessment Center, California State University, Los Angeles.

California Department of Education, Bilingual Education Office. (1986). *Handbook for teaching Pilipino-speaking students.* Sacramento, CA: California Department of Education.

Cohen, A. (1973). The sociological assessment of a bilingual program in California. Doctoral dissertation, Stanford University.

Cruz, I. R. (1990). *Filipino para sa Pilipino I.* Quezon City, Philippines: Phoenix Publishing House.

Cummins, J. (1994). Primary language instruction and the education of language minority students. In C. F. Leyba (Ed.), *Schooling and language minority students: A theoretical framework,* 2nd ed. (pp. 3-46). Los Angeles: Evaluation, Dissemination and Assessment Center, California State University, Los Angeles and California Department of Education, Bilingual Education Office.

Davis, F. B. (1967). *Philippine language-teaching experiments.* Quezon City, Philippines: Phoenix Publishing House.

Department of Education and Culture. (1974). Implementing guidelines for the policy on bilingual education. Department Order No. 25. Manila, Philippines.

Department of Education and Culture. (1976). Rules in orthography of Filipino. Department Memorandum No. 194. Manila, Philippines.

Department of Education, Culture and Sports. (1987). Policy on bilingual education. Department Order No. 52. Manila, Philippines.

Galang, R. (1977). The vernacular in the classroom. In E. Pascasio (Ed.), *The Filipino bilingual* (pp. 102-107). Quezon City, Philippines: Ateneo de Manila University Press.

Galang, R. (1988). The language situation of Filipino Americans. In S. L. McKay & S. C. Wong (Eds), *Language diversity: Problem or resource?* (pp. 229-251). New York: Newbury House.

Gonzalez, A. B. (1971). Reading in a democratic society: The language problem. Unpublished paper.

Gonzalez, A. B. (1974). The social context of the dissemination of Pilipino: A first step towards standardization. Paper read at the Second Conference on Asian Languages, December 16-21, Manila, Philippines.

Gonzalez, A. B. (1980). *Language and nationalism: The Philippine experience thus far.* Quezon City, Philippines: Ateneo de Manila University Press.

Gonzalez, A. B. (Ed.). (1988). *The role of English and its maintenance in the Philippines.* Manila, Philippines: Solidaridad Publishing House.

Gonzalez, A. B. (1996). Evaluating bilingual education in the Philippines: Towards a multidimensional model of education in language planning. In M. L. S. Bautista (Ed.), *Readings in Philippine sociolinguistics* (pp. 327-340). Manila, Philippines: De La Salle University Press.

Gonzalez, A., & Sibayan, B. P. (Eds.). (1988). *Evaluating bilingual education in the Philippines* (1974-1985). Manila: Linguistic Society of the Philippines.

Goulet, R. M. (1971). *English, Spanish, and Tagalog: A study of grammatical and cultural interference. Philippine Journal of Linguistics,* Special monograph no. 1. Quezon City, Philippines: Linguistic Society of the Philippines.

Hemphill, R. (1962). *Background readings in language teaching.* Quezon City, Philippines: Phoenix Publishing House.

Juco, J. M. (1977). Bilingual education under the new constitution. In E. Pascasio (Ed.), *The Filipino bilingual* (pp. 9-15). Quezon City, Philippines: Ateneo de Manila University Press.

Kagawaran ng Edukasyon, Kultura at Isports. (1987). Ang alpabeto at patnubay sa ispeling ng wikang Filipino. Kautusang Pangkagawaran Blg. 81. Maynila, Pilipinas.

Kaplan, R. B. (1982). The language situation in the Philippines. *The Linguistic Reporter* 24 (5): 1-4.

Komisyon sa Wikang Filipino. (1995). Mga tanong at sagot tungkol sa alpabeto at patnubay sa ispeling ng wikang Filipino. Maynila, Pilipinas.

Krashen, S. (1994). Bilingual education and second language acquisition theory. In C. F. Leyba (Ed.), *Schooling and language minority students: A theoretical framework*, 2nd ed. (pp. 47-75). Los Angeles: Evaluation, Dissemination and Assessment Center, California State University, Los Angeles and California Department of Education, Bilingual Education Office.

Lambert, W. E., & Tucker, G. R. (1972). *Bilingual education of children: The St. Lambert experiment*. Rowley, MA: Newbury House.

Laygo, T. M. (1977). *What is Filipino?* Berkeley, CA: Asian American Bilingual Center

Legaretta-Mercaida, D. (1981). Effective use of the primary language in the classroom. In California Department of Education, *Schooling and language minority students: A theoretical framework* (pp. 83-116). Los Angeles: Evaluation, Dissemination and Assessment Center, California State University, LosAngeles.

Leyba, C. F. (Ed.). (1994). *Schooling and language minority students: A theoretical framework*, 2nd ed. Los Angeles: Evaluation, Dissemination and Assessment Center, California State University, Los Angeles and California Department of Education, Bilingual Education Office.

Llamzon, T. A. (1978). *Handbook of Philippine language groups*. Quezon City, Philippines: Ateneo de Manila University Press.

Masangkay, Z., Otanes, F., & Villamin, A. (1977). The Philippine Normal College bilingual experiment. In E. Pascasio (Ed.), *The Filipino bilingual* (pp. 113-116). Quezon City, Philippines: Ateneo de Manila University Press.

National Statistics Office. (1990). *Household population by mother tongue, sex, and region*. Manila, Philippines: National Statistics Office.

Nolledo, J. N. (1992). *The 1987 constitution of the Philippines*. Manila, Philippines: National Book Store.

O'Hare, P. O., & Felt, J. C. (1991). *Asian Americans: Americas fastest growing group*. Washington, DC: Population Reference Bureau.

Otanes, F. T. (1974). Some notes on the educational backgrounds of immigrant Filipino children. Talk given to Operation Manong Volunteers, September 19, Honolulu, Hawaii.

Prator, C. H., Jr. (1950). *Language teaching in the Philippines: A report*. Manila, Philippines: U.S. Educational Foundation in the Philippines.

Ramos, T. V. (1971). *Tagalog structures*. Honolulu: University of Hawaii Press.

Ramos, T. V. (1978). Teaching Philippine culture through language and literature. Unpublished paper.

Ramos, T. V., & Ceña, R. M. (1990). Modern Tagalog: Grammatical explanations and exercises for non-native speakers. Honolulu: University of Hawaii Press.

Ramos, T. V., & de Guzman, V. (1971). *Tagalog for beginners*. Honolulu: University of Hawaii Press.

Schachter, P., & Otanes, F. T. (1972). *Tagalog reference grammar*. Berkeley: University of California Press.

Sibayan, B. P. (1975). Survey of language use and attitudes towards language in the Philippines. In S. Ohannessian, C.A. Ferguson, & E. C. Polome (Eds.), *Language surveys in developing nations: Papers and reports on sociolinguistic surveys* (pp. 115-143). Arlington, VA: Center for Applied Linguistics.

Sibayan, B. P., & Gonzalez, A. B. (1990). English language teaching in the Philippines: A succession of movements. In J. Britton, R. E. Shafer, & R. Watson (Eds.), *Teaching and learning English worldwide*. Clevedon, Avon, England: Multilingual Matters.

Skutnabb-Kangas, T. (1979). *Language in the process of assimilation and structural incorporation of linguistic minorities*. Arlington, VA: National Clearinghouse for Bilingual Education.

Terrell, T. (1981). The natural approach in bilingual education. In California Department of Education, Office of Bilingual Bicultural Education, *Schooling and language minority students: A theoretical framework* (pp. 117-146). Los Angeles: Evaluation, Dissemination and Assessment Center, California State University.

Thonis, E. W. (1994). Reading instruction for language minority students. In C. F. Leyba (Ed.), *Schooling and language minority students: A theoretical framework*, 2nd ed. (pp. 165-202). Los Angeles: Evaluation, Dissemination and Assessment Center, California State University and California Department of Education, Bilingual Education Office.

Tucker, R. G. (1977). The linguistic perspective. In *Bilingual education: Current perspectives (Linguistics)* (pp. 1-40). Washington, DC: Center for Applied Linguistics.

CHAPTER 9

Vietnamese-American Students: Between the Pressure to Succeed and the Pressure to Change

Chung Hoang Chuong

OVERVIEW OF VIETNAMESE MIGRATION

In the twenty years since the end of the Vietnam War in 1975, the United States has resettled more than a million refugees from the three Southeast Asian countries of Vietnam, Cambodia, and Laos (U.S. Committee for Refugees, 1997). In all, there have been four major refugee resettlement movements. The first outpouring occurred in the late part of April, 1975, following the collapse of several governments to Communist troops. Knudsen (1983), Tollefson (1989), and Chung (1994) have extensively documented the relief and resettlement programs set up in a number of Southeast Asian countries which dealt with the flow of the refugees after this date.

Needless to say, the Vietnam War left not only devastation but deep psychological scars on all parties involved. Many young Americans who were sent to Vietnam never came back. Vietnam lost over four million people in the conflict. Poverty and destruction pushed thousands of refugees to seek opportunities for a better life elsewhere, far away from their homeland. Many refugees lived to recount harrowing experiences on open seas during their escape, or the difficulties and problems they endured in make-shift refugee camps. The legacy of the war lingers on, many years after the official end of open conflict.

America was among the countries that kept its door open to the less fortunate and allowed the immigration of war-torn refugees for many years. By the late 1980s, large concentrations of Vietnamese could be found in various parts of the United States, and especially in California. In 1990, the largest Vietnamese population in the United States could be found in Orange County and Los Angeles, California, with a combined total of over 100,000 Vietnamese. Meanwhile, the Vietnamese population in San Jose, California, had reached 55,610, making the city's Vietnamese population the second largest in the state

(Ngin, 1990; U.S. Bureau of the Census, 1993). Today, the presence of Vietnamese immigrants can be easily recognized in many sections of these cities, where large ethnic business centers and storefront windows display signs in the Vietnamese language.

The Vietnamese community is one of the fastest growing Asian-American groups, with the Southeast Asian population having surpassed the one million mark in just twenty years (Immigration and Naturalization Services, 1993; U.S. Bureau of the Census, 1993). The 1990 census showed a total of 593,213 Vietnamese residing in the United States. Among these, 80% were foreign born (U.S. Bureau of the Census, 1993). It might not be a surprise that a mid-decade population count easily reached 750,000, given the continuing influx of immigrants based on a set of special legislations such as the Amerasian Homecoming Act in 1987 and the soon to be discontinued Humanitarian Operation (HO) Program. One cannot disregard the internal population movement or secondary migration, which significantly impacted California in the 1980s. Many refugee families relocated after they had settled in localities across the United States, preferring the opportunities and warmer weather of the Western states. They left their sponsors to move to California, Texas, or Washington to rejoin family members or to take advantage of the various programs available in locales such as Orange County or San Jose, California (Forbes, 1985).

Vietnamese-Americans have made visible and important contributions to many localities and urban centers. Large sections of many cities' downtown areas received a facelift as blocks and rows of Vietnamese ethnic businesses moved in (Chung, 1995). They supplied the electronics industry with highly skilled technicians. Many Vietnamese students made the honor roll, the dean's list, and attained other educational achievements in schools across the country.

In the mid-1990s, American colleges and universities are welcoming the first group of American-born Vietnamese students. These are the children of the first wave of Southeast Asian refugees who arrived in the spring of 1975. These Vietnamese students speak flawless English and are very different from their counterparts who have come to the United States only recently. Aside from their Asian physical features, they are every bit American youngsters, with a baseball cap engraved with their favorite team logo pulled on their heads or clad in fashionable ultra baggy pants.

VIETNAMESE STUDENTS: THREE PROFILES

Most urban school districts in California have at least a few Vietnamese students in their schools. Since the first group of students were enrolled in U.S. schools in 1975, the number of Vietnamese students has continued to increase. During the late 1970s, many school districts were busy developing educational programs or instructional strategies appropriate for the characteristics and backgrounds of the incoming Vietnamese children. By now, various school districts and educators have accumulated quite a bit of information on the Vietnamese and, in many cases, have developed workshops, conferences, and printed materials concerning the education of Vietnamese students. However, changes among the different groups of Vietnamese which have arrived at different times during the last twenty years warrant some rethinking in terms of educational programs and language training approaches. In fact, the Vietnamese population has changed so quickly that much of the material concerning the education of Vietnamese children needs to be updated.

Today, there are many different types of Vietnamese students, displaying a wide range of language skills and educational backgrounds. The Vietnamese students in our schools can be grouped into the following three categories: (1) American-born Vietnamese students, who are English dominant and generally American in cultural demeanor and language; (2) newly arrived Vietnamese students who have come in the last two or three years who tend to be shy and uncomfortable in settings that require strong English language skills; and (3) older immigrant students who have been here for four or more years. This last group feels quite comfortable dealing with day-to-day school activities. They might speak with an accent, but they know how to get around in school settings. This chapter examines the different issues related to the backgrounds of each of these three groups and the educational challenges they face. By becoming aware of these differences, teachers and administrators can come up with various educational strategies and programs which are practical but flexible enough for the ever changing needs of Vietnamese students (Rumbaut & Ima, 1988; Chung, 1994).

Generally speaking, American-born Vietnamese are quite at ease with their peers and with their teachers and encounter virtually no problems in their adjustment to the American classroom setting. The American-born Vietnamese may use discourse styles typical of *MTV* and street English. They may speak "funny" Vietnamese, triggering laughter from their immigrant friends, who don't hesitate to strike back when they fail to use appropriate tones in Vietnamese. They may call their immigrant friends FOBs (Fresh off the Boats), teasing these students about their typical immigrant attire. They may devote less time to their schoolwork than the immigrant students do or talk back to their teachers.

The new Vietnamese immigrant students are easy to spot. They often stay together during recess. Their clothing may be quite distinct until they catch up with more mainstream or current styles. In class, they often prefer to sit in the back row and stay quiet. They work together on class assignments, help each other with homework, and do not mind letting friends "borrow" their answers and ideas. At their own Vietnamese gatherings, however, they are not quiet and shy but quite loud. They may be actively involved in organizing school functions such as parties, fund-raising events, or Vietnamese club picnics. Others may work after school and during weekends. Many look after their younger siblings and act as translators for their parents when they meet with their health care or other professionals. They may be very busy and often have very little time for socialization. As a result, they may be too tired to follow class lectures and fall behind in subject areas that demand a great deal of work or strong English language skills.

Mixed in with these two groups, the "old" immigrant students are somewhere in between. You can still detect a slight Vietnamese accent when they speak English. They may not be as shy as new immigrants and seem to be more at ease in the company of different peers. Usually, they interject comments only when they know the appropriate term. Some attempt to improve their image by following the latest trends. The boys may wear earrings, for example, or their favorite team jerseys two or three sizes too large. They may work and get into car culture with the money they earn. Because they hang out in their own groups and because of their appearance or style of clothing, they are often mistaken for gang members. However, most mind their own business and get involved in positive youth activities. Like the newly arrived immigrants, many concentrate on their school work. Typically, these students have gone through the initial adjustment problem and are fairly well acculturated. At the same time, they can move around comfortably in their own ethnic community and may feel at ease hanging out in Vietnamese cafes or sandwich shops after school or work.

They are an attempt to give the readers a general idea about three broad groups of Vietnamese students. These profiles are not fixed. Indeed, it is important to acknowledge the tremendous variations among individual Vietnamese students. Also most of the descriptions relate to students at the middle and high school levels, not students at the K-5 level.

FIRST CONTACT WITH THE AMERICAN EDUCATION SYSTEM

In 1975 the sudden influx of Southeast Asian refugees into the United States caught many school districts across the country by surprise. They scrambled for whatever information they could get on these newcomers, put together a quick program, hired some bilingual teachers, and hoped for the best. After many workshops, in-services, and professional conferences, educators and other service providers learned to distinguish among the diverse among Southeast Asians and the characteristics of the different waves of refugees, and began to structure a more solid educational plan for them. School district personnel learned about the backgrounds of these children. Many parents of the first wave were educated urbanites. ESL classes helped these refugee children transition into mainstream classes. However, subsequent waves of immigrant children, whose parents had limited educational backgrounds, were not as well prepared and needed a lot more help. More recently, Amerasians and their immediate relatives arrived with even less preparation for schooling and life in the United States. (Chung & Le, 1994). Similarly, newly arrived Vietnamese families who came under the Humanitarian Operation Program (HO Program) typically required assistance in completing even the most basic paperwork for their children's schooling, such as registration forms, vaccination records, and optional enrollment requests.

For the Vietnamese immigrant, initial contact with the American education system was a dramatic experience. Vietnamese children with no English language skills often remained shy and quiet for many weeks, even months. Vietnamese middle and high school students sat through long hours of class staring at their teachers and at indecipherable scribbles on the blackboard. Some communicated with a smile or other expressions or gestures, while others maintained complete silence. On the first day of school, they were overwhelmed with questions: Where can I get my class schedule? Where is the bathroom? Who is the counselor? How do I pronounce my teachers' names? Where do I catch my bus?

Most Vietnamese parents are not aware of the violence and the intimidation their children may face on a daily basis. They believe that if their children just stick to themselves and mind their own business they will be left alone. Unfortunately, that is not generally the case. Ethnic rivalries, gangs, racial tensions, and just plain meanness lead to incidents of violence and confrontation almost every day both in and out of school. For example, one of my students recalled being struck in the face when she did not understand that another student, a bully, wanted her seat on the bus going home (T. M. Ho, class presentation, fall semester, 1996). She tried to conceal the big bruise and not alarm her parents, not knowing how to explain the injury.

Schools with a large Vietnamese student population and Vietnamese-speaking personnel can serve Vietnamese students better with specific programs and bilingual classes designed for Vietnamese LEP (limited English proficient) students. Bilingual peer groups can help new Vietnamese students navigate their way around in the new American schools. However, in schools with very few Vietnamese placed in their school, students are isolated from friends of their own ethnic background. Students who are left to sink or swim learn to fend for themselves and survive in this new urban jungle only after combating many difficulties. Many end up in the streets in the "good care" of bad company.

Often, the first contacts incoming immigrant students have proven to be very important for their future. A pleasant and positive experience may lead to the development of a strong motivation for success. On the other hand, the opposite may be true for those who have a negative experience in interacting with the school board, school personnel, or insensitive peers (Kiang, 1994). They feel rejected by a system so big, so bureaucratic, and so inflexible that the human dimension is lacking. Counselors in charge of hundreds of students find that there is no time for individual problems. Many fall between the cracks, simply give up, and resign themselves to failure in school. For some, peer pressure or lack of family support may lead them to turn to the streets.

AN EDUCATIONAL PROFILE OF VIETNAMESE IMMIGRANT STUDENTS

The profile of the Vietnamese student varies greatly, depending on the student's age. At the high school level, they are typically fully literate in their own language. Immigrant and refugee children usually arrive with some education. They may have received some formal education in their home country and even a few months of language education in the refugee camps (California Department of Education, 1994). One problem many Vietnamese students face is that of proper placement into an appropriate class level due to differences in the organization of instruction by grade level. For example two years of math in Vietnam is roughly equivalent to three years in the United

States (Kelly, 1979). However, the training program in the refugee camp located in Bataan, Philippines, is modeled after the American system. Thus, one year in the PASS Program is equivalent to one year in the United States. It may be feasible to have a committee of Vietnamese educators take on the task of providing guidelines for high school counselors in the task of assessing educational equivalence.

Many Vietnamese parents lower their children's age by one or two years in order to give them time to adjust to a new educational system and to catch up academically (Chung, 1994). As a result, counselors are often confused by the age given by their students. A friend of the author, a counselor at a local high school, observed, "They look and act much older."

Some Vietnamese students may take a little longer to adjust to schools in the United States than others, depending on the degree of similarities and differences in the old and new educational systems. In all cases, their previous educational background and literacy skills positively influence their adjustment to schools in the United States. Not surprisingly, Vietnamese students' adjustment is influenced by their exposure to the Vietnamese educational system.

The Vietnamese educational system, which was modeled after many other education systems and philosophies during their short period of independence, has many pluses and minuses (Do, 1989). On the plus side, Vietnam has a very high literacy rate. It also has an old educational tradition, with the first university having been established in 1070 in the capital city of Thang Long (now Ha Noi). The old system of examination for the mandarinate was observed until the early part of the twentieth century.

In 1917, the new French rule resulted in the shift from traditional Vietnamese education to a standard system of French education (Woodside, 1979; California Department of Education, 1994). After several decades, the French system established itself with the founding of several public institutions controlled by the Services Culturelles Francaises. Many French lycees and Catholic schools coexisted, using French as the medium of instruction.

By the mid 1960s, this French influence was slowly replaced in the South by the state education system with the Vietnamese Quoc Ngu. It was only a matter of time before French education was completely phased out. The pre-1975 education system in Vietnam was influenced by the French colonial period from 1917 to the mid-1960s with many French monolingual programs. After 1960s, they continued in only a limited number of schools which were still controlled by the French Cultural Services until 1970s (Dorais, et al., 1987); however, the Vietnamese language (Quoc Ngu) slowly began to take over in the 1950s with classes taught in the native language. By 1975, very few children were enrolled in any French education programs, with the exception of French foreign language courses at the secondary and postsecondary levels. Therefore, it is wrong to assume that all Vietnamese parents and students can speak French fluently.

Vietnamese students who adhere to the traditional teaching approach and are serious in their school work find the American educational system not as challenging and even easy, at least in the beginning. Others with less prior education and preparation find the task of learning a new language and keeping up with their classmates extremely difficult. Nonetheless, longer study hours and tutorial work after school have helped many Vietnamese immigrant students attain educational success in their new environment.

Despite all the changes brought about by the war, among the Vietnamese, education remains the preferred vehicle for social mobility. The first priority for Vietnamese parents is to select the best school for their children. By word of mouth, they find out quite expediently what school they should send their children to for a quality education. Parents do not hesitate to move to a "good" address, even if they have to pay more for rent or take on another job in order to send their children to a better school. At family gatherings, after the initial greetings and exchange of family news, the topic of children's education inevitably comes up. A typical conversation at such meetings may involve inquiries such as, Where is she going to school? What year is she now at UC Berkeley? When is she going to graduate?

ADJUSTING TO THE NEW EDUCATIONAL SETTING

Although many Vietnamese students have had a few years of education in Vietnam, they still undergo a period of adjustment to the new education system in the U.S. Some of the difficulty may be attributed to their lack of English language skills, although Vietnamese students may initially have an advantage over other students of Southeast Asian background in that the Vietnamese language is alphabetic. This can provide a head start in the area of reading. But beyond this advantage, Vietnamese students have plenty of other tasks to tackle concerning the numerous demands involved in adjusting to life in a new country. Many struggle to cope with the demands of adjusting to a new classroom with a new teacher, new styles of teaching, and new peers.

The traditional styles of teaching employed in Vietnam are markedly different from the methods used in classrooms in the United States today. During the French colonial period, the Vietnamese elite or intelligentsia was educated in the French education system. Some were educated in Vietnam and others studied for a few years in France. Thus, Vietnam had leaders and teachers well versed in French and comfortable in the French system. Some Vietnamese studied in American postsecondary institutions during the period when Americans were providing aid to South Vietnam. During this period, a good number of promising young men in the North were sent to Eastern European countries to obtain degrees and professional certificates. This accounts for the current prevalence of scholars fluent in Russian and trained in the socialist education system. For nearly a decade following the Vietnam War, the socialist model prevailed, until 1986, when Vietnam began a new era of nation-building and development.

Veteran teachers are accustomed to old styles of teaching, because they themselves are the products of the old system and are very slow to change. Xuan Thu Nguyen (1991) pointed out that the methodology employed for teaching in Vietnamese schools has led to the development of a passive attitude on the part of students. Vietnamese teachers prefer the lecture style and believe teaching and learning to be a one-way process, where the teachers teach and the students learn. Further, they do not adjust instruction according to the different levels of their students. It is irrelevant whether students found their instructors' words and sentences comprehensible or not. They must memorize and regurgitate the information for their teachers when asked. Thus rote learning is the dominant learning method which persits to the present day in many schools in Vietnam (Nguyen, 1991; Pham, 1996).

Today, the focus in Vietnam is on the American education system. A group of younger educators are now advocating for an educational model based on the American credit system, with the support of current educational leaders of Vietnam who were trained in the United States. The current sentiment concerning reform in Vietnam is that the educational system needs to be revamped and brought up to a level which prepares Vietnamese students for competion against other workers in the world. However, old habits die hard.

Thus, Vietnamese students bring with them a good deal of good and bad habits. Vietnamese-American students need to get acquainted with the new teaching styles employed in U.S. classrooms. Teachers must give them adequate time to adjust and ease them into new modes of learning. Unfortunately, there is no short cut.

Teachers in the United States often observe that Vietnamese students do not participate in classroom activities enough and that even during recess, they often mingle only with Vietnamese friends. These teachers must understand that Vietnamese students are truly tired of being immersed in an unfamiliar or uncomfortable environment and need a break after long hours of academic instruction provided in English which have rendered them tense and mentally exhausted. They use this time with their peers to inquire about a few points they might have missed in class as well as to provide and receive much needed mutual encouragement and support. It is important that teachers not reprimand Vietnamese students for using Vietnamese. In most instances, it is important to allow them to use their native language when they seek help from their friends both in and out of class.

In Vietnam, mastery learning typically entailed learning everything word for word. They did not have a set of books assigned to each of them. They copied everything from the blackboard. Schools did not house libraries; the closest one may be located in the next city, perhaps more than forty kilometers away. Usually, memorizing answers by test time and reciting verbatim what they had memorized led to good grades, ensuring at least eight or nine points out of a perfect score of ten. The teacher reads from his or her book, usually at a slow pace. He or she often has the only book on the subject in the entire school. Since books are quite expensive in Vietnam, only a few students can afford them. With current economic improvement in large cities, students are able to purchase their own texts while their counterparts in the countryside still struggle.

American classrooms are much more interactive. The teachers often call on students and ask many questions; students are expected to respond and become actively engaged with the material rather than passively absorb information. Students are also expected to work in groups and give oral reports.

Instruction in the two countries also differs in that American teachers typically have a wide array of teaching tools at their disposal, such as posters and charts, the blackboard, a VCR, and an overhead projector. For example, students can actually have an entire lesson based on a video. Instruction may be much easier to comprehend than in Vietnam. But when tested, Vietnamese students may not fully comprehend all the multiple choice items. The test may prove to be more difficult than it appears. Students may panic and wish they could ask the teacher to explain the whole chapter again or ask their neighbors for help. They wrestle with all kinds of questions and feelings as they adjust to the new educational setting in the United States.

Some students manage to survive and succeed in schools by working extra hard. Those who survive the initial phase of adjustment are able to enroll in four-year colleges or universities. There, they encounter new challenges. The small group of Vietnamese students who work extra hard receive praise for their achievements in mainstream or ethnic newspapers. Some even make headlines in national publications. However, they by no means represent the bulk of Vietnamese students who are struggling or in danger of failing. Indeed, a good number cannot cope with the overwhelming demands of a new setting. They simply give up and become involved in other activities. Those who fail may disappear, never to be heard from again. They may find a job or look into other vocational areas and blend into the immigrant communities.

Some schools do a fine job of facilitating adjustment to a new educational system for Vietnamese and other student populations. They work well with a diverse student population, utilizing a variety of educational resources. For example, they may have a good orientation program at the beginning of the school year. This orientation program may include a Vietnamese language booklet explaining the different features of the school. A few slides and an audio tape in Vietnamese may demystify the functions of different offices in the school and the various tasks of key personnel. A Vietnamese student organization can come to the rescue of many new Vietnamese students during the first few weeks of class. Bilingual counselors can offer assistance with initial adjustment concerns and make themselves available by becoming involved in these student clubs. An outgoing message in the native language on the school's telephone menu can assure parents that the school is ready and willing to answer their questions. Teachers can keep their doors open during recess for new students who need their help. These resources are neither difficult to develop nor costly. A library with a good set of bilingual dictionaries can also help incoming students. School announcements can include the names of key individuals that students can approach comfortably who will help answer their questions concerning classes and schedules. It only takes a few good ideas and strong administrative support to help Vietnamese students make a smooth transition into our schools and to make them feel at home.

LEARNING A NEW LANGUAGE

One of the key concerns of educators is what approach or methods they should use to teach a new language. Throughout the 1970s and the 1980s discussions abounded concerning appropriate language teaching methods, such as the Natural Approach (Krashen & Terrell 1983) and Whole Language. Educators were inevitably thrown into debate with one particular approach or another enthusiastically touted at conferences sponsored by organizations such as CABE (California Association for Bilingual Education) or TESOL (Teachers of English to Speakers of Other Languages). It can be safely argued that some methods fit well with certain types of students, while other methods work wonderfully with others.

Vietnamese students are accustomed to a heavily grammar-based approach to language learning. In their home country, instruction was typically centered around spelling, sentence construction, and the memorization of scores of regular and irregular verbs. They were expected to master a list of several hundred irregular verbs. The scenario in ESL classes in the United States is very different. Teachers seem to bombard them with questions, expecting them to participate actively and focus nearly exclusively on oral language instruction. It is not uncommon for teachers to forget grammar instruction and avoid emphasizing conjugations or memorization of irregular verbs for a long time. Vietnamese students may secretly wonder if the teachers are any good, because they do not teach grammar. Writing, too, may not be addressed for some time, in favor of developing oral language skills. In some cases, Vietnamese students are quite surprised at the teacher's poor spelling skills. Many Vietnamese parents are surprised or puzzled when their children come home with little or no written homework.

Actually, the active or interactive method of language teaching may fit well with younger children at the K-6 level, who are typically less shy and are more willing to participate with their classmates. However, for older students, in order to make language classes interesting, writing, spelling, and grammar need to be introduced in tandem with speaking and listening development activities. DeVillar, Faltis, and Cummins (1994) suggest that an approach that strikes a balance between the students' background knowledge and new knowledge can help them to merge slowly into the new mode of learning with sufficient confidence in their teacher. Accordingly, using a familiar context in language teaching can help the students see that the ESL class is a "good" language class. When a teacher has the attention and respect of her Vietnamese students, she can slowly shift to the best language instruction methods currently in use as proven by language practitioners and researchers.

Many Vietnamese college students who are fluent in English experience extreme difficulty with writing. Although they may have good ideas, these ideas may be presented in an awkward manner. Since college instructors usually do not tolerate simple grammatical mistakes, many Vietnamese students may receive bad grades. To make matters worse, many Vietnamese students gravitate toward courses that do not require much writing. They may wait until the end of their senior year before taking the English requirement courses, often receiving just a passing grade. Many Vietnamese students enter the work force with this deficiency, leading to poor work performance and less than satisfactory job evaluations.

In sum, in order to facilitate optimal English language learning, it is critical that Vietnamese students be provided with different types of literacy activities at different levels of instruction. Specifically, it is important that writing exercises be a regular part of English language instruction, particularly at the secondary school level.

FACTORS RELATED TO THE ACHIEVEMENT OF VIETNAMESE STUDENTS

Vietnamese parents tend to view education as the only road for individual advancement. This is true in both Asia and in the United States. Vietnamese parents have such high expectations of their children that their behavior may demonstrate a lack of understanding of the children's real needs and concerns. Many Vietnamese parents apply heavy pressure upon their children hoping that their children will obtain economic stability for the entire family after their graduation. Thus, Vietnamese parents do not hesitate to invest in their children's education. Typically, Vietnamese parents spend long hours at work in order to save money for their children's tuition. Given the family's economic situation, they often expect their children to finish their education in record time.

This kind of pressure can generate various outcomes. Some children perform well under a lot of pressure and tight constraints. Others cannot cope with such high expectations. Vietnamese parents need to know what problems and challenges their children face at school on a daily basis. Then they can provide appropriate support and assistance not only toward academic achievement, but toward social, psychological, and emotional health and wellness.

Immigrant and refugee children often take much longer than other students to complete their assignments in all subject areas. They may spend four or more hours each night reviewing their daily lessons, learning new English words, and finishing their homework. For Vietnamese students who are employed in part-time work in order to supplement their family income, schoolwork may be even more difficult. Lack of time or rest may cause students to fall behind in classwork and homework. They may perform poorly and feel frustrated. Under extreme pressure from their family, quickly school work becomes an unpleasant burden to them. The hours spent in class feel like a punishment and become difficult to tolerate. They may skip classes, and their parents who have their own heavy work schedule often remain unaware of such situations until it is too late to prevent failure.

Recently arrived immigrant students cannot fully understand what teachers say or follow class discussions. It is important to recognize that, caught in this situation, Vietnamese students typically do not dare to ask questions or show enthusiasm in classroom activities. Feeling incompetent in the new language, they do not speak up for fear that they may use a wrong term, which will result in embarrassment and humiliation. The only behaviors Vietnamese students feel safe to display are silence and attentiveness. Thus, most of the time, Vietnamese students are left alone by teachers who have a preference for quiet, obedient students, even while they are forced to attend to the more rowdy or loud students.

THE SUPPORTIVE ROLE OF VIETNAMESE PARENTS

Some teachers and administrators attribute the lack of Vietnamese parental involvement to lack of interest in their children's education. Others believe that the immigrant parents simply do not have the time, inclination, or the educational background to get involved.

It is important to note, however, that Vietnamese refugee families have gone through tremendous upheaval and changes in their lives (Liu & Murata, 1979). They have had to cope with camp life in various refugee centers around the world. Now in the United States, in their struggle to survive, refugee parents have to deal with an array of challenging and daunting tasks. They must learn a new language, attend ESL classes, and enroll in vocational courses to obtain new, marketable skills. In the midst of all these aspects of transition, they need to find a decent paying job. Yet, many Vietnamese parents find that when they have landed the right job, they are left with only a limited amount of time to spend with their children. Limited opportunities for communication and interaction inevitably lead to a widening gap between parents and children. As a result, both their children's schoolwork and social relations may suffer. While parents certainly sense that their children have changed and that something must be done about the widening cultural and communication gap, they may feel that there is little they can do when they have so little time together.

One step that can be taken toward reducing the gap between parents and children, and between parents and schools, is to build awareness among parents. Faced with their own struggles, many Vietnamese parents often do not realize that there are many problems their children face at school. It is not easy for Vietnamese children to navigate between two cultures. They struggle in their effort to identify and negotiate aspects of two cultures with fundamentally different values, mores, and customs. They become involved in a long process of inner reflection and turmoil before they are able to recognize the values that they want to live by.

Yet, for Vietnamese parents, the single most important concern is their children's academic performance. When Vietnamese parents see Cs or Ds on their children's report cards, they quickly conclude that their children do not pay enough attention to their schoolwork and readily chastise them for their poor academic performance. It is critically important for Vietnamese parents to stop and to recognize that their children must reconcile tremendous difficulties posed by their political and historical circumstance.

The Vietnam War has had a negative effect on the quality of education in Vietnam. Additionally, time spent in refugee camps and in preparation for emigration is time spent without consistent educational input. In the United States, students are usually placed into their grade levels according to their age, not their level of education. Thus, many Vietnamese students become quite discouraged when faced with the obstacles of language and lack of basic educational knowledge. Discrepancies between them and their non-Vietnamese peers in terms of academic competence, economic advantage, and various other social and cultural aspects, may make matters worse. Further, counselors faced with a huge caseload may simply forget about the special needs of Vietnamese students. Consequently, Vietnamese students may feel unwanted or ignored both at home and at school. Given such overwhelming pressure, it is critical that parents, counselors, and other school staff intervene to ensure success for Vietnamese students by providing strong support through creative strategies and solutions.

There are many creative ways to bring Vietnamese parents out and to help them participate with enthusiasm in their children's schools. Vietnamese parents can be invited to talk about their immigrant experiences in bilingual- bicultural classes. Parents can be encouraged to read with their children or to take their children to the local museum or academy of science. They may be available to help with assemblies, fund-raising, international cultural events or bake sales. They can also tutor in a number of subjects. Schools can involve parents as partners in the educational process of their children. In turn, schools can also give something back to parents by validating not only their contributions, but also their knowledge, culture, and history.

To promote strong parental support, the issues facing Vietnamese students must be communicated to parents in various ways, through Vietnamese language information pamphlets, parent workshops conducted by bilingual staff members, or presentations made in ESL classes at local adult schools. All participants can discuss the requirements and regulations and academic and social problems that Vietnamese students face at school. Most importantly, these forums can provide opportunities to discuss how Vietnamese parents can help their children in specific and tangible ways. Real cases and concrete examples can be shared among students, staff, and parents. Students feel free to express their experiences, needs, and concerns before an attentive audience. Parents feel empowered by being included in problem prevention and problem-solving. Gradually, Vietnamese parents can be exposed to the notion of being partners in the educational process of their children. Parents who want to be involved can be encouraged to participate in other school activities.

In situations where parents cannot be the primary contact person at home, members of the extended family are great substitutes. Uncles and aunts or older brothers and sisters often carry out the necessary duties involved with the schooling of Vietnamese children. Grandparents are great with students in the lower grade levels. They can be involved both at home and at school in activities that promote literacy, for example, reciting folk poems in Vietnamese or explaining the meanings and the moral lessons hidden in the messages of these melodious verses. A Vietnamese saying, "quyen huynh the phu" (a brother's authorities can substitute those of the father), demonstrates well that variations in the traditional family structure can provide help or support when the mother or father is not available.

With the implementation of these and other creative suggestions, schools can build strong home-school partnerships that can truly benefit Vietnamese students and parents, as well as teachers, counselors, and school administrators.

EFFECTIVE HOME-SCHOOL COMMUNICATION

According to some publications, Vietnamese students' truancy and delinquency is the direct result of Vietnamese single parents families who do not have the time or the inclination to get involved with schools (Long, 1996). Of course, this is a very unfair overgeneralization which fails to acknowledge the harsh reality of life for Vietnamese single mothers or fathers who devote twelve to fourteen hours a day at work and sacrifice everything to send their children to schools and prestigious universities. The important issue here is how schools can foster effective communication with Vietnamese parents.

For most immigrant Vietnamese parents, it is extremely difficult to understand the content of many school notices and bulletins regarding their educational programs. Technical jargon that is common knowledge for mainstream parents may be difficult for Vietnamese parents to comprehend. Thus, Vietnamese parents may rely on their children for translations or call their friends to ask for help, which may or may not lead to reliable, accurate information. Many Vietnamese parents may just ignore school announcements and bulletins if they do not understand them or erroneously determine that the notices are not closely related to their own children's educational programs. Finally, it is a reality that most immigrant parents work extremely hard to survive in this country and often do not have the time or energy to read stacks of paper from their children's schools, especially when they are extremely difficult to comprehend due to the language barrier. In this regard, it is important to note that short and concise messages are often the best kind.

While it is certainly true that many Vietnamese parents are extremely busy with their work, that their English skills are rather poor, and that they do not understand the American education system very well, there are many other reasons for their lack of involvement which are often overlooked. These reasons have to do with the lack of effort on the part of the schools serving the Vietnamese children. The following observations regarding barriers to effective parent-school communication are based upon the author's many years of direct involvement with numerous schools and school districts in California.

1. The school is not "user-friendly." It is often difficult for parents to obtain a satisfactory answer in an expedient manner in telephone communications with school personnel.
2. Parents are contacted only when there is a problem with their children; schools only call to complain about their children's behavior.
3. Messages from school are poorly composed in English or badly translated into Vietnamese. Many times the translated messages do not make any sense in Vietnamese. It appears that many translators are not qualified to handle educational terms which have few equivalents in Vietnamese such as "psychometric," "dean of girls," "special education," and "remedial classes." It is important to remember that effective home-school communication entails writing messages to parents that are both clear and precise. A good rule of thumb with these messages is to check with at least two Vietnamese speakers for accuracy in translations before sending out translated information.

4. There is a general tendency to devalue the role of the language minority parents because of their newness to this country or their lack of English skills. As a result, schools only involve them in simple activities or ask for their help only on rare occasions.

5. It is too common an occurrence that schools lack Vietnamese bilingual personnel who are able to respond to inquiries and questions by Vietnamese parents. Usually, the school secretary is the most knowledgeable person. Yet, one cannot expect that person carrying so many responsibilities to handle translations for all kinds of different language groups. The school or district must provide other bilingual staff to provide services related to Vietnamese students. Recently, in connecting with a local school district for information, I received a message in Vietnamese that dated back to 1993 and had never been erased from the answering machine. Needless to say, the message fortunately related incorrect and outdated information to many newly arrived Vietnamese parents in the district.

To foster ongoing rapport and communication with Vietnamese parents, schools can organize and hold a variety of workshops which would appeal to Vietnamese parents: How to Get Your Children Admitted to UC Berkeley, How to Get Your Children Into a Four-year College, How Can You Help Improve Your Children's Reading Skills? Schools can provide these after-school programs for parents with the confidence that Vietnamese parents will gladly participate. These workshops can provide information about other programs that the school offers. Other sessions may utilize community resources to provide parents with preparation for the citizenship test or evening English as a second language (ESL) programs for working parents. A workshop about filling out different types of government forms would also be most welcome.

SOUTHEAST ASIAN GANGS: MYTHS AND REALITIES

The recent eye-catching headline, "Southeast Asian Gang Takes Hostages at the Good Guys Electronic Store in Sacramento" brought strong reactions from many Vietnamese community members. Some outright disowned and proclaimed that they, the perpetrators, were actually Chinese Vietnamese from the northern part of Vietnam. Others felt that, for too long, the community had not been paying close attention to issues concerning their youth and the changes they are forced to undergo as young immigrants.

The reality is that many Vietnamese parents are caught in a survival struggle, are pressed for time, and can only fervently hope that their children will do well in school. The reality is that many Vietnamese parents cannot believe that some of their own have taken a wrong turn and resort to acts of senseless violence.

This televised incident was not a typical gang story but a tragedy that portrayed a Vietnamese immigrant family caught between two worlds—the traditional world of the older generation and the insensitive, individualistic, and alienating world to which the younger generation must adjust. Unfortunately, there is only a handful of material discussing this "Vietnamese problem" from the perspective of race relations. Recently, an important article on this topic appeared in Feagin and Smith's *The Bubbling Cauldron* (1995). In their chapter, authors Michael Peter Smith and Bernadette Tarallo (1995) provided an ethnographic analysis of the Good Guys incident and discussed the quick assumptions made by the mainstream media in labeling this gang-related incident. Clearly, even the sheriff's department mishandled the case by completely ignoring the role of ethnic culture in the resolution of the matter.

In the late 1980s, when the topic of Southeast Asian gangs regularly made the headlines of local newspapers, I was often contacted to work with law enforcement agencies to find answers or solutions to these problems. Workshops revealed that many officers in the audience believed that Southeast Asian youths were the most vicious and most violent of all gang members. "They stop at nothing," one law enforcement professional remarked. "Since they come from the war, from Vietnam, they bring with them such violent behavior," another officer offered his opinion. "They have an arsenal of handguns, automatic rifles, and the deadly Uzi."

The officers were partially correct. It is true that the level of violence has escalated among many youths, including Vietnamese youngsters. However, it seems erroneous to attribute their violence and carelessness about their own and others' lives to their country of origin or to the long-ceased Vietnam War. The violence they pick up is from the TV set in the living room of overcrowded apartments in San Francisco's Tenderloin district or from their crime-ridden neighborhoods. Johnny Nguyen can literally get his 357 Magnum and AK47 on any street corner. Violence is glamorized and glorified by the media. Johnny Nguyen did not see the war in Vietnam; he is too young. Instead, he saw wars on American movie screens, where Rambo and the Equalizer mercilessly cut down their enemies, or he saw in *Scarface* where it was "pretty cool" to carry an Uzi under a trenchcoat.

Indeed, the sources of these problems can be found right here in America or on the way to America (Conly, et al., 1993; Lewis, 1994). Exposure to violence in the refugee camps, survival needs in the streets of impoverished neighborhoods such as the Tenderloin district in San Francisco, and the difficult adjustment to life in a new society are some of the factors responsible for acts of violence committed by Vietnamese-Americans. These factors may be compounded by the fact that parents are working too hard and simply do not have time for their children. At school, administrators and teachers may not be able to provide a little extra effort or care. Confused over their parental rights and misled on issues related to disciplining their children (i.e., corporal punishment, dating, restrictions), Vietnamese parents may perceive that American society is fraught with violence, teenage problems, unplanned pregnancies, drugs, and diseases. Oftentimes, they feel helpless in witnessing their children become further attracted to the cult of materialism so prevalent in the mainstream media. Faced with the pressure to be accepted, Vietnamese youth may be quick to abandon traditional family values and become preoccupied with cars, walkman players and other electronic goods, styles of clothing, and other things for instant gratification. Many Vietnamese parents may simply give up on trying to reach their children, because resources such as youth programs are either unavailable or unknown to them. Case studies show, however, that when parents make a conscious effort to intervene and work closely with the district personnel in helping their children, these youngsters successfully complete their high school education and move on to college. I personally know a number of students who truly benefited from their parents' help. Spring Diep is but one such student. She is now at San Francisco State University finishing her junior year (personal interview, January 17, 1997).

CONCLUSION

In addition to issues concerning earlier arrivals in the Vietnamese immigrant community, more recent arrivals (Chung, 1992) have raised the importance of rethinking how schools can meet the needs of a changing Vietnamese student population. Perhaps foremost among the matters which call for new strategies and interventions is the development of partnerships with Vietnamese parents and the Vietnamese community. It is important to recognize that many Vietnamese parents are rearranging their lives to pay more attention to their children's education even as they grapple with their daily life struggles. The school can take the critical first step in forging partnerships by helping Vietnamese parents feel wanted and comfortable enough to get involved.

Efforts to involve Vietnamese parents may target a small circle of parents at first, with goals for future expansions. Vietnamese-American children will immediately benefit from the positive effects of this powerful collaboration between parents and schools. Generally speaking, Vietnamese who have resided in the United States for more than five years have many of the survival issues out of the way and are in a position to volunteer their time and advise teachers of changes in the family and community. In working with any group of language minority students, one must examine the needs of students in the context of their family and community. At the same time, parents can work on understanding the problems and needs their children face in the schools and join hands with teachers and administrators to forge an important partnership instrumental in the educational success of their children.

REFERENCES

California Department of Education. (1994). *Handbook for teaching Vietnamese-speaking students*. Sacramento CA: California Department of Education.

Chung, H. C. (1995). Ethnic enterprise in America: Vietnamese nail salons. *San Francisco Urban Institute Quarterly* 1 (1) pp. 9-10.

Chung, H. C. (1994). *Vietnamese students: Changing patterns changing needs*. San Francisco, CA: Many Cultures.

Chung, H. C. (1992). Teaching the content areas to LEP student, *Social Studies Review* 31 (2).

Chung, H. C., & Le, V. (1994). *The Amerasians from Vietnam: A California study*. Rancho Cordova, CA: Southeast Asian Resource Center.

Conly, C., Kelly, P., Mahanna, P. & Warner, L. (1993). *Street gangs: Current knowledge and strategies*. Rockville, MD: U.S. Department of Justice.

DeVillar, A., Faltis, C. A., & Cummins, J. (1994). *Cultural diversity in schools: From rhetoric to practice*. Albany: State University of New York Press.

Do, Q. T. (1989). Notes on education in the traditional culture of Vietnam. *Journal of Vietnamese Studies* 1 (2).

Dorais, L. J., Pilon Le, L., & Nguyen, H. (1987). Exile in a cold land. *Lac Viet Series,* VI. William Joiner Center and Yale Center for International and Area Studies.

Feagin, J. R., & Smith, M. P. (1995). *The bubbling cauldron.* Minneapolis: The University of Minnesota Press.

Forbes, S. (1985). *Residency patterns and secondary migration of refugees resettlement in the United States.* Washington, DC: U.S. Department of Health and Human Services, Office of Refugee Settlement.

Immigration and Naturalization Services. (1993). *Statistical yearbook of the immigration and naturalization services.* Washington, DC: Center for Migration Studies.

Kelly, G. P. (1979). *From Vietnam to America: A chronicle of the Vietnamese immigration to the U.S.* Boulder, CO: Westview Press.

Kiang, P. N. C. (1994). When nothing speaks English only: Analyzing Irish and Cambodian struggles for community development and education equity. In Aguilar San Juan, K. (Ed.) *The state of Asian America.* Boston: South End Press.

Knudsen, J. (1983). Boat people in Southeast-Asian camp. *Bergen Study in Social Anthropology.* University of Bergen, Norway.

Krashen, S., & Terrell, T. (1983). *The natural approach.* San Francisco: Alemany Press.

Lewis, J. (1994). The codes of the streets: Southeast Asians and other newcomers in California's classrooms. *Context,* V (111).

Liu, W., & Murata, A. (1979). *Transition to nowhere.* Nashville, TN: Charter House.

Long, D. P. (1996). *The shattered dream.* Boston: Northeastern University.

Ngin, C. S. (1990). The acculturation pattern of Southeast Asian refugees. *Journal of Orange County* 3 (4).

Nguyen, X. T. (1991). *Language education and culture: A Vietnamese perspective.* Melbourne, Australia: Phillip Institute of Technology.

Pham, M. H. (1996). *Phat Trien Giao Duc va Phat Trien Con Nguoi.* Ha Noi: Nha xuat ban khoa hoc xa hoi.

Rumbaut, R., & Ima, K. (1988). *The adaptation of Southeast Asian refugee youth: A comparative study.* Final report prepared by the Office of Refugee Resettlement. Washington, DC: U.S. Government Printing Office.

Smith, M. P., & Tarallo, B. (1995). Who are the good guys? In M. P. Smith & J. R. Feagin (Eds.), *The bubbling cauldron.* Minneapolis: University of Minnesota Press.

Tollefson, J. (1989). *Alien winds: The re-education of Indochinese refugees.* New York: Preager

U.S. Bureau of the Census. (1993). *1990 census of population: Asians and Pacific Islanders in the United States.* Washington, DC: U.S. Government Printing Office.

U.S. Committee for Refugees. (1997). *World refugee survey.* Washington, DC: US Committee for Refugees.

Woodside, A. (1979). *Vietnam and the Chinese model.* Cambridge, MA.: Harvard University Press.

CHAPTER 10

English Instruction for High Achievement in the Twenty-First Century: A Vietnamese-American Perspective

Mai Dao

The English Language
When the English tongue we speak,
Why is "break" not rhymed with "freak"?
Will you tell me why it's true
We say "sew" but likewise "few";
And the maker of verse
Cannot cap his "horse" with "worse"
"Beard" sounds not the same as "heard";
"Cord" is different from "word";
Cow is "cow", but low is "low";
"Show" is never rhymed with "foe";
Think of "hose" and "dose" and "lose";
And think of "goose" and yet of "choose."
Think of "comb" and "tomb" and "bomb";
"Doll" and "roll" and "home" and "some,"
And since "pay" is rhymed with "say,"
Why not "paid" with "said," I pray?
We have "blood" and "food" and "good";
"Mould" is not pronounced like "could."
Wherefore "done" but "gone" and "lone?"
Is there any reason known?
And, in short, it seems to me,
Sounds and letters disagree.
(Anonymous, 1987)

"The English Language," a poem of anonymous composition, depicts with humor one Vietnamese-American's perspective on the English language. Currently, there is a dearth of English language development programs based on Vietnamese-American perspectives. While educators in the United States are familiar with transitions form various Western languages to another Western language, for example, from French or Spanish to English, they are less familiar with the transfer from various Eastern to Western languages. This chapter examines the linguistic differencs between Vietnamese and English and explores how such differences may affect the English language and literacy development of Vietnamese-American students.

LINGUISTIC BACKGROUND OF VIETNAMESE-AMERICAN
STUDENTS

Vietnamese-American students come from a cultural heritage that has a deep regard for learning in general and for literate people in particular. This is reflected in an educational system and family values that places a strong emphasis on academics. For example, reading is a common pastime among the Vietnamese working class as well as those of higher economic status.

Vietnamese is spoken by more than 69 million Vietnamese people in Vietnam and more than one million in other parts of the world, such as the United States, France, Canada, and Australia (Huynh-Dinh, 1996). In fact, Vietnamese is among the top ten minority language spoken in the United States (California Department of Education, 1989). In California, the Vietnamese-American student population is the second largest minority language group, after the Spanish-speaking student population (California Department of Education, 1996). Vietnamese-Americans are also a significant minority language group in many other parts of the United States.

Vietnamese-American students in public schools display varying levels of Vietnamese and English language competence in the areas of reading, writing, and oral language, depending upon the home environment and educational background. Often, a students' degree of English language proficiency depends largely on the amount of coaching and academic support at home and the quality of English instruction from good teachers who understand these students' language needs.

It is important to consider Vietnamese-American students' proficiency in Vietnamese in the development of English language skills. Typically, these students learn English to a level of proficiency which enables them to function in the community, school, or neighborhood. However, they may or may not receive adequate instruction that supports the development of high academic English language proficiency. Simultaneously, instruction or support in the mother tongue is absent. Under such circumstances, students who do not yet have a strong foundation in Vietnamese lose their ability to communicate in Vietnamese while their English proficiency is still low, because they are in the early stage of the many years required for learning English as second language. Thus, many Vietnamese-American students have acquired only functional levels of English language skills but have lost their mother tongue. Serious communication difficulties arise and affect the students' learning and academic performance (Dao, 1991) because, in school, they cannot fully benefit from instructional assistance provided in either English or Vietnamese; and, at home, they cannot fully benefit from their parents' or other family members' assistance.

Vietnamese-American students traditionally come from families in which parents and grandparents usually educate the children in a variety of ways, by telling stories, sayings, and proverbs; or by reciting or reading Vietnamese literary works. This aspect of the Vietnamese culture is actually a strong basis for literacy development for many Vietnamese children. Unfortunately, this naturally occuring and valuable literacy practice has often been overlooked by many educators, despite the fact that research has demonstrated the significant effect of Vietnamese parents' maintenance of home language and cultural traditions on Vietnamese-American students' academic achievements (Caplan, et al., 1992).

Some Vietnamese-American students are highly literate in Vietnamese and possess a strong formal educational foundation. Of these, some have had limited exposure to English, while others have had several years of formal instruction in English as a foreign language. Those students who have a strong educational background in Vietnamese language and content knowledge tend to be able to transfer their skills, transition into English, and attain academic achievement fairly rapidly. This is consistent with research evidence that shows that the most significant student background variable contributing to academic second language proficiency is the amount of formal schooling students have received in their first language (Collier, 1987; 1995).

There are also Vietnamese-American students who possess limited literacy skills in Vietnamese, due to the lack of or interruption in schooling prior to their arrival in the United States. While they can speak and understand Vietnamese well, they need literacy development and subject matter instruction in Vietnamese in addition to a strong English language development program, for optimal cognitive and academic achievement.

DIFFERENCES AND SIMILARITIES BETWEEN VIETNAMESE AND ENGLISH

This section is designed to help teachers take steps to prevent primary language interference during Vietnamese-American students' English language acquisition process. Additionally, the following will provide an overview of important aspects of the Vietnamese language that are very different from English, as well as parallel forms and structures in Vietnamese that do not exist in the English language. It may thus help teachers to identify appropriate instructional foci for English language learners of Vietnamese linguistic background.

Vietnamese is a distinct language which is not mutually intelligible with any other language. Its linguistic system differs not only from those of Indo-European languages, but also from other Asian languages. Vietnamese has three distinctive characteristics: It is monosyllabic, tonal, and noninflectional. The Vietnamese writing system is in the form of the Roman alphabet (Huynh-Dinh, 1996; Katzner, 1975).

Phonology

Vietnamese Vowels. By and large, Vietnamese vowels are quite similar to the corresponding English vowels, except for subtle differences in pronunciation. The Vietnamese vowels keep the same value in all instances; the sounds of the vowels do not change because of the syllabic environments as they do in English words.

Vietnamese Consonants. With a few exceptions, consonants in Vietnamese are basically similar to those in English. Nevertheless, the distribution and combination of some Vietnamese consonants and vowels differ markedly from the English ones.

Vietnamese does not have consonant clusters such as the English /shr-/ as in shrimp, /skr-/ as in scrooge, /-sks/ as in desks. In Vietnamese, the consonant blends are graphically written with two consonants, but they are not pronounced as a cluster of two consonants; they are pronounced as a single sound; for example, the Vietnamese sound tr in "tre" (bamboo) is not the same as /tr/ as in tremble. This case is comparable to /f/ in phonology and /f/ in phở (noodle soup).

In Vietnamese, there is a distinction between the *unaspirated* /t/, which is pronounced without a puff of air as in tôi (I), and the *aspirated* /t'/, as in thôi (to stop), in initial positions. English has the *aspirated* /t'/ in the initial position but no *unaspirated* /t/ in the initial position.

Unlike English, Vietnamese has numerous diphthongs and triphthongs that are pronounced as single sounds. A diphthong is a combination of two vowels that make one sound in a word (e.g., áo—dress); a triphthong is a combination of three vowels that make one sound in a word (e.g., bưởi—grapefruit).

Monosyllabism. Contrary to English, which is polysyllabic, Vietnamese is monosyllabic, as reflected in the above examples.

Tone. Tone consists of pitch changes within a word that affect its lexical meaning (California Department of Education, 1983; 1994); in other words, a change of tone brings about a change in meaning. There are six tones in Vietnamese, each of which is clearly represented by a diacritical mark either over or under one of the vowels of the appropriate syllable.

Intonation. Intonation has a very limited role in Vietnamese, whereas in English different intonation patterns express differences in the speaker's attitudes. This is an important aspect of the English language that needs to be pointed out to Vietnamese learners of English, so that appropriate expressiveness may be developed in these speakers.

Stress. Stress is another important feature of the English language that the Vietnamese students have to acquire. In English, the change of stress may change or distort a word's meaning and affect its intelligibility (Huynh-Dinh, 1996). However, in Vietnamese, stress has no phonemic value and does not constitute a class of phonemes.

Vietnamese learners of English come from a linguistic background that has a clear set of rules for tones and pronunciation of single and complex vowel combinations. To learn English, Vietnamese-Americans have to learn a different sound system with no clearly stated rules or variations in pronunciation, and inconsistencies in stress and intonation patterns.

Morphology and Syntax

Vietnamese is a noninflectional language. Vietnamese words do not change their morphology to express grammatical categories such as gender, number, tense, case, or mood. There are no prefixes, suffixes, or conjugations for derivations or inflections to mark tenses, plurals, possessives, and so on. When necessary, grammatical meaning is expressed by appropriate function words.

Moreover, Vietnamese does not have pronouns equivalent to the English *it*, *s/he*, or they in the same way they are used in English; such pronouns are only used in Vietnamese for referring to someone lower in social hierarchy. Instead, particles that denote deference are added according to the relationship between the interlocutors. For example, an adult, when referring to a young child, would use **nó** (he). However, the same adult, when referring to a teacher, would add **ấy** and would say **Cô ấy** or **Ông ấy** for Miss or Mister for "she" or "he." This is an instructional focus that needs to be addressed for learners of English as a second language, so that they learn the appropriate use of English feminine, masculine, singular, and plural pronouns; that is, knowing when to use "he," "him," "she," "her," "hers," "mine," and so on.

Plural Form. In English the form of a word changes to reflect the singular or plural; in Vietnamese, the form of the word does not change, and, when alone, does not reflect any number. This is an area of instruction that needs attention because Vietnamese learners of English may omit the final -s when it should be there or may add the -s when it should not be there.

Possessive Form, Adverbs, and -ing Forms. One of the ways to indicate possession in English is the use of the possessive form with apostrophe s, as in "John's book." The apostrophe s, which is pronounced exactly the same as the plural s (with the /-s/, /-z/, and /-iz/ alternatives), may cause Vietnamese learners of English the same problems in pronunciation and in syntax as does the plural form.

Unlike English, Vietnamese does not use suffixes in the following syntactical forms: The -er comparative and -est superlative; -ly adverbs; -ing forms used as nouns; and -ing forms used as adjectives. Because of such distinguishable differences between Vietnamese and English, these forms need to be clearly pointed out to Vietnamese students in order to help them learn to use the English language forms properly.

Verb Tenses and Forms. Great differences exist in the expression of tenses and verb forms in Vietnamese and English. In Vietnamese, the same verb form is used for present, past, and future actions, or for first, second, and third person. Usually the context clues alert the listener concerning the time element of a particular event.

When time is overtly indicated in a Vietnamese sentence, function words or phrases such as "yesterday," "tomorrow," or "when" are added to indicate time as it is done in English. But in English, the time phrase and tense in a sentence must correspond; whereas in Vietnamese, the verb form does not change, whatever the time function word may be.

Eample:
When he was in France he often *spoke* French:
    Hồi   anh *ở* Pháp thì anh *nói* tiếng Pháp thường.
    When (past) he live France then he speak language France often.
When he is in France he often *speaks* French:
    Lúc   anh *ở* Pháp thì anh *nói* tiếng Pháp thường.
    When (present) he live France then he speak language France often.

Like English, auxiliaries are also used in Vietnamese for emphasis or to indicate specific times. But unlike English, in Vietnamese the verb form does not change, whatever the auxiliary word may be. This implies that Vietnamese learners of English may equate English tenses with such auxiliaries, which may not be incorrect in cases such as "I *will eat* bread." However, it would be inappropriate to equate English tenses with Vietnamese auxiliaries in the case of the English present perfect tense, where the auxiliary "have" and the past participle "eaten" are involved in the construction of the sentence—"I *have eaten* bread" Tôi *đã ăn* bánh mì (I already *eat* bread).

Examples of the differences between Vietnamese and English morphology and syntax are provided in Table 10.1.

The description of morphological and syntactical differences between Vietnamese and English in Table 10.1 clearly points to the critical need to teach Vietnamese-American students how to properly use English tenses and to teach them about the various verb forms, particularly the irregular verbs, and other related aspects of English language usage. This also points to the fact that correct usage of English cannot "just be picked up" by learners of English as a second language—an underlying assumption that leads to failure in helping students develop high levels of academic English. From the Vietnamese learners' perspective, English morphology and syntax are extremely complex as it involves learning about various irregularities, the changes of word forms and usage, as well as the breakdown of phrases and word positions in reference to tense changes. Therefore, this area of English language instruction must be extensively covered in appropriate contexts for Vietnamese learners of English to be equipped with the strong foundation needed for progress toward a high level of academic competence in English.

"To be." Vietnamese and English differ in two ways in the use of the verb "to be" in sentences. First, in English, "to be" is an irregular verb that comes in different forms in the present or the past tense—I *am* or *was*, you *are* or *were*, we *are* or *were*, they are or were, s/he *is* or *was*. In Vietnamese, the equivalent of the verb "to be" is là; its form remains the same (là) whether the subjects are first, second, or third person, singular or plural, and whether the tense to be reflected is present, past, or future depending on the context of the sentence.

Secondly, in Vietnamese, "to be" does not occur in all sentences as "to be" would occur in English sentences. In sentences with predicate nouns, "to be" will occur in Vietnamese as "to be" does in English (e.g., Lan is a student). However, in Vietnamese sentences with predicate adjectives, là (to be) does not occur. For example, in English, one would say "Lan is sweet;" in Vietnamese, one would say the equivalent of "Lan sweet." This is another area of verb usage that should be addressed in English instruction for Vietnamese learners of English. Transferring from Vietnamese, new learners of English may omit the verb "to be" and say "Mary nice" instead of "Mary is nice."

Questions. While in English, both types of questions involve rearranging the word order of the verb phrase, in Vietnamese, the word order does not change from the affirmative statement to the corresponding question.

Yes-no questions: In Vietnamese, to turn a statement into a corresponding question, it is simply a matter of adding không at the end of the affirmative statement; however, in English, formulating a question requires changing the verb form to "do" or "did" plus the infinitive verb and breaking down the verb phrase.

WH-questions: WH-questions in English differ from their corresponding statements in two ways: (1) a WH-word (e.g., who, what, when, where, why, which) replaces the appropriate element in the statement and is moved to the beginning of the sentence; and (2) the verb phrase is split up as it is done in yes-no questions. These differences are shown in Table 10.1.

Table 10.1
Vietnamese and English Morphology and Syntax

Vietnamese	English
Uninflected language. *No suffix* -no final -s sound at the end of the word; words do not change their forms to express grammatical categories by way of suffixes	*Inflected*: Use of suffixes for the plural form

Plural

Vietnamese	English
Tôi cần một cuốn *sách*. I need one roll book.	I need a book.
Tôi cần ba cuốn *sách*. I need three roll book. *Possessive form ('s)*	I need three books.
Tôi cần cuốn sách *của* ông Quang. I need roll book property Mr. Quang	I need Mr. Quang's book.

Comparative and superlative

Vietnamese	English
Bill *cao* hơn Minh. Bill tall superior Minh.	Bill is tall*er* than Minh.
Bill *cao* nhất lớp. Bill tall tops class.	Bill is the tall*est* in the class.

-ly adverbs

Vietnamese	English
Cô ấy *đẹp*. (adjective) Miss pretty.	She is pretty.
Cô ấy vẽ *đẹp*. (adverb) Miss draw pretty.	She draws nice*ly*.

-ing forms

Vietnamese	English
Tôi *đi*. I go.	I am go*ing*.
Đi một ngày, học một sàng khôn. Go one day, learn one basket wisdom.	[Go*ing* on] a one-day journey is worth a basketful of wisdom\
Nước *chảy*. Water flow.	Water flows.
Nước *chảy* sạch hơn nước đọng. Water flow clean superior water stagnant.	Runn*ing* water is cleaner than stagnant water.

Questions and Negatives

Vietnamese	English
Q. John có cá vàng *không*? John has goldfish?	*Does* John *have* goldfish?
A. John có cá vàng. John has goldfish.	John has goldfish.
N. John *không* có cá vàng. John not have goldfish.	John *does not* have a goldfish.
Q. John mua *cái gì*? John buy what?	*What has* John *bought*?
A. John mua cá vàng. John buy goldfish.	John has bought a goldfish.

Note the difference in word order and the breaking up of the verb phrase in English, e.g., "What has John bought?"

Tense

Vietnamese	English
The tense of the sentence in Vietnamese can be understood in one of the three tenses, depending on the conversational context:	The verb form expresses the contrast between past and present tenses.
Tôi *mua* áo len và *kiếm* mua giày bốt. I buy sweater and look-for buy boots.	I *am buying* a sweater and *looking* for some boots; I *bought* a sweater and *looked* for some boots; or I <u>will buy</u> a sweater and
The same verb form is used for past, present, and future; the time is inferred from the context, or expressed by auxiliary or	<u>will look</u> for some boots.
function words such as rồi, sẽ:	
Tôi *uống* sửa rồi. I (past) drink milk.	I *drank* milk.
Tôi uống sửa. I drink milk.	I *drink* milk.
Tôi sẽ uống sửa. I intend drink milk.	I <u>*will drink*</u> milk.

Sources: California Department of Education (1983); National Indochinese Clearinghouse (n.d.).

Negatives. Negative statements in English, like questions, are difficult for the Vietnamese learners of English. Negatives involve the same breaking-up of the verb phrase, the same use of "do," and the same irregular behaviors of the verb "to be." In Vietnamese, to change an affirmative statement to a negative one, it is only a matter of inserting the word "not" (**không**) in front of the verb.

From the perspective of the Vietnamese learners of English, formulating questions and negative statements in English is a very involved process. Teachers of English should pay careful attention to helping Vietnamese learners how to properly form English questions and negatives in all tenses.

Articles and Classifiers. The use of the articles a, an, and the is one of the most difficult aspects of English to teach, particularly to learners from an Asian, specifically Vietnamese, linguistic background. In general, a or an is used when one is referring to one instance of something or something indefinite or general, for example, "John ate a cookie"; also, in general, if one wishes to refer to more than one of something or someone indefinite or general, one would use the bare plural of the noun without an article, for example, "John eats cookies." Furthermore, in order to refer to someone or something definite or specific, one uses the article the with both singular and plural nouns, e.g., "John ate the cookie that belonged to his sister" and "John ate the cookies that belonged to his sister." However, there are numerous exceptions to these rules; for example, in the sentence "The goldfish is a member of the carp family," the definite article "the" is used, even though the sentence refers to all goldfish and not just one goldfish in particular.

Moreover, to complicate the matter of teaching and learning English, there are many nouns in English, called mass nouns or noncountable nouns, which cannot occur with "a," "an," or in the bare plural (e.g., water, chalk, furniture, soap, milk). In such instances, it is incorrecty to say "Bring me a soap" or "Bring me soaps." It is also grammatically incorrect to use numbers with mass nouns (e.g., "Bring me three soaps").

Vietnamese also makes a distinction between general and specific, but not through the use of words parallel to the English "a," "an," and "the." Instead, Vietnamese utilizes a system of classifiers; this is, in many respects, parallel to the usage of English mass nouns. The usage of classifiers in Vietnamese applies to all other types of nouns, whether they happen to be comparable to the English mass nouns or not, that is, whether they are nouns that can be counted. Since classifiers are used with all nouns in Vietnamese, such linguistic practice on the part of Vietnamese speakers may transfer into English usage for nonmass nouns or countable nouns, which would be inappropriate in English.

SOCIOLINGUISTIC ASPECTS

The pragmatics (the context of language use) and paralinguistics (nonverbal and other extralinguistic features) of a particular language both reflect the cultural characteristics of a people. For example, the following are informal ways to say "Hello" to a friend in Vietnamese:

1. Look at the friend, nod, and/or give him or her a smile (no linguistic expression)
2. Look at the friend and casually ask **sao?** , which is equivalent to the English "How is it going?"

3. Look at the friend and ask làm gì đó? (What are you doing?), which is comparable to the English "What's up?"

In the last example, if a Vietnamese speaker uses a literal translation to greet someone with "What are you doing?", he may be misunderstood as being nosy in the Anglo-American cultural context.

Vietnamese ways of expressing emotions are in some ways different from Anglo-American ways (Huynh-Dinh, 1996). Most notably, various feelings may be conveyed more often via nonlinguistic symbols such as silence or a smile. The smile may reflect different things. It may convey respect. It may also be used as an expression of apology for a minor offense, as a substitute for "I'm sorry" (e.g., for being tardy to class). It may also indicate "Hi!" or a "Yes" that does not appear overly enthusiastic. The smile may also be used to express embarrassment when one commits an innocent blunder or to show that one sincerely appreciates a certain gesture in lieu of a "Thank you."

There are basic differences between English and Vietnamese in regard to speakers' tendency or preference to use linguistic expression or nonverbal expressions or gestures. While Anglo-American speakers are more inclined to use linguistic expression, Vietnamese-American speakers may prefer to express deep feelings through nonverbal means of communication (Huynh-Dinh, 1996). Table 10.2 illustrates the differences in expressing feelings in Vietnamese and in English.

POSSIBLE PROBLEMS IN LEARNING ENGLISH

Many of the difficulties students of Vietnamese linguistic background may encounter in learning English are the result of linguistic interference—the tendency to carry over the characteristics of his or her first language to the new language. Other difficulties may stem from lack of knowledge about the English language syntax and usage.

Vietnamese speakers may also encounter the following pronunciation problems.

Vietnamese students are not accustomed to sounding out the final consonants in Vietnamese. Thus, when speaking English, they may not make a clear distinction among walk, walks, or walked; between box and boxes; between desk and desks; or between bat and bad.

Table 10.2
Expressing Feelings: Vietnamese v. English

Circumstances/Feelings	Vietnamese	English
Under casual and informal circumstances, to express feelings of thanks or apology.	Silence or a smile	"Thank You" or "I'm sorry"
To acknowledge and show appreciation for a small such as closing the window or passing out books.	Parents and teachers show appreciation nonverbally. They usually do not say to their children or students, but express appreciation with a smile.	Parents and teachers say "Thank you" to their children or students.

Sounds that do not exist in the Vietnamese sound system but occur in English also present problems (Table 10.3).

There is difficulty with the pronunciation of sounds found in both Vietnamese and English systems which are similar but not exactly identical, for example, distinguishing between ship and sheep and vice versa. The sound for "i" in Vietnamese is always pronounced [ee]. Therefore, whenever a Vietnamese speaker sees "i" in a word, she or he may pronounce ship with an [ee] sound. Also, the sound for "a" in Vietnamese is pronounced more like the Spanish or French sound for "a" than the English "a," which is close to but not quite like apple.

For Vietnamese learners of English, one major area of difficulty is learning the grammatical structures of English. This includes learning time relationships and their corresponding sentence structures; verb forms, tenses, and proper usage, especially irregular verbs; and the complex interactions between auxiliaries and suffixes and their various combinations. Moreover, idiomatic expressions and the use of verbs which utilize different prepositions that change the meaning (e.g., pass; pass on; pass out) are complex aspects of English that require extra attention in instruction.

The sociolinguistic aspect of English is another major area of difficulty for Vietnamese students. Learning to use English to communicate appropriately in various social contexts is a difficult process that requires extensive exposure to and interactions within the American cultural environment over a long period of time.

DESIGNING EFFECTIVE ENGLISH INSTRUCTION

The above analysis points to the critical need for the development of a systematic and comprehensive English as a second language instructional program for Vietnamese-American students. But first, educators need to realize the following: It takes an individual four to twelve years of second language development in order to reach a high level of academic proficiency and to be able to compete with native language speakers (Collier, 1989; 1995). Limited-English-proficient students including Vietnamese-American children immersed in mainstream English-speaking classrooms acquire English with impressive speed. However, although they quickly gain native-like English pronunciation and appear quite proficient in English, their proficiency is usually limited to basic interpersonal communication skills, or surface fluency. These students often perform well for a short time, but generally perform poorly in the long run

Table 10.3
English Sounds Not Found in Vietnamese

Consonant Letters	Consonant Sounds	Words
th	/th/	that, those, then, them, though
th	/th/	thin, thought, theft
ch	/ch/	church, chime, chimney
j	/j/	jeep, judge, jean
p	/p/	pin, pot, paper
-l	/-l/	gal, pal, sail, girl
-r	/-r/	car, far, their

(Collier & Thomas, 1989). Their early successful performance in this sink-or-swim situation tends to mislead educators to believing that such an environment is helpful for language minority students. It is critical, however, that educators be reminded that the display of fluency in conversational English among Vietnamese-American children does not necessarily mean that they have already acquired adequate English language skills sufficient for high level academic work and instruction of abstract concepts in English.

Currently the focus of English instruction in the public schools has not gone much beyond emphasizing pronunciation, vocabulary, and the development of basic communication skills. To assume that students from Vietnamese linguistic background will "pick up" grammar on their own is not unlike assuming that math students will "pick up" the ability to derive square roots simply by being exposed to numbers and their square roots. Therefore, curriculum and instruction should not only address basic interpersonal communication skills, which most young Vietnamese-American children have already developed (Huynh-Dinh, 1996), but also provide a strong foundation of the linguistic structures of English. Without such instruction, it is unlikely Vietnamese-American students will achieve the precision in language skills necessary to understand difficult reading materials and to express complex ideas orally and in written form.

Considering Vietnamese Learners' Needs and Perspectives

Greater emphasis should be placed on considering the diverse needs and backgrounds of Vietnamese English language learners. Emphasis needs to be placed on moving away from views that stem from experiences of learning English as native speakers without experience in learning a foreign language for high level academic purposes. Unlike native English speakers in the United States who commonly study French or Spanish to meet a foreign language requirement or to prepare for a vacation in a foreign country, Vietnamese-American students are learning English as a second language in an academic environment where high level, academic English is used, often in a decontextualized manner; that is they have to learn basic skills and abstract concepts in the subject matters in English, the language which they have not yet mastered.

Therefore, in order to properly serve the Vietnamese-American student population, effective and comprehensive English as second language (ESL) programs need to be designed carefully. Developing such programs is not just a matter of selecting proper ESL materials for adoption. Effective programs need to be coordinated schoolwide and based on the input of qualified Vietnamese bilingual professionals who have insight in learning English as a second language.

Good teachers of reading and language arts in public schools normally include a variety of instructional approaches and strategies such as phonemic awareness, phonics, decoding skills, and the phonological and morphological structure of English. This is done from the perspective of designing instruction for students who are fluent native English speakers. The methods used are normally based on the underlying assumption that the students are already familiar with, for example, English sentence structures or word order in their verbal repertoires, which are usually developed before five years of age by native-born English speakers in their natural environments. However, teaching English Syntax to speakers of Vietnamese is an undertaking completely different from teaching syntax to native speakers of English (National Indochinese Clearinghouse, n.d.), since many Vietnamese learners of English have not had such English language exposure or experiences in their homes or communities. There are thus syntactical aspects that must be explicitly pointed out to Vietnamese learners. Vietnamese learners may also need more examples of usage in various contexts, as well as more opportunities for practice in order to fully acquire correct English language structures.

Moreover, careful attention needs to be given to Vietnamese-American students who are not English proficient. Their language needs are quite distinct from the needs of students who are normally considered limited English proficient (LEP). The currently used term LEP seems to encompass a wide range of linguistic proficiency, from slightly to very competent, in oral English. In other words, instructional strategies such as sheltered instruction and cooperative learning are enriching and effective in developing English language skills among students who have basic functional skills in English but need further development in English competency. However, such approaches may not be useful or optimal for those students who cannot speak or understand basic English. Unless instruction or group work involves scaffolding in the primary language, these learning experiences will most likely not be very meaningful.

In brief, it is important to recognize that every Vietnamese-American student has unique experiences in Vietnamese and English. Distinguishing the various language needs of Vietnamese-American students is critical in designing appropriate instructional programs and identifying appropriate instructional strategies for this diverse group of language minority students.

Building on Students' Strengths

Instead of adopting a remedial approach and focusing on the learners' deficiencies, the design of effective instruction for English literacy development of Vietnamese students should start with the areas of strength in these students' backgrounds. This is a basic principle of good pedagogical practice. As mentioned previously, capitalizing on the home support for early literacy development provided in Vietnamese families has been found to correlate to successful academic outcomes for these students.

Cummins's (1981; 1991) common underlying proficiency model explains that skills, knowledge, and concepts learned in any language can be accessed through different languages. Indeed, students who learn to read in their mother tongue are able to transfer many of the reading skills to English (Thonis, 1981). Roberts (1994) lists ample research evidence that low-level literacy skills (i.e., encoding, decoding skills and functional abilities) are generally transferable. Research in programs in the highlands of Vietnam and among Vietnamese-Americans in the United States (Pham, 1994) has shown that such skills do transfer, and first language literacy promotes second language learning (Gudschinsky, 1977). Table 10.4 offers an outline of transferable and nontranferable literacy skills from Vietnamese to second language.

Literacy entails much more than the decoding, encoding, and functional skills mentioned above. It is related to shared knowledge and traditions in a specific social context. Vietnamese-American students who have had prior schooling and literacy experiences, enter American classrooms equipped with the skills and knowledge base necessary to construct meaning and make inferences and predictions. This is referred to as schemata, that is, knowledge representations that include the "knowledge of setting, the identity and function of props, participants' roles and responsibilities, expected activity sequences, rules for interaction, and norms of interpretation" (Saville-Troike, 1991, p. 3).

Vietnamese students' preexisting schemata provide a meaningful context for the interpretation of new language forms. Thus, in designing instruction, educators can capitalize on the funds of knowledge (Moll, et al., 1990) the students bring to the classroom and integrate these resources into the curriculum.

It is important to note, however, that Vietnamese-American students' preexisting schemata have been acquired through social experiences different from those mainstream students have had; that is, their knowledge of "the [learning] setting, the identity and function of props, participants' roles and responsibilities, expected activity sequences, rules for interaction, and norms of interpretation" are all based on the Vietnamese cultural ways and family traditions. This means that in American schools, Vietnamese-American students need to learn to negotiate meaning and function in an entirely new social context. Educators, then, need to teach Vietnamese-American students how to learn new schemata or how to adapt preexisting ones as part of the socialization (i.e., acculturation) process. As shown in Table 10.4, nontransferable literacy skills are the type of inferential skills that depend on extensive knowledge and understanding of values and traditions in the American culture. This is why, in teaching toward effective reading comprehension, it is critical that educators mediate and scaffold learning for the Vietnamese-American students, so that the students can relate what they already know from their culture to the new information situated in the American cultural context; that is, educators need to activate prior (or familiar) knowledge in the construction of new knowledge. The extent of mediation needed for individual Vietnamese-American students necessarily varies according to diverse factors, such as the students' level of acculturation or the degree of similarity between the old and new schooling settings.

Suggestions for English Language Development

Good ESL instruction should include considerations of the student's level of linguistic proficiency. One cannot effectively teach the same content and materials to beginning and advanced learners of English at the same time, using the same methods. There needs to be a clear distinction between non-English proficiency level and varying degrees of limited English proficiency levels; this is not unlike assigning beginning students of Spanish as a foreign language to the basic course or beginning class and placing advanced students in the advanced Spanish course.

For Vietnamese-American students who are non-English proficient, intensive ESL instruction must be provided before they are placed in an all-English academic class where English is the medium of instruction. ESL materials should also have culturally appropriate directions in Vietnamese, just as foreign language textbooks have instructions in English for English-speaking

Table 10.4
Transferable and Nontransferable Literacy Skills from Vietnamese to Second Language

Transferable	Nontransferable
Readiness skills	
-knowledge that written symbols correspond to sounds and can be decoded in order and direction	
-directionality; sequencing	
-ability to distinguish shapes, sounds	
-activation of semantic and syntactic knowledge	
-recognition of some rhetorical devices	
-knowledge of text structure	
-learning to use cues to predict meaning	
-awareness of purposes for reading and writing (e.g., directing behavior, providing information, describing a process)	
-strategies: experimenting, hypothesizing, creating, constructing meaning	
-confidence in oneself as a reader and writer	
-eye movement from left to right on a horizontal line and from top to bottom (same sensorimotor skills required in Vietnamese and English writing systems)	
-identifying position, size, and shape, relationship between capital and lower case letters in Vietnamese and English	
-other skills in the area of auditory discriminationand cognitive development	
Decoding skill	Vietnamese and English
identifying the letters representing vowels and consonants	unrelated, very few cognnants
Comprehension skills, including inferential skills	Inferential skills that require
following tupes of inferential skills:	knowledge and understanding
-developed schemata for the interpretation of meaning.	another culture (e.g., colloquialism, irony, humor,
-listening or reading for the main point	sarcasm, etc.)
-generalizing	
-making logical inferences from known information	
-constructing more complex schemata American societal context)	
-recognizing the meaning of punctuation	
-understanding the concepts of synonyms, antonyms, and homonyms	
Literary and study skills	
-critical reading skills and other study skills needed to learn to appreciate Vietnamese literature	

Sources: California Department of Education, 1983; Pham, 1994; Roberts, 1994; Saville-Troike, 1991.

learners. Such ESL instruction needs to be treated as an important subject and should be provided by qualified teachers trained in English as a foreign language methodology. This leads to a critical question: Is it realistic to require regular classroom teachers to provide effective ESL instruction for Vietnamese-American students? Teacher qualifications and in-service education need to include sensitivity to students' linguistic and cultural backgrounds and levels of language proficiency, and expertise in providing appropriate instructional scaffolding; but is there enough time to adequately train prospective teachers to become sufficiently competent in ESL methodology?

Among the powerful models for use with limited English proficient students are the Canadian dual language immersion model, the European schools model, and the newcomers center being utilized in San Francisco Unified School District. The newcomers centers are beneficial for secondary students. At the elementary level, the dual language program is the most promising of all English language learning models in ensuring long-term academic success for language minority students (Collier, 1995). At the secondary level, the newcomers center provides much needed acculturation and language support. The European schools model, another effective second language program, has been successfully implemented in Europe, Vietnam, and other Asian countries. In these programs, the second language is taught as a subject before it is used as a language of instruction; then, instruction continues in the second language until a high level of grammatical accuracy is attained (Baetens Beardsmore, 1993).

For limited English proficient students, English language development needs to be integrated into the core curricular areas. Foreign language methods, which address the structure of the English language, need to be utilized. Instructional strategies that are appropriately modified for elementary school and high school students to provide explicit language models in meaningful contexts are also critical. Thematic units and subject matter lessons should include not only relevant vocabulary words, but also instruction in how to communicate, explain, and elaborate appropriately and effectively; that is, students also need to be taught appropriate terms and methods of communication, so that they can articulate not only the solutions, but also how they arrive at their solutions. For example, in hands-on science activities, students need to be taught how to describe their observations and findings, as well as how to critically discuss their analyses and conclusions. Language development also needs to be addressed in math, so that students can make meaning out of word problems.

Preparing for Meaningful Learning

There are basic steps to preparing students for meaningful learning, regardless of the teachers' choice of instructional approach, such as the use of learning centers, rotation stations, activities, or various structures in teaching. Simply said, students learn best when the subject matter is organized and presented in a systematic manner that facilitates optimal comprehension. When students understand the lessons, they are more engaged and tend to apply and utilize the English terms that they have learned during the lessons more effectively.

Teachers who have worked with Vietnamese- and Spanish-speaking students at the elementary and secondary levels emphasize the following in providing quality instruction via strong language support in the core content areas for language minority students:

1. Identify ahead of time a list of terms and expressions related to the lesson — not just a few vocabulary words from the standpoint of a native English speaker, but terms which LEP students might need. All necessary high level academic language, including terms necessary for learning abstract concepts, needs to be included. The language of instruction should not be watered down.
2. Request the district, school, or bilingual parent volunteer to have the list translated into the student's primary language.
3. The list should show three corresponding columns: One for English, a second column for visual representation (e.g., a simple sketch or picture), and a third column for equivalent terms or explanations in the student's primary language. The students should be provided with copies of this list.

This type of handout is very helpful for the students who can read. For those who are not yet competent readers, their more competent peers, parent volunteers, or instructional aides can refer to the list to provide assistance. With the use of this well-prepared list, the teacher can be assured that the help provided by peers, parents, or aides is accurate, and not left to chance. The students can take the handout home and study it, allowing for more meaningful learning in class. They may also use the list as a glossary, referring to it whenever they need appropriate words in discussions or for assignments. Parents can also use the list to provide specific support. Without the dual language list, they would not know what to focus on, when assisting with their children's language and concept learning at home.

Before going into the core of the lesson or activity, the teacher needs to allocate time to develop English language learning for language minority students. The teacher needs to utilize media (real objects, pictures, demonstrations, and/or students' native languages) as well as a repertoire of instructional techniques in order to ensure student comprehension of terms and expressions related to the concepts, skills, and information presented in the lesson. Current instructional practice generally entails simply verbally going over a few vocabulary words quickly. It must be emphasized that initially taking more time and using diverse techniques to prepare students for meaningful learning will lead to more effective teaching and learning, not only for Vietnamese-American students but for all students.

During the course of guided practice or activities, the teacher needs to scaffold learning by asking questions and encouraging the students to explain and verbalize their observations. The teacher should allow the students to express themselves in whichever language they are most comfortable. Students may struggle to communicate their ideas in English and opt to elaborate in Vietnamese, in which case it would be a great opportunity for the teacher to reiterate the students' thoughts or ideas in English and model appropriate language use within a situation-specific or relevant context. Vietnamese-American students need plenty of opportunities to practice verbalization of their thought processes before going on to the next step, learning to communicate effectively in writing. Verbal interactions between the teacher and the student is critical for at least two reasons. First, it allows students to practice English and to demonstrate understanding of English terms and usage within the context of the lesson. Second, it allows the teacher to guide and check for understanding, and identify specific areas of comprehension breakdown; this, in turn, allows the teacher to provide appropriate feedback via scaffolding, support, and repetition in specific areas of need. The teacher's key role, then, is to underscore correct English language use by reiterating students' correct communication attempts, providing appropriate scaffolding, and modeling correct communication in English in authentic contexts.

CONCLUSION

If developing English language and literacy for Vietnamese-American and other students is considered a serious matter, it is necessary to recognize that the sink-or-swim approach of letting them "just pick up English" in mainstream classrooms is neither adequate nor acceptable. Acquiring English for academic purposes and high level functioning is a complex, long, and difficult process which requires coherent, well-coordinated, continuous, and systematic instruction, consistently provided at each grade level. As such, systemic change for English language education should be an integral part of school reform efforts. In implementing effective English as a second language instruction, schools need to reconsider the roles and responsibilities of each individual involved: Who are the individuals qualified to teach English as second language? Is it realistic to expect regular elementary classroom teachers and secondary school teachers trained in other subjects to bear the responsibility of teaching English as a second language? Why is the U.S. educational system failing many learners of English in an ideal environment for learning English, the United States, while foreign educational systems are equipping students in non-English-speaking countries with a sufficient English language foundation that allows them to enter and function in U.S. colleges and universities?

If today's educators are to face the challenges of preparing Vietnamese-American students for the twenty-first century, they need to shift away from the practice of teaching simplified language, watered down academics, and cognitively simple tasks of the 1970s and 1980s. Policies need to be based on genuine considerations for effective teaching of English for the limited English proficient learners. Decision makers need to support and ensure the adoption of pedagogical approaches that are more responsive to Vietnamese-American students in all aspects—sociocultural, academic, cognitive, and linguistic. Accordingly, consideration must be given to students' instructional needs and their areas of strength. The importance of the home language and cultural heritage on the academic growth of Vietnamese students must be taken into account. In this vein, schools can begin by tapping into the valuable resources that can be found in Vietnamese-American families and communities.

REFERENCES

Anonymous (1987). The English language. In M. Dao (Ed.), *From Vietnamese to Vietnamese-American: Selected articles* (p. 70). San Jose, CA: Division of Special Education and Rehabilitative Services, San Jose State University.

Baetens Beardsmore, H. (Ed.) 1993. *European models of bilingual education*. Clevedon: Multilingual Matters.

California Department of Education. (1983, 1994). *A handbook for teaching Vietnamese-speaking students*. Sacramento, CA: California Department of Education.

California Department of Education (1989). *Language census report for California public schools—1989.* Sacramento: CA: California Department of Education.

California Department of Education (1996). *Language census report for California public schools—1996.* Sacramento: CA: California Department of Education.

Caplan, N., Choy, M. H., & Whitmore, J. K. (1992). *Indochinese refugee families and academic achievement. Scientific American* 266 (2): 36-42.

Collier, V. P. (1987). Age and rate of acquisition of second language for academic purposes. *TESOL Quarterly* 21: 617-641.

Collier, V. P. (1989). "How long? A synthesis of research on academic achievement in second language." *TESOL Quarterly* 23: 509-531.

Collier, V. P., & Thomas, W. P. (1989). How quickly can immigrants become proficient in school English? *Journal of Educational Issues of Language Minority Students* 5: 26-38.

Collier, V. P. (1995). Acquiring a second language for school. *Directions in Language & Education* 1 (4): 1-11.

Cummins, J. (1981). The role of primary language development in promoting educational success for language minority students. In California Department of Education (Ed.), *Schooling and language minority students* (pp. 3-49). Los Angeles: California State Universtiy, Evaluation, Dissemination and Assessment Center.

Cummins, J. (1991). Interdependence of first- and second-language proficiency in bilingual children. In E. Bialystok (Ed.), *Language processing in bilingual children* (pp. 70-89). Cambridge: Cambridge University Press.

Dao, M. (1991). Designing assessment procedures for educationally at risk Southeast Asian-American students. *Journal of Learning Disabilities* 24 10: 594-602.

Dao, M. (1995, May 1). A matter of teaching and scaffolding: Helping Vietnamese-American students transition. *NABE News* (May 1): 18, 6.

Gudschinsky, S. (1977). Mother-tongue literacy and second language learning. In W. F.Mackey and T. Andersson (Eds.), *Bilingualism in Early Childhood* (pp. 250-258). Rowley, MA: Newbury House.

Huynh-Dinh, T. (1996). *Introduction to Vietnamese culture.* Huntington Beach, CA: Southeast Asian Culture and Education Foundation.

Katzner, K. (1975). *The languages of the world.* New York: Funk & Wagnalls.

Moll, L., Velez-Ibanez, C., & Greenberg, J. (1990). Community knowledge and classroom practice: Combining resources for literacy instruction. In *Handbook for Teachers and Planners: Innovative Approaches Research Project.* Arlington, VA: Development Associates.

National Indochinese Clearinghouse (n. d.). *Teaching English structures to the Vietnamese. Indochinese Refugee Education Guide #11.* Arlington, VA: Center for Applied Linguistics.

Pham, L. (1994). Infant dual language acquisition revisited. *The Journal of Educational Issues of Language Minority Students* 14 (Winter): 185-209.

Roberts, C. (1994). Transferring literacy skills from L1 to L2: From theory to practice. *The Journal of Educational Issues of Language Minority Students* 13 (Spring): 209-221.

Saville-Troike, M. (1991). Teaching and testing for academic achievement: The role of language development. *Focus: Occasional Papers in Bilingual Education*, No. 4. Washington, D.C.: National Clearinghouse of Bilingual Education.

Thonis, E. (1981). Reading instruction for language minority students. In California Department of Education (Ed.), *Schooling and language minority students: A theoritical framework.* Los Angeles: California State Universtiy, Evaluation, Dissemination and Assessment Center.

CHAPTER 11

Hmong-American Students: Challenges and Opportunities

Anthony T. Vang

Hmong-American students are refugees and children of refugees who have immigrated to the United States since 1975. There is very little written about Hmong-Americans, let alone Hmong-American students. When the Vietnam War ended in 1973, many Hmongs in Laos were unwanted or persecuted by the communist Laotian government because of their support for the United States during the war. Hence, the mass exodus of the Hmongs began. The United States became the primary recipient of the Hmong refugees. Once in the United States, the majority of these Hmongs settled in California, Minnesota, and Wisconsin. Half of the California Hmongs live in the San Joaquin Valley (Trueba, et al., 1990). In fact, Fresno, California has the largest concentration of the Hmongs outside of Laos (Trueba, et al., 1993).

This chapter briefly reviews Hmong-American history and illuminates the challenges and difficulties in cultural adaptation and school adjustment which Hmong-American parents and students face, as well as the impact of various sociocultural factors on the education of Hmong students. In addition, this chapter provides concrete suggestions for educators to help Hmong-American students succeed.

HISTORICAL PERSPECTIVE

The Hmong people are a unique group, who, with some dialectic differences, share a unique language and culture. There are about seven million Hmong people scattered around the world. Many of them live in China, North Vietnam, Laos, Thailand, Burma, Australia, Canada, France, Germany, and the United States. The Hmong people have been known by the Chinese and others in Asia as "Miao" or "Meo," which is considered a derogatory name by the Hmongs. Hmong means "free people or human being" (Yang, 1992).

In Laos, the vast majority of Hmong children had limited access to education. The only formal education available in Laos was in the Lao language. Once in school, the Hmong students learned how to read and write in the Lao alphabet and the Lao language. It generally took Hmong children two to three years before they could acquire the Lao language correctly (Bliatout, et al., 1988). Since the Hmong language was not produced in written form until the mid-1950s, many Hmong adults and youths have never experienced the process of becoming literate in their native language.

Why the Hmong People Left Laos

The United States gave up involvement in the Vietnam War in 1973. Two years later, the North Vietnamese and Pathet Lao Communists took over Laos. Suspected of being US spies, the Hmongs became an unwanted people. They had to flee from Laos to escape persecution. On May 12, 1975, a few of the Hmong military leaders and their families were airlifted to safety in Thai camps, but thousands were abandoned, forgotten and left behind to run for their lives through the jungles. Those military leaders who remained were sent to reeducation camps or killed by the communists (Warner, 1995).

Many Hmong people who are now resettled in the United States and other countries had to walk through the dangerous jungles for days before slipping into the Mekong River at night on logs, makeshift rafts, or with "water wings" of bamboo under their arms to escape to freedom. They immigrated as political refugees to the United States, France, Australia, Canada, Argentina, and French Guyana. The largest number of Hmong immigrants in the Western countries, estimated at over 165,000, is in the United States, and the majority resettled in California (U.S. Department of Health and Human Services, 1996), particularly in Fresno and Sacramento.

The Impact of the Secret War in Laos

During the long and dangerous journey from Laos to Thailand, thousands of the Hmong people lost their lives. Many of them were killed by the Lao Communist soldiers, died of starvation or illness, or drowned in the Mekong River. Unfortunately, arriving at the border of Thailand did not end the trauma because many Hmong people lost their families and everything they owned at the border. Take, for example, the story of Kia Lo, a Hmong girl, as reported by Marc Kaufman in the *Philadelphia Inquirer* (1994):

In 1987, Kia Lo, her mother and four brothers and sisters were among thirty-three Hmong transported across the Mekong on a raft by Thai and Hmong smugglers. Fired on by a Thai security patrol, the group emerged from the bushes. After the Thai police confiscated all of their money, one group was allowed to proceed to Ban Vinai, but Kia's group was brought to Baan Haad Bia village. Before dawn the Thai police loaded them onto four boats and sent them back to Laos.

Kia's group... met Pathet Lao soldiers who said they would escort them back to their home area. Instead, the soldiers took them deep into the forest. Kia recalled that they took us to the top of a hill, putting a rope around the adults' necks, they made us sit in a line like we were going to dance. They told the women, "Take your babies off your backs and hold them in front of you." My mother told us, "Now they will kill us." Then the soldiers shot us with rockets and their guns.

Thai fishermen discovered Kia dazed and alone on the riverbank several days later. They took her to a Thai hospital, where an American Embassy official found her and heard her story. The intervention of former Minnesota Sen. David Durenberger allowed the girl to come to America, and she now lives in Minnesota with an uncle. (1994, pp. 15-28)

Refugee Camp Experiences

Some of the Hmong refugees stayed in refugee camps for over ten years; many of the last arrivals were those who had been in camps the longest. However, some of them were lucky enough to be immediately resettled in countries such as the United States, Australia, France, Germany, and Canada. The long-stayers in the camps faced a variety of problems, including poor sanitation, malnutrition, food shortage, and lack of medical services.

In the refugee camps, children were not allowed to go beyond the camp territory. Since it was assumed that refugees would stay only temporarily in Thailand, building schools inside the camps was not a priority of the United Nations High Commissioner for Refugees.

Most of the Hmong children were of school age when they entered the United States. Some of these children had left their country at an early age, while others had been born in the refugee camps. They were too young to know what had happened to them as a result of the Vietnam War and too young to learn the Hmong traditional culture (Podeschi & Xiong, 1990).

Resettlement and Migration Experiences

Many Hmong people experienced life as displaced persons for several years. Most Hmong people in the United States have moved several times, in an effort to bring together family and clans in a new and promising land. Many of the younger Hmong people have never had a permanent home structure (Vang, 1992). Based on the availability of sponsorships, the primary resettlement of the Hmong people was spread out in various locations in the United States such as Alaska, Alabama, California, Colorado, Indiana, Illinois, Kansas, Ohio, Oregon, Oklahoma, Minnesota, Montana, Michigan, Rhode Island, Texas, Washington, and Wisconsin.

The typical migration pattern of a Hmong family was to first establish themselves and become familiar with their new environment. Then, depending on the availability and affordability of housing, employment opportunities, and proximity to family and friends, they would make a secondary migration to another location. Many Hmong families have moved repeatedly from one city to another and then back again, for example, from Minnesota to Fresno, California. The frequent moves of the Hmong families led to high levels of stress and disruption in the children's education. The high rate of transiency also affected the consistency or availability of ESL programs at local public schools.

According to the California Department of Education, in the 1996-97 school year, there were 36,765 Hmong-American students attending public schools in California. The Hmong language was the third most spoken non-native language in California public schools after Spanish and Vietnamese. Eighty-five percent of the Hmong-American students were classified as limited English proficient, with only 15% identified as fluent English speakers (California Department of Education, 1997).

THE INFLUENCE OF HMONG CULTURAL PATTERNS ON FAMILY FUNCTIONS

The Hmong society is characterized by its clans. There are approximately eighteen to twenty-five clans, with each clan comprised of persons sharing the same paternal ancestry. Each clan is distinguished by its last name—Cha, Cheng, Chue, Fang, Hang, Her, Kha, Kong, Kue, Lee, Lo, Moua, Pha, Thao, Vang, Vue, Xiong, or Yang. Clan membership plays an important role in defining social relationships; people with the same clan name are considered brothers and sisters. A man must marry outside his clan. Relationships between clans must be maintained so that marriage can be arranged and proceed smoothly. Men remain members of the same clan all their lives, but women normally move from one clan to another by marriage. Membership in a distinctive, spiritual community is the criterion of clanship. Admission to a clan happens by birth, marriage, or adoption (Yang, 1992). The clans who share a common ancestry and the same basic rituals are more closely related.

A male leader who oversees all relations with other clans directs each clan. The head of the clan has particular powers that permit him to communicate with other clan members on specific issues. Together the clans and the extended family form the basis of the Hmong society's economic, religious, and social well being. In a time of need, Hmongs often turn to their clan for help.

A traditional Hmong household consists of grandparents, parents, children, unmarried brothers and sisters, and grandchildren. The family is the primary institution of the Hmong society. Order and authority in the household are maintained by knowledge of Hmong culture, the ability to communicate with other clans, and respect toward older persons. Younger brothers and sisters respect their older brothers and older sisters; sons and daughters respect their father and mother; and nephews and nieces respect their father's and mother's brothers and sisters, in order of their age.

Marriage Customs

According to the Hmong custom, a father usually has the right to propose marriage for his sons and to judge those proposed for marriage to his daughters. Traditionally, Hmong parents want to see their children marry and have children before they die. Sometimes, Hmong children are forced to marry at a young age because Hmong culture has strict standards of behavior for their children, particularly young girls. For example, if a girl stays after school for a special program or goes to the library accompanied by a male classmate, the girl's parents will most likely pressure her to marry him. In this society, marriage can also be precipitated by the family's need to save face, particularly in situations in which parents feel their children have brought shame to the family (Vang, 1992).

Behaving within the norms of American culture is not in accordance with traditional Hmong family values. More significantly, the Hmong New Year celebration is a time for courtship, when teenagers meet their future spouses. Courtship lasts about three to nine months and marriage follows. The individuals are usually between the ages of fifteen and eighteen. However, some of the young Hmong-Americans today exhibit a strong desire to complete their education before marriage, as they see career opportunities as part of a successful life in the United States.

Roles of Women and Men in Traditional Hmong Society

The patriarchal structure of the Hmong family system plays a significant role in terms of how women are viewed in their society. In Hmong culture, the man is considered to be the head of the household. He has the power and authority to make decisions. He is the breadwinner and has responsibility for the family's economic welfare. The Hmong woman is expected through marriage to become a homemaker and mother. These are the primary roles she is to fulfill during her lifetime.

Traditional Hmong culture is deeply rooted in the lifestyle of an agrarian society and the ways of such a society remain embedded in Hmong families to this day. Agrarian societies are characterized by a high degree of stratification by gender, particularly in the division of labor (O'Kelley & Carney, 1986). In agrarian societies, the man becomes involved in the outer or public sphere, which brings him social prestige and power; the woman is involved in the inner or home sphere, which is given less prestige and power. Women are not considered to be economic producers for the family and society, and they remain close to the home and provide childcare. Men perform the bulk of the agrarian work, which requires long hours and muscular strength.

Change and Conflict. Transplanting the traditional gender role stratification system of the Hmong society into the modern, industrialized workplace of the United States is difficult for the Hmong women, particularly for the young girls who are torn between traditional Hmong culture and American culture. Young Hmong-American girls are faced with this economic reality: if they are unable to complete their high school due to early marriage and pregnancy, they may find themselves in poverty, contributing to the feminization of poverty in this country (Martin, 1991). If young Hmong girls will eventually acculturate to American society, the traditional division of labor in the home will erode. If Hmong girls are expected to do household chores and duties and work outside the home, the traditional division of labor will be a major problem among Hmongs in the future.

THE HMONG FAMILY IN TRANSITION AND CULTURAL CONFLICT

The Hmong families in the United States have undergone tremendous cultural adaptations since their arrival in the United States. The Hmong refugees came to the United States with the expectation of finding a stable home and educational opportunity for their children. However, some of the fantastic hopes of the refugees have disintegrated into disappointment. The resettlement process is often slow and difficult. Some Hmong parents have high expectations about life in the United States, especially in regard to education for their children.

The skills the Hmong parents acquired in their homeland as medical assistants, teachers, military officers, and farmers often do not transfer to this country due to differences in certification and credentialing procedures or in employability. They are forced to rebuild their lives, often working in positions of lower status in order to support their families. Relatives who were left behind in the camps in Thailand may have high expectations for financial support from their relatives in the United States. These adjustments to new roles and added pressure contribute to the stress and acculturation difficulties experienced by many Hmong people.

Now that the brutal tragedy of war is behind them, Hmong parents often speak of their fear in facing what lies ahead: coping with the increasing alienation of their children from what were formerly strong, self-reliant families. Many Hmong-American fathers find it more and more difficult to maintain a strong family unit and assert their role as the head of the family. Hmong children learn English faster and can utilize it better than their parents (Rumbaut & Ima, 1988). They are expected to act as interpreters or instructors and often need to make decisions for adults. Thus, the traditional family structure is challenged and even destroyed, causing considerable tension in the family.

In some cases, the youth have been trained to be tough, quick, and truly independent in getting what they need, one way or another. Many Hmong children have become streetwise in surviving in a harsh environment, but are confused about the values and rules of their families. Living in a host culture with different values, codes, and acceptable behavior, the youths find themselves caught between two cultures. In such a confused state, anxiety enters as a symptom of their state of confusion. A defense mechanism would allow them to cope better with their confusion. Such difficulties in adjusting to a new school and new culture cause many Hmong students to fall behind academically. The dropout rate is unacceptably high. This is largely due to the fact that Hmong children must struggle to adapt to a new culture with barriers of language, culture, and other issues that prevent their full participation in education.

Hmong children adopt new customs and habits fast, contributing to the concerns of Hmong-American parents who want to retain the cultural standards which are associated with respect for and care of elders, proper socialization of children, and maintenance of family. When Hmong adults are asked what worries them most about living in the United States, one of the most frequent answers is the difficulty of raising "good children" who are obedient, responsible, and properly mannered. Young people who are especially peer oriented quickly adopt American customs and behaviors that seem acceptable to the peer groups but are often completely unacceptable to the Hmong-American parents. These conflicts create a severe generation gap in Hmong families, where Americanized Hmong teenagers may flaunt their independence before parents who wish to preserve traditional values.

The Acculturation of Hmong-American Children

The rapid acculturation of the young Hmong children increases the generation gap and sociocultural distance between family members. Some young Hmong children tend to favor English over Hmong and prefer hamburgers, tacos, and hot dogs to traditional Hmong food. Young Hmong children, in adopting American culture, become more expressive. However, traditionally, young Hmong children are not to express anger, frustration, or contempt toward their parents. The communication gap between Hmong parents and their children can grow wider and wider. Understandably, many Hmong parents are confused and fear losing their authority in educating and disciplining their children.

Eventually, one generation will move ahead, and the other generation will be left behind. There is a generation gap between old and young, but who is old and who is young? In a typical Hmong family, instead of one generation gap, there are several. For example, a twenty-two-year-old Hmong man may wonder what has gotten into the kids-why they dress the way they do, dye their hair in a different color, and why they don't study harder in school. The same twenty-two-year-old man may regard a forty-five-year-old Hmong man as a senior citizen, and the forty-five-year-old may speak of "we the younger generation" and "you elders" to still older Hmong adults.

THE EDUCATIONAL BACKGROUND OF HMONG STUDENTS

Many Hmong children in kindergarten to third grade find learning English difficult. Often, their reading and writing skills are far below their grade level, with lack of literacy skills in their own language compounding the problem. Hmong children who have learned the Hmong literacy skills are able to transfer their reading and writing skills to English quite easily. This is because the Hmong language uses the Roman alphabet. It is relatively simple for them to figure out which letters stand for which sounds in English and thus be able to read and write in English.

Those students who are literate in their own language have proven that they have the requisite visual, auditory, and sensorimotor skills, as well as oral language and conceptual development necessary to learn another language (Hakuta, 1985). This means that the student has at least minimum skills and abilities and should be able to progress educationally even when taught in a second language. A positive effect of native language literacy is that it encourages a sense of pride in the student, since he or she is able to read and write in his or her own language. Unfortunately, there are still many Hmong children unable to read or write in their own language because of the unavailability of Hmong bilingual programs.

The Refugee Experience and Its Impact on the Education of Hmong Children

Many young Hmongs must deal with psychological trauma. They suffer from a sense of alienation and separation from their own culture. Some Hmong students may have been sent to the United States while both parents were left behind. Others may have lost their parents through torture and death and must face living in a new land without parents. Others must deal with conflicting messages from their old and new culture, with the old culture still being practiced at home on a daily basis by their parents, and continued exposure to and pressure from the new culture at school. Undoubtedly, these factors have a tremendous impact on Hmong children's academic success in the schools.

Hmong cultural values, beliefs, attitudes, and practices have impacted the Hmong children growing up in America both positively and negatively. The Hmong family's dedication to education is an attitude that has positive implications for children. The school system is a major arena of socialization, and Hmong parents soon recognize the importance that the school has on their children's lives. On the negative side, many factors related to their refugee experience influence the children's academic success or failure.

Relocation can be difficult for children. Having to adjust to new settings, new teachers, and new peers can be a source of educational and social instability for Hmong youth. In addition, Hmong gender issues, as previously noted in this chapter, often negatively impact girls. Some parents may not totally support their daughters' education for fear that they may be "too old" to marry after completing a college education. In fact, many young Hmong women fear this themselves.

However, recent research found that the Hmong girls will challenge the traditional concepts of being girls held by their parents and will seek gainful employment outside their homes (Park, 1998a). The Hmong girls will eventually break away from the traditional female roles cherished in their native country. Furthermore, the study showed that the Hmong-American students have similar levels of educational and occupational aspirations to other Asian-American students. The result pointed out that Hmong students who attend regular classes have higher educational aspirations and better adjustment to the American public school than those who were placed in the English as a second language class.

IMPLICATIONS FOR CLASSROOM TEACHERS AND OTHER EDUCATORS

The teaching and learning styles and expectations in the American educational settings are different from those in Laos. For example, schools in Laos emphasize memorization. In addition, teachers have absolute authority over the behavior and welfare of their students. Students are not encouraged to challenge the intelligence or knowledge of their teachers. Thus, the transition from one style of learning to another is often quite problematic for the Hmong students.

According to Park (1998b), the Hmong students appear to be the most visual learners and have the greatest preference for tactile learning style among all Southeast Asian groups in the study. Therefore, teachers must try to incorporate a variety of teaching strategies when working with Hmong students. The instructional contents should include cooperative learning, visual, and hands-on activities (charts, graphs, semantic maps, graphic organizers, character webs, etc.). Park (1998b) suggests that teachers should try to diversify their teaching styles to match the preferred learning styles of students.

Teachers who are not trained in culturally appropriate teaching styles may actually contribute to the dropout rate of Hmong students. It is important to understand that Hmong students often tend to be silent in the classroom. They do not ask too many questions because they are afraid of being laughed at or of being viewed as less intelligent. Also, it is not culturally appropriate to show off one's knowledge. Thus, these students may not participate in classroom discussions and consequently receive low marks on class participation.

Some Hmong-American students are suspended from school for infractions such as truancy, fighting, and auto theft. Usually their parents are not aware of what has happened to their children, since most school newsletters or permission slips never come to the attention of Hmong parents, and some Hmong-American students frequently forge their parents' signature on school forms. In reality, youngsters are happy to be suspended from school because they consider school subjects to be boring. Further, suspension creates more leisure time for these students to get involved in gangs and illegal activities. Thus, suspension does not appear to be an effective method of discipline for these students.

Case Study I: A Hmong Adolescent's Dilemma

This case study of Kong illustrates many of the problem Hmong-American students' face in the United States. Kong came to the United States as a refugee from Laos in 1990 at the age of thirteen. Kong is a tall, passive, mild-mannered, and rather good-looking young man who dyes his hair brown. His legal entry document states incorrectly that he is three years younger than his actual age. His father was killed during the Vietnam War, and his mother is remarried, leaving him to be raised by an aged grandmother. Kong lives in a two-bedroom apartment in a crime-ridden neighborhood with his uncle, aunt, grandmother, and four cousins. The family subsists on money from Aid to Families with Dependent Children (AFDC).

Kong spent his early childhood with his grandmother in a refugee camp in Thailand. He never went to school before he arrived in Fresno, California. Moreover, he was not literate in any language when he arrived in the United States. He was placed in the eighth grade in a large, racially mixed school where ethnic tensions erupted into fights almost every day. He felt isolated, confused, and utterly lost in his classes. He failed eighth grade twice. He began to skip most of his classes and was arrested once for car theft and another time for driving without a driver's license. He was subsequently suspended from school for a week and placed on probation. Despite advice from the school counselor, the probation officer did not think Kong was prepared to accept help. He had frequent arguments with his aunt and uncle and refused to do household chores. He spent more and more time in the streets. He was bored in school and ashamed to be in classes with students much younger than he was. Interestingly, Kong proposed to work on his problem by transferring to a high school. In order to assist Kong, his school counselor, uncle, and aunt went along with his proposal, but the school refused to place him in a high school until the Immigration and Naturalization Service corrected his legal document. Returning Kong to the same grade in the same school proved to be a major mistake. School officials knew about his criminal record and watched him closely. At the same time, Kong felt that he was being treated unfairly at home. His aunt and uncle did not allow him to go out with friends, and he believed that nobody trusted him, even when he was trying to change.

One day the school counselor noticed that Kong was dressed sloppily and looked extremely thin. Kong told the counselor that he had been living with a friend who was providing him with shelter and food. The next day, the counselor found out through a good information source that Kong had been living in a condemned house with many other youths who had run away from home. Some of them had been arrested several times for auto theft, but because the juvenile justice system in Fresno was overloaded, they were not punished or held accountable in any way.

The efforts of Kong's aunt and uncle to help him fell flat. Kong's own sense of reality was that it was too late to turn back. He believed that his family would never again love him as before and that he was hopelessly behind in school and could never catch up. With an incorrect birthdate on his immigration papers and a poor command of English, he was unable to get a job. He now moved from place to place around the city, one step ahead of the probation officer. Kong's case illustrates well the problems common to many Hmong-American students.

Clearly, the educational system is not prepared to work with these populations. It is extremely difficult to work with Hmong youths when their families feel so powerless. Hmong parents often feel very frustrated because they are unable to express their feelings to the school administrators due to the language barrier. When a Hmong student is suspended from school, Hmong parents feel disgraced, blame themselves for not being able to help their children, and blame the school for not helping them.

One Hmong parent expressed to the author that he was terribly ashamed to have to show his face at the school again and again. He said, "If I had known my children would become wild in this country, I never would have risked my life to escape from the communists." Many Hmong parents are stressed and are faced with depression and feelings of helplessness and powerlessness concerning their relationship with their children's schools. Unfortunately, there is no easy mechanism to deal with the tragic aftermath, disgrace, and shame placed on the family by the experiences prompted by differences in culture and expectations.

It is easy for teachers to regard individual differences based on cultural differences as deviancies or deficits. Understanding the value differences of Hmong students will enable teachers to help students to recognize their own values and to recognize how these values are different from or similar to those of other children in the classroom. It will also help teachers to understand their own culture and values.

An important aspect to be aware of is that Hmong-American children tend to be shy and quiet in the classroom and not ask questions. The cooperative demeanor of Asian students may belie the turmoil, confusion, or hopelessness many Hmong students feel inside. Take the example of May Lia, who was a junior high school student when interviewed by the author in 1996. She was living with her mother and four younger siblings in a two-bedroom apartment. Although she spoke English well, her academic achievement was below average. Her expectation of going to high school was not realistic because there was no role model in her family, and very few in the Hmong community. May Lia needed help with her assignments, but she had no idea where to turn. In addition, she said, "I have lots of problems with my science and history classes. Those subjects are very difficult and boring. I seldom ask questions in the classroom even if I do not understand." The next time the author spoke with May Lia, in December 1996, she had left home, dropped out of school, and moved in with her boyfriend, who was a member of an Asian gang.

Besides facing academic achievement pressure and adjustment problems, Hmong students often have to deal with ethnic tension at school. Fresno, California, is one of the most ethnically diverse cities in the nation. At one high school, students come from eighty-nine different linguistic backgrounds. Some Hmong students have told the author that they think their teachers are not supportive because they are prejudiced against Asians. Sometimes, other students belittle Hmongs for being short, skinny "rice eaters."

The author recalls an event in 1985 when a school administrator was invited to listen to a group of Hmong students express their feelings about ethnic tension on the school campus. Instead of listening to what the students had to say, the administrator began by saying, "Racism is happening everywhere. If anyone plans to press charges against anyone in the school, they would have to agree to report to the police and appear at a court hearing to testify." He also stated that ethnic tension most likely stemmed from a group of students who tended to speak their ethnic languages too often in front of others who could not understand. The meeting had turned into a lecture and warning. The Hmong students were understandably quite disappointed in not being able to express their feelings or get support. They left the meeting feeling guilty for having created problems at school. The words "press charges" and "police" discouraged them from talking to their teachers or counselors.

Parental involvement in a child's education plays an important role in school success. A bridge between home and school can alleviate the isolation between parents and children, which can block communication, create barriers, and widen the cultural gap. There is no doubt that, some twenty-two years after the first Hmong immigrants arrived in this country, American public schools continue to struggle with Hmong parent involvement. Many factors contribute to this, including inadequate funding, lack of bilingual staff and teachers, insufficient time to develop parent involvement programs, lack of knowledge about the Hmong culture, and the continued acculturation difficulties Hmong parents face.

Case Study 2: Lack of Communication Between Hmong Parents and School Personnel

A recent experience demonstrates how various factors can operate to pose difficulties for Hmong students. Pao, a high school senior, was placed in special education classes in his local public school because of his deafness. His hearing loss was due to having been given opium as a baby to keep him quiet during his family's escape from Laos, when they were in danger of Communist attack. He is able to speak fairly clearly and has done well academically. However, he has recently been spending lots of time with his girlfriend, and his grades have dropped. His goal is to become an architect, which requires a five-year college degree.

Due to the drop in his grades, his rehabilitation counselor advised him to attend vocational school for drafting and discouraged him from pursuing a five-year college degree. It is significant that the counselor made such recommendations despite having no background information or knowledge about the Hmong culture, and in particular, not having met with Pao's parents. The counselor remains hesitant about approaching Pao's parents, as they do not speak English well. She has no translator available and does not feel comfortable with the fact that having Pao translate may bias the conference. Because she is not knowledgeable about the Hmong culture, she has no clue where to begin addressing her student's problem, especially regarding obtaining parental involvement. When his parents were asked how Pao was doing in school, however, they answered that he was doing fine. They had no information concerning his grades or the school's recommendation for vocational training.

This is an unfortunate example of the problems brought on by the lack of Hmong bilingual teachers and bilingual counselors. Despite the rapid growth of the Hmong student population in many school districts, few educators have been trained to properly interact with Hmong students and their parents.

Case Study 3: Lack of Hmong Parental Involvement in American Public Schools

Another example illustrates how Hmong parents find it difficult to attend their children's school for special programs, such as back to school night or open house. Blia, a twelve-year-old Hmong girl, could not believe the large number of parents participating in open house at her cousin's private school. She reported how different things were at her own school, which had little parent involvement and how, despite many attempts, her parents never attended any of her school events. Usually, her older sisters became involved, but never her parents.

The parents felt self-conscious about their lack of knowledge about the American school system and feared that they would not know how to act or what to say to their daughter's teacher. Blia, however, felt that her parents were missing an important opportunity to support her and to become familiar with the demands that schools placed on students. When she came home, she was usually instructed to cook dinner, clean, and care for her younger siblings. Only when these tasks were done could she study, which was often not until the early morning hours. She felt that the whole situation was very unfair and that if her parents were more involved in her school and aware of school expectations, they would make fewer demands on her at home.

These two real life stories depict well the gap between Hmong parents and the American public schools. The reality base of the Hmongs and the school system are often at extreme odds with each other. While Hmong families emphasize education as a means to succeed in America, they leave most of the work related to their children's education for the schools to accomplish. Many Hmong parents feel that their involvement would not be helpful, as they may not be literate in Hmong, English, or both and perceive their lack of education as an embarrassment.

STRATEGIES TO INVOLVE HMONG PARENTS IN PUBLIC SCHOOLS

One of the many variables affecting Hmong parents' involvements in schools is their educational background (Trueba, et al., 1990). Most importantly, Hmong parents need information in their own language from the schools as to how they can help their children in the educational process. Communication must be established between parents and the schools so that each party can understand and respect the other's partnership.

One way to increase Hmong parents' involvement in school would be to have them share their culture with teachers, other staff, and students. This could be a stepping stone to greater parental involvement in Hmong children's academic development. Such a model of successful Hmong parent involvement was implemented in Winton School District, a small rural school district in central California. Once a year, Hmong parents organize a cultural program, which includes traditional dance, music, songs, artwork, and food. This event has resulted in parents feeling more welcome at the school. The success of this program would not have been possible without the collaborative efforts and support on the part of the Hmong parents.

Hmong parental involvement in their children's education and their participation in school activities are extremely important. Parent-teacher partnerships during the early grades can be a significant and positive experience in a variety of ways for all parties involved. Such endeavors can provide Hmong parents with opportunities to make decisions and to take on responsibilities toward helping their children's educational growth. Strategies for effectively fostering Hmong parental involvement in their children's education should include the following:

- Reinforcing the shared decision-making responsibilities of teachers and parents through extensive training for all participants.
- Providing training on effective communication strategies for both teachers and parents.

- Providing a well-equipped and accessible Parent Room with bilingual reading materials, television, VCR, and bulletin board.
- Providing an orientation session and a parent handbook for Hmong parents.
- Working with Hmong parents to form a Parent Resource Center in the schools, which can be utilized in planning and organizing family activities within the school and the community.
- Involving Hmong parents in the development of community linkages for schools.
- Working with Hmong parents and community to organize family and community activities.
- Providing Hmong literacy support, including early childhood education and parent education for Hmong parents.
- Teaching Hmong parents communication and interaction skills in relating with their children in an increasingly intercultural context.

Parents can play a significant role in assisting teachers, administrators, and children in classrooms and with various school activities. Parent-teacher meetings can help Hmong parents understand their children's behavior and academic achievement and help Hmong parents gain new insight and information about schools programs. Teachers can regularly provide Hmong parent's information about their children's progress, and also enable Hmong parents by sharing common concerns, frustrations, and successes toward helping the children.

An open-door school policy will help Hmong parents to understand school operations and goals and will encourage Hmong parents to volunteer in classrooms or extracurricular activities. A collection of Hmong reading materials may be made available on loan for families. If Hmong parents do not speak English, an interpreter should be made available to assist in communication between teachers and Hmong parents. Hmong parents can be strongly encouraged to spend time each month in their child's classroom either as a volunteer or as an observer, depending on their interest and skill level. Classroom time can help establish positive teacher-parent relationships. Finally, to the extent that it is feasible, school districts need to hire bilingual English-Hmong teachers.

HMONG PARENTS' ATTITUDE TOWARD EDUCATION

Parents are children's first and most important teachers. Parents can give their children a good start in life by equipping them with strong academic skills, which can increase their chances for success in school. Parents can organize extracurricular activities such as trips to the zoo, museums, and libraries. The home curriculum can include reading with and to the children, writing, and discussions about the importance of community events, as well as participation in various types of sports activities. This type of home environment can help build the foundation of children's learning, and linguistic and social development. Hmong parents can learn practical strategies on how to help their children with homework assignments and how to keep track of their children's progress in school.

Although Hmong families are certainly diverse and distinct, there are some cultural imperatives that remain fairly consistent across the culture and apply to all Hmong families. One of these imperatives is the importance of maintaining and keeping the Hmong language intact. Further, many parents feel that knowledge of the Hmong language can be beneficial to success in America, since being bilingual typically opens up many professional opportunities.

A recent study on Hmong parents' attitudes of bilingual education found that the majority of Hmong parents support bilingual education. Most Hmong parents feel that it results in greater development of knowledge and that it facilitates the learning of various subject matter. Most of the Hmong parents surveyed agreed that it was important that their children maintain their primary language (Lee & Shin, 1996). Despite what may be indicated by the current conservative political climate, Hmong parents apparently support the many advantages and benefits a well-implemented bilingual education can provide.

Pioneer Elementary School in Merced, California, offered a Hmong bilingual program from kindergarten through the third grade until the end of 1998. This program was abandoned when California passed Proposition 227 to partially ban the implementation of bilingual education in public schools. At each grade level, there are four Hmong bilingual teachers who possessed the Hmong BCLAD (Bilingual, Cross-cultural, Language and Academic Development) credential.

At this school, the Hmong children who have demonstrated their academic skills in English are also proficient in writing, reading, and speaking in their primary language. Since Hmong parents support Hmong language acquisition and maintenance, their support can be critical in the success of both their children and the school district. Bilingual education can be a tool that builds confidence and trust between families and schools, and instills in the children recognition of and respect toward both American and Hmong cultures.

LOOKING TOWARD THE FUTURE

Despite memories of a brutal past, unforgettable personal tragedies, and the difficulties of linguistic and cultural differences, many Hmong-American students are doing well academically and are successfully integrating into mainstream society. The number of Hmong-American high school and college graduates has increased dramatically across the country. For example, in 1987, Avonne Vang, a graduate in nursing from California State University, Fresno, was awarded the President's Medal, the highest honor bestowed by the university on a student. At Fort Miller Junior High School, in Fresno, California, twenty-six out of seventy-four of the school's March 1995 Honor Roll students were Hmong children (*Falcon Newsletter,* 1995). Most recently, in 1997, twelve Hmong-American high school students graduated as valedictorians in the Fresno Unified School District (Fresno Unified School District, 1997).

However, many Hmong children are still facing English language difficulty, as indicated by the results of the California Achievement Test (CAT). Many Hmong elementary and secondary students' knowledge of reading and writing is far below their grade level, and others are neither proficient in their primary language nor English, even though they were born in the United States. For example, in spring 1996, the author went to supervise his student teachers at a school in Merced County, California. He found five fourth grade Hmong students and their bilingual aide sitting outside of the classroom. He asked the bilingual aide why these students were not in class. The Hmong aide stated that it was because the Hmong children were classified as limited English proficient (LEP) and, therefore, not qualified to take the CAT. When the author asked the students in Hmong, "How long have you been here in America?" One replied, "Three years," and the others said, "We think the four of us were born here in Merced."

What Can Schools Do?

Despite problems and limitations, schools can help Hmong-American students achieve educational goals by implementing the following suggestions:

1. Provide both pre-service and in-service teacher training that includes useful information about Hmong culture to help teachers reach their Hmong students more effectively. Schools can provide incentives for both certified and classified employees to study the Hmong language and culture. Cummins (1989) points out that the transition from one style of learning to another is problematic for both teachers and students in intercultural settings. Teachers who are not trained in culturally appropriate teaching skills may actually contribute to the Hmong dropout rate. For example, American teachers need to know that Hmong children tend not to ask questions, not because they are shy and quiet, but because cultural codes dictate that deference and silence is appropriate when in the presence of authority figures such as the teacher. Further, American teachers could reach more of their Hmong students if they better understood their nonverbal cues and body language.

2. In order to increase the number of Hmong teachers and counselors, school districts probably have to "grow their own." Beginning in elementary schools, future teacher clubs can be formed to encourage Hmongs to complete their education and consider teaching as a career.

3. Schools can reach out more to Hmong parents and encourage them to keep their children in school and to be more actively involved in the education of their children. They need to know that in America, teenage marriages and childbearing usually prevent opportunities for graduation from high school or college.

4. Schools could offer tutoring and academic counseling after school, utilizing bilingual volunteer tutors or college students for a mentor program. A few schools, such as Fremont Elementary in Merced County, California, and Jane Adam in Fresno, California, already have such programs in place, and the results are encouraging.

5. Schools in California are already in the process of developing a more multicultural curriculum, but what will this mean for Hmongs, who are a tiny minority and who have not been in the United States long enough to make a strong impact on social and educational policy? Realistically speaking, to what extent can public schools offer Hmongs a sense of their own culture and national background? An alternative approach may be to develop their own "after hour schools" to supplement the public school curriculum and to give young people a sense of their special heritage as other minority groups such as Jews, Armenians, and Japanese-Americans have done. Such supplemental schools might help Hmong youngsters come to terms with their identity, which they need in order to succeed in American society.

CONCLUSION

For the Hmong people, a people that is already grieving for the loss of homeland, family, and stability, failing in education or dropping out of school is a tragedy that has effects beyond the school. It signifies the loss of potential talent and contribution to American society at large and the Hmong-American community in particular. Thus, we must all work to reduce and to eventually eliminate the educational failure and dropout rate among Hmong students. Towards this end, special programs need to be instituted in schools as an integral part of the Hmong children's education. Such programs require the support and input of all educators, administrators, and the Hmong community.

Teachers, counselors, and aides are in a unique position to establish relationships with the Hmong students and to communicate with their parents. They can provide ongoing assessments and continuous follow-up support of Hmong children's needs. Educators also play a crucial role in fostering a comprehensive approach to facilitating the educational process among parents, administrators, and the community. Therefore, a practical step schools can take is to develop programs that bring Hmong limited English proficient (LEP) students and their parents together in building literacy skills both in Hmong and in English and to provide inservice training for teachers and aides concerning the Hmong language, culture, and bilingual methodology. Not only will such training equip teachers with a clear understanding of how to work with and teach Hmong children better, it will also enhance the overall academic achievement of Hmong LEP students.

It is critical for schools to provide family literacy programs for Hmong parents and to encourage Hmong parents' participation in all school activities. Hmong parents should be encouraged to write and produce stories of their own lives, to create their family history, and to create a bridge between the past and the future of their children. The texts produced by family members can be used to enhance the curriculum of various subjects. In sum, parental involvement in American public schools would improve the quality of educational programs for Hmong children, enhance opportunities for access to bilingual materials or programs, promote high academic achievement, and reduce grade repeats and absenteeism among Hmong children and youths.

REFERENCES

Bliatout, B., Downing, B., Lewis, J., & Yang, D. (1988). *Handbook for teaching Hmong-speaking students*. Folsom Cordova Unified School District, Southeast Asian Community Resource Center, CA.

California Department of Education (1997). *Language census report*. Sacramento, CA: California Department of Education.

Cummins, J. (1989). *Empowering minority students*. Sacramento, CA: California Association for Bilingual Education.

Falcon Newsletter. (1995, March). Fort Miller Middle School. Fresno, CA.

Fresno Unified School District. (1997). *California basic educational data system report for high school graduates*. Fresno, CA: Fresno Unified School District.

Hakuta, K. (1985). *Mirror of language: The debate on bilingualism*. New York: Basic Books.

Kaufman, M. (1994). Allies abandoned: The United States enlisted the Hmong to help fight the cold war. Now it is shunning them during the peace. *Philadelphia Inquirer*, February 27, pp. 15-28.

Lee, B., & Shin, F. (1996). Hmong parents' perceptions of bilingual education. *CAAPAE Newsletter*, Spring, pp. 10-15.

Martin, G. (1991). Family, gender, and social policy. In L. Kramer (Ed.), *The sociology of gender* (pp. 323-345). New York: St. Martin's Press.

O'Kelley, C., & Carney, L. (l986). *Women and men in society*. Belmont, CA: Wadsworth.

Park, C. (1998a). *A comparative study of educational and occupational aspirations: Southeast Asian and Anglo students*. Paper presented at the Annual Conference of American Educational Research Association, April, San Diego, California.

Park, C. (1998b). *A comparative study of learning style preferences: Southeast Asian and Anglo Students*. Paper presented at the Annual Conference American Educational Research Association, April, San Diego, California.

Philadelphia Inquirer, February 27, 1994, pp. 15-28.

Podeschi, R., & Xiong, V., (1990). *The Hmong and American education: The 1990s*. Milwaukee: University of Wisconsin.

Rumbaut, R. G., & Ima, K. (1988). *The adaptation of Southeast Asian refugee youths: A comparative study*. San Diego: California State University.

Trueba, H. T., Cheng, L. R. L., Ima, K. (1993). *Myth or reality: Adaptive strategies of Asian Americans in California*. Washington, DC: Falmer Press.

Trueba, H., Jacobs, L., & Kirton, E. (1990). *Cultural conflict and adaptation*. New York: Falmer Press.

U.S. Department of Health and Human Services, Office of Refugee Resettlement. (1996). *Profiles of the Hmong communities in the United States*. Washington, DC: U.S. Department of Health and Human Services.

Vang, A. (1992). *The academically proficient Hmong high school girl dropouts*. Doctoral dissertation, University of San Francisco.

Warner, R. (1995). *Backfire: The CIA's secret war in Laos and its links to the war in Vietnam*. New York: Simon & Schuster.

Yang, D. (1992). *Minority cultures of Laos: Kammu, Lua', Lahu, Hmong, and Iu-Mien*. Sacramento, CA: Folsom Cordova Unified School District, Southeast Asia Community Resource Center.

CHAPTER 12

Mong Linguistic Awareness for Classroom Teachers

Paoze Thao

INTRODUCTION

Since 1975, over 1.1 million Southeast Asians (SEA) have been resettled in the United States. The United States Department of Health and Human Services (1995) tabulated the statistics for the numbers of SEA arrivals based upon their country of origin and indicated that 235,569 were refugees from Laos. The author estimated that 50% of those from Laos were ethnic Mong and that their numbers may have increased to 165,000 nationwide in 1997. Though a new statistical tabulation is not available, North and Yang (1988) presented data showing that the majority of the Mong population concentrates in three states—California (57%), Minnesota (13%), and Wisconsin (13%)—and the rest is scattered throughout twenty-seven states. Due to their lack of formal education in Laos and illiteracy in their own language, the Mong have experienced tremendous difficulties. These factors have affected their social and educational adjustment in the United States (Thao, 1994, 1997, 1998).

This chapter presents a brief discussion of the historical and cultural background of the Mong; the historical development of the Mong orthography; the characteristics of Mong students; a comparative discussion of the two regional Mong dialects and English in the areas of phonology, morphology, and syntax; and sociolinguistic aspects. The author also suggests some of the typical difficulties that Mong students may experience when acquiring English. The objective of this chapter is to provide linguistic information for classroom teachers and other educators to help them provide a smooth transition for Mong students.

DEFINITIONS OF TERMS

In the past, several terms have been coined for Mong by the Chinese, their neighbors, and Western scholars. The term 'Miao' was historically used by the

Chinese and was loosely translated as 'barbarian' (Bernatzik, 1947). This term is related to the Annamese word, Meau' transliterating for cat. 'Mong-tse' was also used by the Old Chinese historical work *Schudjing*, which compared Mong language with the howling or the cry of the hyena. Terrien explained the meaning of the Chinese character for 'Meau,' transliterating a cat's head. When agricultural activities are involved, the term 'Meau' in Chinese character, consists of two parts: 'Miao' for 'plant' and the bottom part 'tse' for 'field' whereas 'tse' is translated as an ethnicity. As a result, 'Meau-tse' means the 'son of the soil, the farmers, who do not belong to the Great Nation.' Schotter referred in the Chinese Kweichow province to designate 'Meau' as all non-Han people (Bernatzik, 1947, p. 7). Other researchers have used the spelling of 'Meo' as called by their hosts, the Laotians and the Thai (Barney & Smalley, 1953; Binney, 1968; Haudricourt, 1972; Savina, 1924). However, all the terms mentioned have negative connotations. The Mong prefer to be called 'Mong' or 'Hmong' although the origin of the word 'Mong' or 'Hmong' is unknown. The term 'Mong' or 'Hmong' refers to a classless egalitarian ethnic group who calls themselves 'Mong' or 'Hmong.'

The author uses 'Mong' over the other terms for several reasons. First, the terms, 'Miao,' 'Meau,' 'Mong-tse,' 'Meau-tse,' and 'Meo,' have historically negative connotations. The spelling 'Mong' does not deviate too much from the original terms and maintains consistency in the spelling from the perspectives of historical and comparative linguistics. Therefore, it makes more sense to change the spelling from 'Miao,' 'Meau,' 'Mong-tse,' 'Meau-tse,' 'Meo,' to 'Mong' rather than to 'Hmong.'

Second, a report pointed out that "General Vang Pao established the Mhong Language Council in February, 1982, in response to the resolutions passed at two consecutive national Hmong conferences," which were held in June, 1980, in Minneapolis, Minnesota, and in December, 1980, in Santa Ana, California (Thao & Robson, 1982). General Vang Pao appointed twelve members to the Hmong Language Council: six members from the Mong Leng (Blue Mong) community and six members from the Hmong Dawb (White Hmong) community. The author was one of the appointed members. The committee members met at the University of Minnesota in Minneapolis, Minnesota on August 12-14, 1982, through the sponsorship of the Center for Applied Linguistics. The role of the council was to conduct studies to standardize the Mong language. Through the committee's experience of literary search, they agreed that it was necessary to change the consonantal phoneme from /hm/ to /mh/ and the spelling of the initial spelling of the term from '*Hm*ong' to '*Mh*ong' (Thao & Robson, 1982).

Third, the spelling of the term 'Hmong' only occurred in Laos (Yang, 1975) and was based solely on sociopolitical and economic factors rather than on sound academic disciplines, such as linguistics. Because there is no obstruction of the airstream in the oral cavity in the articulation of the sound [h] (a pair of [ ] is used to denote phonetic symbols), it is classified as a voiceless fricative (due to its hissing sound at the glottis) as well as a voiceless glottal glide and is used as a consonant by itself or as a glide combining with other sounds. With the articulation of the sound [h] in English, there is an aspiration of a small puff of air that occurs immediately following the articulation of the oral stops /p/, /t/, and /k/

(a pair of slashes / / is used for phonemic representation) if they are syllable initial preceding a stressed vowel as in pin [ph], tick [th], and kin [kh] and thereby are aspirated voiceless stops. If these three oral stop sounds occur after syllable initial /s/, as in spin [p], stick [t], and skin [k], they are unaspirated voiceless stops. The pairs of sounds [p] and [ph], [t] and [th], [k] and [kh] are the allophones (the predictable phonetic variants) of the phonemes /p/, /t/, and /k/, respectively. Because of this, linguists generally consider this aspiration a minor aspect in the American English phonology. This means that aspiration does not change the overall phonemic representation of the phonemes /p/, /t/, and /k/ within the broader phonological context (Fromkin & Rodman, 1993, 1998). By the same token, in Mong phonology, there are four pairs of nasal sounds used between the two Mong dialects (Blue Mong and White Hmong) that share the same aspiration feature as in English. These pairs of sounds consist of [m]/[hm], [ml]/[hml], [n]/[hn], and [ny]/[hny]. The Blue Mongs (Mong Leng) use the full voiced nasals [m], [ml], [n], and [ny]; whereas the White Hmongs articulate devoiced or voiceless nasals [hm], [hn], [hml], and [hny]. Compared to English, though these pairs of sounds are spelled differently by the two Mongs, they are the predictable phonetic variants or the allophones of the same phonemes /m/, /ml/, /n/, and /ny/, respectively. Thus, the aspiration feature for these four pairs of sounds does not change the overall phonemic representation of those phonemes in Mong. For this reason, the term 'Hmong' is spelled 'Mong.'

Fourth, the decision to use the spelling 'Mong' is not new. Researchers, such as Lyman (1974, 1979), Thao (1994, 1997, 1999), and Xiong (Xiong & Xiong, 1983), have used the spelling 'Mong.' The term 'Mong' was derived from 'Mong-tse' by simply clipping 'tse' from the term. The term is firmly supported by the perspectives of historical and comparative methodology of linguistics. In addition, the spelling 'Mong' does not deviate too much from the other terms.

Fifth, the spelling 'Mong' will simplify library listings. Researchers tend to examine their literary search with the initial spelling 'm' for 'Mong' rather than 'hm' for 'Hmong.' The Mong and non-Mong would spell the term with an initial /m/ sound rather than /hm/, when they hear it for the first time.

Sixth, on a separate but related issue, the U.S. government is very sensitive to this naming issue. A neutral terminology, 'Highlander,' was coined to include the Mong/Hmong, Iu Mien, Lao Lue, Khamu, and Lao Theung (North & Yang, 1988). Highlander is a broad term lumping together all the minority ethnic groups coming from the highlands of Laos; the Laotians were referred to as Lowlanders.

Seventh, on July 22, 1995, in Denver, Colorado, Chee Yang, Colonel 'Bill' F. Bilodeaux, Christine Cook, and the American Tribute Committee with the cooperation from Colonel Frank Bales, Generals Harry C. Aderholt, Jim Hall, Steve Ritchie, Art Cornelius, and the Mong veterans paid special tribute to the 40,000 Mong soldiers who died during the Vietnam War as part of the U.S. secret army in Laos and to the 15,000 Mong soldiers who were wounded in the line of duty between 1961 and 1975. This tribute was to commemorate them for the first time in the history of the United States. A symbolic 'M' was posted on the hill behind the background of the stage to represent the 'Mong' people. Colonel Hang

Sao accepted the medal of honor on behalf of the Mong soldiers who fought and died in this war (Thao, 1996, 1997).

MONG HISTORICAL AND CULTURAL BACKGROUND

The Mong is an ethnic tribe who migrated from China in the eighteenth century to settle in Laos. As a people, the Mong have a history of more than 5,000 years. It is difficult to obtain a good estimate of the Mong population worldwide since no official census has been conducted. However, the population may have reached six million. Xiong (1989) broke down the demography of Mong according to various sources as cited by different authors at different times (Garrett, 1974; Tsaj, n.d.; Yang, 1975) and confirmed this statistic.

The Mong assisted France during its colonial rule in Southeast Asia between 1893 and 1947 and the United States during its secret war in Laos against the Communists during the Vietnam War between 1962 and 1975. After the United States withdrew its troops from Southeast Asia, the Mong suffered political persecution. In 1976, the U.S. Congress recognized the Mong as former CIA (Central Intelligence Agency) employees and authorized the Department of State to admit some Mong refugees to the United States.

The Mong family, being the most important unit in the Mong society, is the basic nurturing institution. It includes all its extended family and its clan. Its political system is closely tied to the original clan system and remains strongest at the local level, where most of the decisions are made. The traditional Mong survived in a self-sufficient and agricultural economy. Spiritually, the Mong were traditionally animists. *Webster's New World Dictionary* defines animism as "the belief that all life is produced by a spiritual force, and that all things in nature have souls" (Hackett, 1984). Animism is a belief system that combines supernatural power, ancestor worship, superstition, and spirit worship (Thao, 1994). Though many Mongs were animists, it is estimated that half of the Mong population in the United States have converted to Christianity.

As a consequence of the long war in Laos during the Vietnam War, education for Mong adults who are now in the United States was totally disrupted. Their lack of formal education and marketable skills and their illiteracy in their own language make it difficult for them to live in a technologically developed country such as the United States. The language barrier continues to impede their ability to achieve their full potential as contributing members in the society. Based on the statistics provided by the California Department of Education, as of March 1, 1996, of 34,000 Mong students currently enrolled in California public schools, 31,156 were identified as limited English proficient (LEP) students (California Department of Education, 1997). This reveals a crisis in Mong education in America.

HISTORICAL DEVELOPMENT OF MONG LITERACY

There was no historical evidence suggesting that the Mong had a writing system before 1909, when Rev. Samuel Pollard, a British missionary of the Bible Christian Mission (formerly the United Methodist Mission) developed The Pollard Script (Pollard, 1919, p. 173; Hudspeth, 1939, p. 173) to complete the translation of the New Testament into Hwa Miao under the supervision of Rev. William H. Hudspeth in China, which was published by the British and Foreign Bible Society in 1917 (Pollard, 1919). The Pollard Script is not mutually intelligible to today's Mong in the United States. Except for The Pollard Script, the Mong depend upon oral tradition. They continue to pass on their skills and their social values through oral tradition from father to son, from mother to daughter, and from generation to generation.

In the 1950s, along with the entry of Christianity to Laos, came the development of Mong literacy. Many Mong became Christians through the mission of the Christian and Missionary Alliance (CMA) headquartered in New York (now in Colorado Springs, Colorado). Rev. Xuxu Thao, the first Mong president of the Lao Evangelical Church, recalled and asserted in his memoir that 5,000 Mong and 2,000 Khamu were converted to Christianity in the 1950s (Thao, 1994, 1997). This massive conversion took place when the Andrianoffes, an American missionary couple, arrived to spread the gospel in the province of Xieng Khouang, Laos. After this, one of the immediate and critical issues faced by the CMA was the illiteracy of the Mong and Khamu tribes. They could neither read nor write Lao. Both tribes had no records of ever having their own writing systems.

Following the CMA conferences from 1951-1953 in Saigon, South Vietnam, two missionary linguists were assigned the task of developing the orthographies for the Mong and the Khamu tribes. In this manner, Christian literacy and Bible translation could be done in both languages. In turn, they could comprehend the Christian doctrines, which are the foundation of Christian faith (Thao, 1994, 1997). Barney (1957) acknowledged that, in June 1951, he went to Xieng Khouang, Laos to "set the task of reducing the Mong language to writing" (p. 68). Smalley (1982) also confirmed his mission with Barney in his presentation about the history of the development of the romanized popular alphabets (RPA) to the Mhong Language Council at the University of Minnesota on August 12, 1982, in Minneapolis, Minnesota. Smalley reported that he "went to Luang Prabang province of Laos to study Khamu language whereas Barney to Xieng Khouang to study Mong Leng." Barney developed proficiency in the Mong language and romanized it successfully into the romanized popular alphabet (RPA) system. At that time, Barney was referred to by many Mongs as 'Thanh Mong' or 'Mister Mong.' Even today, many Mong remember him as 'Thanh Mong.' Smalley, trained as a linguist, assisted Barney in refining the RPA system (Smalley, 1976). Unfortunately, in 1953, the Communists took over the province of Xieng Khouang, Laos. As a consequence, all American missionaries were evacuated for a short time. When the Mong RPA system was completed, it was submitted to the Royal Lao government in 1954 for approval but was repudiated. Smalley informed the author that the Lao government decreed that no minority language was to be written in any script but Lao (Smalley, 1997, personal communication, 21 August). This means that the Mong have not been able to use the system officially in Laos until today. Thus the RPA system was put on hold officially by the Lao government (Thao, 1994, 1997, 1999).

CHARACTERISTICS OF THE MONG LEARNERS

Linguistically, the Mong can be classified into two major groups: 'Mong Leng,' or Blue Mong and 'Hmong Dawb,' or White Hmong. This classification involves the speakers of the two major regional dialects of the Mong, including the new generation of learners enrolled in public schools across the United States and around the world.

In the past, several terms have been used for the Blue Mong. The term 'Mong Leng' has been used synonymously with the term 'Blue Mong.' The author wants to caution against the use of another term, 'Mong Ntsuab' (Green Mong). The term 'Mong Ntsuab' has a negative historical connotation. The Mong Leng (Blue Mong) object to the use of 'Mong Ntsuab' or 'Green Mong,' whenever it is used. They find it offensive and are intimidated by it. The term refers to a subgroup of the Mong who anachronistically practiced a cult of cannibalism. This subgroup no longer exists. White Hmong refers to that group's ceremonial dress, and no negative connotation is attached to it. The Blue Mong are proud of their name, which translates to 'veins of the Mong,' implying that they carry the life blood for all Mong.

The Mong Leng (Blue Mong) and Hmong Dawb (White Hmong) have interwoven their bonds through marriage for centuries; surprisingly, they have preserved their linguistic and cultural purity and have respected each other's differences. Both groups have lived with each other harmoniously for centuries. In fact, the two Mongs interface with each other in a system of checks and balances within the Mong society. The social, religious, educational, and political systems of the two groups have their own dynamics and are absolutely symmetrical and well balanced within the Mong society. However, Mong Leng call themselves 'Mong' and White Hmong (Hmoob Dawb) 'Hmong.'

Major Dialectal Differences

The linguistic division between the Mong Leng and the Hmong Dawb cuts across all the Mong membership, customs, and various Mong who wear costumes of different colors (Bliatout, et al., 1988). It is very difficult to estimate the numbers of speakers of these two regional dialects in the United States. The two Mong regional dialects may be spoken by similar or equal numbers of people. However, there are more Mong Leng than Hmong Dawb in the mainland China and many Hmong Dawb admitted that their ancestors were Mong Leng. Though these two Mong dialects seem to be mutually intelligible, there is a difference between them (Geddes, 1976).

This linguistic difference between the two Mongs can be compared to the differences in pronunciation of British English, American English, and Australian English. Some Mong even compare the difference to that between English and Spanish. Many Mong Leng have become bidialectal and switch from one dialect to the other. Practically, Mong Leng tend to have an easier time speaking Hmong Dawb, but the reverse does not hold. For the most part, the differences tend to center around the pronunciation of certain sound segments and sound combinations (Purnell, 1970; Smalley, 1976).

In terms of the linguistic mutual intelligibility between Mong Leng and Hmong Dawb, Smalley (1994) observed that their lexicons "seem to be completely different" (p. 245) and "do not seem to correspond with each other at all" (pp. 98-99). Table 12.1 presents some samples from their lexicons.

Several researchers have noted that the differences lie in pronunciation, with the exception of the suppletions. This pronunciation difference is fairly consistent in sounds, sound segments, and sound combinations. They can be predictably matched with their corresponding sounds in Mong Leng and Hmong Dawb (Purnell, 1970; Smalley, 1976, 1994). Table 12.2 illustrates a systematic sound correspondence between the two Mong dialects.

The differences between the two Mong regional dialects have a major impact on Mong children's acquisition of dual language.

Besides this linguistic difference, another way to classify the Mong is by the colors of their traditional costumes: *Mong Sib, Mong Dlub* (Black Mong), *Mong Ntsuab* (Green Mong), *Mong Txaij* (Striped Mong), *Mong Quasnpaab* (Flowery Mong), *Hmong Dawb* (White Hmong) (Thao, 1994).

Language Change

The second major characteristic involves the sociolinguistic aspect of language change. The generation of the Mong parents in the United States today have lived in three different countries: Laos, Thailand, and the United States. They have intermixed language, referred to as 'diglossia,' a term coined by Fergerson (Giglioli, 1972). This means that their lexicons may include words borrowed from their hosts, such as Chinese Mandarin, Lao, French, Thai, and English. Transmigration from country to country in the last two centuries has resulted in the use of interlingua among themselves. This influences their children's language acquisition.

Example:

Mong Leng:	*Peb moog tom **tajlaj**, moog yuav **txivlaum fuabxeeb** hab moog saib*
Hmong Dawb:	*Peb mus tom **tajlaj**, mus yuav **txivlaum huabxeeb** thiab mus saib **cinema**.*

Table 12.1
Samples of Lexical Differences Between the Two Mong Dialects

Mong Leng (Blue Mong)	Hmong Dawb (White Hmong)	Meaning in English
dlaim choj	daim pam	a blanket
ntsab	txhuv	rice
paamdlev	puamhub	mint
txivkwj	yawglaus	husband of aunt
pujnyaaj	phauj	aunt
lub qwg	lub laujkaub-fwj	a kettle
taujqab	taujdub	lemon grass
lub xaabcum	lub kos	fire iron
tug kaabcuam	tus khib	an instrument used to carry firewood on the back

Table 12.2
Sound Correspondence Between the Two Mong Dialects

Corresponding Sounds	English Meanings	Mong Leng (Blue Mong)		Hmong Dawb (White Hmong)	
Consonants	Mong/Hmong	/m/	*M*oob	/hm/	Hmoob
	heavy	/ny/	*ny*aav	/hny/	*hny*av
	a bag	/n/	*n*aab	/hn/	*hn*ab
	water	/dl/	*dl*ej	/d/	*d*ej
	to run	/dlh/	*dlh*a	dh/	*dh*ia
	to break	/ndl/	*ndl*ais	/nt/	*nt*ais
	the sound of a boiling rice porridge	/ndlh/	*ndlh*ij*ndlh*uj	/nth/	*nth*ij*nth*uj
Irregular Consonants	to respect	/ f /	*f*wm	/h/	*h*wm
Vowels	a foreigner	/aa/	m*aa*b	/a/	m*a*b
	a woman=s dress	/a/	taabt*a*b	/ia/	tabt*ia*b
Irregular vowel sounds	to say	/a/	h*a*s	/ai/	h*ai*s
	a female	/u/	p*u*j	/o/	p*o*j (p*o*g)
	to cause	/ua/	k*ua*s	/o/	k*o*m
	to go	/oo/	m*oo*g	/u/	m*u*s
Tone	a horse	/-- g/	nee*g*	/--s/	nee*s*

English: We go to market, go buy peanuts, and go watch movie.
                  We go to the market, buy peanuts, and watch a movie.

In this example, they use a Mong sentence pattern mixed with a Lao lexicon '*tajlaj*' for market, with a Chinese Mandarin lexicon "*txivlaum fuabxeeb*" for peanut, and with a French lexicon '*cinema*' for movie.

Mong children in public schools today are heavily influenced by their parents' use of language, especially borrowed words from ancient Chinese Mandarin, Lao, Thai, French, and English. Though many of them speak English fluently, they can hardly speak proper Mong. In another words, they experience tremendous culture and language loss. As shown in the following examples, too often Mong children basically translate word for word, from English to Mong.

Example:		
English	*Mong Leng (Blue Mong)*	*Hmong Dawb (White Mong)*
I wear shoes.	*Kuv naav qhaus.*	*Kuv hnav qhaus.*
	Proper use: *Kuv rau qhaus*	Proper use: *Kuv rau qhaus.*
My father	The phrase *kuv tug txi* (my husband) is confused with *kuv txiv* (my father).	The phrase *kuv tus txiv* (my husband) is confused with *kuv txiv* (my father).

Many Mong students today speak Mong by translating directly from English to Mong. The phrase and sentence illustrated above are some of the examples of the way Mong children transfer the concepts of English language (L2) to their native language (L1). What really happens is that Mong students learn the Mong language informally from their parents (L1) without the social and cultural context of the Mong culture, and they receive formal education inside and outside of the school setting within the social and cultural context of American culture. When they translate the literal meaning from English to Mong without the social and cultural context of the Mong culture, the meaning becomes semantically anomalous. This direct translation affecting the semantics, as shown in the examples, has caused a major concern among Mong parents.

Many Mong students face a dilemma. They are caught between the macroculture and the Mong culture, and between their native language (L1) and English (L2). In order to develop proficiency bilingually in Mong and English, both languages need to be taught and reinforced equally within the social and cultural contexts of both cultures. This is a very critical issue in language instruction. Mong students are taught to assimilate into the macroculture but lack reinforcement from their parents at home. As a result, they feel disjointed and confused about both cultures and do not know how to respond in a culturally appropriate manner. This is why language instruction cannot take place without social and cultural contexts; that is, language instruction cannot occur in isolation. It must be immersed in content areas in both Mong and English. Mong students have been taught formally in academic settings without the reinforcement of the social and cultural context from their parents at home. They learn the Mong language informally at home, without any academic support for the Mong language at school. Thus, the gap between home and school widens. As a consequence, language use for Mong children becomes disorderly and confused.

CHARACTERISTICS OF THE MONG LANGUAGE

The Mong language was classified by linguistic typologists as a subgroup of the Sino-Tibetan language family of Asia. Arlotto (1972) considered it as one of the pre-Sinitic languages and asserted that "within China itself, among the few remaining pre-Sinitic languages we have the Miao-Yao family, spoken by scattered remnants of what once undoubtedly was a widespread and flourishing family" (p. 52). This means that the Mong had long existed prior to 1300 b.c. Chang (1972) indicated that the term 'Miao' occurred as early as the *Book of Documents*, and the Miao people had been in contact with the Chinese at least since the Shang-Chou Dynasty. According to Michael (1986), the Shang Dynasty and the Chou Dynasty are dated 1725-1123 b.c. and 1123-221 b.c., respectively.

Despite the Mong language's mutual unintelligibility with any other languages spoken in Asia, linguists have grouped it with one of the marginalized languages called the Mien, under the Mong-Mien (Miao-Yao) language family (Smalley, 1994). The Mong orthography currently and widely used is based on the refinement of the romanized popular alphabet (RPA) system. This RPA system was devised based upon the phonemic principle. Since it is phonemic based rather than ideographic or character based, the RPA system automatically dichotomizes the Mong dialects along the regional pronunciation differences between Mong Leng (Blue Mong) and Hmong Dawb (White Hmong). This is one reason why the RPA system has not been adopted by all Mong. Currently, there are no writing systems that are better than the RPA system to satisfy the Mong's desire. The RPA remains the sole writing system because it is easy to learn and use. Though the RPA system is consistent and absolutely symmetrical, the spellings vary from dialect to dialect and from ideolect to ideolect (language of the individual), depending upon the geographic region of origin of the individual Mong.

Mong Phonology

The Mong language shares the same sentence structure with English. A Mong sentence structure depicts a subject + verb + object (SVO) pattern, e.g., '*Kuv hlub koj.*' "Kuv (subject*)* + hlub (verb) + koj (object)" that transliterates into "I love you" in English. Notice that each word ends with a consonant. These endings are not consonantal phonemes as in English; they represent the tone markers ku*v*, hlu*b*, ko*j*. The Mong do not pronounce tone-markers like the inflectional endings in English. Due to the nature of the Mong language, derivational phonology and morphology are not an essential part of its repertoire.

Phonologically, Mong is a tonal language. Though linguists classify it as a monosyllabic language family, it contains sizable numbers of disyllabic and polysyllabic words. A typical Mong lexicon consists of a consonant, a vowel, and a tone marker, (e.g., 'kuv' *k* is a consonant, *u* the vowel, and *v* the tone marker). The Mong language is comprised of sixteen vowel phonemes, sixty-three segmental phonemes, and eight different tone sandhi markers.

Mong Vowel Phonemes. The Mong language consists of sixteen vowel phonemes: ten monophthongs (seven oral vowels and three nasal vowels; see Table 12.3) and six diphthongs—the combination of two single vowels (Thao, 1997) or a single vowel plus a glide (Fromkin & Rodman, 1993).

1. Ten monophthongs: seven monophthongs and three nasal monophthongs
    Seven oral monophthongs: /i/, /e/, /w/, /u/, /o/ , /a/, and /ə/
    Three nasal monophthongs: /ee/ [eŋ], /aa/* [aŋ] and /oo/ [oŋ]
    (The spellings look like diphthongs but they are nasal monophthongs.)
    * Used by Mong Leng only.
2. Six diphthongs:
    Three open diphthongs: /ia/**   /ua/   /uə/
    Three closed diphthongs: /ai/   /aw/   /au/
    ** Used by Hmong Dawb only.

Mong Consonantal Phonemes. There are sixty-three segmental phonemes in

Table 12.3
Mong Vowel Phonemes

	Front		Central		Back	
	Unrounded	*Rounded*	*Unrounded*	*Rounded*	*Unrounded*	*Rounded*
High	/i/	/w/				/u/
Middle (Nasal)	/e/ /ee/ [eŋ]		/ə/			/o/ /oo/[oŋ]
Low (Nasal)					/a/ /aa/ [aŋ]	

the Mong language: nineteen single consonants, twenty-four double consonantal blends, sixteen triple consonantal blends, and four quadruple consonantal blends.

1. Nineteen single consonants:

p	t	d**	r	c	k	q	?	f	
x	s	h	v	z	m	n	l	w	y

2. Twenty-four double consonantal blends:

pl	dh**	dl*	ts	tx	ph	th	rh	ch	
kh	qh		np	nt	nr	nc	nk	nq	xy
ml	ny		ng	hl	hm**	hn**	ng		

3. Sixteen triple consonantal blends:

plh	dlh*	tsh	txh	nph	npl	nth	ndl	nts
nrh	nch	ntx	nkh	nqh	hml**	hny**		

4. Four quadruple consonantal blends:

nplh	ndlh	ntsh	ntxh

*   Used by Mong Leng only.
**   Used by Hmong Dawb only.

Table 12.4 illustrates the combined existing phonemes used by both Mong Leng (Blue Mong) and Hmong Dawb (White Hmong) with some exceptions.

Eight Mong Tone Markers. The Mong lexicon could not have been fully constructed without the tone markers. A lexicon in the Mong language always consists of a consonant, a vowel, and a tone marker. The tone marker is always situated at the end of each word or is always followed by a vowel. The following letters represent the RPA symbols for the tone-markers. There are eight different vocal tones in the Mong language (Table 12.5).

Stress. One of the characteristics that distinguish English from Mong is the use of stress. In English, one or more syllables in each content word is stressed.

Examples:
1. (a) subject (noun)   The subject of a story (stress on the first syllable)
    (b) subject (verb)   He'll subject us to his boring stories. (stress on the second syllable)
2. (a) pervert (noun)   My neighbor is a pervert. (stress on the first syllable)
    (b) pervert (verb)   Don't pervert the idea. (Stress on the second syllable)
Mong does not use stress.

Intonation. English is different from Mong in the area of prosodic suprasegmental features. Mong language uses the eight different tones to distinguish the semantics of the words. See Table 12.5, whereas English uses intonation and pitch.

Example:
1. What did you put in my drink, Fue?
2. What did you put in my drink, Fue?

In the first sentence the questioner asks what Fue put in the drink; the questioner in the second sentence is asking if someone put Fue in the drink.

Mong Morphology

Morphology is defined as "the study of the internal structure of words; the

Table 12.4
Mong Consonant Phonemes

Manners of Articulation	Labial			Dental	Alveolor			Palatal		Velar		Glottal
Points of Articulation	bilabial	labio-lateral release	labio-dental	apico dental	apico alveolar lateral	apico alveolar affricate	apico post alveolar	palatal	palatal affricate release	velar	back velar	glottal
Stops and Affricates vl. unaspirated	p	pl		t	(d)	ts		c	tx	k	q	?
vl. aspirated	ph	plh		th	(dh)	tsh		ch	txh	kh	qh	
vd. unaspirated					dl		r					
vd. aspirated					dlh		rh					
vd. prenasal unaspirated	np	npl		nt	ndl	nts	nr	nc	ntx	nk	nq	
vd. prenasal aspirated	nph	nplh		nth	ndlh	ntsh	nrh	nch	ntxh	nkh	nqh	
Fricatives vl.			f			x		s				h
vd.			v					z				
nasal vl.	(hm)	(hml)		(hn)					(hny)			
vd.	m	ml		n					ny	ng 1 [ŋ]		
Liquid vl.				hl								
vd.				l								
Glides			W 2					y				

Sources: Adapted and compiled from Smalley, W. A. (1976, p. 89) and Ratliff, M. S. (1986, p. 16).
Note: vl. = voiceless; vd. = voiced; ( ) = used only in Hmong Dawb
1. tl, tlh, ntl, ntlh, and is changed to dl, dlh, ndl, ndlh, and ng. (Mong Literacy Volunteer, Inc. [1980]).
2. Phoneme addition proposed by Rev. Xeng Pao Thao in consultation with George Linwood Barney.

Table 12.5
Mong Tone Markers

RPA Symbol		Mong Leng (Blue Mong)	Hmong Dawb (White Hmong)	English Meaning
- **b**	high	cua**b**	cua**b**	trap
		ti**b**	ti**b**	to pile up
- **j**	high falling	cua**j**	cua**j**	number nine
		ti**j**	ti**j**	older siblings
- **v**	mid rising	cua**v**	cua**v**	counterfeit
		ti**v**	ti**v**	to resist, to oppose, to opt against
-	mid	cua-	cua-	wind
		ti-	ti-	near, close to
- **s**	mid low	cua**s**	cua**s**	father of son=s wife
		ti**s**	ti**s**	wing, to name
- **g**	mid low	cua**g**	cua**g**	to reach to breathy
		ti**g**	ti**g**	to turn, to reverse, to spin around
- **m**	low glottalized	cua**m**	cua**m**	to press together
		ti**m**	ti**m**	because of
- **d** low rising and a predictable variant of - **m**		- ti**d**	- ti**d**	- there, over there

component of the grammar which includes the rules of word formation." (Fromkin & Rodman, 1993, p. 511; 1998, p. 530). As previously stated, Mong is a noninflected language. Though most of the Mong lexicons consist of monosyllables, disyllables, and polysyllables, they do not change their forms. Since Mong lexicons do not take on the affixes (prefixes, suffixes), English morphology is difficult for Mong students. The following illustrate some of the difficulties that Mong students may encounter.

-s/-es Inflections. As previously discussed, compared to English, the Mong language maintains the same form. It does not carry -s/-es inflections in plural forms and in third person singular present tense forms.

Examples:
Mong Leng:	*Kuv*	*muaj*	*ib*	*tug**	*cwjmem.* (singular)
Hmong Dawb:	*Kuv*	*muaj*	*ib*	*tus**	*cwjmem.* (singular)
English:	I	have	a	(clf.)**	pen.
Mong Leng:	*Kuv*	*muaj*	*ntau*	*tug*	*cwjmem.* (plural)
Hmong Dawb:	*Kuv*	*muaj*	*ntau*	*tus*	*cwjmem.* (plural)
English:	I	have	many	(clf.)	pens.
Both Mong:	*Kuv*	*yuav*	*ib*	*lub*	*tsho.* (singular)

| English: | I | buy | a | (clf.) | shirt. |

| Both Mong: | *Kuv* | *yuav* | *kaum* | *lub* | *tsho.* (plural) |
| English: | I | buy | ten | (clf.) | shir**t**s. |

Mong Leng:	*Nwg*	*yuav*	*ib*	*lub*	*tsho.* (singular)
Hmong Dawb:	*Nws*	*yuav*	*ib*	*lub*	*tsho.* (singular)
English:	He	buy**s**	a	(clf.)	shirt. (singular)

Mong Leng:	*Nwg*	*yuav*	*kaum*	*lub*	*tsho* (plural)
Hmong Dawb:	*Nws*	*yuav*	*kaum*	*lub*	*tsho* (plural)
English:	He	buy**s**	ten	(clf.)	*shirts* (plural)

*   Mong Leng (Blue Mong) uses mid low breathy tone /-g/; Hmong Dawb (WhiteHmong) uses mid low tone (-s).
** Classifier

Forming Nouns. In Mong, adding the word "**kev**" in front of a word changes its grammatical category to noun. Keep in mind that inflectional morphology does not exist in the Mong language. In English, adding prefixes (pre-, circum-, trans-, post-, etc.) and suffixes (-ment, -ion, -ance, -ion or -ia, -ty, -ism, etc.) to a root stem, normally changes the grammatical category. By the same token, inflectional morphemes can coexist with derivational morphemes and tend to surround the derivational morphemes (e.g., neighborhood —> neighborhood**s**; I sing/he sin**gs**). However, in Mong, there are no noun declensions like those in English (Table 12.6).

Grammatical Gender. In Mong, there is no grammatical gender (masculine or feminine) like French, Spanish, and English, e.g. *le* jardin (the garden), *la* maison (the house). Though the Mong use 'tub' meaning 'son' and 'ntxhais' meaning 'daughter' to denote genders (masculine or feminine), the Mong language does not have grammatical genders as in English.

Examples:

Mong Leng:	*txaistog* (both masculine and feminine)	
Hmong Dawb:	*txaistos* (both masculine and feminine)	
English:	wait**er** (masculine)	wait**ress** (feminine)

Mong Leng:	*tub* fuabtais (masculine)	*ntxhais* fuabtais (feminine)
Hmong Dawb:	*tub* huabtais (masculine)	*ntxhais* huabtais (feminine)
English:	prince (masculine)	princess (feminine)

The use of the term 'tub,' meaning 'son,' or 'ntxhais,' meaning 'daughter,' placed

Table 12.6
Derivational Morphology in Mong and English

Mong Leng (Blue Mong)		Hmong Dawb (White Hmong)		English Meaning
kev	tswjfwm	kev	tswjhwm	govern**ment**
kev	qeeglug	kev	qeeslus	criter**ion** (criter**ia**)
kev	txavtawm	kev	txiavtawm	subtrac**tion**
kev	thuam	kev	thuam	critic**ism**
kev	paabcuam	kev	pabcuam	assist**ance**
kev	puamtsuaj	kev	puamtsuaj	casual**ty**

before 'fuabtais' in Mong Leng or 'huabtais,' in Hmong Dawb meaning 'king,' marks the gender of the lexicon.

Words Borrowed from Ancient Chinese Mandarin, Lao, French, and English. Since the Mong lived in China, Laos, the refugee camps in Thailand, and the United States, they have borrowed words from ancient Chinese Mandarin, Lao, French, Thai, and English lexicons, as illustrated in Table 12.7.

It is estimated that the Mong had borrowed approximately 10% of their lexicons from ancient Chinese Mandarin. All Mong lexicons ending with '-xeeb' were borrowed from Ancient Chinese Mandarin.

Mong Syntax

Word Order. Syntactically, Mong sentences follow the English sentence patterns of SVO (subject + verb + object).

Example:		(S)	(V)	(O)
	Both Mong:	*Kuv*	*hlub*	*koj.*
	English:	I	love	you.

Table 12.7
Borrowed Words from Ancient Chinese Mandarin, Lao, French, and English

Ancient Chinese Mandarin		
Mong Leng *(Blue Mong)*	*Hmong Dawb* *(White Hmong)*	*English* *Meanings*
txivlaum fuabxeeb	txivlaum huabxeeb	peanut
xhwjxeeb	txhwjxeeb	special
thaajyeeb	thajyeeb	peace
pheejyig	pheejyig	reasonable, cheap

Lao		
Mong Leng *(Blue Mong)*	*Hmong Dawb* *(White Hmong)*	*English* *Meanings*
khoom	khoom	things
xabnpum	xabnpum	soap
tajlaj	tajlaj	market
faisfab	faisfab	electricity
laa-voos	la-voos	dancing

French			
French	*Mong Leng* *(Blue Mong)*	*Hmong Dawb* *(White Hmong)*	*English* *Meaning*
kilomètre	kilomev	kilomev	kilometer
Français (e)	Faabkis	Fabkis	French
cinéma	xine (ma)	xine (ma)	movie

English			
English	*Mong Leng* *(Blue Mong)*	*Hmong Dawb* *(White Hmong)*	*English* *Meaning*
America	Amelikas	Amesliskas	America
okay	okhe	okhe	okay
church	tshawj	tshawj	church

However, the lexical category of adjective in Mong does not follow the word order of English. In English, adjectives precede nouns, (e.g., a big house); in Mong, the adjectives are placed after the nouns similar to French, (e.g., *lub tsev luj*, ('the house big'). Therefore, word order in English may be difficult for Mong students.

Inflection Endings. In Mong, there are no -ed forms in past tenses as in English.

Examples:

Both Mong:	*Kuv*	*hlub*	*koj*	*nubnua.*	(present)
English:	I	love	you	today.	(present)
Both Mong:	*Kuv*	*hlub*	*koj*	*tseb nua.*	(past tense)
English:	I	lov*ed*	you	last year.	(past tense)

Though the Mong language does not take on any inflections in past tenses as in English, the Mong express their tenses through adverbial phrases, such as today, yesterday, tomorrow, and so on.

There are no -ing forms in participles in Mong as in English.

Example:

Both Mong:	*hlub*	—>*hlub*
English:	love	—>lov*ing*

The Mong do not move subjects and verbs around in interrogative sentences as in English, but insert the word '*puas*' (question) between the subjects and the verbs to change the declarative sentences into interrogative sentences.

Examples:

Both Mong:	Kuv	*puas*	hlub	koj?
English:	I	(question)	love	you?
—>	Do	I	love	you?
Both Mong:	Koj	*puas*	hlub	kuv?
English:	You	(question)	love	me?
—>	Do	you	love	me?

The Mong insert the word '*tsi*' (not) before the verb or the modal auxiliaries to change the declarative sentences into negative sentences.

Examples:

Both Mong:	Kuv	tsi	hlub	koj.
English:	I	(negative for not)	love	you.
—>	I	do not	love	you.
Both Mong:	Kuv	tsi	noj	mov.
English:	I	(negative for not)	eat	rice.
—>	I	do not	eat	rice.

In Mong, there are no verb conjugations as in French or English. Conjugation is an act or a presentation of a complete set of inflected forms of verbs while being conjugated to signify different tenses and mood.

Examples:

Mong Leng:	*Kuv*	*hu*	*ib*	*zaaj*	*nkauj.* (present)
Hmong Dawb:	*Kuv*	*hu*	*ib*	*zaj*	*nkauj.*
French:	Je	chante	une	(clf.)	chanson.
English:	I	sing	a	(clf.)	song.

Mong Leng:	*Kuv*	*hu*	*ib*	*zaaj*	*nkauj.* (past tense)
Hmong Dawb:	*Kuv*	*hu*	*ib*	*zaj*	*nkauj.*
French:	J'ai	chanté	une	(clf.)	chanson.
English:	I	*sang*	a	(clf.)	song.

Mong Leng:	*Kuv*	*hu*	*ib*	*zaaj*	*nkauj.* (future)
Hmong Dawb:	*Kuv*	*hu*	*ib*	*zaj*	*nkauj.*
French:	Je	chant*erai*	une	(clf.)	chanson.
English:	I	*will sing*	a	(clf.)	song.

Classifiers. The Mong language is different from English in the use of classifiers. The Mong always use classifiers (clf.) in front of nouns to denote or express their morphology or semantics. Center for Applied Linguistics (n.d.) defines the function of classifiers as "words which come just before the noun, and which combine with it and its modifiers in several ways to express many of the ideas that English expresses by means of suffixes—like plurals, possessives, e.g., a glass of water, a stick of gum" (p. 6).

Examples:

Both Mong:	*ib*	*lub*	*tsev*
English	a (one)	(clf.)	house
Mong Leng:	*ib*	*dlaim*	*tab*
Hmong Dawb:	*ib*	*daim*	*tiab*
English:	a (one)	(clf.)	dress

TYPICAL DIFFICULTIES FOR MONG STUDENTS LEARNING ENGLISH

The following illustrate some of the typical difficulties that Mong students may have.

Pronunciation Problems

Pronunciation problems are the result of the direct transference from Mong consonantal sounds that correspond directly with English mainly due to the correct places and the manners of articulation (Table 12.8).

Beginning Sounds.

Examples:

/b/	/v/	/w/	/z/	/j/
*b*at	*v*at	*w*in	*z*one	su*gg*est

/z/	/θ/	/t/	/ð/	/d/
vi*s*ion	*th*ick	*t*ick	*th*ey	*d*ay

Table 12.8

Comparison of the Articulation of Mong and English Consonants

English Sounds	H/Mong Sounds	Eng. Place of Articulation	H/Mong Place of Articulation	Eng. Manner of Articulation	Mong/Hmong Manner of Articulation
/p/ as in spin	/p/	bilabial	bilabial	voiceless stop, unaspirated	voiceless unaspirated stop, affricate
/p/	/ph/	bilabial	bilabial	voiceless stop, aspirated	voiceless aspirated stop, affricate
/b/	/np/	bilabial	bilabial	voiced bilabial	voiced prenasalized, unaspirated, affricate
/t/ as in stick	/t/	alveolar	apico-dental	voiceless stop, no aspiration	voiceless unaspirated, stop, affricate
/t/ as in tick	/th/	alveolar	apico-dental	voiceless stop aspiration	voiceless aspirated, stop, affricate
/d/ as in dog	/dl/	alveolar	apico-alveolar lateral	voiced stop	voiced unaspirated, stop, affricate
/d/ as in dog	/d/	alveolar	apico-alveolar lateral	voiced stop	voiced unaspirated, stop, affricate
/k/ as in skin	/k/	velar	velar	voiceless unaspirated stop	voiceless unaspirated, stop, affricate
/k/	/kh/	velar	velar	voiceless aspirated stop	voiceless aspirated, stop, affricate
	/g/	velar	velar	voiced stop	voiced prenasalized unaspirated stop, aff.
	/nk/	velar	velar		
	/l/	alveolar	apico-dental	voiced lateral liquid	voiced lateral, liquid
	/hl/	-	apico-dental	-	voiceless lateral liquid
	/r/	alveolar	apico-postalveolar	voiced liquid	voiced unaspirated, stop, affricate
	/rh/	-	apico-postalveolar	-	voiceless aspirated, stop, affricate
/w/	/w/	bilabial and/or velar	labio-dental	glide	glide
/z/	/z/	alveolar	palatal	voiced fricative	voiced fricative
/j/ or /dz/	/nts/	palatal	apico-alveolar affricate	voiced affricate	voiced prenasalized unaspirated stop, aff.
	/hm/	-	bilabial	-	voiceless nasal, aspirated
	/ml/	-	labio-lateral release	-	voiced nasal
	/hml/	-	labio-lateral release	-	voiceless nasal, aspirated
/h/	/n/	alveolar	apico-dental	nasal	voiced nasal
	/hn/	-	apico-dental	-	voiceless nasal
	/ny/	-	palatal-affricate release	-	voiced nasal
	/hny/	-	palatal-affricate release	-	
/ng/ as in sing	/ng/ [ç]	velar (syllable final)	velar (syllable init/final)	velar	nasal
/θ/	-	interdental	-	voiceless fricative	-
/ð/	-	interdental	-	voiced fricative	-

Consonantal Clusters. Mong consonantal blends are pronounced as digraphs in English. Therefore, Mong students may have difficulties with the spelling of many English silent consonantal clusters.

Example:
cor*ps* /s/   *thr/θr*/ough   ba*th*/θ/   ba*the* /ð//

Ending Sounds. Mong students do not pronounce ending sounds of consonants or vowels as in English (e.g., ba/t/, bat/s/), including the allomorphs of the plural and past tense morphemes. Allomorphs are the phonetic variants of the regular plural and past tense morphemes. Thus, it is difficult for them to use the correct morphemes and to pronounce them correctly.

Example:

Plural allomorphs:	/-s/	/ - z /	and	/-əz/
	cat*s* / s /	dog*s* /z/		bush*es* /-əz/
Past tense allomorphs:	**/-d /**	/ -t /	and	/-əd/
	call*ed* /d/	walk*ed* /t/		want*ed* /əd/

Vowel Sounds. In Mong, there are seven vowel phonemes /i/, /e/, /w/, /u/, /o/, /a/, and /ə/ and three nasal vowel phonemes (/ee/, /aa/, and /oo/). In English, there are twelve vowel phonemes. This means that the Mong do not have the following lax (short) vowel phonemes that correspond to those in English.

Examples:
/I/   as in bit   /ɛ/ as in bet
/U/ as in butt   and   /æ/ as in bat

Mong students may experience difficulty and confusion in distinguishing the new lax (short) vowels /I/, /ɛ/, and /U/ and the tense vowel /æ/ phonemes because they are incompatible with and nonexistent in Mong.

Examples:
bet /ɛ/ vs.   bait /e/   vs.   bat /æ/
bit /I/ vs.   beat /I/

Vowel Digraphs. Mong students may have problems with English vowel digraphs. Vowel digraphs are the combinations of two vowel sounds as illustrated in Fromkin and Rodman (1993, p. 183; 1998, p. 219).

Examples:

	oo	*wo*	*ough*	*ew*	*ue*	*oe*
as in	*too*	*two*	*through*	*threw*	*clue*	*shoe*

The spelling of these vowel digraphs in English may confuse Mong students. This is because of their unfamiliarity with the forms of the English digraphs. All the digraphs presented in the examples above are spelled in different forms but are pronounced all the same with the /u/ sound. In contrast, /oo/ is a nasal vowel phoneme (nasal monophthong) in Mong and is pronounced /oη/ instead of /u/.

Modal Auxiliaries

Several terms have been used for modal auxiliaries. These terms include modals, auxiliaries, or helping verbs. The role of modal auxiliaries, or helping verbs, in the semantics of English is to express the degree of greater consideration, politeness, tentativeness, permission, ability, possibility, willingness, obligation, prediction, and so on. Modal auxiliaries in English need to be taught to Mong students so that their language is not harsh or rude. It is important that Mong students know how to use English modal auxiliaries appropriately. Proper language use, including the use of proper modal auxiliaries in an appropriate manner, speaks volumes about the individual's academic training, experience, and child-rearing practices. Thao's study (1985) on the corresponding modal auxiliaries between Mong and English indicated that individuals who do not know how to use modal auxiliaries appropriately use language that sounds very demanding (Table 12.9).

Mong Verb Formation

Time, Mood, and Tenses. Mong verbs take the same forms when indicating time, mood, and tenses.

Example:

Both Mong:	*Kuv*	*hu*	*nkauj* (for all tenses)
English:	I	sing	a song. (present)
	I	sang	a song. (past tense)
	I	will sing	a song. (future tense)

Compared to English, Mong verbs do not take on the various inflectional forms when indicating the tenses. However, this does not mean that the Mong do not have tenses. Mong tenses can usually be expressed by adverbial phrases, such as yesterday, today, and tomorrow.

Examples:

Mong Leng:	*Naagmo,*	*kuv*	*hu*	*nkauj.* (past tense)
Hmong Dawb:	*Naghmo,*	*kuv*	*hu*	*nkauj.*
English:	Yesterday,	I	*sang*	a song.

Mong Leng:	*Nubnua,*	*kuv*	*hu*	*nkauj.* (present)
Hmong Dawb:	*Hnubno,*	*kuv*	*hu*	*nkau*j.
English:	Today,	I	*sing*	a song.

Mong Leng:	*Pigkig,*	*kuv*	*hu*	*nkauj* (future)
Hmong Dawb:	*Tagkis,*	*kuv*	*hu*	*nkauj.*
English:	Tomorrow,	I	*will sing*	a song.

Verb Serialization. Verb serialization is a special feature in the sentence construction in the Mong language. The Mong like to use two main verbs in one clause or in one sentence without using a conjunction to separate them.

Examples:

Mong Leng:	*Kuv*	*moog*	*ua si.*	
Hmong Dawb:	*Kuv*	*musua*	*si.*	
English:	I	go	do	play.

--->	I	play.		
Mong Leng:	*Kuv*	*moog*	*kawm*	*ntawv.*
Hmong Dawb:	*Kuv*	*mus*	*kawm*	*ntawv.*
English:	I	go	learn	book.
--->	I	study.		

Owensby asserted that Mong verbs shared this feature with Chinese languages (Bliatout, et al., 1988, p. 56). He asserted that Mong students may use two main verbs in one clause or in one sentence without using a conjunction to separate them. This type of error may be caused by the transference of the concept of verb serialization when forming sentences in English.

PRACTICAL SUGGESTIONS FOR CLASSROOM TEACHERS AND OTHER SERVICE PROVIDERS

Though today's Mong students are being raised in the United States, their parents try to balance their traditional Mong life style with certain elements of mainstream American culture. However, the language barrier continues to impact the rate of adjustment for Mong students, particularly at the K-12 level. Mong students must know how to adapt selectively to maintain a balance between Mong and American culture, cope with the pressure of becoming academically proficient in English by integrating content areas quickly, and meet their teachers' and their parents' high expectations. However, it is easier said than done. In reality, some Mong students' English language proficiency level is so limited that they cannot be mainstreamed. They may not have attained a high academic achievement level compared to other Asian-American students, but they have certainly made impressive progress in the last two decades.

Mong students may experience difficulties in the areas of phonology, morphology, syntax, and semantics. However, these difficulties vary from student to student, depending on the length of residence in the United States and the degree of exposure to English both at home and at school.

The following outlines some practical suggestions for teachers and service providers working with Mong students, so that they may effectively help Mong students acquire the English language. It is impossible to provide every detail in

Table 12.9
Mong and English Modals

Mong Leng (Blue Mong)	Hmong Dawb (White Hmong)	English Modals
tau	tau	can, could, may, might
yuav	yuav	will, would, shall
yuavtsum	yuavtsum	must, would, should
ibtxwm *	ibtxwm *	used to
muaj peevxwm	muaj peevxwm	dare, have the ability to
maamle, le-maam,	mam, li-mam,	may, might, shall
maam, le	mamli, li	should

* *Ibtxwm* is used in the sense of *used to* and is not a modal in Mong but functions as an adverb or an adverbial phrase.

every area of difficulty Mong students experience; therefore, only some of the most typical difficulties are highlighted.

Phonology

The Mong orthography was phonemically based on the romanized popular alphabets (RPA). Thus, its consonantal phonemes consist of single, double, triple, as well as quadruple consonantal blends. Compared to English, though there are more consonants in Mong than in English, Mong students may have problems with phonemic awareness and the pronunciation of certain sounds in English.

Initial Sounds.   /b/ /v/ /w/   /z/ /j/ /z/ /θ/ /t/ /δ/ /d/

One effective way to teach pronunciation is to use minimal pairs. For example, if Mong students have problems pronouncing the sounds /r/, /v/, /θ/ and /δ/, teachers may select minimal pairs containing the sounds that their Mong students can articulate and contrast with those they cannot (e.g., from *l*ice to *r*ice; *f*an to *v*an; ba*th* /θ/ to ba*the* /δ/).

Consonantal Clusters. All ending sounds, including plural and past tense allomorphs.

Examples:
Ending Sounds:	cor**ps**	throu**gh**	
plural allomorphs:	/-s/	/-z/	/-∂z/
past tense allomorphs:	/-d/	/-t/	/-∂d/

Short Vowels. Certain lax (short) vowels in English (e.g., /i/, /u/, /ɛ/, /æ/) are difficult for Mong students because they do not exist in the inventory of the Mong language. In addition, the English prosodic suprasegmental features, which include pitch, stress or accent, and intonation, as discussed earlier in this chapter, are difficult for Mong students.

Vowel Digraphs. Mong children may have some difficulties with the vowel digraphs in English. They may not be able to understand why different letters represent a single sound. The underlined vowel digraphs in the following words represent /u/.

Examples:
t<u>oo</u>   tw<u>o</u>   thr<u>ou</u>gh   thr<u>ew</u>   cl<u>ue</u>   sh<u>oe</u>

Morphology

Compared to English, the Mong language is nonderivational. Thus, the following concepts should be taught in a consistent and explicit manner.

Ending Sounds. Teachers may need to constantly remind the Mong students that all lexical words in English ending with inflections are pronounced. They may help Mong students break the polysyllabic words in English into syllables and morphemes and make comparisons to Mong lexicons.

Affixes. Because Mong language is considered nonderivational, the use of affixes (prefixes and suffixes) and root morphemes is foreign to Mong students. In addition, they do not pronounce the inflectional endings. This means that Mong lexicons maintain the same forms so derivational morphology is not an essential part of the Mong language.

Subcategorization. Subcategorization is defined as the part of the lexical entry of a lexicon that specifies which syntactic categories can and cannot occur with it.

Examples:
to be interested <u>in</u> something (always followed with the preposition <u>in</u>)
to be fond <u>of</u> something (to be fond is always followed by the preposition <u>of</u>)
to sleep, to weep, to stop (verbs that are classified as intransitive verbs and cannot be followed by a direct object).

Suppletive Forms. Suppletive forms or suppletions are the exceptions to the rule, that is, the plural forms of the following words that do not follow the regular plural rule:

Examples:
Man/men   fish/fish   woman/women   child/child*ren*   deer/deer

Syntax

Inflected Forms. The Mong syntax follows the English sentence patterns of subject + verb + object (SVO). Therefore, Mong students are not used to the various inflected forms of verb tenses, which make it very difficult for them to form correct sentences in English. The difficulty lies with the concepts of noninflected forms which include the tenses (present, past, gerund, past participle, progressive forms, etc.), noun possessives, gender, and pronoun cases (me, mine).

Word Order. Word order in Mong varies from that of English. In English, adjectives precede nouns; whereas in Mong, adjectives are placed after the nouns that they modify.

Serial Verb Construction. Mong students may use a series of verbs strung together without conjunctions to separate them in the same sentence. This is the result of language transfer of the serial verb construction in Mong to English.

Semantics

Semantics is the study of meanings of language, so that an individual can make sense out of the words, phrases, and sentences that are strung together to derive meanings. Part of the semantics involves the use of homonyms, synonyms (including polysemous words, such as man and boy), antonyms, phrases, sentences, and pragmatics. Semantics may be one of the most difficult areas for Mong students. Typical difficulties include the use of idioms, metaphors, and articles.

Idioms. Idioms are expressions that tend to be frozen in form and violate the syntactic rules.

Examples:
once in a blue moon   for the time being
give a hand   making ends meet

Metaphors. Metaphors are expressions that do not take on the literal meaning of the sentences.

Examples:
The sea never sleeps.
The walls have ears.

While native speakers of English take knowledge of the use of articles for granted, Mong students may experience great difficulty differentiating between the use of indefinite (a, an) and definite (the) articles. Mainstream teachers should address the use of articles in their lessons as part of the Mong students' English language development.

CONCLUSION

According to the model minority myth, Asian students are focused, goal oriented, studious, hard working, and successful. Thus, teachers may assume that their Mong students share these characteristics. However, this may not be true, as many did not receive any formal education in Laos and have encountered many difficulties in their social and educational adjustment to life in the United States.

Nevertheless, generally speaking, the future looks very promising for Mong students. It is expected that they will excel in all areas of academic disciplines, advance to their full potential, successfully acculturate into the American society, acquire the socioeconomic mobility, and contribute greatly to the advancement of life in the United States. With increased understanding of the linguistic as well as social, cultural, and psychological factors affecting Mong students, preservice and in-service teachers can assist them in the educational process by successfully integrating them into an atmosphere of high academic achievement and guiding them to become responsible contributing members of society.

It is recommended that school districts provide bilingual and bicultural approaches to teaching and learning. School districts should not immerse Mong students into monolingual English classrooms without sufficient support from their native language. The following are some critical elements that teachers and school districts could take to ensure the successful implementation of high quality educational programs for Mong students:

1. Adequate bilingual Mong staff would be very beneficial to assist Mong students to make a smooth transition from the elementary school level to the secondary school level. Using trained bilingual and bicultural staff with linguistic and cultural knowledge of the Mong appears to be one of the most effective approaches in educating the Mong students. The bilingual staff may ameliorate the cultural and educational problems and facilitate the learning, as well as the acculturation of Mong students.
2. School districts should make every attempt to hire teachers who have been trained in the cross-cultural, language academic development or bilingual cross-cultural, language academic development (CLAD/BCLAD) to teach the Mong students. Preservice teachers who have been trained in CLAD and BCLAD could also help to make a smooth transition for Mong students.
3. Mong students could benefit from services of para-educators—paraprofessionals with a combination of skills and training from various disciplines. There are many effective ways to educate the Mong-speaking students. Preservice and in-service teachers and para-educators do not have to be Mong-Americans to deliver services to them effectively. Those who have a deep commitment and passion for their profession and

are willing to go out of their way to make things happen for Mong students can make a big difference in the lives of these young people. Education goes beyond ethnic, political, racial, and socioeconomic lines.

REFERENCES

Arlotto, A. (1972). *Introduction to historical linguistics*. Lanham, Maryland.: University Press of America.

Barney, G. L. (1957). Christianity: Innovation in Meo culture. M.A. thesis, University of Minnesota.

Barney, G. L., & Smalley, W. A. (1953). Third report on Meo (Miao): Orthography and grammar. Mimeo.

Bernatzik, H. A. (1947). *Akha and Miao*. New Haven, CT: Human Relations Area Files.

Bertrais, Y. (1964). *Dictionnaire Hmong (Meo Blanc)-Francais*. Vientiane, Laos: Mission Catholique.

Binney, G. A. (1968). *The social and economic organization of two White Meo communities in Thailand*. Washington, DC: Advanced Research Program Agency.

Bliatout, B., Downing, B., Lewis, J., & Yang, D. (1988*). Handbook for teaching Hmong-speaking students*. Folsom, CA: Folsom Cordova Unified School District, Southeast Asia Community Resource Center.

California Department of Education. (1997). *Language census*. Sacramento, CA: California Department of Education.

Chang, K. (1972). *The reconstruction of proto-Miao-Yao tones BIHP*. Berkeley: University of California and Academia Sinica.

Fromkin, V., & Rodman, R. (1993). *An introduction to language*, 5th ed. Fort Worth, TX: Harcourt Brace College.

_____. (1998). *An introduction to language*. 6th ed. Fort Worth, TX: Harcourt Brace College.

Garrett, W. E. (1974). The Hmong of Laos: No place to run. *National Geographic*. (January): 78-111.

Geddes, W. R. (1976). *Migrants of the mountains: The cultural ecology of the Blue Miao (Hmong Njua) of Thailand*. Oxford: Clarendon Press.

Giglioli, P. (1972). *Language and social context*. New York: Penguin Books.

Hackett, A. P. (1984). *Webster's NewWorld Dictionary*. New York, NY: Warner Books.

Haudricourt, A. G. (1972). *Problèmes de pholologie diachronique*. Paris: Centre National de la Recherche Scientifique.

Hudspeth, W. H. (1939). *Stone-gateway and the flowery Miao*. London: Cargate Press.

Lyman, T. A. (1974). *Dictionary of Mong Njua (Green Miao), a Miao (Meo) language of Southeast Asia*. The Hague: Mouton.

_____. (1979). *Grammar of Mong Njua (Green Miao): A descriptive linguistic study*. Sattley, CA: Blue Oak Press.

Michael, F. (1986). *China through the ages: History of a civilization*. Boulder, CO: Westview Press.

Mong Literacy Volunteer, Inc. (1980). Phoneme spelling change. Minutes of September 13, 1980, meeting in Joliet, Illinois.

National Indochinese Clearinghouse. (1978). *The Hmong language: Sentences, phrases, and words*. General Information Series #15. Arlington, VA: Center for Applied for Linguistics.

_____. (1978). The Hmong language: Sounds and alphabets. General Information Series #14. Arlington, VA: Center for Applied Linguistics.

North, D., & Yang, D. (1988). *Profiles of the highland Lao communities in the United States*. Washington, DC: Office of Refugee Resettlement, U.S. Department of Health and Human Services, Social Security Administration.

Pollard, S. (1919). *The story of the Miao*. London: Henry Hooks.

Purnell, H. (1970). Toward a reconstruction of proto Miao-Yao. Ph.D. dissertation, Cornell University.

Quincy, K. (1988). *Hmong: History of a people*. Cheney, WA: Eastern Washington University Press.

Ratliff, M. S. (1986). The Morphological functions of tone in White Hmong. Doctoral Dissertation, University of Chicago.

Savina, F. M. (1920). *Abécédaire Meo-Français* (Hmong-French Reader). Hanoi: Imprimerie d'Extrème Orient.

_____. (1924). *Histoire des Miao*. Paris: Societe des Missions Etrangères.

Smalley, W. A. (1976). The Problems of consonants and tone: Hmong (Meo, Miao), In *Phonemes and orthography: Language planning in ten minority languages of Thailand*. (pp. 85-123). Canberra: Australian National University.

_____. (1982). History of the development of the Hmong romanized popular alphabet. Presentation and handout to the Hmong Language Council, August 12, Minneapolis, Minnesota: University of Minnesota. The nature of the meeting was to conduct studies to standardize the Mong language.

_____. (1994). *Linguistic diversity and national unity: Language ecology in Thailand*. Chicago: The University of Chicago Press.

_____. (1997). Personal Communication with the author, August 21.

Thao, C., & Robson, B. (1982). *Interim report of the Mhong Language Council Conference August 12-14, 1982*. Washington, DC: Center for Applied Linguistics.

Thao, P. (1985). Teaching modals in Mong ESL classes. M.A. departmental paper, Northeastern Illinois University.

_____. (1994). Mong resettlement in the Chicago area (1978-1987): Educational implications. Ph.D. dissertation, Loyola University of Chicago.

_____. (1997). *Kevcai siv lug Moob* (Foundations of Mong language). Marina, CA: PT Publishing.

_____. (1999). *Mong education at the crossroads*. Lanham, MD: University Press of America.

Thao, S. (1996). *Ncu txug txajntsig Moob I/II* (Special tribute commemorating the Mong I/II], Video. Fresno, CA: S. T. Universal Video.

Tsaj, C. (n.d.). *Hmoob nyob Pa Tawg teb* (The Hmong in Wenshan). Guyane, France: Association Communaute Hmong.

U.S. Department of Health and Human Services. (1988). *Profiles of the highland Lao communities in the United States*. Washington, DC: Government Printing Office.

U.S. Department of Health and Human Services. (1995*). Report to Congress FY 1995*. Washington, DC: Government Printing Office.

Xiong, L., Xiong, J, & Xiong, N. L. (1983). *English-Mong-English dictionary*. Milwaukee, WI: Hetrick Printing.

Xiong, X. D. (1989). Txooj Moob huv nplajteb (The Mong in the world), *Txooj Moob* (May): 4, 8-12.

Yang, D. (1975). *Les Hmong du Laos face au developpement*. Vientiane, Laos: Edition Siaosavath.

CHAPTER 13

Scars of War: Educational Issues and Challenges for Cambodian-American Students

Khatharya Um

CONTEXT FOR UNDERSTANDING THE CAMBODIAN DIASPORA

The communist victory in Cambodia, Laos, and Vietnam in 1975 brought an end to the Second Indochina War, America's longest war, but it also created conditions for protracted conflict, political and socio-economic upheaval, and ultimately, mass refugee exodus. For the Cambodian people, who have little prior history of overseas migration, 1975 also marked the beginning of the diaspora that saw to the displacement and resettlement of close to one million Cambodians. Some 146,346 refugees from Cambodia were admitted to the United States between 1975 and 1994, constituting approximately 13%, of the total 1,180,538 Southeast Asians and Amerasians that were resettled in the United States (Office of Refugee Resettlement, 1994). At large, Southeast Asians constitute the single largest category of refugees to be resettled in the US in the post-1965 period and the fastest growing segment of the Asian-Pacific-American (APA) population.

The Southeast Asian American community has become much more visible in recent years for at least two reasons: (1) the community has seen rapid growth, and (2) the community has concentrated in distinct geographical areas due to postresettlement or secondary migrations. This increase in visibility has both positive and adverse consequences. Public perceptions of Southeast Asian communities are polarized. At one extreme, is the image of refugees as being helpless and dependent, lacking the necessary requisites for effective transition into the post-industrial American society and economy. In this sense, the community is seen to be at risk. At the other extreme are the presumptions of economic and scholastic achievements, exemplified by the numerous valedictorians, visible presence on college campuses and booming ethnic enterprises. While inspirational, the media's focus on individual success stories such as that of the Cambodian girl who struggled and succeeded despite her limited English proficiency to win a spelling bee, contributes to the oversimplification and generalization of the Cambodian experience, which, in turn, masks the myriad education-related problems confronting youths of refugee families. The implications of such stereotyping for policies and programs are, by extension, grave.

Despite the frequent tendency to view Southeast Asians as a homogenous community in the United States, to lump them generically as Indochinese, the communities that came into being in the aftermath of the Vietnam War reflect tremendous diversity among groups and within groups. The complexity of the refugee experience points to the importance of looking at the timing, context, and process of migration in the study of adaptation. Depending upon the time of exit from the home country and arrival in the United States, Cambodian refugee cohorts, for instance, reflect vast socioeconomic and experiential differences. During the Khmer Rouge regimes (1975-1979) infliction of systematic class persecution, endemic starvation, and hard labor resulted in the death of over 1 million Cambodians, more than one-seventh of the population, with a disproportionate percentage of the educated, professionals, and urbanites being killed. The demographic profile of refugees who eventually escaped to the border camps following the collapse of the Communist regime (resettled in third countries in the early 1980s) reflects this politico-historical experience. The Cambodian refugee community, at large, consists of a high percentage of people of the peasant or lower socioeconomic class or those who had successfully hidden their upper-class background. In comparison with the smaller group of refugees who were resettled in 1975, the overwhelming majority of the later arrivals were less educated, more rural in origin, and generally less endowed with the skills, or the "human capital," that are generally deemed essential for successful resettlement.

In addition to the temporal factor, the context and process of migration also have implications for adjustment-related issues such as physical and mental health. In addition to the trauma of displacement shared by all refugees, the post-1979 cohorts endured and survived chronic starvation, unimaginable violence under the Khmer Rouge, and endemic perils of flight, of minefields, insurgency, and banditry. Once in border camps, they were further diminished by a life of uncertainty and divested of their sense of self-determination in critical aspects of their daily routine. Their physical safety, access to food, and future welfare depended on forces beyond their control-international politics, immigration policies and officers, and regional politics as they determined the degree of receptivity to refugees on the part of host and resettlement countries. This learned helplessness has direct implications for their adjustment in the postresettlement context and particularly for their capacity to regain their sense of self-sufficiency.

The ability of refugees to make successful transition towards integration, however, depends as much upon the host context as it does on pre-resettlement experiences. Success is reflective of the adaptive resources of the individual refugee and community as much as it is of opportunities and condition that exist for capitalizing upon those resources. In short, it depends equally upon the context *into* which refugees are being resettled, as it does the context *out* of which they emerge. Intrinsic human capital notwithstanding, the state and condition of local economies and politics do determine opportunities and constraints for the optimization of those resources. Given their low level education and skill, Cambodian refugee employment is highly concentrated in the manufacturing sector which is tremendously vulnerable to economic vicissitudes. Thus the economic welfare of large segments of the refugee population depends upon the continued vitality of these rather volatile sectors of American economy.

Be it in terms of economic or social adjustment, the tribulations that continue to affect the lives of refugee families-poverty, racism, urban violence, crime-deter successful adaptation as much as the trauma that they experienced and carry with them into exile. These adverse conditions that confront refugee families, in turn, are linked in very significant ways to student academic performance. Temporal and contextual factors, therefore, are critical in accounting for variations in the degree of individual and community resiliency, as well as accounting for the patterns and dynamics of the response to change. An understanding of the issues and concerns of Cambodian refugee communities must involve the examination of these multiple dimensions—cultural, structural, historical, generational—as they affect the adaptation of Cambodian students and their families. People working with Cambodian refugee families must determine not only the extent to which each of these factors bears upon the process of adjustment and integration, but they must also determine how these forces interface with and reinforce each other to generate compounded adverse consequences.

WAR, REVOLUTION, AND ENCAMPMENT: CHAKKENGES TO CRITICAL ASPECTS OF CAMBODIAN SOCIAL AND CULTURAL INSTITUTIONS

Of exile, Barudy (1987) points out that it "is never the fulfillment of a wish; it is a 'forced choice,' necessary to escape danger and survive. It always involves a break or a *repetition* of the break in the individual's personal and social history which began with the repression" [my emphasis]. While refugees have some commonalties with other immigrants, it is this contextual particularity that distinguishes the refugee condition from voluntary migration. What further separates the Cambodian refugee experience from that of other Southeast Asian groups is the compounding nature and concomitant intensity of the dislocation experience. For the Cambodian people, the disruption generated by war and revolution was multilevel as well as multidimensional. The nature and scope of dislocation extended from the individual, to the communal, to the nation-state, and involved structural, sociocultural, and psychical dimensions. Revolutionary transformation and turmoil consumed everyone living under the Communist regime, regardless of age, gender and class. By extension, the disruption, whether systematic or incidental, affected fundamental aspects of Cambodian culture and society, from the social consciousness of her people to the structural and functional integrity of key institutions.

To a regime such as that of the Khmer Rouge, which sought totalistic control over its populace, any force that commanded traditional loyalty was viewed as a challenge to the state. Buddhism, the nucleus of Khmer weltenschaung and the basis of its cultural, literary, social, and spiritual tradition, was banned. Bonzes were forcefully defrocked and sent to work camps or summarily put to death, while the *vat* (Buddhist monasteries), which traditionally constitute the social and spiritual center of the village, were transformed into rice granaries or makeshift prisons. The undermining of Buddhism was one aspect of that overall process of institutional destabilization. Despite subsequent efforts towards cultural restoration, the implication of this institutional weakening continues to register in diaspora, depriving the community of one of the cementing forces.

Just as Buddhism was seen as being oppositional to the secular faith of communism, so were family and community ties perceived as a threat to the regime. The policy of mass and repeated relocation was motivated, therefore, not by economic imperatives but by the need of the totalitarian state to undercut communal ties to ensure absolute loyalty and undermine potential resistance. The institution of family, which is the locust of Khmer social identity and primordial relations, was systematically attacked. During the Khmer Rouge regime, working age Cambodians were assigned to age and gender-based mobile work brigades and subjected to constant uprooting. As one refugee recalled, "In all four years under A-Pot ('the wretched Pot'), I had nothing. Just a *krama* (a scarf), a spoon that I had made myself, and one set of clothing. I knew no village, no home. My [work] team was sent everywhere. They did not want us to stay in any one place too long for fear that we would get to know the locals too well" (S. Khon, personal interview, Oakland, Califomia,1989). Assignment to work teams in which members not only worked but lived, and ate together, meant the purposive fragmentation of the family unit and systematic reintegration of individual members into a new organization. In some cases, children as young as five years of age were separated from their parents, and subjected to systematic indoctrination.

The Cambodian social and economic lives, thus, were reorganized into a new hierarchy. Parents, who traditionally were accorded a place second only to Buddha within the Khmer cultural universe, were made subordinate to the omnipotent state. Children were taught that they now belonged to *Angka* (The Organization). For young adults, the state replaced parents and kin in the selection of marriage partners and the sanctification of marital relationship. Endemic fear, suspicion, and chronic starvation further atomized the individual and threatened the integrity of the family: "There are no more parents or children. We owe our life and loyalty only to *Angka*. It was as if we were no longer a family with thoughts and respect for each other. We no longer relate to each other the same way" (Um, 1990, p. 254). The Khmer Rouge motto *sok muy, kbal muy* (one strand of hair, one head) encapsulates the credo of the regime which deemphasizes the individual for the good of the group. Among surviving Cambodian refugees, the legacy of trauma is reflected in the fear of, and unquestioning obedience to, authority and the high degree of fatalism. Furthermore, the undermining of critical institutions such as the family and religion divests the diasporic community of the structural cohesion and support necessary for facilitating resettlement.

Other consequences of this history of dislocation are less tangible but equally salient to the discussion of adaptation. For a culture that is based significantly on oral tradition, the degree of rupture that was inflicted by the decimation of one-seventh of the population is immeasurable. Thus, while culture is a significant component in addressing education-impacted issues, it is important to recognize that fundamental aspects of Cambodian cultural norms and institutions have been significantly affected by historical and generational factors. The cultural dimension of refugee community studies, therefore, must be situated simultaneously within the contexts of continuity and change.

In sum, the recent history of the Cambodian people is one of dislocation and disempowerment. Destabilization of traditional institutions and social relations did not end with exit from the home country; it continues during the process of migration, through the period of encampment, and in resettlement, with detrimental consequences for the sustained viability of the Cambodian social support system. For many Cambodian refugees who survived the Khmer Rouge experience and for whom flight often resulted in further loss of family members through separation and death, the years of languishing in refugee camps were marked by uncertainty, artificiality, and concomitant social psychosis that further aggravated the unraveling of the social fabric of family and community. In this regard, it is significant to note that Cambodians experienced a much longer period of encampment than other Southeast Asian refugee groups, averaging 3 to 5 years. The implications of the refugee camp experience are wide ranging and persist long after exiting from the camp. Educational disruption, dependency, and a sense of fatalistic helplessness ultimately resulted from camp policies that discouraged institutionalization of economic and educational pursuits as a deterrent against permanent border settlement. In less than a decade of turmoil, a culture once based upon agrarian tradition came to produce a new generation who knew only that rice came from the UN trucks.

IMPORTANCE OF HOST ENVIRONMENT

Adjustment is affected not only by the legacies of dislocation and trauma but also by postresettlement experiences and the political relationship of the refugee community with the receiving society. Even for refugees with the necessary adaptive resources, resettlement is not without considerable challenge. While studies of refugee adaptation consistently point to the self-sufficiency and preparedness of the 1975 cohort to gain access to employment, very few studies report the significant downward mobility, particularly of the educated elite. The tendency to equate employment, even underemployment, with "successful" adaptation disregards the frustration that many high-achieving refugees feel about the un/under fulfillment of their life aspirations. Moreover, where educational and occupational achievements have been possible, social and cultural alienation continues to inculcate a sense of marginalization. Regardless of economic standing, given that the majority of Cambodian-Americans are of the majority -identified group in their home country, the effects of being reduced to minority status in the highly racialized American society are multiple and grave. Whereas differentiation and marginalization are the lived experiences that contradict the loftier rhetoric of pluralistic democracy, many continue to be preoccupied with the homeland, partly as a way of rationalizing and coping with their present condition. The dream of the return to the ancestral land is, therefore, "a pragmatic solution to the dilemma of being part of two contexts, two countries and two sets of norms and values, which may not only be different, but in most cases contradictory" (Al-Rasheed, 1994, p. 200). This preoccupation not only deters the prospect for planting permanent roots in the new place of resettlement but also deflects critical resources in terms of leadership, capital, and attention away from the refugee community in America, which is floundering in fundamental ways.

REINTERPRETATION, RENOVATION, RECONSTRUCTION: CULTURE AND COMMUNITY IN DIASPORA

The refugee experience involves not only aspects of disruption but also of recollection, selection, interpretation, modification, and reconstruction. In the process of moving from the destruction of all that is familiar towards integration into everything that is new, a refugee has to learn to make sense of his or her world that, in essence, has been turned upside down. Thus, analyses of refugee adaptation in the United States cannot be confined to examining the disconnection in their experience. They must also highlight the continuities that are present in the transition from one culture to another; that is, in addition to articulating the aspects of marginalization and helplessness refugees face, the Cambodian people's undeniable resiliency that is demonstrated at individual, family, and community levels must also be emphasized.

Refugees are in many ways a selective population, not only in terms of their decision to flee but in their ability to survive. This, in itself, is a critical adaptive resource that they have brought with them. Despite the United States government policy of dispersal, an ethnic community has been re-established through secondary and tertiary migration. Ethnic based mutual assistance agencies, cultural and professional associations, Buddhist temples and Cambodian Christian churches have all emerged as key institutions for the gathering and dissemination of critical information, for the pooling and sharing of scarce resources. Since its inception in 1989, the Cambodian Network Council, based in Washington D.C., has served as the umbrella organization for the Cambodian mutual assistance agencies, providing the community with a political presence in the national policy and advocacy arenas, while institutions such as the United Cambodian Community and the Cambodian Association of

America, both of Long Beach, California continue to provide leadership at the local and regional levels. These institutions, among others, provide support and structure for those who have been stripped of even the most basic sense of family and community. Refugees turn to these community institutions for information about jobs, housing, parenting advice, peer support and culturally appropriate interventions in times of life crises. For instance, because mental health clinics carry a certain social stigma associated with mental illness, Cambodian families often turn to Buddhist monks for solace through counseling, prayers, and holy ablution, essentially through venues that are comprehensible within the Khmer cultural universe.

More importantly, these institutions serve as important loci for the articulation and reaffirmation of ethnic identity and homeland culture, as it is remembered. In a world of whirlwind changes, they yield that security of sameness, a context, however fleeting, where traditional norms in regards to social status, leadership, authority, and relations of obligation, are still valid and legitimated. Participation in community functions becomes a way for the diasporic Cambodian community to "live out the tension embedded in the 'experiences of separation and entanglement,' of living here and remembering/desiring another place" (Clifford, 1994, p. 15). At various religious ceremonies and cultural events, Cambodian-Americans immerse themselves in momentary reprieve in the reconstituted world of familiar sights, sounds, and smell, in the adornment of traditional dress, in the partaking of traditional food, music, and religious chants. Inside the walls of Buddhist temples or ceremonial halls, the community is brought together in the affirmation of cultural and ethnic identity, of continuity in a world of disruption and rupture. Though weddings are now abridged and religious festivals charted not in accordance with cosmology but practicality (i.e., made to coincide with weekends, for instance, in order to facilitate community participation), they remain important cementing forces for a community that is often fractionalized along class, gender, generational, and political lines. In this context, the community, even in diaspora, can be imbued it with a reconstituted ethos.

In promoting new partnership, schools may look to these community based organizations (CBOs) as a resource and a conduit for accessing the refugee community. Access to bilingual and bicultural staff afforded to the schools through this relationship can facilitate outreach to families, such as through the provision of quality primary language translation and materials, and culturally and experientially appropriate technical assistance. In discussing the role of community-based organizations in promoting home-school partnership, the executive director of the Cambodian Association of Greater Philadelphia points out the critical link between these institutions and the community: "They (CBOs) can understand the problem because they live there, they've been there, they come from there, they're one of them" (National Coalition of Advocates of Students, 1997, p. 72).

RESETTLEMENT AND THE CHALLENGES OF ADAPTATIONS

Over the last two decades since the initial resettlement, the Cambodian-

American community has developed and evolved, both in terms of numerical growth and in terms of importance in the economic and sociocultural tableau of American society. Following the admission of the initial cohort of 4600 Cambodians in 1975 (Office of Refugee Resettlement, 1988), successive resettlement initiatives led to an exponential increase in numbers and complexity in the socioeconomic composition of the refugees admitted. Nevertheless, comprehensive and systematic studies of the Cambodian refugee population remain relatively scarce which impedes access to, and implementation of, effective and efficient service delivery. The community assessment that does exist (National Association For the Education and Advancement of Cambodian, Laotian and Vietnamese Americans, 1995; Ima and Rumbaut, 1983) points to inherent vulnerabilities among Cambodian-American refugees and immigrants. The legacies of war, revolution, and exile are registered in the adjustment challenges that the community encounters in resettlement. Because of the decimation of the educated class, the surviving, diasporic community reflects a high percentage of people with low level of formal education; 64.3% of Cambodian adults have less than a high school education, compared to 39.4% Vietnamese and 24.4% of the mainstream population (National Association For the Education and Advancement of Cambodian, Laotian and Vietnamese Americans, 1995). Analysis based on the 1990 census reveals that 24% of Cambodians in the 25-44 age group and 40.8% of those in the 45-65 cohort have no formal education at all. A study of the San Diego Cambodian community (Rumbaut and Ima, 1988) indicates an average of less than three years of formal education among the adults. The scarcity of the educated and entrepreneurial classes, along with the destruction of familial and communal support networks, constrain the ability of the Cambodian refugee community to mobilize internal social and economic resources. Of direct significance to education is the absence of support for students. Parents often feel ill-equipped to provide their children with academic assistance after a certain grade level. Advocacy for the students is also constrained by the scarcity of community leadership. Without institutional backing and mediation, refugee parents, particularly those without much familiarity with formal educational systems, feel tremendously disempowered in their dealings with schools and bureaucracies.

Economic Marginality

Lack of education and transferable skills among a high percentage of Cambodian refugees, furthermore, has resulted in employment concentration in highly vulnerable economic sectors; approximately 38% of Cambodian workers are employed in manufacturing sectors with machine operator/assembler and precision/craft accounting for 15.6% and 23.8% respectively (National Association for the Education and Advancement of Cambodian, Laotian and Vietnamese Americans, 1995). In Massachusetts, for instance, the downsizing of Wang Industries severely affected the Cambodian-American community, which had grown in response to the employment opportunities within that sector, and resulted in an increase in welfare dependency. Statistics on labor participation and income level obscure the fact that many refugees hold multiple, low-paying jobs without employment security, health and retirement benefits. With over 40% continuing to live below poverty line, Cambodian refugees constitute not only a community in transition, but one clearly at risk.

Social Marginality and Mental Health

In addition to structural constraints, the adjustment process of Cambodians is complicated by subjective factors. Being a refugee "means being engaged in a kind of lifelong psychological balancing act" (Wicker and Schoch, 1987, p. 17). The experiences of dislocation caused by displacement and exile may foster a sense of marginality long after their arrival in the United States. Indeed, many refugees seems to continue to exist in a discontinuous state of being, caught between the inability to free oneself from the past and the uncertainty of the future: "Sometimes, I don't know what is real anymore... the past, the present.... I used to say to myself, 'This can't be real; it must be a nightmare, and I will wake up.' Except that nightmare never ends. I just got used to it" (A. Thong, personal interview, San Diego, March, 1989). As a result of the unanticipatory, and often secretive nature of the escape, the perilous journey resulting in more deaths and disappearances of friends and relatives, compounded by the inability to communicate with the home country during the mid-1970s to late 1980s, many Cambodian refugees feel a sense of unresolved business. For Khmer Buddhists, the inability to perform appropriate funereal rites has contributed to the deterring of the healing process and further impeded the achievement of a sense of closure to these tragic life experiences. These various factors all contribute to keeping many Cambodian refugees in a state of limbo and perpetuate their continued preoccupation with the ancestral homeland, hence prolonging their sense of being uprooted.

For many refugees, particularly among the post-1979 cohort, adaptation to a new context thus entails greater challenges than those posed by the market place. Language and cultural bafflers not only impede access to the job market but keep segments of the refugee population in linguistic isolation. This is particularly true of the elderly. Speaking of his daily existence, an elderly Cambodian gentleman reflected that "I stare at the wall and blink until three o'clock, when the children come home from school. Then there is noise and activity; there is life" (A. Ung, Personal interview, San Diego, December, 1992). Cultural differences, in norms and expectations, are also the basis of many adjustment issues. For the majority of Cambodian refugees who come from a more agrarian background, negotiating the transition from a rural existence to life in a postindustrial society can be a highly daunting and disorienting process. The notions of mutual assistance, life-long obligations and patronage, are obfuscated by the deep sense of alienation prompted by the postmodern environment of the United States. Whereas the Khmer social system is based upon personal relationships and a sense of communalism, the impersonal nature of the welfare and social service bureaucracies of America can be tremendously alienating for the new arrivals and exacerbate the high degree of insecurity and uncertainty many refugees feel. Adaptation-related stress may compound the traumas incurred during the migration process and induce high levels of depression and post-traumatic stress disorder symptoms among Cambodian refugees. As a result of the compounding effects of their politico-historical experiences and persistent sociocultural and economic marginalization, Cambodian refugees manifest a degree of fatalism that is significantly higher than that of other refugee communities.

In a different sense, the circumstances for the younger generation may be even worse. Those who were too young to remember the Khmer Rouge years can neither relate to their parents' traumatic experiences nor empathize with their adjustment difficulties. Nevertheless, they live under the constant shadow of the trauma with which their parents struggle. In addition, many are culturally disconnected from the home culture and traditionalism of their parents and older siblings, and are understandably resistant to the demands for conformity they encounter at home.

Changing Dynamics of Cambodian Refugee Families

In addition to the need to adapt to external changes with regard to jobs and social institutions, Cambodian refugee families must struggle to adjust to changes within the family which the immigration experience has prompted. As assets and resources are redefined by the new social and economic contexts, many aspects of tradition loose their relevance. Power relations within the family and within the community are consequently altered. The Khmer Rouge years witnessed forced separation of family members and an astonishing death rate among the male population who were either systematically killed or had died of harsh labor and starvation. Nearly two decades after the end of the Khmer Rouge regime, the demography of Cambodia continues to reflect an imbalance in gender ratio. Thus, the high percentage of fragmented families and widowhood within the Cambodian refugee community (in some locales, the percentage of widows may be as high as 25% [Rumbaut and Ima, 1983]), has led to the displacement of the male figure as the head of household and to the alteration in gender roles and relations within the family. In many instances, women are now compelled by economic necessity to seek employment outside of the home. While Cambodian women have always played critical economic roles, their economic contributions are now the primary, and not simply supplementary, source of family income. In the refugee camps, international relief agencies avoided being criticized for feeding warring soldiers by issuing food assistance only to women and girls (Ledgerwood, 1990). This situation continues in the United States where many Cambodian families are dependent upon the government program of Assistance to Families with Dependent Children in which the check is often made in the mother's name.

For Cambodian women, greater access to economic resources, whether through public assistance or low-skill employment, means increased independence; even housewives now find that they can generate supplemental income through engagement in home industry such as piecework sewing. Enhanced economic mobility and independence of Cambodian women, however, contrast with the real or perceived economic demotion of the Cambodian males; as one Cambodian-American man pointed out, "We now have to live under the wings of our wives" (S. Ol, personal interview, Long Beach, July, 1990). These changes fundamentally affect relational dynamics within the family, upsetting traditional gender hierarchy, and calling into question basic assumptions about gender roles and relations. Shifts in traditional power relations contribute to the increase in domestic violence and divorce rates within the Cambodian- American community (Ledgerwood, 1990) and hence to the continued erosion of the Cambodian social fabric.

Parent-Child Relations

Role reversal and altered power relations are also manifested in parent-child relations. From a cultural context which places youth at the bottom of the social hierarchy where they are to be seen but not heard, Cambodian refugee youths are often moved into an unprecedented position of power by their ability to adapt better and more rapidly than the adults. Given the adults' limited education and English language skills, children in many refugee families have assumed the role of linguistic and cultural brokers, with powers to mediate, filter, and manipulate information. One parent who was informed by school personnel that her child was failing academically was shocked to discover that, contrary to what her son had been telling her, F does not mean "fine." Another parent explained the nature of his total reliance upon his children in this way: "We are blind and mute; the children are our bridge to the outside world" (T. Lim, personal interview, Sonoma, January, 1990). In view of this role reversal, it has been argued that filiarchy, a system whereby children assume power positions, has emerged in the Cambodian-American social context The power of children to access confidential correspondence can interfere with effective home-school relations, especially if such relations are reliant exclusively upon written and telephone communication.

Alterations to the parent-child relationship have led to Cambodian youth being forced to assume responsibilities inappropriate for their age. This, coupled with the mounting disempowerment that Cambodian parents feel, has a definite effect on family dynamics. Some Cambodian youths have used their newfound leverage to disregard parental authority, sometimes threatening to report their parents for purported child abuse when subjected to strict discipline, or when their freedom is being curtailed n other ways. Feeling the loss of control over their children and being unfamiliar with American laws, Cambodian parents may opt for extremist recourse of either resorting to traditionally sanctioned corporal punishment or abdicating completely their parental roles as disciplinarians. Their predicament is evident: "When we discipline our children, the police comes to take us to jail. When we don't do anything and our children err, we, as parents, are blamed. We no longer know what to do" (S. Tith, personal interview, San Francisco, March, 1991).

Another area of contention in parent-child relationship is communication. Differential rate of acculturation is often the basis of intergenerational conflicts, exacerbated in many cases by the children's loss of the primary language in the process of acquiring English. Communication is often reduced to a unidirectional flow of parental commands and imperatives. Even families who understand the need to be more expressive and interactive may find their intention constrained by demanding work schedules and the burden of their own adjustment difficulties. Nonetheless, whereas parents tend to attribute this lack of communication and expressiveness to culture or survival demands in a new environment, Cambodian youths often interpret it as family dysfunctionalism and lack of parental care and concern. In many instances, this reinforces their sense of alienation from their own family and ethnic community, and further justifies the dismissing attitudes they exhibit toward their own parents and other Cambodian adults.

Marginality and Identity

The effects of all these changes are felt equally by the youth and by the adults. Like their parents, children of refugee families often find themselves having to navigate the multiple demands and conflicting pressures to conform. They are subjected to the competing influence of the home culture, the school culture, the street culture and societal culture at large: "The immigrant child is exposed to the conflicting values of home, peer group, school, to clashing definitions of the good life, and to the tug-and-pull of competing loyalties" (National Coalition of Advocates for Students, 1997, p. 4). Some can effectively negotiate the necessary delicate balance and can function in multiple worlds, but many falter. Traditionally, the socialization of youth occurs and is reinforced at home, at school, and in society. Cambodian youths in the United States receive messages from each of these arenas that are often conflicting and polarizing. At school and through the media, they are socialized to believe in individualism, assertiveness, and independence. At home, they are confronted with the pressure to adhere to the traditional Cambodian values of collectivism, self-effacing modesty, gender and age hierarchy. From mainstream society, they learn that English is the language of power. At home, they see in their parents' and their own limited English proficiency, the epitome of social and economic marginality. From mainstream society and the media, they acquire consumerist and materialist values.

At home, they live in poverty, in neighborhoods replete with forces proffering alternative venues to economic "success," that is crime and delinquency. In a racialized society which lumps all Asian-Americans into a homogenous grouping, youth from refugee families are sometimes entrapped by the image of the model minority, with its generalized ascription of success and wealth. Meanwhile, at school and in the work place they are confronted with the disempowerment that comes with their linguistic and educational disadvantages. Many are overwhelmed by the inherent tension between their desire to live up to expectations, whether societal, communal, or familial, and the educational obstacles that they encounter. The sense of failure that they have internalized is further aggravated by the survivor's guilt many refugees feel.

In a society that identifies Cambodia and everything Cambodian with nothing more than the killing fields and with politically and socioeconomically disenfranchised refugees, many Cambodian youths have come to internalize these messages. They have come to associate their parents—their Cambodian-ness, and their refugee-ness—with social stigmas and regard them as possessing no inherent usefulness for success in America. This contributes to intergenerational conflict and the progressive disempowerment not only of parents and guardians but of the youth themselves. Often shame translates into loss of self-esteem as they struggle with their own identity, that is, their Cambodian-ness and refugee-ness. Within the school's social hierarchy in which immigrant students are ranked at the bottom, this Filipino student's remark captures the disparaging treatment of Cambodian students in the public schools: "A white guy was calling us names, like 'Cambodian'—very derogatory names. We beat him up" (National Coalition of Advocates of Students, 1988, p. 60). It is thus not surprising that many reject their ethnic and cultural identity and, being unable to overcome social and cultural marginality, find themselves in perpetual limbo.

In an environment in which they are made to feel psychologically, intellectually or physically unsafe, students cannot be expected to focus on academic pursuits. As one student put it, "Sometimes you can't concentrate in class because there is trouble, like when somebody calls you a name or gives you a bad look or pushes you. You can't talk back, and then you are so mad and all you can think about is revenge, so you can't concentrate" (Koschmann, 1987, p. 185). For many non-English speaking students, linguistic constraint reinforces the sense of helplessness and vulnerability: "What can you do? They say bad things to you, but you can't talk to them because you can't talk English. So they just keep on doing it, and you keep on doing nothing. Then one day you get in a fight" (Koschmann, 1987, p. 185). Because of their political experiences and cultural predisposition, some students communicate their frustration in other inarticulated ways. In their comparative study of refugee youths, Rumbaut and Ima (1988) referred to the expressive withdrawal of Cambodian students whereby students choose not to confront problematic situations at school, but simply to drop-out.

The relationship between school climate and school retention is well-documented in the existing body of scholarship. Adding to the urgency of the issue are the recent findings of the Asian Law Caucus (1997), which documented a disconcerting increase of hate crimes in schools and college campuses. In working towards reform, schools need to place policy priority on the creation of an environment that is conducive to personal and intellectual growth. Such an environment must reflect not just tolerance of diversity but its celebration through curriculum, program, and the overall school climate as it is shaped by the attitude of faculty and staff. Given the perilous absence of positive reinforcement, for refugee youths, it is imperative that the core curriculum integrate fundamental components of Southeast Asian histories, cultures and the contributions that these communities have made to the overall enrichment of American culture and society. A well designed and effectively implemented multicultural curriculum would provide not only intellectual enrichment but also help diffuse racial and ethnic tensions, which are usually rooted in fear and spawned by ignorance.

IMPLICATIONS FOR THE SCHOOLING AND EDUCATION OF CAMBODIAN AMERICAN STUDENTS

While all population movements necessarily entail some degree of uprootedness, forced migration imposes a compoundingly multi-dimensional character onto the dislocation that is unparalleled in its scope and intensity in other experiences. As such, refugee students and their families have particular needs and concerns that are not shared by other immigrant communities. Given the diversity of the Cambodian refugee community at large, both among and within groups, the issues and concerns vary in nature, scope, and intensity. In order to effectively address those needs, school staff must be cognizant of the diversity of the Cambodian-American student population that is reflected along generational, class, and gender lines. Existing literature and studies of Southeast Asian refugees 'have addressed the issues of the "1.5 generation," those youths who immigrated in their adolescence, having been imbued with aspects of the traditional culture in the formative years but have also been acculturated by their immersion in the American educational system. What is glaringly absent, however, are the voices and concerns of the group which I term the "1.8 generation," and those of the second generation. The "1.8 generation" refers to the cohort of refugee youths who arrived in their pre-adolescent years, often too young at the time of migration to have had anything 'more than an intuitive affinity with the traditional culture. Most have little difficulty with the English language but have virtually no command of their primary language; a few may have some comprehension of the primary language but are not necessarily conversant in it. Their issues and those of the second generation differ from the older cohort, the "1.5 generation," to the extent that they do not revolve as much around problems of English language acquisition, except perhaps in mastering academic English. These cohorts are concerned more with intergenerational and identity issues, in addition to their adolescent anxieties. While generational factor is one dimension of difference within the refugee student population, it is also important to note that class, gender, and personal experiences are important mediating variables in educational achievement Educational pursuit has frequently been prematurely interrupted by the need to secure early employment to help support the family, particularly for young Cambodian males, or by pressure to marry early in the case of young Cambodian women.

Overall, many of the challenges facing youths of refugee families are not academic. For instance, problems that appear to be learning disorders may, in fact, be rooted in nonacademic factors. Addressing the needs of refugees, therefore, must begin with an understanding of the historical and personal experiences that critically impact the educational experience. Further, the tremendous diversity of refugee experiences must be recognized. Educators and people working with refugee families need to be aware of the conscious and unconscious assumptions that they may have about individuals and ethnic groups-assumptions about students' value systems, aptitudes, predisposition, learning styles, and capabilities.

It must be recognized that the refugee experience may not have allowed for the development of academic preparedness and school readiness. Given the disruptions in their educational experience, refugee youths may enter American schools with social and intellectual development which do not match their age. A-sixteen-year-old in high school may in fact have had only a few years of formal education but have lived through experiences that would defy the imagination of the average adult in America. Assumptions about social and intellectual development are further challenged by the attempt of some refugee parents to minimize the effects of educational disruption by reporting an age lower than the actual age of their children. This issue has been brought to the fore in instances when seemingly underaged girls are married off or in cases of socially overdeveloped youth manifesting behavioral problems in school. Sensitive and responsive education of refugee students, therefore, begins with the knowledge of the student population. Further, the willingness and ability to be flexible in pedagogical methods, policies, and efforts to accommodate variations in learning styles, educational experiences, psychosocial development, and situational particularities are also critical.

Being cognizant of the historical experiences of refugees, however, should not lead to the presumption that all refugee students are traumatized beyond reprieved and, as a result, are academically dysfunctional. All too often, students' capabilities and aspirations are stunted, not by inherent deterrents but by low expectations. In many instances, English learners are informally tracked by the classes they are advised to take and by the information that they are given or not given. A common complaint among limited English proficient (LEP) refugee students is that they are not being given the same information as other high-achieving students, particularly in regard to postsecondary educational options. A survey of Southeast Asian refugee students at Berkeley revealed that 98% received college information from older siblings and friends rather than from teachers and counselors; while in high school, most were given information about vocational programs or junior colleges but rarely about four-year institutions (Urn, 1997).

Similarly, the tendency to adhere to the generalized image of the cohesive and supportive Asian family disregards the reality of fragmentation, informal adoptions, and reconstituted households that are common features of the refugee community. A study of the Cambodian refugee community in San Diego revealed that over 50% of the households were headed by single parents (Rurnbaut & Ima, 1988). Koschmann (1987), in her study of Cambodian youth in an eastern city, also documented the complexity of the Cambodian families, including informal adoptions and kinship relations that differ from what may be on record in official immigration documents. In some instances, families may have informally adopted orphans or unaccompanied minors out of a sense of altruism or obligation to friends and relatives. Moreover, it is not uncommon to find households reconstituted of unrelated individuals who came together for pratical reasons, such as shared housing costs or companionship. Given the changing dynamics and composition of the Cambodian family, it is quite possible that the adults responsible for the youth may not be the natural parents but older siblings or extended family members. It is critical that, in their ongoing efforts to promote home-school relations, schools recognize this complexity within the refugee community which extends far beyond the conventional definition of family.

IMPLICATIONS FOR HOME-SCHOOL RELATIONS

Different understandings of roles and responsibilities of family members have also complicated home-school relations. Within the traditional Khmer social hierarchy, educators command a highly respected position because of the responsibilities entrusted to them. Traditionally, education is regarded as a lifelong process, aimed at the total development of the individual, thus extending beyond the academic realm into the civic and the moral. The role of a teacher is therefore that of instructor, mentor, counselor, a lifelong guide. One Cambodian parent commented, "We respect and regard the teachers like the second parents. Therefore, we have no need to teach the kids because the teachers already teach them" (National Coalition of Advocates of Students, 1997, p. 4). There is a Khmer saying that reflects the level of trust that Khmer parents place in educators: "Do as you wish, just keep his/her skin and bone." This statement expresses the underlying values that Cambodian parents hold, that a teacher's use of corporal punishment is acceptable as long as he or she exercises it for the betterment of the child and does not cause permanent injury. As a result of the differences in expectations, issues about rights and responsibilities are, by extension, unclear. A Cambodian father reflected, "In Cambodia, once children were registered in schools, everything was taken care of by the teachers. As parents, brothers, and sisters, we had no right to interfere in the system regarding our children's education" (National Coalition of Advocates of Students, 1997, p. 4). Once in the United States, Cambodian parents are understandably confused by the seeming inability of the school system to provide strict accountability for the students. One parent commented, "After they (students) are dropped off at school, parents have no way of knowing what they do or where they go. It is the responsibility of the school to monitor them. My daughter missed school for nearly a month but the school never informed me until it was too late. She was already in trouble" (S. Chhum, personal interview, San Francisco, March, 1992). Given their histories and cultural predispositions, Cambodian parents are often reluctant to question school policies and decisions or to actively advocate for their children. This, however, should not be interpreted as lack of concern for their children's education and welfare but understood as stemming from fear of authority figures and the absolute faith refugee families have in the educational system.

Home-school relations and parent-child communications are also undermined by the different understandings of the goal and objectives of education. The American educational system values subject areas beyond the core academic content areas, such as art and music, as well as extracurricular activities such as sports, photography, and participation in student organizations. Cambodian parents tend to view these interests and activities as unimportant and distracting from the educational focus on the core content areas. For them, education is much more narrowly defined. As such, they are less supportive of their children's interests and desire for participation in what they deem to be superfluous activities. This discrepancy between the notion of Cambodian parents as to what constitutes core education and that instilled by the American educational system poses problems particularly for female Cambodian youths, who are subject to stricter control than their male peers. Culturally, Cambodian girls have strictly prescribed roles of social conduct and are generally not allowed to participate in unchaperoned social activities. Furthermore, they are expected to assume their full share in household responsibilities starting from early adolescence. Rigid rules govern gender interactions; dating is a virtually non-existent concept, and disagreement over the permissibility of dating is a common source of family conflict where the exercise of corporeal punishment could lead to real or alleged cases of child abuse. In view of these cultural constraints, there are high expectations in regard to sexual virtues. Parents sanctify marital relations, with arranged marriages still being quite commonplace, although the number has decreased in recent years. Many Cambodian parents, therefore, fear that their daughters' virtue will be compromised by the level of freedom and peer pressure in America. That is an impetus towards pressuring for early marriages. Rather than dismissing such decisions as being backward or irrational, or advocating outcomes that may further erode the cohesion of the Cambodian family, educators need to view these issues from the families' cultural and situational perspectives and assist them in exploring options and alternatives.

Schools and the average Cambodian family also differ in their understanding of support. Schools may base their notion of parent involvement on assumptions of middle-class American family dynamics, such as parents assisting their children with school work, attending parent-teacher conferences, and participating in school activities. Cambodian refugee families' involvement in their children's educational life, however, is shaped by their cultural understanding of their roles and obligations and by the pragmatics of their daily lives. In view of their low educational background and limited English, many Cambodian refugee parents feel incapable of providing academic support to their children. Efforts to involve the home and family in the education of Cambodian students, therefore, must seek to introduce limited English speaking parents to new ways of sharing in their children's educational life, such as promoting primary language-based activities or having children read to parents who may be illiterate. Because Cambodian parents feel very limited in their role in the education of their children, they tend to confine their notion of support to the provision of the fundamental necessities so that the children have only to concentrate on educational pursuits. Coming from a socioeconomic context where the pursuit of learning is a luxury not readily afforded to everyone, Cambodian parents may view their willingness and ability to free their offspring from economic obligations as the ultimate expression of support.

BUILDING A COMMUNITY OF EFFECTIVE SCHOOLING

Presently, many schools find themselves severely overextended. When escalating demands are continually met with diminishing resources, however, schools are necessarily compelled to reassess their situations and, in many instances, to recognize the need for new approaches. Resources need to be redefined, old partnerships strengthened, and new ones created. Both educators and the constituent community must recognize that effective education involves responsibilities and challenges that cannot be undertaken by any one party alone. Recognition of mutual dependence is the basis for collaborative relationships that are built upon trust and equity. All too often, discussions of school reform stops short of any proposal for the restructuring of power relations. Family and community involvement, however, is not reducible to parent education and "training," a term that is problematic in and of itself because of the deficit view of language minority parents that it implies. True involvement means the elevation of parents and guardians to positions of power within the school structure. It means giving them access to and a voice in the decision- and policy-making arenas. It requires close collaboration and shared accountability.

To achieve these goals, schools need to become a safe place for all students and their families, especially for those who have been historically marginalized. As a member of the San Francisco Board of Education pointed out, "Immigrant children in our schools enter an educational system that's foreign, where the language is incomprehensible, where the faces of classmates are of many colors, and where parents feel unconnected and frustrated. It is alarming, but not surprising, that so many of our students fail and drop out of school" (National Coalition of Advocates of Students, 1988, p. 66). In promoting greater family and community involvement in the educational process, schools must (1) honestly assess the situation and identify the root problems that impede diversification and inclusion; (2) adopt a new paradigm, if necessary, for promoting collaborative efforts among diverse constituents; (3) establish a shared definition and vision of partnership; and (4) provide personnel with the tools to work effectively with language minority students and their families. In efforts to increase community inputs, some schools have taken the initiative to formulate a linguistically and culturally accessible instrument to assess the needs of the community. In other instances, schools, community-based organizations, and the families collaborate in formulating meeting agendas rather than operating on the basis of one party imposing its agenda onto others. This process allows parents to establish their own priorities of needs and concerns and thus fosters community involvement and helps schools to recognize and include the diverse immigrant and refugee communities. All too often, family involvement programs have approached the English-learning communities as if they are a homogenous entity, lumping together preliterate refugees and those from the rural areas with well-to-do, cosmopolitan, and multilingual immigrant parents simply because their children are designated as being limited English proficient.

Only with the appropriate information and accurate profiles of the communities and student populations that they are to serve can schools develop programs that effectively address issues and concerns of their community. This endeavor, however, necessarily begins with a paradigm shift away from the conventional deficit view of immigrant parents to one that values their input and attributes critical importance to their role in the educational process. If the spirit of equity and genuine partnership that schools espouse to believe in is to become a reality, schools must not only heed the needs of family and community concerns, but do so on the stakeholders' terms. This may entail school staff participating in community forum conducted in primary languages (with English translation) rather than the other way around, held in the community rather than at the school site, and at a time that accommodates the families' schedules rather than that of the school staff. For one educator, the rich learning experience that came from participating in such a community forum, has been invaluable: "I certainly understand parents better. It's really good to sit in a group and be the language minority, to get the perspective of how it feels from the other side, and it helps me to understand the hesitation to speak on the part of parents" (National Coalition of Advocates of Students, 1988, p. 95). It is through the process of involvement and collaboration that parents experience empowerment, and new leadership can develop within the community. Empowered parents can then recruit and mentor other parents and family members.

Home-school-community collaborations not only promote academic performance and retention but can also yield critical resources for the schools, allowing schools to do more with less. In working to enhance existing curriculum to more meaningfully reflect the cultural and historical experiences of the student population, institutions can tap into community resources. The funds of knowledge, mined from the cultural and experiential reservoirs of families, can form the bases of many culturally authentic, family-centered curriculum. In the San Joaquin Valley, a school's community garden brought parents and grandparents into the schools. It provided a rare opportunity for members of multiple generations to work alongside one another and for previously unrecognized talents and skills of refugee elders to be publicly re-validated. Similarly, a Seattle high school successfully implemented an integrated, hands-on curriculum in science, language arts, math, and social studies by utilizing parents' expertise in fishery and gardening. Using this concept, schools can tap into the vast body of knowledge of traditional medicine that abounds among the older generation of Southeast Asians to introduce, for instance, herbology as an integrated component of the science curriculum.

In addition to enriching the schools' academic programs, strengthening links between the home, school, and community can also reduce further fragmentation of refugee students' lives and psyche. If education is to be meaningful, it must bear relevance to the students' lives and experiences. The frustration of this refugee youth speaks loudly to the need for curricular reform: "I sit in this classroom and listen to the noise about the American Civil War and about civics. Who cares? For me, the reality is the streets and money and getting a good paying job. What do these people know about war and history, about life? I lived through the war" (Tenhula, 1991, p. 119). For the United States, the Vietnam War was one of the most scarring chapters of its history, and a community of over one million Southeast Asian refugees stand as the living legacy of that experience. It is inexcusable that a whole new generation of Americans can move through the nation's high schools and colleges without knowing anything about the role of Southeast Asians in our collective history. Including the mosaic of voices, cultures and experiences that define true American history and civilization is not simply an enrichment of our educational curriculum; it is the core curriculum that reflects the realities of America's pluralist democracy.

CONCLUSION

All migration entails dislocation. For Cambodian refugees, however, the diaspora was forced, unanticipated, and abrupt, resulting in a deep and lasting sense of trauma, dislocation, and loss that has persisted through multiple stages before, during, and after migration. It is the nature and degree of the dislocation that distinguishes the refugee condition from that of other immigrant experiences and that creates the tremendous challenges in the adjustment process of Cambodian refugees. With the fracturing of their familiar, orderly social world, refugees experience the loss of coherent structure in which one's roles and relations are clearly defined, where norms and expectations are readily understood, and behavior strictly prescribed. For the Cambodian people, war, revolution, genocide, and diaspora have destabilized their fundamental social and cultural institutions. Forced into a new social, economic, and cultural context, they must reconcile and adjust not only to changes in the external world but, even more disconcerting, to changes within the family. In other migration contexts, the institution of the family can serve as the last remaining stabilizing force in the face of upheaval; for most Cambodian refugees, however, this support structure has been weakened by the progressive fracturing of the family institution. Simply making the adjustment-whether educational, economic, or social-not to say anything about achieving excellence, is in itself a daunting challenge.

Despite certain commonalties shaped by their refugee condition, the Cambodian student population, like that in any other immigrant and refugee community, is quite diverse. The timing and process of migration as important determinants of the sociology and demography of refugees converge with factors of class, age, and gender to account for variations in the issues and needs that impact upon adaptation, including educational adjustment. Depending upon their background and experiences, Cambodian students and their families are differentially equipped to deal with the challenges that confront them; hence, their needs and concerns vary.

Because the refugee condition is marked by such a pervasive sense of dislocation, the schooling process must not contribute to further disorientation and fragmentation. Education must be aimed not simply at the inculcation of knowledge but at the total development of the individual-the intellectual, the spiritual, the moral, the civic. Schooling is, therefore, as much about imparting information as it is about fostering critical thinking, as much about building the foundation of knowledge as it is about inculcating self-esteem and a sense of personal and social responsibility. In this totalistic approach to education, there is an inherent recognition of the need for collaboration and of the undeniable interdependence of the various forces and institutions that impact the overall development of the individual student. The family, the school, and the community are critical stakeholders and agents in this process, and collaboration among them must be effected if we are to ensure a positive outcome. This supracommunity, however, is only as enduring and viable as the force that cements the relationships within it. That glue is trust, which can be extremely difficult to establish among peoples and communities so long imbued in the culture of fear. Trust stems from mutual respect and acknowledgment of a common goal; at the basis of any effective working relationship is the conviction that all stakeholders are working towards the same end, one that supersedes their individual or institutional interests. It begins with the recognition of the "we" in this process, of our own roles, responsibilities, and of our interdependence. A Cambodian poem speaks eloquently to the essence of this interconnectedness: "If I fail as a parent, as a son he fails." To this I add, that if we fail as educators, they will fail as students, and if we, collectively, fail as a community, they will fail as citizens.

REFERENCES

Al-Rasheed, M. (1994). The myth of return: Iraqi Arab and Assyrian refugees in London. *Journal of Refugee Studies* 7, (2/3).

Asian Law Caucus (1997). *Anti Asian crimes audit 1996*. San Francisco, CA: Asian Law Caucus.

Barudy, J. (1987). Therapeutic value of solidarity and hope. In D. Miserez (Ed.), *Refugees: The Trauma of exile*. Norwell, MA: Martinus Nijhoff.

Clifford, J. (1994). Diasporas. *Cultural Anthropology* (summer): 1-48.

Koschmann, N. (1987). *The resettlement process of Southeast Asian refugee adolescents: Making it in America*. Doctoral dissertation, Cornell University, New York.

Ledgerwood, J. (1990). *Changing Khmer conceptions of gender*. Doctoral dissertation, Cornell University, New York.

National Association for the Education and Advancement of Cambodian, Laotian and Vietnamese Americans (1995). *A Profile of the Cambodian, Hmong, Laotian and Vietnamese people in the United States*. Fort Lauderdale, FL: National Association for the Education and Advancement of Cambodian, Laotian and Vietnamese Americans.

National Coalition of Advocates for Students. (1988). *New voices: Immigrant students in US public schools*. Boston, MA: National Coalition of Advocates for Students.

National Coalition of Advocates for Students. (1997). *Unfamiliar partners: Asian parents and US public schools*. Boston, MA: National Coalition of Advocates for Students.

Office of Refugee Resettlement. (1988). *Annual report to Congress*. Washington DC: U.S. Government Printing Office.

Office of Refugee Resettlement. (1994). *Annual report to Congress*. Washington DC: U.S. Government Printing Office.

Rumbaut, R., & Ima, K. (1988). *The adaptation of Southeast Asian refugee youth: A comparative study*. Final report by the Office of Refugee Resettlement. Washington DC: U.S. Government Printing Office.

Sham, Y. (1989). *The frontier of loyalty*. Middletown, CT: Wesleyan University Press.

Tenhula, J. (1991). *Voices from Southeast Asia: The refugee experience in the United States*. New York, NY: Holmes and Meier.

Um, K. (1990). *Brotherhood of the pure: Communism and nationalism in democratic Kampuchea*. Doctoral dissertation, University of California at Berkeley, California.

Um, K. (1996). Issues facing Southeast Asian students in education. Paper presented at the National Asian Family-School Partnership Conference, Boston, Massachusetts, October 30, 1996.

Um, K. (1997). Resettlement into Limbo. In *Unfamiliar partners: Asian parents and US public schools*. Boston, MA: National Coalition of Advocates for Students.

Wicker, H. R., & Schoch, H. K. (1987). Refugees and mental health: Southeast Asian refugees in Switzerland. In D. Miserez (Ed.), *Refugees: The trauma of exile*, Norwell, MA: Martinus Nijhoff.

CHAPTER 14

Linguistic Perspective on the Education of Cambodian-American Students

Wayne E. Wright

On April 17, 1975, Pol Pot and his murderous Khmer Rouge regime captured the Cambodian capital and took over the country. They emptied the cities, drove the entire population into the countryside, and forced the people to perform hard agricultural labor under slave-like conditions. All institutions, including the schools, were abolished. For nearly four years, Cambodians were subjected to starvation, disease, and execution. Former government workers, teachers, professors, and other members of the educated elite were systematically executed, with between one and three million people put to death during the course of the Cambodian genocide. At the end of 1978, the Vietnamese invasion brought an end to the Killing Fields of Cambodia, and hundreds of thousands of Cambodians fled to the Thailand border. From the United Nations-supported border camps, Cambodian refugees had the opportunity to relocate and settle in other countries, such as the United States (Chandler, 1993).

Between 1975 and 1977, approximately 6,000 Cambodian refugees resettled in the United States (Table 14.1). This first wave of refugees consisted mostly of former government leaders and other members of the urban elite who were able to escape just before the Khmer Rouge take over.

Between 1978 and 1987, over 134,000 Cambodians were allowed to resettle in the United States (see Table 14.1). This second wave of refugees makes up the majority of the Cambodians in the United States. In general, these refugees had rural backgrounds and were less educated than those of the first wave (Smith-Hefner, 1990). Most refugees from this group have had a difficult time adjusting to life in the United States. Their rural backgrounds and lack of education, combined with trauma from the Khmer Rouge years, have made it difficult for the adult family members to learn English and find employment.

Table 14.1
Cambodian Refugees Admitted to the United States

Fiscal Year	Total
1975	4,600
1976	1,100
1977	300
1978	1,300
1979	6,000
1980	16,000
1981	27,100
1982	20,234
1983	13,114
1984	19,849
1985	19,131
1986	10,054
1987	1,539

Cambodian Immigrants Admitted to United States

1988	9,629
1989	6,076
1990	5,179
1991	3,251
1992	2,573
1993	1,639
1994	1,404
1995	1,492
1996	1,568

Sources: Data for 1975-1987: Ouk, M., Huffman, F. E., & Lewis, J. (1988, p. 23, adapted with permission) and U.S. State Department, Office of Refugee Resettlement. (1978, p.12). Data for 1988-1995: U.S. Immigration and Naturalization Service. (1995). Data for 1996: U.S. Immigration and Naturalization Service. (1996).
Note: INS data based on immigrants admitted to the United States by country of birth.

Consequently, the majority of the refugees from this group still fall below the poverty line (Ledgerwood, 1990).

The third wave of refugees is quite small. Cambodian refugee admissions to the United States dropped significantly after 1986 (Table 14.1), and by 1993 the Thailand refugee camps were completely closed. All those who remained in the border camps were repatriated back to Cambodia. Recently, political changes have made it possible for some Cambodian-Americans to sponsor their immediate relatives, where immigration directly from Cambodia had been nearly impossible prior to 1992. It is unlikely that there will be another influx of Cambodian immigrants as large as that witnessed in the early 1980s.

As more and more Cambodian refugees were resettled in the United States, and as families relocated in order to find better economic opportunities and to be closer to relatives, large Cambodian communities began to develop in several U.S. cities, including Long Beach, Oakland, San Diego, and Stockton (California); Lowell (Massachusetts); Chicago (Illinois); Dallas, Houston, and Austin (Texas); St. Paul (Minnesota); and Seattle (Washington), to name a few.

In these emerging Cambodian communities, Cambodian-American children quickly made up significant portions of the local school population.

By 1996, Khmer-speaking students made up one of the top five language groups in fifty California school districts. Eight of these California school districts (Oakland, Fresno, Long Beach, Los Angeles, San Diego, Lodi, Stockton, Modesto) had a Khmer-speaking student population numbering between 1,047 and 8,043 (California Department of Education, 1996).

While Cambodian students in the early 1980s were almost exclusively recent arrivals, the majority of Cambodian-American students in K-12 educational institutions today have never been to Cambodia and have no recollection of the refugee camps. Some were born in refugee camps but came to America as babies. Many are the American-born children of parents who were in refugee camps before immigrating to the United States. Many students in elementary schools today are the American-born children of Cambodian-Americans who were educated in American schools. Despite the decline in Cambodian immigration rates, the Cambodian-American student population in many school districts is continuing to show steady growth rates (Table 14.2).

Although most Cambodian-American students today were born and/or raised in the United States, they struggle with language learning and have many educational needs. This chapter discusses the linguistic background of Cambodian-American students in the United States and the implications of this background for educational programs. Next, the Khmer[1] (pronounced Khmai) language and writing system are examined and compared with English, with a focus on areas of difficulty for students learning English. Finally, general

Table 14.2
Enrollment of Cambodian-American Students in California Schools, 1981-1996

Census	LEP	FEP	Total
1981	2,474	419	2,893
1982	5,166	650	5,816
1983	6,695	937	7,632
1984	8,399	1,434	9,833
1985	10,730	2,005	12,735
1986	13,907	2,723	16,630
1987	15,665	3,914	19,084
1988	17,274	4,283	21,557
1989	18,111	4,614	22,725
1990	19,234	5,243	24,477
1991	20,055	5,452	25,507
1992	20,752	5,903	26,655
1993	21,040	7,219	28,259
1994	21,467	7,481	28,948
1995	21,028	8,071	29,099
1996	20,645	9,056	29,701

Note: LEP = limited English proficient; FEP = fluent English proficient.
Sources: Data for 1981-1988: Ouk, M., Huffman, F. E., & Lewis, J. (1988, p. 26) Adapted with permission. Data for 1989-1996: California Department of Education (1996).

strategies and suggestions for working with Cambodian-American students are offered.

LINGUISTIC BACKGROUND OF CAMBODIAN-AMERICAN STUDENTS

Although most Cambodian-American students were born in the United States, Khmer remains the first language of the home. Most older parents do not speak English well and speak to each other exclusively in Khmer. Even younger parents who speak English fluently prefer to speak Khmer with each other at home. Parents usually speak Khmer to their children, and newborn children are raised almost exclusively in the native language. At home, children typically watch Cambodian videotapes and cable programs, listen to Khmer music, and hear their parents and older relatives speak Khmer on the telephone and with neighbors. In established Cambodian communities, children often accompany their parents to Cambodian shops where Khmer is the dominant language of interaction.

However, Cambodian-American children born or raised in the United States are also exposed to a great deal of English, even before they enter school. The television is a major source of English language influence. The radio, and American audiotapes and CDs also provide substantial English language exposure. Children hear English when they go with their parents to American supermarkets, department stores, and fast food restaurants.

Once children enter school, they quickly realize that English is the dominant language of that environment. School-aged children report that they continue to speak Khmer to their parents, but speak both Khmer and English with their siblings and friends. As time goes on, however, children begin to use English more and more at home.

Many people assume that if students are limited in English proficiency, they must be fully proficient in their native language. However, with the exception of a small number of recent immigrants, this assumption does not hold true for most Cambodian-American students. Although students come from Khmer dominant parents and homes, learn to speak Khmer first, and receive much Khmer exposure in their communities, their primary language is not fully developed. Ouk, Huffman, and Lewis (1988) observed that in Cambodia, children had many opportunities to develop vocabulary, concepts, and reasoning skills through stories told by parents, grandparents, relatives, neighbors, and from the preaching of Buddhist monks at local temples. In America, the television, VCR, stereos, and movies have replaced these oral Khmer activities. As a result, children are exposed to less complex language and have less practice in higher order thinking skills in their native language.

Once Cambodian-American students enter American schools, they begin to lose their first language rapidly. Linguists have documented that most immigrant languages are lost by the third generation (Dicker, 1996). However, Cambodian-American parents and community leaders have been shocked to observe rapid language loss among first- and second-generation children. Smith-Hefner (1990) documented the dismay of Boston-area parents and community leaders as they observed their Cambodian-American children lose their native language. Language loss is a source of great pain and shame in the Cambodian family and community, because Cambodians believe there is a strong connection between Khmer language and identity.

The high degree of exposure to English and the rapid loss of the first language appear to suggest that Cambodian-American students learn English quickly, effortlessly, and fluently. However, one should not jump to this conclusion. Many Cambodian-American college students report that they struggle with reading and writing in English. Many Cambodian-American students struggle at universities which require a writing proficiency exam for graduation. It is not uncommon for Cambodian-American students to take the test many times before they are able to pass or, for some, to transfer to universities where such exams are not required or can be waived with coursework in order to complete their degrees. Many choose fields such as accounting and engineering, because in these fields the use of English in speaking, reading, and writing appear less demanding.

The California Department of Education collects data on the English language proficiency of language minority students in K-12 schools. California has the largest population of Cambodians in the United States, with the city of Long Beach encompassing the largest Cambodian population outside of Cambodia. While each state, district, school site, and community are unique, the data from California reveals patterns that are reflective of Cambodian-American students throughout the country.

In California, parents of entering students are asked to complete a home language survey. If a language other than English is used at home, the students are given an oral English exam to determine their level of English language proficiency. Students are then classified as limited English proficient (LEP) or fluent English proficient (FEP). There are varying degrees within the LEP category, with *A* being little or no proficiency, to *E* being near fluent. The language census data, however, only distinguishes between LEP and FEP students.

It should be noted that there are some limitations of the LEP designation, including cultural and linguistic bias inherent in the exam. These limitations, however, will mostly affect the levels within the LEP category, rather than the LEP-FEP distinction. It should also be noted that the term LEP is viewed by this author and many others as a negative label focusing on what students can not do rather than on what they can do. While more positive terms such as "English language learner" are preferred, the term LEP is used here because it is the classification used in the available student data.

Table 14.2 shows the enrollment of Cambodian-American LEP- and FEP-designated students in California schools from 1981 to 1996. As data are not available for student populations based on Cambodian ethnicity, these totals offer the best estimate of the number of Cambodian-American students enrolled in California schools.

Table 14.2 shows that in California, the Cambodian-American LEP and FEP student population has grown since 1981 from 2,893 students, to 29,701 students in 1996. By comparing the Cambodian immigration data from Table 14.1 and student enrollment data in Table14. 2, student growth prior to 1990 appears to be a combination of immigration and American-born children, whereas growth after 1990 appears to be almost exclusively from American-born children.

In a similar manner, the total number of LEP and FEP students increased steadily until 1994 when the number of LEP students began to decrease slightly but the number of FEP students continued to increase. This may suggest that 1994 was the peak year, and that the LEP and FEP populations will continue to decrease and increase, respectively, over the next decade with the number of FEP students eventually outnumbering LEP students. However, Table 14.2 shows that LEP Cambodian-American children outnumber FEP Cambodian-American children by a ratio of 2 to 1. Thus, despite high exposure to English in the home and community, English dominant classrooms, and a high degree of primary language loss, the majority of Cambodian-American students are not yet fluent English speakers.

An interesting picture is revealed when the data are distributed across grade level (Figure 14.1). Only 192 out of 2,181 Cambodian-American children entered kindergarten as fluent English speakers in 1996. In fact, the majority of elementary-school-aged Cambodian-American children (K-5) were classified as limited English proficient. Cambodian-American LEP students also outnumber FEP students in the middle schools (grades 6-8). Only in the high schools, did FEP students slightly outnumber LEP students.

Given the fact that the majority of the students represented in Figure 14.1 started their education in kindergarten, it may be possible to identify some trends from the graph as if it were a continuum across time. Looking at the data in this light, we see that the number of Cambodian-American LEP students decreases significantly each year after second grade, and that the number of Cambodian-American FEP students continues to increase until it surpasses the number of LEP students in the ninth grade. This suggests that, as Cummins (1981) has argued, it takes from five to seven years to fully master a new language.

Figure 14.1

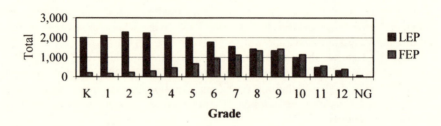

California Khmer LEP & FEP by Grade (1996)

Source: California Department of Education, Educational Demographics Unit (1996).

IMPLICATIONS FOR INSTRUCTION IN ENGLISH

It is important to keep in mind the difference between basic interpersonal communication skills (BICS) and cognitive academic language proficiency (CALP) as described by Cummins (1981). It is critical to remember that the English language Cambodian-American students have learned prior to schooling is derived primarily from television and peers. Playground English is markedly different from the cognitively demanding academic language of the classroom. This is not always apparent in the primary grades, but once children move on to the intermediate grades and secondary levels of schooling, the lack of academic language poses great difficulty and causes struggles with lectures, text books, and written assignments. Limited English proficient Cambodian-American students need direct and well-defined English language development (ELD) programs in order to help them acquire the vocabulary and higher order thinking skills they will need to succeed academically.

Many Cambodian-American children come from impoverished homes with parents who lack formal education. Thus, educators should not assume that parents can readily assist their children with homework assignments. Many children do not have books at home and rarely see their parents model literacy behaviors common in mainstream middle-class homes. Some students enter kindergarten never having held a pencil or heard a book read aloud by an adult.

Most Cambodian-American students lack development in their native language and thus have a weak foundation upon which to develop English language and literacy skills. Bilingual educational programs, where Khmer language and literacy skills are developed and then transferred to English literacy, offer a good solution to the problem of fostering strong literacy and English language skills (Marquez, 1997). Where bilingual programs do not exist, administrators and teachers need to find other ways to provide Cambodian-American students with primary language instruction and support. This will help develop a solid linguistic foundation in children, which will better prepare them to learn a second language.

CONTRASTIVE DESCRIPTION OF KHMER AND ENGLISH

The Khmer language is the major modern representative of the Mon-Khmer language family and is part of the Austro-Asiatic language family (Huffman & Proum, 1978). With 5,932,800 speakers in Cambodia, it is the country's national language and spoken by approximately 90% of the population. There are regional differences in spoken Khmer just as there are in English. To the skilled listener, various Khmer accents often belie the region of origin in Cambodia. There are approximately 1,130,400 speakers of Khmer outside of Cambodia, including Thailand, Vietnam, Laos, China, France, and the United States (Grimes, 1996).

Phonology

Khmer is nontonal and has a high percentage of disyllabic words. Huffman (1970) identified eighteen consonant and thirteen vowel phonemes (sounds).

Table 14.3
Initial Consonant Sounds and Clusters

Similar in both Khmer and English	English Only (no Khmer equivalents)
b as in '*b*it'	*g* as in '*g*ate'
ch as in '*ch*at'	*j* as in '*j*ug'
d as in '*d*uck'	*r* as in '*r*ip'
h as in '*h*e'	*sh* as in '*sh*ip'
k as in '*k*it'	*th* as in '*th*igh'
m as in '*m*an'	*th* as in '*th*y'
n as in '*n*o'	*w* as in '*w*e'
p as in '*p*ot'	*wh* as in '*wh*at'
s as in '*s*at'	*z* as in '*z*oo'
t as in '*t*ake'	*zh* as in 'mea*s*ure'
y as in '*y*ou'	*dw* as in '*dw*ell'
kl as in '*cl*ay'	*gr* as in '*gr*ound'
pl as in '*pl*ay'	*gw* as in '*Gw*en'
sk as in '*sk*ill'	*qu* as in '*qu*ick'
sl as in '*sl*ip'	*shr* as in '*shr*ine'
sm as in '*sm*art'	*spl* as in '*spl*it'
sn as in '*sn*ap'	*squ* as in '*squ*elch'
sp as in '*sp*ot'	*thr* as in '*thr*ow'
st as in '*st*op'	*thw* as in '*thw*ack'
sw as in '*sw*im'	*tw* as in '*tw*enty'

Source: Ouk, M., Huffman, F. E., & Lewis, J. (1988, p. 70). Adapted with permission.

There are eighty-five two-place initial consonants /CC-/ and two three-place initial sequences /CCC-/. Of the thirteen vowel phonemes, there are ten short vowels and three short diphthongs. These vowel phonemes can stand alone or be combined to form thirty-one different vowel sounds.

Many of the consonant and vowel phonemes in Khmer and English are similar. However, some English consonant and vowel sounds do not exist in Khmer and vice versa (Table 14.3).

Many of the initial consonant sounds are the same in the initial position for both Khmer and English, for example, the /s/ in the English word *sun* and the Khmer word សក់ /sɑk/ "hair." However, when these Khmer consonants are in the final position they are not fully pronounced, but merely "stop" the word at the point of initial pronunciation. For example, in the English word "cut" the final /t/ is fully pronounced, but in the Khmer word កាត់ /kat/ "to cut," the word is stopped by placing the tongue in the /t/ position, and no air is released to produce the sound.

Khmer and English have many initial consonant clusters, but in Khmer, there are no consonant clusters in the final position. For example, both Khmer and English could have an /str/ initial consonant cluster, as in *strong* and ស្ត្រី

/strəy/ "woman," but only English has consonant clusters in the final position, such as /nth/ in the word *ninth*.

English has approximately fourteen vowel sounds, whereas Khmer has approximately thirty-one. However, not all fourteen English vowel sounds are present in the thirty-one Khmer vowel sounds (Table 14.4). This could pose a significant difficulty for Cambodian students learning English.

There are thirty-three Khmer consonant symbols (Table 14.5). Unlike English, where a letter's name and sound(s) are often different (e.g., h, w, x, y, etc.), in Khmer, the consonant's name and sound are the same. This could also be a source of difficulty for English language development of Cambodian students.

Morphology and Syntax

Most English verbs change according to tense (e.g., walk, walked, walking). Some English verbs change into completely different words according to tense, (e.g., go-went; see-saw; take-took), and some English verbs do not change at all (e.g., hit, bet). Khmer verbs do not change, and the tense is made known through the context of the sentence:

ខ្ញុំទៅសាលា   /kñom tɨw saalaa/ I go to school

      I   go school

ខ្ញុំទៅសាលាម្សិលមិញ   /kñom tɨw saalaa mselmiñ/ I went to school yesterday

      I   go school yesterday

ខ្ញុំនឹងទៅសាលាស្អែក   /kñom nɨŋ tɨw saalaa sʔaɛk/ I am going to school tomorrow

      I   will go school tomorrow

The English verb *to be*, is complex and has many forms (I *am*, I *was*, I *have been*; You *are*, You *were*, You *have been*; She *is*, She *was*, She *has been*; etc.). Khmer has only two forms of *to be*, គឺ /kɨɨ/ "to be" and ជា /ciə/ "to be." Most of the time, these two forms can be used interchangeably, together (with /kɨɨ/ preceding /ciə/), or not at all:

នេះម្ដាយខ្ញុំ ។ /nih mdaay kñom/ This is my mother.

      this mother I

នេះគឺម្ដាយខ្ញុំ ។ /nih **kɨɨ** mdaay kñom/ This is my mother.

      this be mother I

នេះជាម្ដាយខ្ញុំ ។ /nih **ciə** mdaay kñom/ This is my mother.

      this be mother I

នេះគឺជាម្ដាយខ្ញុំ ។ /nih **kɨɨ ciə** mdaay kñom/ This is my mother.

      this be be mother I

As a result, the conjugations of both regular and irregular English verbs present an extraordinary learning task for Cambodian-American students.

Table 14.4
English Vowel Sounds

Similar to Khmer	Not in Khmer
|iy| as in b*ea*t	|I| as in b*i*t
|ey| as in b*ai*t	|ε| as in b*e*t
|ə| as in b*u*t	|æ| as in b*a*t
|a| as in f*a*ther	|u| as in b*oo*k
|uw| as in b*oo*t	
|ow| as in b*oa*t	
|ɔ| as in b*ou*ght	
|ay| as in b*i*te	
|aw| as in b*ou*t	
|oy| as in b*o*y	

Source: Ouk M., Huffman, F. E., & Lewis, J. (1988, p. 74). Adapted with permission.

Table 14.5
Khmer Consonants

	Voiceless or "Small Voice"		Voiced or "Large Voice"		
	Unaspirated	Aspirated	Unaspirated	Aspirated	Nasals
Velars	ក	ខ	គ	ឃ	ង
	/kaa/	/khaa/	/kɔɔ/	/khɔɔ/	/ŋɔɔ/
Palatals	ច	ឆ	ជ	ឈ	ញ
	/caa/	/chaa/	/cɔɔ/	/chɔɔ/	/ñɔɔ/
Retroflexes (pronounced as dentals)	ដ	ឋ	ឌ	ឍ	ណ[1]
	/daa/	/thaa/	/dɔɔ/	/thɔɔ/	/naa/
Dentals	ត	ថ	ទ	ធ	ន
	/taa/	/thaa/	/dɔɔ/	/thɔɔ/	/nɔɔ/
Labials	ប	ផ	ព	ភ	ម
	/baa/	/phaa/	/pɔɔ/	/phɔɔ/	/mɔɔ/
Misc.	យ	រ	វ	ឝ	
Voiced	/yɔɔ/	/rɔɔ/	/lɔɔ/	/wɔɔ/	
Voiceless	ស	ហ	ឡ	អ	
	/saa/	/haa/	/laa/	/aa/	

Source: Ouk M., Huffman, F. E., & Lewis, J. (1988, p. 71). Adapted with permission.
[1] This nasal is in the voiceless, or small voice series.

   English pronouns also vary according to context, with multiple forms for *I*
(me, my, mine), *you* (your, yours), *he* (him, his), *she* (her, hers), *we* (our, ours),

and *they* (them, their, theirs). Khmer pronouns do not change according to the syntax of the sentence, but change depending on who one is talking to. This will be discussed in the Sociolinguistic Aspects section. English has gender based third person pronouns (he, his, him; she, her, hers), but the Khmer third person pronoun, គាត់ /kŏət/, is gender free.

The English articles (a, an, the) have no Khmer equivalents. Therefore, developing familiarity with the use of appropriate articles would be a daunting task even for Cambodian students who have been educated in the United States for many years. In Khmer, definite and indefinite objects are determined through the context of the conversation or the use of other clarifying words in the sentence:

សានទិញបាល់ ។ /san tiñ bal/ San bought a/the ball.

           San buy ball

សានទិញបាល់មួយ ។ /san tiñ bal muəy/ San bought a ball.

           San buy ball one

សានទិញបាល់នោះ ។ /san tiñ bal nuh/ San bought that ball.

           San buy ball that

Another difficulty lies with English nouns. Most English nouns have singular and plural forms (e.g., cat-cats; ox-oxen; mouse-mice), while some English nouns have one form for both singular and plural usage (e.g., water, air, blood, cheese). Khmer nouns have one form only, and the number is clarified by the context of the sentence:

លីមានខ្មៅដៃ ។ /lii miən kmaudaɛ/ Lee has (a) pencil(s).

           Lee have pencil

លីមានខ្មៅដៃពីរ ។ /lii miən kmaudaɛ pii/ Lee has two pencils.

           Lee have pencil   two

លីមានខ្មៅដៃច្រើន ។ /lii miən kmaudaɛ craən/ Lee has many pencils.

           Lee have pencil   many

Word order in English and Khmer varies slightly. Both frequently follow a basic SVO (subject + verb + object) order, as in the sentence "Sok hit the ball." One major difference is the placement of modifiers. English modifiers are placed in front of the noun or verb they are modifying, as in *blue house*. Khmer modifiers follow the noun or verb as in "*house blue*" for "*blue house*."

The order of words in a noun phrase is somewhat fixed in English, but in Khmer there is greater flexibility. The order in Khmer is frequently the near reverse of English, which could confuse Cambodian students:

	Khmer	English
អាវស	/aaw sɑɑ/	white shirt
	shirt white	

អាវសខ្ញុំ   /aaw sɑɑ kñom/   my white shirt
                  shirt white I

អាវសថ្មីរបស់ខ្ញុំ   /aaw sɑɑ thməy rɔbah kñom/   my new white shirt
                  shirt white new of   I

Semantics and Lexicon

Both Khmer and English use compound words to create new vocabulary. For example, the English word *spaceship* is a combination of the words *space* and *ship*, and the Khmer word for *zoo*, សួនសត្វ is made up of the word សួន /suən/ "garden" and សត្វ /sɑt/ "animal." Khmer and English both contain words borrowed from other languages which developed through contact with other groups and the sharing of new objects, concepts, and ideas. Khmer has borrowed extensively from Pali and Sanskrit for religious and political vocabulary. Additionally, regional trade led to the introduction of loan words from Chinese. During the French Protectorate years in Cambodia (1863—1953), many French words were borrowed to describe new cultural items, the French educational system, secondary school subject matter, and bureaucratic terminology (Huffman & Proum, 1978). Further, American military presence during the Lon Nol years (1970-1975) led to the adoption of some English words.

When Cambodians first arrived in the United States, they faced many new objects, concepts, and ideas for which there were no Khmer equivalents (e.g., computer, hamburger, fax, zip code, etc.). Many of these terms can be explained in Khmer, but often require several words. For example, *homework* would have to be described as កិច្ចការសាលាធ្វើនៅផ្ទះ /kec kaa saalaa twəə nɨw ptĕah/, which is literally "school work to do at home." It is much easier to borrow the English word for this concept, ហូមវឺក /houmwək/ "homework," which is now common practice among Cambodian-American parents, students, and bilingual school personnel. Likewise, many Khmer speakers will use an English word in a Khmer utterance, even though an equivalent Khmer or standard French loan words exists. They may choose to do this because they are more familiar with the concept in English than in Khmer, the English term may be shorter or easier to say, or the Khmer term may not completely encompass the same meaning as the English term. For example, most Cambodian-Americans from a rural background did not have access to telephones in Cambodia, whereas telephones are an important part of their daily life in the United States. The Khmer word for *telephone* is ទូរស័ព្ទ /tuurɔɔsap/; however Cambodian-Americans usually use the word តេឡេហ្វូន /teileifoun/ "telephone" because they became familiar with the object here. Another example is the use of the word *call*. In English, people *call* each other on the telephone. There is a Khmer word for *call*, ហៅ /hau/, but it cannot be used in the sense of *call* someone on the telephone. In Khmer, a person would *telephone to* someone: ទូរស័ព្ទទៅ /tuurɔsap tɨw/ or តេឡេហ្វូនទៅ /teileifoun tɨw/. However, most Cambodian-Americans prefer to use the English word *call* in their Khmer conversations because it is shorter, easier to say, and has a precise meaning.

Writing System

The Khmer writing system has its own unique set of characters, derived from a form of the ancient Indian Brahmi script (Huffman & Proum, 1978). Both the Khmer and English writing systems are phonetically based, with consonant and vowel symbols representing specific sounds that are combined to form words. However, the Khmer writing system is much more precise than English in its sound-symbol relationships. While spelling rules for English are followed by long lists of exceptions, in Khmer, consonant and vowel symbols have clearly defined sounds, and rules for combining these sounds are very consistent. The irregularity in spelling of many English words can pose a serious problem for Cambodian students learning English.

Both Khmer and English are written left to right, and top to bottom. Khmer consonants form the base of the left to right line, and vowels, feet (secondary consonant characters), and diacritic marks can be written on the same line as the consonants, or combinations of up to two levels above and/or two levels below the consonant line. There are no spaces between Khmer words. Instead, spaces are used in much the same way commas are used in English.

There are two main varieties of Khmer script. One script is used for regular writing tasks (ក ខ គ ឃ ង). It is the main script used in the body of texts of books and newspapers and is the script taught to students in school. The other is a calligraphy-type script and is commonly used for newspaper headlines, book titles, shop signs, advertisements, and names (ក ខ គ ឃ ង). The calligraphy type script mostly follows the basic shape of the letters in the regular script, but some symbols differ enough to have to be learned separately.

Pragmatics and Sociolinguistic Aspects

Language reflects the culture of the speakers. Language naturally highlights the social structure and items important to that culture. In Cambodian culture, great importance is placed on family, age, and social status. In Khmer, family and kinship terms are complex, with distinct terms for siblings, aunts, and uncles by age and sometimes gender. For example, in English, terms for siblings are usually divided only by the gender, as in *brother* and *sister*. In Khmer, the primary division of siblings is based on age, with បង /baaŋ/ referring to older siblings, and ប្អូន /pʔoun/ referring to younger siblings. The gender terms ប្រុស /proh/ "male" and ស្រី /srəy/ "female" are added to specify whether that sibling is male or female. Thus, បងប្រុស /baaŋ proh/ is "older brother" (literally older sibling male), and ប្អូនស្រី /pʔoun srəy/ is "younger sister" (literally younger sibling female). Family kinship terms are also used as terms of address for almost everyone in Cambodian society. Kinship terms often substitute for generic pronouns. For example, a Cambodian child who wants to say "I love you" to his mother would say កូនស្រឡាញ់ម៉ាក់ /koun srɑlaañ maak/ which is literally "child loves mother."

Khmer pronouns reflect the age and social status of the speaker and the person he or she is speaking to or about. For example, in the case of the first person pronoun *I*, in addition to the use of kinship terms as first person pronouns, there is a generic form, a form for speaking to monks, a form used by monks when speaking to others, a form for addressing royalty, and a condescending form. Huffman and Proum's *English-Khmer Dictionary* (1978), offers thirteen different categories for the second person pronoun *you*, with variations for gender, politeness, age, relationship, and social status. Kinship terms can also be used as second person pronouns. Therefore, when learning English, Cambodian students may be bewildered to see this relative lack of variation in language levels, especially during the initial stage of English development.

Khmer verbs also vary according to the social status of the speakers, who the speakers are talking about, and the context of the conversation. For example, there are multiple Khmer forms of the English verb *to eat*. The form used by two people having a conversation would depend on who they are, where they are, and what they are talking about. If they were at a formal meeting, they would use a polite form. If they were close friends going out for a bite to eat, they could use the colloquial form or even one of the vulgar forms. The form would vary if they were talking about a dog, a monk, or the king. Cambodian students would be perplexed to see this relative lack of variation in English to reflect age and social status differences during the initial stage of English development.

The structures and conventions of names differ in English and Khmer. Traditionally in Cambodia, the family name is listed first, followed by the given name. This is the opposite of the American system in which the family name is the last name, and the given name is the first name. Traditionally, Cambodian wives keep their own family name and do not take the family name of the husband. Thus, the last names of Cambodian children frequently differ from their mothers'.

Americans often create nicknames by using the first part of a given name (e.g., Jeff for Jeffrey; Pat for Patrick; etc.). In contrast, Khmer nicknames most often come from the end of the name. For example, siblings named Sarom, Sarun, Sarith, Sareth, and Sarin would have as their nicknames Rom, Run, Rith, Reth, and Rin, respectively.

Names are very personal in Cambodian culture, and people in high status positions are often called by their title or position as a sign of respect. For example, teachers are held in high esteem, and it is considered rude to call a teacher by his or her name. It is a great honor to be called "teacher." In America, most teachers do not like to be called "teacher" and prefer to be called by their proper address and last name (e.g., Mr. Brown, Mrs. Sanchez, etc.). Understandably, Cambodian-American students are confused when their teachers say, "Don't call me teacher!" in response to what is considered a term of great respect in Cambodian culture.

POSSIBLE PROBLEMS AND DIFFICULTIES OF CAMBODIAN STUDENTS LEARNING ENGLISH

Pronunciation

Cambodian-American students have difficulty pronouncing English sounds for which there are no Khmer equivalents, such as the words in the second column of Table 14.3. Cambodian-American students also have trouble with ending consonant and consonant cluster sounds. For example, the may pronounce *friend* as *frien, lamp* as *lam,* and *desk* as *des.* Contractions are also problematic for these students, because the meaning is based on the final consonant clusters. For example, *can't* is often pronounced *can.* The final /s/ is very difficult for Cambodian-American students to produce, and students are often marked down on oral English grammar tests because the evaluator interprets their failure to add a final /s/ to plurals and third person singular verbs (e.g., he take*s*) as a grammatical error rather than a pronunciation problem.

Grammar

Changes in pronouns and verbs seem to be the most problematic for Cambodian-American students. Since Khmer pronouns and verbs do not change, students have trouble when they try to translate their own thoughts into English. The tense structure and rules governing pronouns need to be learned by Cambodian-American students as a new concept, and they need modeling of these structures in order to master them.

Cambodian-American students sometimes have problems with the third person pronouns and may use the wrong gender when referring to someone. For example, a Cambodian-American student might say "That girl, *he* hit me."

The use of articles is another area of difficulty for Cambodian-American students. Often they leave out the articles *a, an,* and *the* because these words do not exist in Khmer.

Beginning ESL students may also have difficulty with word order. Some Cambodian-American children may say "the car red" instead of "the red car." However, most seem to catch on to the reverse order of English rather quickly.

Vocabulary

Cambodian-American students often confuse English words which only differ at the final consonant or cluster, substituting, for example, *bag* for *back* or *think* for *thing.* Some interference comes from Khmer with words that have direct counterparts in English, but are used differently in the two languages. For example, the Khmer word for *open,* បើក /baək/, is used much in the same way as it is in English (e.g., *open* the door, *open* the book, *open* a bank account), but it is also used to mean *turn on* something, such as a lamp or the television. Thus, Cambodian-Americans often say in English "*Open* the light" or "*Open* the TV."

Spelling and Writing

Since the two writing systems are completely different symbol wise, there is usually no interference between the Khmer writing system and the English system. If anything, literate Khmer students find the linear, single layer writing system and the spacing between words in English very simple. Most writing errors result from the problems having to do with pronunciation, grammar, and vocabulary, as discussed earlier. For example, Cambodian-American students may spell words as they hear and pronounce them, leaving off final consonant sounds and the final /s/ in plurals and verbs.

Sociolinguistic Aspects

Younger Cambodian-American students learn the sociolinguistic aspects of English fairly quickly as they interact with their teachers and other English speakers. Older new immigrant Cambodian-American students may need longer periods of time to learn the subtleties of communicating American style in areas such as taking turns, making polite interruptions, nodding the head, or adding "uh-huhs" during the conversation to indicate active listening, and using culturally appropriate ways to make excuses.

In general, Cambodian-American students may seem quieter than other students. This can be partially attributed to the fact that many Cambodian-American children are frequently if not constantly told by their parents to respect their teacher. Some children interpret this to mean that they are not to interrupt the teacher or ask any questions. However, their participation and behavior resemble that of other students as they become accustomed to American schools.

STRATEGIES FOR ENGLISH LANGUAGE DEVELOPMENT

When the implementation of a Khmer bilingual program is not feasible, Cambodian-American students need to be placed in classrooms that utilize specially designed academic instruction in English (SDAIE),[2] or "sheltered" English instruction. In SDAIE classrooms, the instruction is in English, but the teachers employ special techniques and practices to make the core content subjects comprehensible for English language learners. SDAIE instruction needs to be delivered by qualified teachers who possess credentials or training authorizing them to work with limited English proficient (LEP) students (California Department of Education, 1990).

In SDAIE classrooms at the elementary level, programs that stress a balanced literacy approach appear to offer the best support for Cambodian-American students. In balanced literacy programs, great emphasis is placed on reading and writing for authentic and meaningful purposes. Teachers read aloud to their students several times a day from literature with rich language and engage students in activities to help them construct meaning from text. Teachers offer direct reading and writing instruction, serve as a literacy model for their students, and provide ample time for both guided and individual practice in reading and writing. These teachers reward effort and observe children carefully to individualize instruction for each child.

Teachers need to make an effort to expose Cambodian-American children to as many different genres of literature as possible, especially in the area of nonfiction books. Primary grade (K-2) teachers who only use fiction in instruction do not prepare students for the demands of nonfiction reading that students face in the intermediate grades (3-5) and secondary levels (6-12) of education.

Many Cambodian-American students have few books in their homes. Teachers need to make an effort to help provide Cambodian-American children with more reading materials at home. Teachers could take students on frequent trips to the school and public libraries, loan books to them from the classroom library, or have students make their own books to take home and read independently or with family members. Since many Khmer parents do not speak or read English, teachers may encourage parents to read aloud to their children in Khmer. For parents who are illiterate in Khmer, teachers could have students read aloud daily to their parents.

Although the emphasis in SDAIE classrooms is on developing English literacy and content knowledge through English, there are still steps administrators and classroom teachers need to take in order to provide students with Khmer primary language support. For example, bilingual Khmer teacher aides may be hired to provide primary language support to students during their acquisition of English. These aides can preview and review lessons and stories in Khmer, work with Cambodian-American students to develop oral language and higher order thinking skills, and teach core concepts. This can provide Cambodian-American students with some background in the various subjects areas and prepare them to receive more comprehensible input (Krashen, 1985) and understand the key concepts during the teacher's lesson. Khmer aides who are literate in Khmer can utilize Khmer language books and materials with their small groups. After-school Khmer language classes may also be held and taught by parent volunteers, aides, or bilingual classified staff members.

SDAIE classrooms are ideal assignments for Cambodian-American teacher candidates with strong English skills. Most of these candidates possess oral language skills in Khmer which they can use to provide primary language support for their Cambodian-American students. In addition, they are able to communicate directly with parents and can serve as an important role model for their students.

In addition to SDAIE instruction, every classroom or program with limited English proficient Cambodian-American children needs a separate and distinct direct English language development (ELD) component. Where the focus of SDAIE is to make core content subjects comprehensible in English, the focus of ELD instruction is to develop oral language skills and vocabulary. It is imperative that students receive at least thirty minutes of ELD instruction a day at the elementary level, and one or two hours of intensive ELD instruction at the secondary level.

It is imperative to note that a strong, balanced literacy program does not replace ELD instruction. Rather, strong ELD instruction supports the balanced literacy program. For example, when children are learning to read, they often rely on picture cues in the story for meaning. However, the picture is of little help if students do not know the word for it in English. Additionally, without adequate oral language development, students may learn to decode unfamiliar words but fail to comprehend the meaning of the words or the text. ELD instruction helps students develop the vocabulary for words they will encounter in reading in all subject areas.

Limited English proficient Cambodian-American students need a combination of specially designed academic instruction in English; a strong, balanced literacy program; primary language support; and English language development. Only with this combination of powerful instruction and support can Cambodian-American students be prepared for the demands of listening, speaking, reading, and writing in English to be encountered in mainstream classrooms in the upper grades and secondary schools.

WORKING WITH CAMBODIAN-AMERICAN STUDENTS

Suggestions for Administrators

Place Cambodian-American students classified as limited English proficient in SDAIE classrooms taught by qualified teachers.
Recruit Cambodian-American teachers with strong English language skills for SDAIE instructional settings.
Recruit bilingual aides to provide primary language support in the classrooms.
Ensure that classroom teachers are utilizing their bilingual Khmer aides effectively.

Suggestions for Teachers

Become familiar with the similarities and differences between Khmer and English in order to better understand the areas of difficulty for Cambodian-American students learning English.
Get acquainted with the background of your Cambodian-American students.
Implement a balanced literacy program.
Read aloud to children several times a day from various genres, especially nonfiction.
Find ways to help students have books and other reading materials at home.
Implement a strong, distinct English language development program.
Use bilingual aides to preview and review lessons and stories in Khmer, and develop oral language, higher order thinking skills, and concepts in the primary language.
Acquire Khmer language materials for use in instruction and learning.

NOTES

1. In common usage, *Khmer* and *Cambodian* are used interchangeably to describe both the language and the ethnicity. In this chapter, *Cambodian* and *Cambodian-American* are used exclusively to describe members of this ethnic group, and *Khmer* is used exclusively to describe the language.
2. The pronunciation of the acronym SDAIE means "to regret," or "to be sorry" in Khmer. Avoid using this term with Khmer students and parents.

REFERENCES

California Department of Education (1990). *Bilingual education handbook: Designing instruction for LEP students.* Sacramento, CA: California Department of Education.

California Department of Education (1996). *Language census report for California public schools.* Sacramento, CA: California Department of Education.

Chandler, D. (1993). *A history of Cambodia.* Chiang Mai, Thailand: Silkworm Books.

Cummins, J. (1981). The role of primary language development in promoting educational success for language minority students. In California State Department of Education (Ed.), *Schooling and language minority students: A theoretical framework* (pp. 3-49). Los Angeles: Evaluation, Dissemination and Assessment Center, California State University.

Dicker, S. J. (1996). *Languages in America: A pluralist's view.* Philadelphia: Multilingual Matters.

Grimes, B. F. (Ed.). (1996). *Ethnologue: Languages of the world* (13th ed.). Dallas, TX: Summer Institute of Linguistics. Available on-line: www.sil.org/ethnologue/

Huffman, F. E. (1970). *Cambodian system of writing and beginning reader.* Ithaca, NY: Southeast Asian Program, Cornell University.

Huffman, F. E., & Proum, I. (1978). *English-Khmer dictionary.* New Haven, CT: Yale University Press.

Krashen, S. D. (1985). *The input hypothesis: Issues and implications.* London: Longman.

Ledgerwood, J. (1990). Changing Khmer conceptions of gender: Women, stories and the social order. *Dissertations Abstracts International* Vol. 51-01A, p. 0207.

Marquez, M. *Developing a K-5 Khmer (Cambodian) bilingual program.* Audio cassette of the CABE 1997 Annual Meeting. San Diego: The Sound of Knowledge.

Ouk, M., Huffman, F. E., & Lewis, J. (1988). *Handbook for teaching Khmer-speaking students.* Folsom, CA: Folsom Cordova Unified School District.

Smith-Hefner, N. J. (1990). Language and identity in the education of Boston-area Khmer. *Anthropology & Education Quarterly* Vol. 21, pp. 250-268.

U.S. Immigration and Naturalization Service. (1996). Fiscal year detailed run data.

U.S. Immigration and Naturalization Service. (1995). *Immigration and naturalization yearbook.* Washington, DC: Demographics Department.

U.S. State Department, Office of Refugee Resettlement. (1978). *Refugee Reports.* Vol. 8, p. 12.

Index

About the Contributors

LI-RONG LILLY CHENG is professor of communicative disorders, and assistant dean of Student Affairs and International Development, College of Health and Human Services, San Diego State University. She is also director of the International Institute for Human Resources Development in Health and Human Services and a fellow of the American Speech-language Hearing Association. She has researched bilingual language acquisition, language and culture, cross-cultural communication, and speech-language pathology among the bilingual population.

MARILYN MEI-YING CHI is professor of language/literacy education and coordinator of the Chinese Bilingual Teaching Credential Program, Division of Teacher Education, San Jose State University. She has published six books and numerous articles on early literacy, Chinese-American children's literature, and the linguistic and cultural backgrounds of Chinese-American students. Her current research projects focus on English-Chinese bilingual and biliteracy development and learning processes and how limited English proficient Asian children acquire English as a second language in multiple contexts.

HAROLD CHU is professor and director of the Center for Bilingual-Multicultural-ESL Education, Graduate School of Education, George Mason University. He is the author of six books and numerous chapters and articles on bilingual-multicultural-ESL education; language arts; assessment; comparative analyses between Korean and English, Japanese and English; Korean and American, and Japanese and American cultures.

CHUNG HOANG CHUONG is associate professor of Asian American Studies and head of the Vietnamese-American Studies Center, San Francisco State University. He taught the first Vietnamese-American studies course at the University of California at Berkeley in 1981. His research focuses on various aspects of forced immigration and refugee adaptation.

MAI DAO is assistant professor in the Division of Teacher Education and the Division of Special Education and Rehabilitative Services, San Jose State University, California. Her publications focus on English as a second language methods, assessment and instruction of limited English proficient students, at-risk students, and Southeast Asian refugee families.

ROSITA G. GALANG is professor and chairperson of the Department of International and Multicultural Education, University of San Francisco. She has served as president of the National Association for Asian-Pacific Bilingual Education. She has written numerous articles and handbooks on the linguistic and cultural backgrounds of Filipino immigrants and their education in the United States.

KUNIE KIKUNAGA is a native speaker of Japanese and a graduate of Tsuda College, Japan. She currently teaches Japanese at Stanford University, California. Her current research focuses on Japanese as a second /foreign language (JSL), ESL, immigrant children in Japan, and the application of technology in education.

EDMUNDO F. LITTON is director of Asian and Pacific Student Services and assistant professor of education at Loyola Marymount University, Los Angeles. He has taught in high school bilingual classrooms in the Philippines and elementary school in the United States. His research topics include teacher preparation and language and educational issues that affect the Filipino community.

TINA YAMANO NISHIDA is an adjunct faculty at the University of California, Los Angeles and teaches courses on the educational experiences of Asian-Pacific Americans. Having been raised in both Japan and the United States, her bilingual and bicultural background has shaped both her areas of research and professional experience. She has conducted research for the Asia Pacific Economic Cooperation (APEC) Education Foundation, coauthored articles on rethinking the current U.S.-Japan educational exchange and assessing American community colleges in Japan, and has taught at various universities in Japan, including Waseda, Jochi, and Geidai.

CLARA C. PARK is associate professor of education and coordinator of the single subject Korean bilingual teacher education program at the College of Education, California State University, Northridge. She has published numerous articles and chapters on effective strategies for Korean and Asian-American students. She has conducted research concerning the learning style preferences and educational and occupational aspirations among high school students of Asian and other ethnic backgrounds. She is the founding president of the California Association for Asian and Pacific American Education and past president of the Korean-American Educators' Association. She is a member of the Bilingual and Crosscultural Advisory Panel of the California Commission on Teacher Credentialing and was a member of the Ethnic Advisory Council for California Superintendent of Public Schools.

PAOZE THAO is assistant professor at the Center for Collaborative Education and Professional Studies, California State University, Monterey Bay. A native of Laos and ethnic Mong, he came to the United States as a refugee. He was a supervisor for the refugee services of Travelers and Immigrants Aid, director of Outreach for the Chicago District Office for the U.S. Immigration and Naturalization Service, and a training and research specialist for the Multifunctional Resource Center for Bilingual Education, Wisconsin Center for Education Research, College of Education, University of Wisconsin, Madison. His research and publications focus on Southeast Asian culture, second language acquisition, cultural aspects of student behavior, and parental and community involvement.

KHATHARYA UM is assistant professor of Asian American studies, University of California, Berkeley. She has served as president of the National Association for the Education and Advancement of Cambodian-, Laotian-, and Vietnamese-Americans (NAFEA) and is the current vice president of the Cambodian Network Council. She has published numerous articles on the politics and developments in Southeast Asian American communities and in Southeast Asia. Her research areas include diaspora studies, with an emphasis on refugee and resettlement policies, transnationalism, and community development.

ANTHONY T. VANG is assistant professor and coordinator of the Southeast Asian bilingual teaching credential program, Department of Teacher Education, California State University, Stanislaus. He came to America as a refugee and served as executive director of a social service agency helping Southeast Asian refugees in Fresno, California. His research focuses on Southeast Asian refugees' cultural conflict and adaptation, bilingual teacher training, and Hmong parent involvement in education.

DAVID WHITENACK is assistant professor of (Spanish) bilingual education, Division of Teacher Education, San Jose State University. He is a sansei (third generation) Japanese-American and has studied Japanese as an adult. His research interests include preservice and beginning teacher development, specifically pertaining to the instruction of non-native English-speaking students.

WAYNE E. WRIGHT is a bilingual Khmer-English mentor teacher in Long Beach, California. He has studied the Khmer language for nine years, including advanced Khmer at Cornell University. From 1993 to 1994, he volunteered in Cambodia, providing technical assistance to local organizations, and served as the department head of English at the Institute of Economics in Phnom Penh. He was a member of the bilingual Khmer Subcommittee, Bilingual and Crosscultural Advisory Panel, California Commission on Teacher Credentialing.

ISBN 0-89789-602-5